"In *Augmented Education in the Global Age*, Daniel Araya and Peter Marber chronicle AI's astonishing disruption of social life. They shine a much needed light on AI's tectonic impact on how we work, which will, in turn, have a significant effect on how we learn. The volume is an extended interrogation, filled with vital questions concerning a future where augmented intellect is a reality with which we will need to be reconciled. With an extraordinarily diverse range of contributors, the volume explores not only how humans and new technologies will collaborate more closely in the coming years, but also what those collaborations will portend for industry, power, and what it means to be human".

Dr. Christopher Ankersen, *NYU Center for Global Affairs*

"Araya and Marber have assembled a wide range of insights into the future of work and education amidst the rise of artificial intelligence – an obvious 'gray rhino' phenomenon heading straight at us and giving us a choice act wisely or not. This important compilation is a must read for anyone who cares about strategic planning that can both avert the economic and social risks that come with AI and harness its power for positive progress".

Michele Wucker, *The Gray Rhino: How to Recognize and Act on the Obvious Dangers We Ignore*

AUGMENTED EDUCATION IN THE GLOBAL AGE

Augmented Education in the Global Age: Artificial Intelligence and the Future of Learning and Work is an edited collection that explores the social impact of Artificial Intelligence over the coming decades, specifically how this emerging technology will transform and disrupt our contemporary institutions. Chapters in this book discuss the history of technological revolutions and consider the anxieties and social challenges of lost occupations, as well as the evolution of new industries overlapping robotics, biotechnology, space exploration, and clean energy. Chapter authors unpack the nature of augmented education, from revamping curriculum and personalizing education, to redesigning workplace learning for an algorithmic era. Ultimately the book discusses policy and planning for an augmented future, arguing that work and learning are undergoing a metamorphosis around creativity and innovation amid a new global era and the race against automating technologies. Bringing together expert perspectives from around the world, this exciting, informative collection of research and analysis helps educators, policymakers and analysts navigate the future of work and learning amid rapid and accelerating technological change.

Daniel Araya is a Senior Fellow with the Centre for International Governance Innovation and Senior Partner with the World Legal Summit.

Peter Marber is a noted author and scholar who currently teaches at Harvard University and Johns Hopkins' Carey Business School.

AUGMENTED EDUCATION IN THE GLOBAL AGE

Artificial Intelligence and the Future of Learning and Work

Edited by Daniel Araya and Peter Marber

Designed cover image: © Getty Images

First published 2023
by Routledge
605 Third Avenue, New York, NY 10158

and by Routledge
4 Park Square, Milton Park, Abingdon, Oxon, OX14 4RN

Routledge is an imprint of the Taylor & Francis Group, an informa business

© 2023 selection and editorial matter, Daniel Araya and Peter Marber; individual chapters, the contributors

The right of Daniel Araya and Peter Marber to be identified as the authors of the editorial material, and of the authors for their individual chapters, has been asserted in accordance with sections 77 and 78 of the Copyright, Designs and Patents Act 1988.

The Open Access version of this book, available at www.taylorfrancis.com, has been made available under a Creative Commons Attribution-Non Commercial-No Derivatives 4.0 license.

Trademark notice: Product or corporate names may be trademarks or registered trademarks, and are used only for identification and explanation without intent to infringe.

Library of Congress Cataloging-in-Publication Data
Names: Araya, Daniel, 1971- editor. | Marber, Peter, editor.
Title: Augmented education in the global age : artificial intelligence and the future of learning and work / edited by Daniel Araya and Peter Marber.
Description: New York : Routledge, 2023. | Includes bibliographical references and index.
Identifiers: LCCN 2022052474 | ISBN 9781032122939 (Hardback) | ISBN 9781032137773 (Paperback) | ISBN 9781003230762 (eBook)
Subjects: LCSH: Education. | Artificial intelligence--Educational applications. | Artificial intelligence--Forecasting.
Classification: LCC LB1028.43 .A93 2023 | DDC 371.33/463--dc23/eng/20230120
LC record available at https://lccn.loc.gov/2022052474

ISBN: 978-1-032-12293-9 (hbk)
ISBN: 978-1-032-13777-3 (pbk)
ISBN: 978-1-003-23076-2 (ebk)

DOI: 10.4324/9781003230762

Typeset in Bembo
by SPi Technologies India Pvt Ltd (Straive)

An electronic version of this book is freely available, thanks to the support of libraries working with Knowledge Unlatched (KU). KU is a collaborative initiative designed to make high quality books Open Access for the public good. The Open Access ISBN for this book is 9781003230762. More information about the initiative and links to the Open Access version can be found at www.knowledgeunlatched.org.

CONTENTS

Foreword   *x*
List of Contributors   *xiii*

    Introduction   1
    Daniel Araya and Peter Marber

PART I
Augmented Work in the Global Age   11

1   Augmenting Human Intellect: A Conceptual Framework   13
    Douglas C. Engelbart

2   Reimagining Education and Workforce Preparation in Support of the UN's Sustainable Development Goals   30
    Jin Michael Fung and Samira Hosseini

3   The Bio Revolution: Innovations Transforming Economies, Societies, and Our Lives   48
    Michael Chui, Matthias Evers, James Manyika, Alice Zheng, and Travers Nisbet

4   Help Wanted in Space: The Impact of Artificial Intelligence on Employment in the Cosmos Economy   75
    Jack Gregg

5 The 21st-Century Imperative for Universities: Redesigning
   Higher Education for the Climate Problem   90
   Ruth DeFries

6 The Turing Trap: The Promise & Peril of Human-Like
   Artificial Intelligence   103
   Erik Brynjolfsson

PART II
Augmented Learning in the Global Age   **117**

7 AI and Education: Will the Promise be Fulfilled?   119
   Alexandros Papaspyridis and Jason La Greca

8 Proceed with Caution: The Pitfalls and Potential of AI
   and Education   137
   Kelly Shiohira and Wayne Holmes

9 Extending Biological Intelligence: The Imperative of
   Thinking Outside Our Brains in a World of Artificial
   Intelligence   157
   Annie Murphy Paul

10 Education for a Post-Work Society: AI, the Liberal Arts and
   the Future of Leisure   172
   Jon K. Burmeister

11 The Most Valuable Intelligence Is Not Artificial:
   Great Books, Free Minds, and St. John's College   188
   Peter Marber

12 Chinese Globalization: BRI and the Future of Higher
   Education   206
   Daniel Araya and Michael A. Peters

PART III
Policy and Planning for the Augmented Future   **219**

13 A New Generation Artificial Intelligence Development Plan 221
   The State Council of the People's Republic of China

14 US National Security Commission on Artificial Intelligence 234
Eric Schmidt

15 Training the "Workforce of the Future": The Integration of New Technologies in Work-Based Higher Education Programs in Germany and the United States 245
Inez von Weitershausen

16 How India Is Building Learning Technologies at Scale 260
Tarun Wadhwa

17 AI ≠ UBI: Income Portfolio Adjustment to Technological Transformation 274
Aleksandra K. Przegalinska and Robert E. Wright

Index *300*

FOREWORD

A primary challenge for any sentient creature born into our complex world is to find its place in the frameworks that define it. In developed countries, children spend the first fifteen years or more of their lives searching for their place in the world. Much of that learning takes place informally, through interactions with parents, relatives, friends, social institutions, and, not least, plain old mucking about, giving each a unique set of formative experiences. Childhood and adolescent experiences are the invisible sorting process by means of which society leads us into our adult roles.

But for the sake of strength and cohesion, we also want all children to pass through certain experiences that define the common framework of their given geography and turn a collection of people into a society. That framework may encompass many dimensions – history, geography, cultural traditions, economic activities, governance and laws—as well as the development of essential skills – language, basic mathematics, creativity, music, traditional and modern crafts, agility and dexterity, strength and stamina, working in teams and on projects, and so forth.

We call such experiences "education" and they are the means by which young people are exposed and led into the kinds of roles offered by a given society using the time-honored methods of teachers and classrooms. In developed countries, children spend some twelve years in such education. In less developed countries, they may receive only six, reflecting the narrower ranges of roles offered by their societies. A young person who successfully navigates such education is or was deemed to be equipped for life in jobs for which he or she has successfully qualified.

But this is a historic view of education in which a syllabus evolves gradually over decades, matching the evolution of the host society. This is no longer the case.

A young worker today will pass through multiple jobs over the course of a career. And careers are also extending from 60 to 65 to 70 years. Even within a given job, the processes, the mechanisms supporting these processes, and the tools and priorities for managing these processes will evolve significantly within ten years or less. Some jobs disappear completely, requiring not just incremental change, but wholesale re-education.

In many jobs, continuous learning has become part of the job as new technologies are introduced, new processes are put in place, and new products are manufactured. Workers must adapt to these or risk becoming irrelevant and unemployable. Some of that learning is provided by employers, who may even go as far as providing simulators for devices or processes that are being readied for deployment, sometimes as games. But much is still acquired by observing and interacting with co-workers or it is self-taught from books, videos, and online training. Learning may be part of the annual appraisal process, motivating workers to develop their skills.

Henry Ford's invention of the production line was the birth of such continuous learning. Today's adaptations are delivered via the Internet with its vast banks of knowledge in multiple formats and languages and its rich tools for delivering such education, culminating, perhaps, in the virtual environments of Facebook's Metaverse.

What lies beyond those vast Internet libraries and the Metaverse? Historically, the need for training or learning is driven by inventions, such as computers, but their deployment lags years or even decades behind the inventions themselves. Re-training a workforce may be the longest stage in the deployment of new technologies. But over the last century, the rates of penetration of new technologies have also been accelerating—electricity, telephones, radios, private cars, monochrome televisions, color televisions, microwave ovens, personal computers, and mobile telephones. Each deployment wave was shorter than the last, until, for example, mobile telephone penetration reached 50% of the total world population in less than 30 years even in the poorest countries.

We live in an age of prolific innovation, where penetration rates are limited by the users' ability to self-train. Indeed, designers build on the knowledge they know we already have with previous generations of industrial tools or domestic appliances. Their products progressively internalize that knowledge to enable us to deal with ever greater complexity. Invention, training, and usage converge.

The rapid adoption of enterprise computing in the period 1960 to 1980 was led by basic bookkeeping, but fairly quickly also began to be used for process management, in particular for planning. It is a short step from planning to "What-if" games and from there to simulating or modeling possible outcomes drawing on human thinking processes rooted in game playing. With Augmented Intelligence (AI) providing support, the potential for playing games increases exponentially, and training becomes the art of game playing among the participants in a given industry using real money.

As invention, usage and training converge, the world turns more quickly. How long can this acceleration continue? Will we reach a point where technical innovation so far outpaces training that we hit a barrier, like the sound barrier, where the speed of change exceeds our ability to exploit it ? But wait, what if the training came first, instead of afterward? Simulators are already a step in that direction, but the development of the simulated process or product still comes first. And the product design still starts today and looks forward.

What if we started from a desired outcome, an outcome that we could describe, that is feasible or at least plausible, but for which there is no evident starting point or path. Like winning a game of chess. In fact, we do this already. It is one of the ways to plan to climb a major mountain. You start from the summit and find ways down. So go further and ask an AI to search for new endpoints. Not extrapolations of what we know today, but unknown, unimaginable, and yet constrained destinations and then have it work how to connect that distant goal with our present starting point. Can we jump through the training barrier?

What lies beyond *h. sapiens* and its limited imaginations? Is there some creature or organization of creatures that will replace Carbon-based lifeforms? Do we evolve into "The Matrix" where human life is purely virtual? Or does it lead to a savage partition of the race, as in H. G. Wells' "War of the Worlds"? Coming soon to a Multiverse near you!

Colin Harrison

CONTRIBUTORS

Daniel Araya is a Senior Fellow with the Centre for International Governance Innovation and Senior Partner with the World Legal Summit. Dr. Araya is a regular contributor to Forbes, The Brookings Institution, and Singularity Hub where his work contributes to research on autonomous systems in global governance. He has been invited to speak at a number of universities and research centers including the US Naval Postgraduate School, Harvard University, the American Enterprise Institute, the Center for Global Policy Solutions, Stanford University, the University of Toronto, UC Santa Cruz, and Microsoft Research. His newest books include *Augmented Intelligence* (2018), and *Smart Cities as Democratic Ecologies* (2015). He has a doctorate from the University of Illinois at Urbana-Champaign.

Erik Brynjolfsson is the Jerry Yang and Akiko Yamazaki Professor and Senior Fellow at the Institute for Human-Centered AI and Director of the Digital Economy Lab at Stanford University. He is also the Ralph Landau Senior Fellow at the Institute for Economic Policy Research and Professor by Courtesy at the Graduate School of Business and Department of Economics at Stanford University; and a Research Associate at the National Bureau of Economic Research. He is the author or coauthor of seven books, including *Machine, Platform, Crowd: Harnessing Our Digital Future* (2017), *The Second Machine Age: Work, Progress, and Prosperity in a Time of Brilliant Technologies* (2014), and *Race against the Machine: How the Digital Revolution Is Accelerating Innovation, Driving Productivity, and Irreversibly Transforming Employment and the Economy* (2011) with Andrew McAfee, and *Wired for Innovation: How Information Technology Is Reshaping the Economy* (2009) with Adam Saunders.

Jon K. Burmeister is a professor of philosophy and religious studies at the College of Mount St. Vincent. He combines a background in the history of philosophy (e.g., Plato, Hegel, Nietzsche) with investigations of contemporary social, ethical, and technological questions. A National Endowment of the Humanities grant winner, Dr. Burmeister has published numerous articles and the book *On Language: Analytic, Continental, and Historical Contributions*. He previously taught at Boston College where he also earned his PhD.

Michael Chui is a partner at the McKinsey Global Institute (MGI), McKinsey's business and economics research arm. He leads research on the impact of disruptive technologies and innovation on business, the economy, and society. Michael has led McKinsey research in such areas as data analytics, social collaboration technologies, the Internet of Things, artificial intelligence, robotics and automation, and biological technologies. He is on the boards of the James Irvine Foundation and the Asia Society of Northern California, and also is a member of the Council on Foreign Relations. Dr. Chui earned his doctorate at Indiana University.

Ruth DeFries is a professor of ecology and sustainable development at Columbia University in New York and co-founding dean of the Columbia Climate School. Her highly regarded research quantifies how land use changes affect climate, biodiversity, and other ecosystem services, as well as human development. She has also developed innovate education programs in sustainable development. In addition to over 100 scientific papers, she is committed to communicating the nuances and complexities of sustainable development to popular audiences through her books *The Big Ratchet: How Humanity Thrives in the Face of Natural Crisis* and *What Would Nature Do?: A Guide for Our Uncertain Times*. Dr. DeFries was elected as a member of the US National Academy of Sciences, received a MacArthur "genius" award, and is the recipient of many other honors for her scientific research.

Douglas C. Engelbart was an American engineer and inventor, and an early computer and Internet pioneer. He is best known for his work on founding the field of human–computer interaction. While at Stanford's Augmentation Research Center Lab, his work led to the creation of the computer mouse, the development of hypertext, networked computers, and precursors to graphical user interfaces. These were demonstrated at the now-famous "The Mother of All Demos" in 1968. Engelbart's Law, the observation that the intrinsic rate of human performance is exponential, is named after him. During his lifetime he won many awards including the National Medal of Technology, the Lemelson-MIT Prize, the ACM Turing Award, the BCS Lovelace Medal, the Norbert Wiener Award for Social and Professional Responsibility, and the Computer History Museum Fellow Award, among others.

Matthias Evers is a thought leader in the field of AI/ML-driven science and is currently. Chief Business Officer of Evotec, a life science company in Germany focused on delivering new therapeutics. He was previously a partner at McKinsey & Co. where he worked for more than two decades. Dr. Evers earned his doctorate at the Center for Molecular Neurobiology at the University of Hamburg.

Jin Michael Fung is an Executive Director in the Institute for the Future of Education at Tecnologico de Monterrey, leading efforts to generate, transfer, and disseminate applicable knowledge about educational innovations, and seeking disruptive global solutions for the future of higher education and lifelong learning. He was formerly Deputy Chief Executive at SkillsFuture Singapore, where he led the development of a comprehensive education and training ecosystem under the national SkillsFuture movement, which has become a global reference for workforce skills development and lifelong learning. He was the Founding President of the Higher Education Planning in Asia Association, and serves on several global boards and committees.

Jack Gregg is an acclaimed writer and educator focused on the commercialization of space. Dr. Gregg has served as the Founding Dean of Northrop Grumman's Space Sector Corporate University, and he was the Executive Director of the California Space Authority. Gregg has also held leadership positions at Loyola Marymount University, the University of California-Irvine, California State University-Long Beach, and the University of California-Riverside. His seminal book, *The Cosmos Economy: The Industrialization of Space*, was published in 2021. He earned his bachelor's from the University of Miami, his MBA from the University of California-Irvine, and his doctorate from Pepperdine University.

Wayne Holmes is a learning sciences and innovation researcher, who is based at University College London. For almost a decade, he has focused on the application of Artificial Intelligence (AI) to both enhance and further understand learning, and its ethical and social implications. He also advises UNESCO on the pedagogical, ethical and social implications of AI for education (including co-leading UNESCO's 'AI in Education: Guidance for Policymakers' and 'Teaching AI for K12' portal. Dr. Holmes has co-authored three books about AI and education, including: *Artificial Intelligence in Education. Promise and Implications for Teaching and Learning* (2019).)

Samira Hosseini is the Director of the Writing Lab at the Institute for the Future of Education within Tecnologico de Monterrey, where she also is a Research Professor at the School of Engineering and Sciences. Dr. Hosseini has published more than 60 scientific articles and serves on editorial boards for *Computers & Electrical Engineering*, *E-Learning*, *Journal of Big Data*, *Artificial Intelligence in*

Education, among other periodicals. She obtained her BSc degree from the University of North Tehran, and her MSc degree in Polymer Chemistry and a PhD degree in Biomedical Engineering from the University of Malaya.

Jason La Greca is a Senior Program Manager at Microsoft Higher Education Experiences based in Australia. Jason is a passionate advocate of transformative learning and teaching, accessibility, and language preservation through technology. He has taught extensively across K-12 and higher education, where he was able to share his obsession with languages and linguistics. At Microsoft, he works with hundreds of organizations to drive transformation and to improve outcomes for millions of learners worldwide. He holds degrees from Western Sydney University and the University of New England.

James Manyika is a senior partner at McKinsey & Company and chairman and director of the McKinsey Global Institute. In addition to leading research on technology, the digital economy, the future of work, and competitiveness, James has worked with chief executives on issues related to innovation, digitization, and other global trends. A Rhodes Scholar, he received his DPhil, MSc, and MA from Oxford in AI and robotics, mathematics, and computer science, and his BSc in electrical engineering from the University of Zimbabwe as an Anglo-American Scholar. He is a fellow of the American Academy of Arts and Sciences, a distinguished fellow of Stanford's AI Institute, and a fellow of the Royal Society of Arts.

Peter Marber has been a thought leader on globalization, public policy, and human capital formation for more than three decades. An award-winning money manager, he currently serves as a chief investment officer for emerging markets at Aperture Investors and has held senior positions at Loomis, Sayles & Co., and HSBC. Dr. Marber also is a distinguished lecturer at Harvard University and Johns Hopkins, and he previously taught at Columbia University and NYU's Center for Global Affairs. He has published dozens of articles and seven books including *Brave New Math: Information, Globalization, and New Economic Thinking in the 21st Century* (2015) and *The Evolution of Liberal Arts in the Global Age* (with Araya, 2017). His most recent book is *Quid Periculum? Measuring & Managing Political Risk in the Age of Uncertainty*, published in 2021. He is a Fellow of the Royal Society for Arts and the Royal Astronomical Society and a member of Chatham House. Marber earned his doctorate from the University of Cambridge.

Travers Nisbet manages banking strategy and partnerships at Chime, and is a fellow at the Institute for Advanced Studies in Culture at the University of Virginia. He previously was a business analyst at Mckinsey & Co. in San Francisco for several years, and he earned his bachelor's degree from the University of Virginia.

Contributors **xvii**

Michael A. Peters has spent the last three decades researching and writing about some of the enduring issues in education. He has written over eighty books, including *The Global Financial Crisis and the Restructuring of Education* (2015), *Paulo Freire: The Global Legacy* (2015) both with Tina Besley, *Education Philosophy and Politics: Selected Works* (2011); and *Education, Cognitive Capitalism and Digital Labour* (2011), with Ergin Bulut. He is a Distinguished Professor at Beijing Normal University, China, and Emeritus Professor at the University of Illinois, Urbana-Champaign. He is the executive editor of the journal, *Educational Philosophy and Theory*, and editor of three international E-journals, *Policy Futures in Education*, *E-Learning and Digital Media*, and *Knowledge Cultures*. Peters has acted as an advisor to governments on these and related matters in Scotland, NZ, South Africa, and the EU. He was made an Honorary Fellow of the Royal Society of NZ in 2010 and awarded honorary doctorates by the State University of New York (SUNY) in 2012 and the University of Aalborg in 2015.

Alexandros Papaspyridis is the Tertiary Education Industry Director for the Asia region of Microsoft, covering India, Greater China Region, Asia Pacific, Australia, and Japan. His focus is the Digital Transformation of Higher Education to enable the future student cohorts to prosper in the Fourth Industrial Revolution which helps universities leverage AI. He has been with Microsoft since 2008 working in Central and Eastern Europe, MENA, and Asia Pacific Japan. He is an advisory member at the National University of Singapore's Centre on AI Technology for Humankind, and a board advisor at Imperial College, London where he has conducted research on innovation ecosystems. Dr. Papaspyridis holds a PhD. in Electronics Engineering, a Master's in Management and a Bachelor's in Electrical Engineering from Imperial College, London. He also holds the Microsoft Professional Program certificate in Artificial Intelligence.

Annie Murphy Paul is an acclaimed science writer whose work has appeared in the *New York Times*, the *Boston Globe*, *Scientific American*, *Slate*, *Time*, and *The Best American Science Writing*, among many other publications. She is the author of three books including *Origins* and *The Cult of Personality*. Paul is currently a Learning Sciences Exchange Fellow at the Jacobs Foundation, has been a fellow at New America, and has also received the Spencer Education Reporting Fellowship and the Rosalyn Carter Mental Health Journalism Fellowship. She has spoken to audiences around the world about learning and cognition; her TED Talk has been viewed by more than 2.6 million people. A graduate of Yale University and the Columbia's Graduate School of Journalism, she has served as a lecturer at Yale and as a senior advisor at Yale's Poorvu Center for Teaching and Learning. Her latest book is the bestseller *The Extended Mind: The Power of Thinking Outside the Brain*.

Aleksandra K. Przegalinska is a Senior Research Associate on AI, Robots, and the Future of Work at Harvard Law School. She is also Associate Professor and heads the Human-Machine Interaction Research Center at the AI in Management Program at Kozminski University in Poland. She previously conducted postdoctoral research at the Massachusetts Institute of Technology in Boston. In 2021 Aleksandra joined the American Institute for Economic Research as a Visiting Research Fellow. Her work focuses on the future of work seen through the lens of emerging technologies, as well as in natural language processing, humanoid artificial intelligence, social robots, and wearable technologies. She is the co-author of *Collaborative Society* (MIT Press) with Dariusz Jemielniak. She graduated from The New School for Social Research in New York and earned her PhD in the philosophy of artificial intelligence at the University of Warsaw.

Eric Schmidt is a renowned technologist, entrepreneur, and philanthropist. He served as Google's Chief Executive Officer and Chairman from 2001 to 2011, where he pioneered Google's transformation from a Silicon Valley startup to a global leader in technology. Prior to Google, Eric was the Chairman and CEO of Novell and held technical positions at Xerox Palo Alto Research Center (PARC), Bell Laboratories, and Zilog. Dr. Schmidt was elected to the National Academy of Engineering in 2006 and inducted into the American Academy of Arts and Sciences as a fellow in 2007, and has published three books. He became the Chairman of the Department of Defense's Innovation Board in 2016 and was also a member of NASA's National Space Council User Advisory. He is currently Chairman of the National Security Commission on Artificial Intelligence. Eric holds a bachelor's degree in electrical engineering from Princeton University and a master's degree and PhD in computer science from the University of California, Berkeley.

Kelly Shiohira is an Executive Manager at JET Education Services, a non-profit focused on improving education in Africa. She specializes in literacy and the use of technology for education, and has contributed to prominent projects including the *Bridges to the Future Initiative South Africa* and the *PSET CLOUD*, an ambitious initiative to leverage interoperability, AI, and the principles of self-sovereign identity to enable credential fluency and data-driven decisions about education and the world of work. Her recent publications include *AI K-12 Curricula: A Mapping of Government-Endorsed AI Curricula* and *Understanding the Impact of Artificial Intelligence on Skills Development*. She holds degrees from the University of Florida, the University of Pennsylvania, and Rhodes University.

The State Council of the People's Republic of China is the chief administrative authority of the People's Republic of China. Constitutionally synonymous with the Central People's Government, the State Council is Chaired by the premier and supervises the administrative functions of the Chinese government.

Tarun Wadhwa is an entrepreneur, strategist, lecturer, and writer working at the intersection of tech and public policy. His work has appeared in *Forbes, Foreign Policy, Fortune, CNN Business, The Economist, The Wall Street Journal, MarketWatch, Digital-Life-Design, Venture Beat, Huffington Post*, and many other publications. He was previously a Nonresident Fellow at Atlantic Council's GeoTech Center, a Visiting Fellow at Emory University's Department of Political Science, and a Visiting Instructor at Carnegie Mellon University's College of Engineering where he co-taught the popular *Exponential Innovation* course. Tarun is the Founder of Day One Insights, a strategy and advisory firm focused on technological convergence, corporate reinvention, and social impact. He is also co-founder and CSO of Rsq Labs, a consultancy focused on machine learning, cryptography, and blockchain-based finance.

Inez von Weitershausen is a Research Associate at MIT's Good Companies, Good Jobs Initiative. Her ongoing work on cross-national differences in the organization and implementation of systems for training, education, and reskilling has informed MIT's Task Force on the Work of the Future and has been featured in MIT's edX course *Shaping Work of the Future*. She has also explored topics involving comparative regulation and public policy as a Visiting Fellow at the Centre for Analysis of Risk and Regulation at the London School of Economics. Inez holds a PhD. in International Relations from the London School of Economics, a Master of Law & Business degree from Bucerius Law School and WHU Otto Beisheim School of Management, and an MA in Politics, History, and Area Studies from the University of Bonn.

Robert E. Wright is a Senior Research Fellow at the American Institute for Economic Research (AIER). He has published over two dozen major books and edited collections, including AIER's *The Best of Thomas Paine* (2021) and *Financial Exclusion* (2019). He has also published numerous articles for the *American Economic Review, Business History Review, Independent Review, Journal of Private Enterprise, Review of Finance*, and *Southern Economic Review*, among other journals. Robert has taught business, economics, and policy courses at Augustana University, NYU's Stern School of Business, Temple University, and the University of Virginia. He earned his PhD in History from SUNY Buffalo in 1997.

Alice Zheng is the principal at RH Capital in San Francisco where she invests in early-stage women's health companies across the life sciences, digital health, and consumer sectors. She previously led McKinsey & Company's women's health practice. Dr. Zheng started her career as a physician and was a resident at Mount Sinai St. Luke's and Mount Sinai Roosevelt hospital in New York. She earned her BS, MPH, and MD degrees at the University of Michigan and an MBA from Harvard Business School.

INTRODUCTION

Daniel Araya and Peter Marber

As the social theorist Marshall McLuhan observes, "First we build the tools, then they build us". This observation—that tools or technologies shape human development—has never been more applicable than it is today. With a capacity to think, act, and even learn like human beings, artificial intelligence (AI) has begun catalyzing deep structural changes in the nature of learning and work. AI now sits at the center of a constellation of emerging technologies including robotics, machine learning, cloud computing, genomics, 3D printing, quantum encryption, 5G telecommunications, and many others. Taken as a whole, these disparate technologies constitute what we might call the "AI Revolution".

Much like the Industrial and Agricultural Revolutions of the past, AI represents a new techno-economic paradigm. Like electricity, AI is the quintessential "dual-use" technology with enormous potential to shape the nature of work and learning. Much as the steam engine, the printing press, and the internal combustion engine, AI and other data-driven technologies now provide tools for substantially augmenting human capabilities across a range of social and economic domains. This edited collection explores the features of human augmentation through the lens of education and work with the purpose of contributing to research and policy analysis for a changing global era.

Augmenting Work and Education

Since its inception some 60 years ago, AI has evolved from an arcane academic field into a powerful driver of social transformation. Indeed, AI has become the quintessential "general purpose" technology. While conventional forecasts on technological change often make the mistake of assuming that disruptive

DOI: 10.4324/9781003230762-1

innovation simply replaces old technologies on a one-to-one basis, the reality is that general-purpose technologies like AI tend to disproportionately replace old systems with dramatically new infrastructure, boundaries, and capabilities. What we are now experiencing is a system shift in which the combination of human ingenuity and machine technologies are becoming foundational to a new kind of society.

For much of recorded history, human beings have toiled under the weight of ignorance, scarcity, and disease. But in the last 2/10 of one percent of recorded history, we have witnessed a dramatic acceleration in economic output. The combination of the Industrial Revolution, the globalization of the world's economy over the last century, and now the AI Revolution is providing modern societies—developing and industrialized—with the capacity to transform certain kinds of human labor while also advancing unique human capabilities.

Of course, speculating on how technology might reshape modern societies is not new. In 1930, John Maynard Keynes predicted a life of wealth and leisure as technology reduced the need for labor across advanced economies. Unfortunately, the reality has been something else altogether. Wages and income for the majority of households in advanced economies have barely risen since the 1970s. Winner-take-all policies have fostered a degree of wealth inequality across industrialized countries that has not been seen since the Gilded Age.

Around the world, newly educated workers in developing countries now compete with workers in advanced economies. In this Global Age, many young workers are largely dependent upon "gigs" and short-term contracts, while older workers are confronted with corporate downsizing and the looming threat of labor automation. Some forecasts suggest that as much as 50% of what constitutes "work" today could be automated by 2050, with virtually every type of job requiring some form of upskilling.

Nonetheless, there is more to this AI Revolution than meets the eye. Even as AI, robotics, machine learning, and other forms of labor automation eliminate many current professions, historical cycles of innovation would suggest that new occupations and entirely new industries are just over the horizon. What seems clear is that we now stand at an inflection point in the evolution of work and learning. Where the Agricultural Revolution harnessed domesticated animals for farming, and the Industrial Revolution leveraged machines for mass production, so today the AI Revolution is advancing computers to augment human intelligence. In the context of education, handwriting is on the "school wall". As an industry, education—like many other sectors of the economy—is undergoing an enormous transformation. Much as the quaint one-room schoolhouse of 19th-century America and Great Britain were slowly displaced by factory-styled institutions, so education systems today are undergoing a similar metamorphosis.

In this brave new world, "work" as we know it may become increasingly precarious. In fact, many experts now suggest that a "post-work" era is on the horizon. While not inevitable, such a possible future is worth discussing. In fact, there is already considerable academic research and popular media discourse examining the changing nature of work. Yet many questions remain: Will new jobs be created or is humanity on the cusp of an entirely new and different era? How do people and governments prepare for a world in which traditional occupations become obsolete? What jobs will be in demand in the future? How do we educate populations for this future? What public policies should be considered? Can this future be more inclusive and more environmentally sustainable? These are the kinds of questions that *Augmented Education in the Global Age* seeks to understand.

Part I: Augmented Work in the Global Age

Part I probes our current technological revolution and considers the anxieties surrounding lost occupations—along with the promise of new social and economic opportunities. While there have been technological revolutions in the past, the convergence of a large number of general-use technologies suggests a very uncertain future. These chapters examine the idea of augmenting human civilization, along with new economic and labor opportunities in industries overlapping energy, agriculture, space, medicine, and education.

Chapter 1 begins with an excerpt from Douglas Engelbart's seminal 1962 report *Augmenting Human Intellect: A Conceptual Framework*. For many experts, Engelbart's work represents a watershed moment in modern computing and a vision for the future of human social evolution. Written at the famed Stanford Research Institute, the report has influenced a wide range of technology pioneers including Bill Gates, Steve Jobs, and Robert Metcalfe, to name only a few. Engelbart presciently laid out concepts that eventually became the basis for the Internet and World Wide Web, the "mouse", hypertext, the graphical user interface (GUI), and other tools that we now take for granted. More importantly, his report promoted an entirely new way of thinking, communicating, collaborating, and learning with computers. His simple vision—now so relevant to 21st-century society—was to augment our collective capability to solve complex problems and tasks, while also freeing human beings from mundane, repetitive, and time-consuming chores that could simply be automated. Indeed, Engelbart's description of technology "augmenting" human capabilities is both an inspiration for this collection and a common theme running throughout many of its essays.

In **Chapter 2**, Jin Michael Fung and Samira Hosseini build on the theme of augmented intelligence in the context of a new education-for-work paradigm linked to the United Nations Sustainable Development Goals. As they explain, the shelf life of a contemporary occupation is anticipated to fall to a remarkably short five years even as AI and automation become increasingly predominant. Fung and Hosseini suggest that individuals will need to update and refresh their skills at least eight times during their 40-year careers to remain relevant at their workplace. This will require both advanced and developing nations to reshape lifelong learning and skills development systems to build more sustainable economies and societies in the future. As the authors conclude, there is an urgent need for thoughtful education policies coordinated with employers, industry associations, educational institutions, trade unions, non-profits, and government.

In contrast to many pessimistic forecasts about the future of AI, **Chapter 3** highlights the phenomenal daily advances in what a McKinsey team of researchers calls the "Bio Revolution". Across the natural sciences, AI is transforming old industries and creating new industries to improve human well-being and the environment. Building on AI, a McKinsey team argues that new digital technologies have the potential to alleviate and help solve many of humanity's greatest challenges in healthcare, food production, and climate change, while also creating new industries, new occupations, and new research areas.

In **Chapter 4**, space expert Jack Gregg highlights the economic and employment opportunities in building what he calls the "Cosmos Economy". While space-based technologies have historically been limited to a few governments, more than 80 countries now operate space programs with thousands of private-sector companies exploring the commercialization of our galaxy. Across this vast burgeoning ecosystem, AI and related technologies can help in augmenting deep space research, and in exploring places where humans cannot go… yet. By using AI and related technologies, Gregg believes that many jobs will be created in activities ranging from meteorological forecasting and advanced telecommunications to mining, metallurgy, sustainable energy production, and tourism. Rather than automation, the challenge today, he suggests, is a shortage of qualified workers.

In **Chapter 5**, Columbia's Climate School's inaugural dean Ruth Defries reminds us that the existential threat of climate change may have a silver lining: It offers not only an opportunity to solve critical ecological challenges and produce new jobs but also to build a better future. Much as in the past, universities and higher education institutions must evolve to create new knowledge, new strategies, and new workforce programs that support human flourishing in the context of a carbon neutral future. As Defries concludes, this will require not only new curriculums but a reconfiguration of studies away from single research areas and toward truly multidisciplinary education—much of which will rely heavily on AI.

Chapter 6 concludes Part I with Stanford economist Erik Brynjolfsson's examination of the age-old debate over whether machines will boost productivity and increase leisure or simply drive social dislocation. He asks us to consider the power shift accompanying the AI Revolution: As "machines become better substitutes for human labor, workers lose economic and political bargaining power and become increasingly dependent on those who control the technology". Much like Engelbart, Brynjolfsson draws a distinction between using AI to *automate* (i.e replace) versus using AI to *augment* human labor. As he observes,

> when AI is focused on augmenting humans rather than mimicking them, humans retain the power to insist on a share of the value created. What is more, augmentation creates new capabilities and new products and services, ultimately generating far more value than merely human-like AI.

While he agrees that both types of AI can help humanity, he cautions that there are currently disproportionately higher incentives for automation than augmentation among companies, investors, and policymakers.

Part II: Augmented Learning in the Global Age

Technology has continually reshaped the human condition and profoundly augmented the way we learn: From the abacus to calculators to smartphones; from papyrus to chalkboards to laptops; from hunting through library stacks, to scanning microfiche, to searching the Internet. The AI Revolution is expected to impact many industries and sectors around the world, with education being among the most important.

While public schooling, as we know it, was born roughly 200 years ago—around the time of the first Industrial Revolution—AI is now a game changer in this domain. AI had only been slowly adopted by the education sector, but in the wake of the COVID-19 pandemic, adoption has accelerated. For example, Zoom and other videoconference programs used AI technologies to optimize connections and compress data transfer to improve video quality and augment the user experience. More recently, applications such as ChatGPT and DALL-E have provided a window into the ways in which AI will augment research and writing across a range of tasks— from writing software to formulating business ideas to enhancing artwork. Looking forward, AI applications will increasingly be woven into all stages of learning and education including course design, personalized tutoring, record keeping, and task automation. Part II explores the applications and impact of AI in education and what it means for learning and living now and into the future.

Chapter 7 opens with a practitioner's view on AI and education from professional software developers at Microsoft. With decades of experience in schools around the world, Alexandros Papaspyridis and Jason La Greca document how AI is being used in both higher education and K-12 classrooms. The authors guide us through real-world examples of AI in curriculum design, student training, remediation, grading, and even special-needs education. They also remind us of the ethical considerations that should underpin the design of AI in the education domain.

In **Chapter 8**, Kelly Shiohira and Wayne Holmes stress that AI is ultimately a tool, but not a perfect one. As they wisely point out,

> AI is not machines that think independently. AI is merely a set of human-created algorithms that aim to mimic some human thought processes, such as decision-making. They do so to a greater or lesser extent, using a range of database techniques (machine learning approaches such as supervised, unsupervised, reinforcement and deep learning), all of which depend on huge amounts of data and knowledge-based techniques.

Sometimes, those data and techniques can be biased and inaccurate, requiring thoughtful and ethical design *before* implementation. The authors suggest a few key guidelines for managing accuracy, bias and fairness, transparency, privacy, safety, and *human* editability to address potential problems or unforeseen consequences in the evolution of AI. Most importantly, Holmes and Shiohira remind us that educational AI should be designed for the public good with the proverbial Rawlsian veil of ignorance—guaranteeing everyone an equal opportunity to prosper, not just a select few.

Best-selling author Annie Murphy Paul argues that the most impressive advances in the future of education and work will be "through a partnership of digital smarts and human smarts", or what Englebart called human augmentation. In **Chapter 9**, she asks us to ponder "natural intelligence—the capacities of our biological brains", in order to broaden our understanding of the human mind. Instead of the binary computer as a metaphor for the human brain, she suggests thinking of it more as a "magpie"—the resourceful bird that constructs nests "from the materials around them, weaving the bits and pieces they find into their trains of thought". Set beside the brain-as-computer metaphor, she suggests, the brain-as-magpie is a very different kind of analogy with very different implications for how educational curriculum should be designed.

In **Chapter 10**, philosopher Jon Burmeister asks and answers the very basic questions: What will people do if their lives are no longer dominated by traditional work, and what kind of education would best serve them in such a world? Up until only a few generations ago, humans toiled from teen years through old age, with much shorter lifespans than we find in the 21st century. According to Nobel-winning economist Robert Fogel, individual leisure time has more than quintupled since the late 19th century to approximately 250,000 hours as people start work later in life, retire earlier, and live longer. With AI, this trend should continue for decades. Burmeister notes that the ancient Greeks developed the "liberal arts" approach because it was "precisely the right sort of education for those who do not need to work—not because their work was done by machines but because it was done by human servants". Building on Aristotelian ideas of happiness, Burmeister argues that a broad liberal arts education may be the best preparation for a future with more time for *a-telic* pursuits: Active, mindful activities that are done for their own sake, rather than to achieve a particular end. According to Burmeister, a liberal arts education helps us to discover the human pursuits that make life worth living.

In **Chapter 11**, author and scholar Peter Marber argues that higher education should be focused on cultivating the most human qualities of creativity and cooperative problem-solving. In his view, this accomplishes two things at the same time: Both addressing claims by employers who want more creative employees, and those of workers who want more personal fulfillment from their work. Surprisingly, he finds these demands interrelate and are tied to *free thinking*. Marber notes, "Only by thinking freely can we cultivate creative and critical minds, which is also how we build our individual identities". One higher education template for this approach to learning can be found at America's St. John's College through its Great Books curriculum and focus on dialogue. Echoing Burmeister, Marber believes that not only can this style of liberal arts education help build the creative skills that employers seek, but it can also lead to greater personal fulfillment and the analytical mindset needed for a functioning democracy.

Part II ends with **Chapter 12** in which scholars Daniel Araya and Michael A. Peters consider the global implications of AI on learning. Exploring the influence of China's Belt and Road Initiative (BRI) in reshaping global higher education, Araya and Peters speculate on the future of learning across emerging economies. Stretching across Asia, the Middle East, Africa, and Europe, China's BRI is often portrayed as simply a trade network for Chinese exports, but the authors argue that it represents a much broader platform for social and cultural integration. China's economic re-emergence is a unique historical event but it also reflects the return of Asia to the center of the global economy. While English-speaking countries have dominated higher education for over two centuries, things are changing. Just as Anglo-American power has been ceding economic ground to China in recent decades, so China's influence in education across developing countries could represent a tipping point in the global order. The chapter builds the case that by using AI, Chinese universities will drive a new stage of globalization across emerging economies in the rise of a complex multipolar system.

Part III: Policy and Planning for an Augmented Future

Building on changes in the nature of work and learning, Part III discusses policy and planning for an augmented future. Most education systems today have been designed to support an industrial laborforce. In the wake of disruptive technologies like AI, however, governments will need to adapt education systems to a rapidly evolving digital economy. Part III investigates the policy challenges and choices that are emerging in a competitive AI-driven world. AI and other digital technologies are now central to global innovation, with national competitiveness directly tied to data-driven capabilities and strategies. All nations, large or small, developed or advanced, will need to address this new and complex reality.

Chapter 12 begins with a document examining China's AI policy and planning in the context of a changing global order. Excerpted from a national strategic document produced by China's State Council, the chapter outlines the country's soaring ambition to become the world leader in AI by 2030. More than a remarkable vision, the chapter details how the country intends to build next-generation AI technologies, coordinate AI innovation platforms, and accelerate the training and development of high-end human talent. Leveraging AI to enhance China's enormous education system is key to the country's long-term planning. Indeed, technology-augmented human capital development undergirds the country's robust innovation strategies.

Chapter 14 considers the US response to China's growing geopolitical influence. In 2019, the US government established the National Defense Authorization Act and tasked a blue-ribbon panel with making recommendations. That commission, led by former Google chairman Eric Schmidt, produced a report highlighting the need for AI talent development in the United States, along with accelerating advances in AI and associated technologies. One thing that Schmidt and his group make very clear: The United States faces many technical skills gaps across industries when it comes to AI. As this excerpted report observes, time is of the essence in the race with China.

In **Chapter 15**, Inez von Weitershausen of MIT investigates the growing mismatch between employers' needs and workers' skills in advanced economies, and how higher education is responding to such concerns. Drawing on case studies in Germany and the United States, she finds that the influence of German industry is stronger than in America where universities tend to shape collaborations with the private sector. These differences result in diverging levels of comparability and standardization of programs which, in turn, influence both countries' ability to train the workforce of the future.

Of course, the United States and China are not the only centers of technological innovation in the world. Let's not forget another large and rising economy in this Global Age: India. In **Chapter 16**, Tarun Wadhwa reminds us that India will be the world's most populous country for many decades to come. Indeed, the quality of India's education system will determine the country's broader socio-economic trajectory. What will Indians need to prosper and compete in a world economy where knowledge and innovation have become globalized? Making the most of the country's "demographic dividend" will require using technology to improve the availability and relevance of learning materials and methods. To that end, India's government, industry, investors, and entrepreneurs are focusing on leveraging the proliferation of digital technologies to facilitate the growth of enormous learning platforms. Given the scale of India's population, the country's successes and failures may hold key lessons for many other countries as well.

Part III concludes with **Chapter 17**. In the 2020 US presidential election, candidate Andrew Yang gained notoriety by proposing his "Freedom Dividend", a universal basic income (UBI) policy offering a $1,000 monthly stipend for all American adults to help deal with job displacement partially due to automation and AI. Are such UBI policies needed given these technological changes? Aleksandra K. Przegalinska and Robert Wright of the American Institute for Economic Research caution that it may be premature to roll out UBI programs. Yes, they agree, rapid changes are occurring, but at speeds that individuals and employers are adapting to without mass unemployment. While not dismissing the idea completely, they argue that governments can always act quickly with income support as many did during early COVID-19 lockdowns.

As the many insightful chapters in this collection remind us, AI is fundamentally reshaping industrial societies and this is no time to bury one's head in the sand. Indeed, the history of technological revolutions is a history of social anxiety and social challenges. The current AI revolution is driving a vast creative explosion in robotics, autonomous systems, network computing, renewable energy infrastructure, space-based telecommunications, and machine learning. What is clear is that there is much at stake. When it comes to the future of "human augmentation", today's public policies could be the difference between a dystopian future or one of progressive fairness, innovation, and prosperity. We hope that this edited collection contributes to the discussion of what can be done and needs to be done in order to to prepare us for this era of Promethean change. It is, perhaps, the most important debate of our time.

PART I
Augmented Work in the Global Age

1

AUGMENTING HUMAN INTELLECT

A Conceptual Framework

Douglas C. Engelbart

1.1 Introduction

1.1.1 General

By "augmenting human intellect" we mean increasing the capability of a man to approach a complex problem situation, to gain comprehension to suit his particular needs, and to derive solutions to problems. Increased capability in this respect is taken to mean a mixture of the following: More-rapid comprehension, better comprehension, the possibility of gaining a useful degree of comprehension in a situation that previously was too complex, speedier solutions, better solutions, and the possibility of finding solutions to problems that before seemed insoluble. And by "complex situations" we include the professional problems of diplomats, executives, social scientists, life scientists, physical scientists, attorneys, and designers—whether the problem situation exists for 20 minutes or 20 years. We do not speak of isolated clever tricks that help in particular situations. We refer to a way of life in an integrated domain where hunches, cut-and-try, intangibles, and the human "feel for a situation" usefully co-exist with powerful concepts, streamlined terminology and notation, sophisticated methods, and high-powered electronic aids.

Man's population and gross product are increasing at a considerable rate, but the *complexity* of his problems grows still faster, and the *urgency* with which solutions must be found becomes steadily greater in response to the increased rate of activity and the increasingly global nature of that activity. Augmenting man's intellect, in the sense defined above, would warrant full pursuit by an enlightened society if there could be shown a reasonable approach and some plausible benefits.

This report covers the first phase of a program aimed at developing means to augment the human intellect. These "means" can include many things—all of which appear to be but extensions of means developed and used in the past to help man apply his native sensory, mental, and motor capabilities—and we consider the whole system of a human and his augmentation means as a proper field of search for practical possibilities. It is a very important system to our society, and like most systems its performance can best be improved by considering the whole as a set of interacting components rather than by considering the components in isolation.

This kind of system approach to human intellectual effectiveness does not find a ready-made conceptual framework such as exists for established disciplines. Before a research program can be designed to pursue such an approach intelligently so that practical benefits might be derived within a reasonable time while also producing results of long-range significance, a conceptual framework must be searched out—a framework that provides orientation as to the important factors of the system, the relationships among these factors, the types of change among the system factors that offer likely improvements in performance, and the sort of research goals and methodology that seem promising.[1]

In the first (search) phase of our program, we have developed a conceptual framework that seems satisfactory for the current needs of designing a research phase. Section 1.2 contains the essence of this framework as derived from several different ways of looking at the system made up of a human and his intellect-augmentation means.

The process of developing this conceptual framework brought out a number of significant realizations that the intellectual effectiveness exercised today by a given human has little likelihood of being intelligence limited; that there are dozens of disciplines in engineering, mathematics, and the social, life, and physical sciences that can contribute improvements to the system of intellect-augmentation means; that any one such improvement can be expected to trigger a chain of coordinating improvements; that until every one of these disciplines comes to a standstill and we have exhausted all the improvement possibilities we could glean from it, we can expect to continue to develop improvements in this human-intellect system; that there is no particular reason not to expect gains in personal intellectual effectiveness from a concerted system-oriented approach that compare to those made in personal geographic mobility since horseback and sailboat days.

The picture of how one can view the possibilities for a systematic approach to increasing human intellectual effectiveness, as put forth in Section 1.2 in the sober and general terms of an initial basic analysis, does not seem to convey all of the richness and promise that was stimulated by the development of that picture. Consequently, Section 1.3 is intended to present some definite images that illustrate meaningful possibilities derivable from the conceptual framework presented in Section 1.2—and in a rather marked deviation from ordinary technical writing, a good portion of Section 1.3 presents these images in a fiction-dialogue style as a mechanism for transmitting a feeling for the richness and promise of the possibilities in one region of the improvement space" that is roughly mapped in Section 1.2.

The style of Section 1.3 seems to make for easier reading. If Section 1.2 begins to seem unrewardingly difficult, the reader may find it helpful to skip from Section 1.1.2 directly to Section 1.3. If it serves its purpose well enough, Section 1.3 will provide a context within which the reader can go back and finish Section 1.2 with less effort.

In Section 1.4 (Research Recommendations), we present a general strategy for pursuing research toward increasing human intellectual effectiveness. This strategy evolved directly from the concepts presented in Sections 1.2 and 1.3; one of its important precepts is to pursue the quickest gains first, and use the increased intellectual effectiveness thus derived to help pursue successive gains. We see the quickest gains emerging from (1) giving the human the minute-by-minute services of a digital computer equipped with computer-driven cathode-ray-tube display, and (2) developing new methods of thinking and working that allow the human to capitalize upon the computer's help. By this same strategy, we recommend that an initial research effort develop a prototype system of this sort aimed at increasing human effectiveness in the task of computer programming.

To give the reader an initial orientation about what sort of thing this computer-aided working system might be, we include below a short description of a possible system of this sort. This illustrative example is not to be considered a description of the actual system that will emerge from the program. It is given only to show the general direction of the work and is clothed in fiction only to make it easier to visualize.

Let us consider an augmented architect at work. He sits at a working station that has a visual display screen some three feet on the side; this is his working surface, and is controlled by a computer (his "clerk") with which he can communicate by means of a small keyboard and various other devices.

He is designing a building. He has already dreamed up several basic layouts and structural forms and is trying them out on the screen. The surveying data for the layout he is working on now have already been entered, and he has just coaxed the clerk to show him a perspective view of the steep hillside building site with the roadway above, symbolic representations of the various trees that are to remain on the lot, and the service tie points for the different utilities. The view occupies the left two-thirds of the screen. With a "pointer", he indicates two points of interest, moves his left hand rapidly over the keyboard, and the distance and elevation between the points indicated appear on the right-hand third of the screen.

Now he enters a reference line with his pointer and the keyboard. Gradually, the screen begins to show the work he is doing—a neat excavation appears on the hillside—revises itself slightly, and revises itself again. After a moment, the architect changes the scene on the screen to an overhead plan view of the site, still showing the excavation. A few minutes of study, and he enters on the keyboard a list of items, checking each one as it appears on the screen, to be studied later.

Ignoring the representation on the display, the architect next begins to enter a series of specifications and data—a six-inch slab floor, twelve-inch concrete walls eight feet high within the excavation, and so on. When he has finished, the revised scene appears on the screen. A structure is taking shape. He examines it, adjusts it, pauses long enough to ask for handbook or catalog information from the clerk at various points, and readjusts accordingly. He often recalls from the "clerk" his working lists of specifications and considerations to refer to them, modify them, or add to them. These lists grow into an evermore-detailed, interlinked structure, which represents the maturing thought behind the actual design.

Prescribing different planes here and there, curved surfaces occasionally, and moving the whole structure about five feet, he finally has the rough external form of the building balanced nicely with the setting and he is assured that this form is basically compatible with the materials to be used as well as with the function of the building.

Now he begins to enter detailed information about the interior. Here the capability of the clerk to show him any view he wants to examine (a slice of the interior, or how the structure would look from the roadway above) is important. He enters particular fixture designs, and examines them in a particular room. He checks to make sure that sun glare from the windows will not blind a driver on the roadway, and the "clerk" computes the information that one window will reflect strongly onto the roadway between 6 and 6:30 on midsummer mornings.

Next, he begins a functional analysis. He has a list of the people who will occupy this building and the daily sequences of their activities. The "clerk" allows him to follow each in turn, examining how doors swing, and where special lighting might be needed. Finally, he has the "clerk" combine all of these sequences of activity to indicate spots where traffic is heavy in the building, or where congestion might occur, and to determine what the severest drain on the utilities is likely to be.

All of this information (the building design and its associated "thought structure") can be stored on a tape to represent the design manual for the building. Loading this tape into his own clerk, another architect, a builder, or the client can maneuver within this design manual to pursue whatever details or insights are of interest to him—and can append special notes that are integrated into the design manual for his own or someone else's later benefit.

In such a future working relationship between human problem-solver and computer "clerk", the capability of the computer for executing mathematical processes would be used whenever it was needed. However, the computer has many other capabilities for manipulating and displaying information that can be of significant benefit to the human in nonmathematical processes of planning, organizing, studying, etc. Every person who does his thinking with symbolized concepts (whether in the form of the English language, pictographs, formal logic, or mathematics) should be able to benefit significantly.

1.1.2 Objective of the Study

The objective of this study is to develop a conceptual framework within which could grow a coordinated research and development program whose goals would be the following: (1) To find the factors that limit the effectiveness of the individual's basic information-handling capabilities in meeting the various needs of society for problem-solving in its most general sense; and (2) to develop new techniques, procedures, and systems that will better match our needs' problems and progress of society. We have placed the following specifications on this framework:

1. It provides perspective for both long-range basic research and research that will yield practical results soon.
2. It indicates what this augmentation will actually involve in the way of changes in working environment, in thinking, in skills, and in methods of working.
3. It establishes a basis for evaluating the possible relevance of work and knowledge from existing fields and for assimilating whatever is relevant.
4. It reveals areas where research is possible and ways to assess the research, be a basis for choosing starting points, and indicate how to develop appropriate methodologies for the needed research.

Two points need emphasis here. First, although a conceptual framework has been constructed, it is still rudimentary. Further search, and actual research, are needed for the evolution of the framework. Second, even if our conceptual framework did provide an accurate and complete basic analysis of the system from which stems a human's intellectual effectiveness, the explicit nature of future improved systems would be highly affected by (expected) changes in our technology or in our understanding of the human being.

1.2 Conceptual Framework

1.2.1 General

The conceptual framework we seek must orient us toward the real possibilities and problems associated with using modern technology to give direct aid to an individual in comprehending complex situations, isolating the significant factors, and solving problems. To gain this orientation, we examine how individuals achieve their present level of effectiveness and expect that this examination will reveal possibilities for improvement.

The entire effect of an individual on the world stems essentially from what he can transmit to the world through his limited motor channels. This in turn is based on information received from the outside world through limited sensory channels; on information, drives, and needs generated within him; and on his processing of that information. His processing is of two kinds: that which he is generally conscious of (recognizing patterns, remembering, visualizing, abstracting, deducing, inducing, etc.), and that involving the unconscious processing and mediating of received and self-generated information, and the unconscious mediating of conscious processing itself.

The individual does not use this information and this processing to grapple directly with the sort of complex situation in which we seek to give him help. He uses his innate capabilities in a rather more indirect fashion, since the situation is generally too complex to yield directly to his motor actions, and always too complex to yield comprehensions and solutions from direct sensory inspection and use of basic cognitive capabilities. For instance, an aborigine who possesses all of our basic sensory-mental-motor capabilities, but does not possess our background of indirect knowledge and procedure, cannot organize the proper direct actions necessary to drive a car through traffic, request a book from the library, call a committee meeting to discuss a tentative plan, call someone on the telephone, or compose a letter on the typewriter.

Our culture has evolved means for us to organize the little things we can do with our *basic* capabilities so that we can derive comprehension from truly complex situations, and accomplish the processes of deriving and implementing problem solutions. The ways in which human capabilities are thus extended are here called augmentation means, and we define four basic classes of them:

1. ***Artifacts***: Physical objects designed to provide for human comfort, for the manipulation of things or materials, and for the manipulation of symbols.
2. ***Language***: The way in which the individual parcels out the picture of his world into the concepts that his mind uses to model that world, and the symbols that he attaches to those concepts and uses in consciously manipulating the concepts ("thinking").
3. ***Methodology***: The methods, procedures, strategies, etc., with which an individual organizes his *goal-centered* (problem-solving) activity.
4. ***Training***: The conditioning needed by the human being to bring his skills in using Means 1, 2, and 3 to the point where they are operationally effective.

The system we want to improve can thus be visualized as a trained human being together with his artifacts, language, and methodology. The explicit new system we contemplate will involve artifacts computers, and computer-controlled information-storage, information-handling, and information-display devices.

The aspects of the conceptual framework that are discussed here are primarily those relating to the human being's ability to make significant use of such equipment in an integrated system.

Pervading all of the augmentation means a particular structure or organization. While an untrained aborigine cannot drive a car through traffic, because he cannot leap the gap between his cultural background and the kind of world that contains cars and traffic, it is possible to move step by step through an organized training program that will enable him to drive effectively and safely. In other words, the human mind neither learns nor acts by large leaps, but by steps organized or structured so that each one depends upon previous steps.

Although the size of the step a human being can take in comprehension, innovation, or execution is small in comparison to the overall size of the step needed to solve a complex problem, human beings nevertheless do solve complex problems. It is the augmentation which means serving to break down a large problem in such a way that the human being can walk through it with his little steps, and it is the structure or organization of these little steps or actions that we discuss as *process hierarchies*.

Every process of thought or action is made up of sub-processes. Let us consider such examples as making a pencil stroke, writing a letter of the alphabet, or making a plan. Quite a few discrete muscle movements are organized into the making of a pencil stroke; similarly, making particular pencil strokes and making a plan for a letter are complex processes in themselves that become sub-processes to the overall writing of an alphabetic character.

Although every sub-process is a process in its own right, in that it consists of further sub-processes, there seems to be no point here in looking for the ultimate bottom of the process-hierarchical structure. There seems to be no way of telling whether or not the apparent bottoms (processes that cannot be further subdivided) exist in the physical world or in the limitations of human understanding.

In any case, it is not necessary to begin from the bottom in discussing particular process hierarchies. No person uses a process that is completely unique every time he tackles something new. Instead, he begins from a group of basic sensory-mental-motor process capabilities and adds to these certain of the process capabilities of his artifacts. There are only a finite number of such basic human and artifact capabilities from which to draw. Furthermore, even quite different higher order processes may have in common relatively high-order sub-processes".

When a man writes prose text (a reasonably high-order process), he makes use of many processes as sub-processes that are common to other high-order processes. For example, he makes use of planning, composing, and dictating. The process of writing is utilized as a sub-process within many different processes of a still higher order, such as organizing a committee, changing a policy, and so on.

What happens, then, is that each individual develops a certain repertoire of process capabilities from which he selects and adapts those that will compose the processes that he executes. This repertoire is like a tool kit, and just as the mechanic must know what his tools can do and how to use them, so the intellectual worker must know the capabilities of his tools and have good methods, strategies, and rules of thumb for making use of them. All of the process capabilities in the individual's repertoire rest ultimately upon basic capabilities within him or his artifacts, and the entire repertoire represents an inter-knit, hierarchical structure (which we often call the *repertoire hierarchy*).

We find three general categories of process capabilities within a typical individual's repertoire. Some are executed completely within the human integument, which we call explicit-human process capabilities; there are those possessed by artifacts for executing processes without human intervention, which we call *explicit-artifact* process capabilities; and there are what we call the *composite* process capabilities, which are derived from hierarchies containing both of the other kinds.

We assume that it is our H-LAM/T system (human using language, artifacts, methodology, in which he is trained) that has the capability and that performs the process in any instance of use of this repertoire. Let us look within the process structure for the LAM/T ingredients, to get a better "feel" for our models. Consider the process of writing an important memo. There is a particular concept associated with this process—that of putting information into a formal package and distributing it to a set of people for a certain kind of consideration—and the type of information package associated with this concept has been given the special name of *memorandum*. Already the system language shows the effect of this process—that is, a concept and its name.

The memo-writing process may be executed by using a set of process capabilities (in intermixed or repetitive form) such as the following planning, developing subject matter, composing text, producing hard copy, and distributing. There is a definite way in which these sub-processes will be organized that represents part of the system methodology. Each of these sub-processes represents a functional concept that must be a part of the system language if it is to be organized effectively into the human's way of doing things, and the symbolic portrayal of each concept must be such that the human can work with it and remember it.

If the memo is simple, a paragraph or so in length, then the first three processes may well be of the explicit-human type (i.e., it may be planned, developed, and composed within the mind) and the last two of the composite type. If it is a complex memo, involving a good deal of careful planning and development, then all of the sub-processes might well be of the composite type (e.g., at least including the use of pencil and paper artifacts) and there might be many different applications of some of the process capabilities within the total process (i.e., successive drafts, revised plans).

The set of sub-process capabilities discussed so far if called upon in proper occasion and sequence, would indeed enable the execution of the memo-writing process. However, the very process of organizing and supervising the utilization of these sub-process capabilities is itself a most important sub-process of the memo-writing process. Hence, the sub-process capabilities as listed would not be complete without the addition of a seventh capability—what we call the *executive* capability. This is the capability stemming from habit, strategy, rules of thumb, prejudice, learned method, intuition, unconscious dictates, or combinations thereof, to call upon the appropriate sub-process capabilities with a particular sequence and timing. An executive process (i.e., the exercise of an executive capability) involves such sub-processes as planning, selecting, and supervising, and it is really the executive processes that embody all of the methodologies in the H-LAM/T system.

To illustrate the capability-hierarchy features of our conceptual framework, let us consider an artifact innovation appearing directly within the relatively low-order capability for composing and modifying written text, and see how this can affect a (or, for instance, your) hierarchy of capabilities. Suppose you had a new writing machine—think of it as a high-speed electric typewriter with some special features. You could operate its keyboard to cause it to write text much as you could use a conventional typewriter. But the printing mechanism is more complicated; besides printing a visible character at every stroke, it adds special encoding features by means of invisible selective components in the ink and special shaping of the character.

As an auxiliary device, there is a gadget that is held like a pencil and, instead of a point, has a special sensing mechanism that you can pass over a line of the special printing from your writing machine (or one like it). The signals this reading stylus sends through the flexible connecting wire to the writing machine are used to determine which characters are being sensed and thus to cause the automatic typing of a duplicate string of characters. An information-storage mechanism in the writing machine permits you to sweep the reading stylus over the characters much faster than the writer can type; the writer will catch up with you when you stop to think about what word or string of words should be duplicated next, or while you reposition the straightedge guide along which you run the stylus.

This writing machine would permit you to use a new process of composing text. For instance, trial drafts could rapidly be composed of re-arranged excerpts of old drafts, together with new words or passages which you stop to type in. Your first draft could represent a free outpouring of thoughts in any order, with the inspection of foregoing thoughts continuously stimulating new considerations and ideas to be entered. If the tangle of thoughts represented by the draft became too complex, you would compile a reordered draft quickly. It would be practical for you to accommodate more complexity in the trails of thought you might build in search of the path that suits your needs.

You can integrate your new ideas more easily, and thus harness your creativity more continuously, if you can quickly and flexibly change your working record. If it is easier to update any part of your working record to accommodate new developments in thought or circumstance, you will find it easier to incorporate more complex procedures in your way of doing things. This will probably allow you to accommodate the extra burden associated with, for instance, keeping and using special files whose contents are both contributed to and utilized by any current work in a flexible manner—which in turn enables you to devise and use even-more complex procedures to better harness your talents in your particular working situation.

The important thing to appreciate here is that a direct new innovation in one particular capability can have far-reaching effects throughout the rest of your capability hierarchy. A change can propagate up through the capability hierarchy; higher-order capabilities that can utilize the initially changed capability can now reorganize to take special advantage of this change and of the intermediate higher-capability changes. A change can propagate *down* through the hierarchy as a result of new capabilities at the high level and modification possibilities latent in lower levels. These latent capabilities may previously have been unusable in the hierarchy and become usable because of the new capability at the higher level.

The writing machine and its flexible copying capability would occupy you for a long time if you tried to exhaust the reverberating chain of associated possibilities for making useful innovations within your capability hierarchy. This one innovation could trigger a rather extensive redesign of this hierarchy; your way of accomplishing many of your tasks would change considerably. Indeed this process characterizes the sort of evolution that our intellect-augmentation means have been undergoing since the first human brain appeared.

To our objective of deriving orientation about possibilities for actively pursuing an increase in human intellectual effectiveness, it is important to realize that we must be prepared to pursue such new-possibility chains throughout the *entire* capability hierarchy (calling for a system approach). It is also important to realize that we must be oriented to the *synthesis* of new capabilities from reorganization of other capabilities, both old and new, that exist throughout the hierarchy (calling for a "system-engineering" approach).

1.2.2 The Basic Perspective

Individuals who operate effectively in our culture have already been considerably "augmented". Basic human capabilities for sensing stimuli, performing numerous mental operations, and for communicating with the outside world, are put to work in our society within a system—an H-LAM/T system—the individual augmented by the language, artifacts, and methodology in which he is trained. Furthermore, we suspect that improving the effectiveness of the individual as he operates in our society should be approached as a system-engineering problem—that is, the H-LAM/T system should be studied as an interacting whole from a synthesis-oriented approach.

This view of the system as an interacting whole is strongly bolstered by considering the repertoire hierarchy of process capabilities that is structured from the basic ingredients within the H-LAM/T system. The realization that any potential change in language, artifact, or methodology has importance only relative to its use within a process' and that a new process capability appearing anywhere within that hierarchy can make practical a new consideration of latent change possibilities in many other parts of the hierarchy—possibilities in either language, artifacts, or methodology—brings out the strong interrelationship of these three augmentation means.

Increasing the effectiveness of the individual's use of his basic capabilities is a problem in redesigning the changeable parts of a system. The system is actively engaged in the continuous processes (among others) of developing comprehension within the individual and of solving problems; both processes are subject to human motivation, purpose, and will. To redesign the system's capability for performing these processes means redesigning all or part of the repertoire hierarchy. To redesign a structure, we must learn as much as we can of what is known about the basic materials and components as they are utilized within the structure; beyond that, we must learn how to view, to measure, to analyze, and to evaluate in terms of the functional whole and its purpose. In this particular case, no existing analytic theory is by itself adequate for the purpose of analyzing and evaluating overall system performance; pursuit of an improved system thus demands the use of *experimental* methods.

It need not be just the very sophisticated or formal process capabilities that are added or modified in this redesign. Essentially any of the processes utilized by a representative human today—the processes that he thinks of when he looks ahead to his day's work—are composite processes of the sort that involve external composing and manipulating of symbols (text, sketches, diagrams, lists, etc.). Many of the external composing and manipulating (modifying, rearranging) processes serve such characteristically "human" activities as playing with forms and relationships to ask what develops, cut-and-try multiple-pass development of an idea, or listing items to reflect on and then rearranging and extending them as thoughts develop.

Existing, or near-future, technology could certainly provide our professional problem-solvers with the artifacts they need to have for duplicating and rearranging text before their eyes, quickly and with a minimum of human effort. Even so apparently minor an advance could yield total changes in an individual's repertoire hierarchy that would represent a great increase in overall effectiveness. Normally the necessary equipment would enter the market slowly; changes from the expected would be small, people would change their ways of doing things a little at a time, and only gradually would their accumulated changes create markets for more radical versions of the equipment. Such an evolutionary process has been typical of the way our repertoire hierarchies have grown and formed.

But an active research effort, aimed at exploring and evaluating possible integrated changes throughout the repertoire hierarchy, could greatly accelerate this evolutionary process. The research effort could guide the product development of new artifacts toward taking long-range meaningful steps; simultaneously competitively minded individuals who would respond to demonstrated methods for achieving greater personal effectiveness would create a market for the more radical equipment innovations. The guided evolutionary process could be expected to be considerably more rapid than the traditional one.

The category of "more radical innovations" includes the digital computer as a tool for the personal use of an individual. Here there is not only promise of great flexibility in the composing and rearranging of text and diagrams before the individual's eyes but also promise of many other process capabilities that can be integrated into the H-LAM/T system's repertoire hierarchy.

1.2.3 Detailed Discussion of the H-LAM/T System

1.2.3.1 The Source of Intelligence

When one looks at a computer system that is doing a very complex job, he sees on the surface a machine that can execute some extremely sophisticated processes. If he is a layman, his concept of what provides this sophisticated capability may endow the machine with a mysterious power to sweep information through perceptive and intelligent synthetic thinking devices. Actually, this sophisticated capability results from a very clever organizational hierarchy so that pursuit of the source of intelligence within this system would take one down through layers of functional and physical organization that become successively more primitive.

To be more specific, we can begin at the top and list the major levels down through which we would pass if we successively decomposed the functional elements of each level in search of the "source of intelligence". A programmer could take us down through perhaps three levels (depending upon the sophistication of the total process being executed by the computer) perhaps depicting the organization at each level with a flow chart. The first level down would organize functions corresponding to statements in a problem-oriented language (e.g., ALGOL or COBOL), to achieve the desired overall process. The second level down would organize lesser functions into the processes represented by first-level statements. The third level would perhaps show how the basic machine commands (or rather the processes which they represent) were organized to achieve each of the functions of the second level.

Then a machine designer could take over, and with a block diagram of the computer's organization, he could show us (Level 4) how the different hardware units (e.g., random-access storage, arithmetic registers, adder, arithmetic control) are organized to provide the capability of executing sequences of the commands used in Level 3. The logic designer could then give us a tour of Level 5, also using block diagrams, to show us how such hardware elements as pulse gates, flip-flops, and AND, OR, and NOT circuits can be organized into networks giving the functions utilized at Level 4. For Level 6, a circuit engineer could show us diagrams revealing how components such as transistors, resistors, capacitors, and diodes can be organized into modular networks that provide the functions needed for the elements of Level 5.

Device engineers and physicists of different kinds could take us down through more layers. But rather soon we have crossed the boundary between what is man-organized and what is nature-organized, and are ultimately discussing the way in which a given physical phenomenon is derived from the intrinsic organization of sub-atomic particles, with our ability to explain succeeding layers blocked by the exhaustion of our present human comprehension.

If we then ask ourselves where that intelligence is embodied, we are forced to concede that it is elusively distributed throughout a hierarchy of functional processes—a hierarchy whose foundation extends down into natural processes below the depth of our comprehension. If there is any one thing upon which this "intelligence depends" it would seem to be *organization*. The biologists and physiologists use the term "synergism" to designate (from *Webster's Unabridged Dictionary*, Second Edition) the "...cooperative action of discrete agencies such that the total effect is greater than the sum of the two effects taken independently..." This term seems directly applicable here, where we could say that synergism is our most likely candidate for representing the actual source of intelligence

Actually, each of the social life or physical phenomena we observe about us would seem to derive from a supporting hierarchy of organized functions (or processes), in which the synergistic principle gives increased phenomenological sophistication to each succeedingly higher level of organization. In particular, the intelligence of a human being, derived ultimately from the characteristics of individual nerve cells, undoubtedly results from synergism.

1.2.3.2 Intelligence Amplification

It has been jokingly suggested several times during the course of this study that what we are seeking is an "intelligence amplifier" (the term is attributed originally to W. Ross Ashby).[2,3] At first, this term was rejected on the grounds that in our view one's only hope was to make a better match between existing human intelligence and the problems to be tackled, rather than to make man more intelligent. But deriving the concepts brought out in the preceding section has shown us that indeed this term does seem applicable to our objective.

Accepting the term "intelligence amplification" does not imply any attempt to increase native human intelligence. The term "intelligence amplification" seems applicable to our goal of augmenting the human intellect in that the entity to be produced will exhibit more of what can be called intelligence than an unaided human could; we will have amplified the intelligence of the human by organizing his intellectual capabilities into higher levels of synergistic structuring. What possesses the amplified intelligence is the resulting H-LAM/T system, in which the LAM/T augmentation means represent the amplifier of the human's intelligence.

In amplifying our intelligence, we are applying the principle of synergistic structuring that was followed by natural evolution in developing the basic human capabilities. What we have done in the development of our augmentation means to construct a superstructure that is a synthetic extension of the natural structure upon which it is built. In a very real sense, as represented by the steady evolution of our augmentation means, the development of "artificial intelligence" has been going on for centuries.

1.2.3.3 Two-Domain System

The human and the artifacts are the only physical components in the H-LAM/T system. It is upon their capabilities that the ultimate capability of the system will depend. This was implied in the earlier statement that every composite process of the system decomposes ultimately into explicit-human and explicit-artifact processes. There are thus two separate domains of activity within the H-LAM/T system: that represented by the human, in which all explicit-human processes occur; and that represented by the artifacts, in which all explicit-artifact processes occur. In any composite process, there is cooperative interaction between the two domains, requiring interchange of energy (much of it for information exchange purposes only). Figure 1.1 depicts this two-domain concept and embodies other concepts discussed below.

Where a complex machine represents the principal artifact with which a human being cooperates, the term "man-machine interface" has been used for some years to represent the boundary across which energy is exchanged between the two domains. However, the "man-artifact interface" has existed for centuries, ever since humans began using artifacts and executing composite processes.

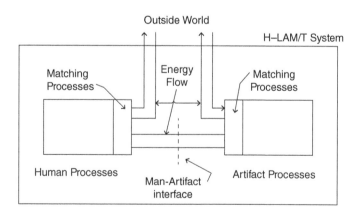

FIGURE 1.1 The two sides of the H-LAM/T system.

Exchange across this "interface" occurs when an explicit-human process is coupled to an explicit-artifact process. Quite often these coupled processes are designed for just this exchange purpose, to provide a functional match between other explicit-human and explicit-artifact processes buried within their respective domains that do the more significant things. For instance, the finger and hand motions (explicit human processes) activate key-linkage motions in the typewriter (couple to explicit-artifact processes). But these are only part of the matching processes between the deeper human processes that direct a given word to be typed and the deeper artifact processes that actually imprint the ink marks on the paper.

The outside world interacts with our H-LAM/T system by the exchange of energy with either the individual or his artifact. Again, special processes are often designed to accommodate this exchange. However, the direct concern of our present study lies within the system, with the internal processes that are and can be significantly involved in the effectiveness of the *system* in developing the human's comprehension and pursuing the human's goals.

Acknowledgement

October 1962

SRI Summary Report AFOSR-3223 • Prepared for: Director of Information Sciences, Air Force Office of Scientific Research, Washington DC, Contract AF 49(638)-1024 • SRI Project No. 3578 (AUGMENT 3906).

Click here for scan of the original printed report [PDF/Print | eReader]

See also About Doug's 1962 Report for more resources.

Notes

1 Kennedy and Putt (see Ref. [1] in the list at the end of the report) bring out the importance of the conceptual framework to the process of research. They point out that new, multi-disciplinary research generally finds no such framework to fit within, that a framework of sorts would grow eventually, but that an explicit framework-search phase preceding the research is much to be preferred.

2 The reference is to p. 42 of B. C. Vickery's *Classification and Indexing in Science* which is Ref. [26] at the end of the report.

3 The reference is to *The Measurement of Meaning*, which is Ref. [27]

References

1. Kennedy, J. L. and Putt, G. H., "Administration of Research in a Research Corporation," RAND Corporation Report P-847 (20 April 1956).
2. Ashby, Ross, *Design for a Brain* (John Wiley & Sons, New York City, NY, 1960).
3. Ashby, Ross, "Design for an Intelligence-Amplifier," *Automata Studies*, edited by C. E. Shannon and J. McCarthy, pp. 215–234 (Princeton University Press, Princeton, 1956).

4. Korzybski, A, *Science and Sanity*, 1st Ed. (International non Aristotelian Library Publishing Co., Lancaster, PA, 1933).
5. Whorf, B. L., *Language, Thought, and Reality* (MIT & John Wiley & Sons, Inc., New York City, NY, 1956).
6. Bush, V., "As We May Think," *The Atlantic Monthly* (July 1945).
7. Newell, A. (editor), *Information Processing Language-V Manual* (Prentice-Hall, Inc., Englewood Cliffs, NJ, 1961).
8. McCarthy, J., "LISP 1.5 Programmer's Manual," Computation Center and Research Laboratory of Electronics, MIT (14 July 1961).
9. Gelernter, H., Hansen, J. R., and Gerberich, C. L., "A Fortran Compiled List-Processing Language," *Journal of the Association for Computing Machinery*, Vol. 7, pp. 87–101 (April 1960).
10. Yngve, V. H., "Introduction to COMIT Programming," Technical Report, Research Laboratories of Electronics and Computation Center, MIT (5 November 1961).
11. Yngve, V. H., "COMIT Programmer's Reference Manual," Technical Report, Research Laboratories of Electronics and Computation Center, MIT (5 November 1961).
12. Perlis, A. J. and Thornton, C., "Symbol Manipulation by Threaded Lists," *Communications of the ACM*, Vol. 3, No. 4 (April 1960).
13. Carr, J. W., III, "Recursive Subscripting Compilers and List-Type Memories," *Communications of the ACM*, Vol. 2, pp. 4–6 (February 1959).
14. Weizenbaum, J., "Knotted List Structures," *Communications of the ACM*, Vol. 5, No. 3, pp. 161–165 (March 1962).
15. Licklider, J. C. R., "Man-Computer Symbiosis," *IRE Transactions on Human Factors in Electronics*, Vol. 1, pp. 4–11 (March 1960).
16. Ulam, S. M., *A Collection of Mathematical Problems*, p. 135 (Interscience Publishers, Inc., New York, NY, 1960).
17. Good, I. J., "How Much Science Can You Have at Your Fingertips?" *IBM Journal of Research and Development*, Vol. 2, No. 4 (October 1958).
18. Ramo, S., "A New Technique of Education," *IRE Transactions on Education*, Vol. 1, 37–42 (June 1958).
19. Ramo, S., "The Scientific Extension of the Human Intellect," *Computers and Automation* (February 1961).
20. Fein, L., "The Computer-Related Science (Synnoetics) at a University in the Year 1975," unpublished paper (December 1960).
21. Licklider, J. C. R. and Clark, W. E., "On-Line Man-Computer Communication," *Proceedings Spring Joint Computer Conference*, Vol. 21, pp. 113–128 (National Press, Palo Alto, CA, May 1962).
22. Culler, G. J. and Huff, R. W., "Solution of Non-Linear Integral Equations Using On-Line Computer Control," Ramo-Wooldridge, Canoga Park, California, paper for presentation *at SJCC, San Francisco* (May 1962).
23. Teager, H. M., "Real-Time, Time-Shared Computer Project," report, MIT, Contract Nonr-1841(69) DSR 8644 (1 July 1961).
24. Teager, H. M., "Systems Considerations in Real-Time Computer Usage," paper presented at *ONR Symposium on Automated Teaching* (12 October 1961).
25. Randa, Glenn C., "Design of a Remote Display Console," Report ESL, R-132, MIT, Cambridge, Massachusetts (available through ASTIA) (February 1962).

26. Vickery, B. C., *Classification and Indexing in Science*, p. 42 (Academic Press, Inc., New York, 1959).
27. Osgood, C. E., Suci, G. J., and Tannenbaum, P. H., *The Measurement of Meaning* (University of Illinois Press, Urbana, IL, 1957).
28. National Science Foundation, *Current Research and Development in Scientific Documentation No. 6 NSF-60-25*, p. 104 (National Science Foundation, May 1960).

2
REIMAGINING EDUCATION AND WORKFORCE PREPARATION IN SUPPORT OF THE UN'S SUSTAINABLE DEVELOPMENT GOALS

Jin Michael Fung and Samira Hosseini

Introduction

When envisioning what the future of work may hold amid automation and ubiquitous AI, one theme is prominent: A dedication to the need for reskilling, upskilling, and multi-skilling of the workforce, independent of the area of activity (Fung, 2020a). In the rapid evolution of the job market, both management and workers must respond to constant disruptions and change in order to remain relevant as contributing employees (Fung, 2020a, 2020b, Fung and Lim, 2019; Tucker, 2019). Embracing change as a constant, companies need to embrace the mindset of continuous transformation and incorporate leadership that promotes agility and support for talent identification and development. During the past few decades, the workforce has undergone a rapid transformation from traditional skill sets to upgraded tech-intensive competencies emphasizing the mastery of analytical functions, programming, product and digital marketing, human-computer interactions, mathematical computing and data-driven monitoring, planning, and informed decision making. The annual reports of the World Economic Forum (WEF) present a list of competencies required to remain employable in the increasingly competitive job market. The necessary skills perceived by WEF are a clear affirmation that a pivot is needed in preparing human talents for all aspects of the future workplace. According to these reports, 50% of employed individuals will require reskilling if they intend to remain relevant within the job market. This is at a time when the Future of Jobs Survey announces a state of emergency in the upskilling of around 40% of workers within six months or less. To unleash the full potential of the workforce and reduce the evident skills gaps, enhanced technology adoption and on-demand skill development will be necessary components (Forum, 2020).

DOI: 10.4324/9781003230762-4

As a newly emerging competency, WEF declares a set of self-management skills including "active learning, resilience, stress tolerance and flexibility" as highly essential for the future of job market inclusion. Such skills are particularly meaningful in light of the multitude of disruptions the world is experiencing. These disruptions can be classified into the following: (1) Technological advancements and digital transformation (displacement of jobs due to automation and robotics); (2) shifting demographics (an aging population and a long-term significant decline in birth rate; hence, the need for better, extended training programs for the workforce); (3) longevity (multiple stages of life that may require different skills and a continuous process of upgrading and expanding competencies); (4) globalization and localization (intertwined economic and supply chain initiatives that switch reflexively from global to local levels); and (5) global pandemics and endemics (including the recent COVID-19 pandemic and economic breakdowns that followed lost jobs and other created opportunities which require accessing new skills). In this inevitable paradigm shift, a strong partnership between stakeholders, including higher education institutions, governments, nonprofit and philanthropic organizations, and policymakers is more necessary than ever. This transition, however, will take time and resources. It is estimated to take up to two months to upgrade skills related to content writing, sales and marketing, two to three months to develop skills related to product development, data and AI/ML, and four to five months to acquire cloud computing and engineering skills. Smart planning and the bounty of technological advancements could leverage the multiple dimensions of this revolutionary approach to talent development and maintenance (Forum, 2020).

One such example is the SkillsFuture movement that originated in Singapore as a means to foster skills mastery and develop new competencies among the population of the country, covering diverse demographics and age brackets. The movement is based upon four main thrusts: Helping individuals make informed decisions regarding their education and careers, developing a high-quality education system compatible with the new needs of the ever-evolving workplace, promoting employer recognition and career development on the basis of skills mastery, and developing a culture of lifelong learning. The overarching principle that drives the efforts of this movement is the ideal of preparing the nation's population for the new and upcoming demands of the professional world and equipping them with the skills needed to develop an inclusive society (Fung, 2020b; Fung, Taal, & Sim, 2021; Mourshed and Fung, 2021).

One initiative under the movement is an alliance between SkillsFuture Singapore, a Singaporean government agency responsible for reskilling the workforce, Singapore's publicly funded polytechnics and Generation, a global nonprofit dedicated to skilling and positioning learners for the workforce. The initiative targeted specific skills gaps in the labor market by providing training in an entirely new manner. Identifying the need to invest in mid-career workers (aged 40 or above), the initiative provided 8- to 12-week training bootcamps for specific, tech-related positions which were comprised of technical modules and importantly on mindset and soft skills development. As the training programs were designed based on extensive interviews with employers on their needs, high placement rates were achieved for graduates into full-time jobs within the respective tech industries. The lessons learned from the initiative illuminated the following: (1) Training was of interest to young learners and also attracted considerable attention (30%–50%) from those aged 40 or above; (2) while all learners demonstrated proficiency in the acquired skills, the over 40 groups encountered challenges, including lower levels of self-confidence and ageism when dealing with employers; (3) this lack of self-esteem could be addressed through mock interviews, mentorship, and conducting job fairs (Mourshed and Fung, 2021).

Another key player in this paradigm shift, and in closing the skills gaps, is higher education. By implementing new strategies and educational models, higher education institutions can nurture the future workforce by cultivating skills that are urgently demanded by headhunters and employers. One such model is Tec-21 offered by Tecnologico de Monterrey, a leading higher education institution in Mexico with 31 campuses across the country, over 94,000 students, and nearly 11,000 faculty members. This educational model is based on four main components: (1) Challenge-based learning; (2) flexibility; (3) a memorable university experience; and (4) inspiring professors. The goal of Tec-21 is "to provide comprehensive education and … strengthening the skills of the next generations to develop the competencies required to become leaders who will face the challenges and opportunities of the 21st-century". (Casanova et al., 2019). Tec-21 seeks to develop a list of competencies in students ranging from self-knowledge and management, innovative entrepreneurship, and social intelligence for a commitment to ethics and citizenship, reasoning to address complexity, communication, and digital transformation. Through disciplinary and transversal competency development strategies, students are prepared to practice and expand their leadership skills, entrepreneurship spirit, humanistic outlook, and international competitiveness (Casanova et al., 2019). The implementation strategy of the Tec-21 model is presented in Figure 2.1. This educational model is offered in blocks of information units that students undertake over the course of 18 weeks. In weeks 6, 12, and 18 (i-Weeks), the learning dynamic changes whereby faculty members and students immerse themselves in a highly experiential and challenge-based learning environment outside the classroom. Activities during these i-Weeks involve receiving trainings, and subsequently signing up for social service activities, while i-Semester is an entire semester dedicated to working within an industrial environment to focus on addressing real-world problems (Bulle, 2021; Olivares et al., 2021).

Beyond these examples of effective educational innovation, the significant role AI can play in the education landscape and how it may evolve in the future should not be underestimated. Based originally upon the ability to predict outcomes or choices on the basis of numerical analytical methods such as linear regression to

Reimagining Education and Workforce Preparation for UN's SDGs   33

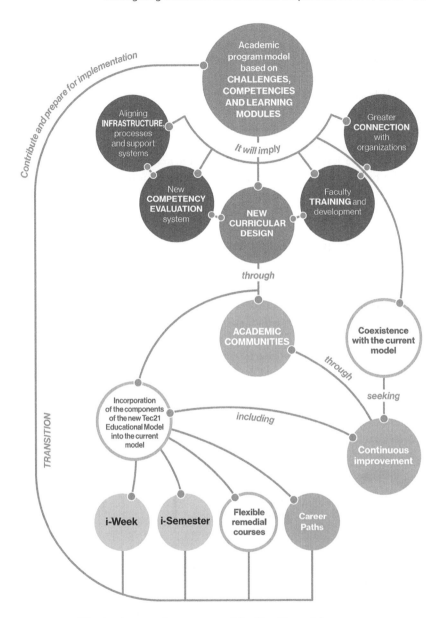

FIGURE 2.1 The implementation strategy of the Tec-21 model.

approximate a function with a given set of parameters (UNESCO, n.d.-a; Chen, Chen, & Lin, 2020), AI has developed into a full-fledged field in and of itself. This powerful tool is capable of taking teaching and learning to new levels and evolutionary dimensions while the ethical considerations around AI have always been subject to careful reflection. In teaching, AI can be used to monitor classroom responses and emotional state to tune the class to the general mood and bring students' attention to the lecture (Hernandez-de-Menendez, Morales-Menendez, Escobar, & Arinez, 2021). Tracking multiple aspects of students' behavior and biometric signs to determine if students' focus on the contents of the course has particularly proven to be useful in remote or digital classes (Wampfler, Klingler, Solenthaler, Schinazi, & Gross, 2019). For students, in turn, AI might be used for determining affinity toward specific subjects or fields of study (Martínez et al., 2021). It can also help generate content and assessments for students to practice what they have learned (Yangsheng, 2021). Integrating AI features within the industry-oriented educational environment can open various windows of opportunity to higher levels of on-demand education that is tuned to the need of individual learners.

A New Paradigm for Higher Education

As we rethink the future of work, it is necessary to reimagine the future of education and how it can serve as a scaffold for both academic attainment and skills mastery, a thriving environment that provides work experience and studies within curricula and prepares graduates to be ready to enter and continue as productive, long-term participants in the labor market. These goals require a new paradigm for skills and knowledge acquisition (Fung and Lim, 2019), a paradigm that is nonlinear and highly flexible to remain responsive, relevant, and effective toward the changing needs of the job market. To achieve these goals, we need to work in an ecosystem approach involving multiple stakeholders, to build a future of education that is FAIR, an acronym for **F**it for purpose; **A**ccessible; **I**nclusive; and **R**elevant and Responsive (Figure 2.2).

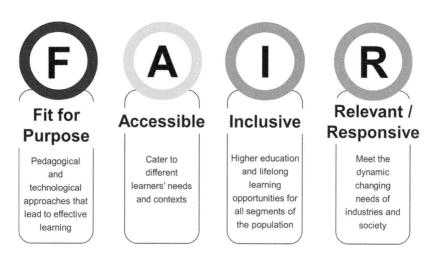

FIGURE 2.2 FAIR: a vision for the future of education, as advocated by the Institute for the Future of Education.

Fit for Purpose

In line with the pursuits of the SkillsFuture and Tec-21 models, higher education institutions will need to redesign their curricula not just for traditional students, but also to cater to nontraditional learners (i.e., adult learners and working professionals). Institutions will have to explore and make the best use of educational technologies, including massive online open courses (MOOCs), virtual reality (VR), augmented reality (AR), and simulation experiences, to meet the needs of learners across diverse backgrounds (educational achievements, age, professional competencies, constraints, etc.). A reverse thinking process that envisions the end purpose, together with a mindset of growth that is open to change and understands the current and future demands of the workplace, can be employed to successfully design and develop fit-for-purpose curricula.

Accessible

One of the potential barriers to skills development is the accessibility of education and training opportunities. Modular short-cycle programs to acquire specific work skills offered to individuals—like those provided by SkillsFuture—increase the likelihood and pace of upskilling workers at all levels. Akin to the policy interventions taken by the Government of Singapore, stakeholders and policymakers across nations should consider subsidizing such training programs as an investment toward economic development by making lifelong learning more affordable. In that regard, "Creating a regulatory and legislative framework that gives people choices over how they create the multiple stages of their life will be the priority for governments". (Gratton and Scott, 2016).

In Mexico, TecMilenio, a private higher education institution that is part of Monterrey Institute of Technology and Higher Education, offers alternative pathways for learners to advance in their competencies and careers. These include multiple degrees designed for working professionals who can pursue their studies at a personally desired pace and upgrade their skills selectively as the need becomes apparent. Moreover, a vast number of online courses (i.e., languages, mechatronics, human development, science of happiness, etc.) are open to all learners from 12 to 100 years old [5]. In addition, the Alternative Credentials Unit under the Institute for the Future of Education (IFE) has graduated more than 800 adults from data science and coding bootcamps. And the MOOCs offered by IFE have engaged more than 560,000 learners on EdX, and nearly 1.4M learners on Coursera (MOOCS, n.d.). A dedicated Vice Rectory for Lifelong Learning has been set up within Tecnologico de Monterrey, training 127,000 lifelong learners through more than 1,300 programs in the 2021–2022 academic year alone.

Inclusive

The inclusiveness theme represents a commitment to provide more equitable opportunities for all learners as one of the priorities of this educational model. The "I" within the matrix of FAIR aims to provide learners across age demographics and different socio-economic statuses with quality educational opportunities. For example in Singapore, specific interventions are put in place to enable low-wage workers to grow through progressive wage models and upgrade their work skills with corresponding increase in wages. Special programs are offered in basic literacy and numeracy training, in addition to basic digital training, to help those without such requisite competencies to level up and gain access to more learning opportunities. These aspects of inclusiveness gained even greater significance during the COVID-19 pandemic, whereby those who were displaced from their jobs were able to find other jobs through reskilling.

In countries with dispersed geographies, the digital divide between urban and rural settings and the lack of access to online systems for sustained learning in marginalized areas have contributed to a considerable gap in skill development which may not be easy to close. For the past eight years, the Líderes del Mañana program (Leaders of Tomorrow) has strengthened the principles of meritocracy, inclusion, and social mobility in Mexico. This program developed by Tecnologico de Monterrey forms a strong support system for nurturing students from low-income backgrounds through scholarship opportunities to study and grow in professions and transform their community in the future (2020, 2020). A study of the program's graduates demonstrated that, as professionals, they earn twice the salary of their peers while their average wage is 235% higher than those who did not earn a university degree. Leaders of Tomorrow have enjoyed a 22% higher rate of employability and a 50% greater chance of being formally hired. Their employment packages typically include 60% higher benefits than average, while 77% of this group of graduates hold high-profile positions in corporate businesses (lideresdelmanana, 2020).

TPrize, another initiative within IFE, issues annual calls for solutions to provide disadvantaged communities life-long learning opportunities with a strong emphasis on inclusion and diversity across Latin America and the Caribbean region (TPrize, n.d., http://tprize.mx/en/). Winners are awarded funding for their innovative projects in addressing the designed educational challenge for the year. The TPrize winners are also provided access to Growth, a personalized support and acceleration program. The solutions of TPrize target different educational levels (primary, secondary, higher education, and lifelong learning), and cater to various contexts (i.e., rural or urban) to reduce gaps across gender, race, indigenousness, and socioeconomic backgrounds. Over the past two years, TPrize has awarded ten winners from Mexico, Colombia, Chile, Brazil, Guatemala, Peru, and the USA who have successfully raised capital, gathered sponsorships, expanded their operation to other countries within the region, and have impacted tens of thousands of learners throughout Latin America and the Caribbean. One of the winners of TPrize was LAB4U, a project that has reached and benefited 16,000 students. LAB4U consists of a set of tools that aim to close the gap in quality education and access to laboratory assignments in rural and urban schools alike. Another winning project was "Ser Maestro" ("Being a teacher" in Spanish), a project centered on the identification, recognition, and training of rural setting teachers in order to develop their full potential as educators. This project has reached 130,000 beneficiaries in various rural settings upgrading their skills and abilities in a multitude of schemes.

Relevant/Responsive

To maintain relevance in the future job market, individuals must be aware of and respond to the present and future demands of the industry. One of the deficiencies of the current education system is the lack of effective communication with industry which, in turn, prevents both parties from developing a mutual understanding of the current needs and forecasting requirements for the future. The previously provided examples, the SkillsFuture movement and Tec-21 education model have successfully addressed this challenge through the alignment of training provisions with stated industry needs. It is vital for higher education to create active engagement with the industry, understand their skills needs, and thereby construct detailed competency mappings and curriculum design that effectively serve both industry and education. The challenge-based learning scheme of Tec21, for instance, involves students in solving the current questions of the industrial sector, and through the process developing the required skills to find solutions to these challenges. This development of competency and skills frameworks (incorporated in programs such as SkillsFuture and Tec21 educational model) creates a common taxonomy that is referenced by employers, training institutions, and government agencies providing quality assurance and funding support for continuous skills mastery, thereby providing a common language to building an integrated skills development system. Frequent refreshes of such frameworks are necessary to keep up-to-date with changes in industrial skills needs, and powerful tools such as AI and ML can be leveraged on big datasets from multiple sources to produce job-skills insights that are used to refine the curricula within higher education.

Five Challenges to be Addressed

In light of FAIR as a new vision for the future of education, higher education institutions have the imperative of assuring Quality and Relevance, while placing an increasing emphasis on Access, Inclusion, and Efficiency. To attain these goals, a number of challenges must be addressed including, but not limited to, (1) skills development to support job mobility of all workers and the transformation of

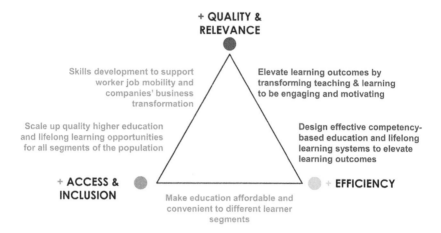

FIGURE 2.3 The imperatives for higher education institutions to deliver a future of education that is FAIR.

corporate businesses; (2) scaling up the quality of higher education and lifelong learning opportunities for all population segments; (3) transforming teaching and learning experiences to be engaging and motivating to enhance learning outcomes; (4) designing effective, competency-based education and lifelong learning systems catering to traditional and nontraditional learners; and (5) ensuring that education is affordable and convenient to different learner segments within society (Figure 2.3). To ensure that such qualities form the pillars of the future of education, collective efforts and investments at different levels and layers of society are required. Governments and policymakers, education institutions and stakeholders, nonprofits and philanthropic organizations, and diverse industrial sectors must develop as a strong alliance to address one of the agreed-upon fundamental priorities of humanity: Quality Education.

Quality Education: A Global Target

One of the enduring core challenges for humanity is to ensure that equal opportunities for well-being, growth, and progress are provided for all the 7.96 billion inhabitants of planet Earth. In the year 2000, the United Nations (UN) held a historic event in which a set of global targets, the Millennium Development Goals (MDGs), was presented (United Nations, 2015). With reducing extreme poverty and universal primary education as two of the main areas of focus, the eight MDGs became the social priorities of nations over the course of the next 15 years. Through implementing a multitude of strategies, the MDGs met some essential milestones and played a significant role in securing progress in the least privileged regions of the globe. However, after a robust review and consultations with administrations, civil societies, industries, knowledge-based organizations,

FIGURE 2.4 The seventeen Sustainable Development Goals (SDGs) of the United Nations.

Source: United Nations (https://sdgs.un.org/goals).

and citizens, it was agreed to continue with a number of the goals beyond 2015 (Fox & Stoett, 2016; Lopez-Tapia et al., 2022; Sachs, 2012).

In September 2015, the UN announced the 2030 Agenda for Sustainable Development Goals (SDGs) as a response to the urgent needs of the planet. All 193 Member States agreed on these new global missions and proposed 169 specific action plans in the economic, social, and environmental spheres to transform profoundly the current state of nations and to secure the future for the present and future generations (Figure 2.4). This international call to action was summarized into 17 targets as follows: (1) No Poverty, (2) Zero Hunger, (3) Good Health and Well-being, (4) Quality Education, (5) Gender Equality, (6) Clean Water and Sanitation, (7) Affordable and Clean Energy, (8) Decent Work and Economic Growth, (9) Industry, Innovation and Infrastructure, (10) Reduced Inequalities, (11) Sustainable Cities and Communities, (12) Responsible Consumption and Production, (13) Climate Action, (14) Life Below Water, (15) Life On Land, (16) Peace, Justice, and Strong Institutions, and (17) Partnerships for the Goals.

Adhering to the 2030 Agenda to Ensure Quality Education

Several years after this call for global action, multiple studies measured the contributions made toward the advancement of each SDG and analyzed the progress framework for each goal (Fraisl, Campbell, & See 2020; Nagy, Benedek, & Ivan, 2018). Even though the UN Statistics Division together with the Organization for Economic Co-operation and Development (OECD) developed a global SDG indicator database to keep track of the progress, the indicators are neither simple to measure nor easy to interpret. Indeed, as the Head of the World Bank's Development Economics Data Group, Haishan Fu, pointed out "Implementing the SDGs and measuring and monitoring progress toward them will require much more data than are currently available, with more accuracy, better timeliness, greater disaggregation, and higher frequency" (Dang & Serajuddin, 2020; Maurice, 2016).

It has been emphasized that progressing evenly toward all 17 SDGs is crucial, although preserving uniformity in addressing differences and inequalities may appear as a significantly greater challenge (Liu et al., 2021; Xu et al., 2020). Evenness in the progress made toward the SDGs is highly important as it determines the achievement of the goals in their entirety. While studying the gap in achievements and addressing the SDGs is in itself a call for comprehensive studies and analyses, herein we focus the discussion on the interfaces between each of these SDGs and SDG4 (Quality Education). It is evident that "Education is at the heart of sustainable development and the SDGs. For people to live sustainably, they need to learn" as stated by UNESCO (UNESCO, n.d.-b). We aim at garnering the attention of higher education institutions, industry, government agencies, and policymakers to the intertwined network of global targets that are the current priorities of nations across the globe. Additionally, it is hoped that this analysis will function as an invitation to higher education researchers to take a fresh look at the current state of progress toward the SDGs since participation of the scientific community and the resulting scholarly findings serve as powerful indicators of SDGs progress or lack thereof (Asatani, Takeda, Yamano, & Sakata, 2020; Kickbusch & Hanefeld, 2017; Marron, Naughton, & Oaks, 2019).

The Intertwined Matrix of SDGs and the Relationship with Education (SDG4)

The complex network and knotted fabric of SDGs require considerable attention from stakeholders at all levels. While each SDG has a specific target, it is hard to define them outside the context of Agenda 2030 as a whole. We have categorized these 17 goals into three main spheres including Social (SDGs 4,5,8,10,16,17), Environmental (SDGs 11–15), and Infrastructure (SDGs 1–3,6,7,9), and analyzed the impact of each sphere on education.

Social Sphere

In the Social sphere, issues pertaining to gender, and social inequalities, in addition to economic growth, prove to have an impact on quality education (SDG4). Gender disparities, under-representation, and intellectual gender bias span from pedagogy to work opportunities for girls and women. From a scholarly perspective, although SDG 5 is the most researched goal and has received tremendous attention from the academic community, it is one of the least accomplished milestones of the 2030 Agenda. Poor families often favor boys when investing in education (SDG 1) and the belief that females are not suitable candidates for studying certain areas of science and technology remains common across distinct demographics (Anne, 2017; Laufer et al., 2021), while in the workplace female professionals are less likely to be offered senior positions (Guemouria, Acebo, Rosales-Lopez, & Hosseini, 2021). Furthermore, decent work and economic growth are a direct function of quality education and skills development. For SDG 8 to become a reality, "access to information and education needs to improve, societal debates need to become more inclusive and paradigm shifts need to happen". (Stoian, Monterroso, & Current, 2019). Additionally, inequalities have a profound impact on all aspects of our civil rights and providing opportunities and equal access to social good (SDG 10). Broadly, inequality can penetrate many layers of the social fabric ranging from political (civic and inequality before the law), income (wealth inequality), opportunity (inequality in life options and access), treatment (agency and responsibility inequality), and membership (inequality in the context of the society) (Mount, 2008). Moreover, it is crucial to build efficient, reliable, and inclusive institutions at all levels in society and ensure "responsive, inclusive, participatory, and representative decision-making" that allows educators and students to become global citizens and/or life-long learners (Platform, n.d.; UNESCO, 2018).

So it is seen that in the case of Social SDGs, the absence of justice and reliable and accountable institutions can be a substantial hindrance in achieving stable socioeconomic growth, the even distribution of opportunities (SDG 10), decent work opportunities, and environment (SDG 8), as well as quality education (SDG 4) (Silander, 2021). To address this, stakeholders at all levels (the triumvirate of Government, Academia, and Industry) should ensure that enacted laws and implemented social programs substantively protect disadvantaged and vulnerable populations, and raise consciousness about the existence of societal inequalities which, in turn, would lead to more innovative solutions.

Environmental Sphere

Progress in the environmental sphere stems from our responses to natural causes, in addition to strategies that we design and undertake to further advance a sustainable setting for the inhabitants of the planet earth. SDG 11, for example, can be facilitated through consolidating nationwide and local expansion programs and growth strategies across the world. Lifelong learning, in particular, can play a crucial role in securing sustainable social and economic progression (UNESCO). In regard to sustainable consumption practices, safe and sustainable practices diminish the rate of depletion of natural resources (SDG 14 and SDG 15), limit the use of toxic constituents (SDG 3 and SDG 6), and minimize contaminating emissions, thereby honoring the anticipated needs of future generations. It is estimated that annually 1.3 billion tons of food (valued at US$1 trillion) are wasted due to unsustainable consumption (SDG 12) or poor transportation (SDG 9). The irresponsible use of energy, on the other hand, limits the access for many across the world who need to acquire even the minimum means for learning (UNESCO, n.d.-c). Educational institutions at all academic levels can encourage and involve students to provide answers to the most pressing questions of humanity with respect to responsible consumption and production (Kaliampos & Kohl, 2020). Evidence suggests that similar to the two previously discussed SDGs, climate change can have a direct impact on the education sector in various ways, including the destruction and loss of local educational infrastructure and materials, mortality or physical harm to students and educators, and through the emotional and psychosocial impacts involved (UNICEF, 2019). A collective response to SDG 13 is required to preserve Earth as a habitable planet for the current and future generations. Moreover, a massive culture change is needed for each individual to understand the urgency of climate actions and to take responsibility toward addressing the immediate needs of the planet. Studies indicate that didactic methods for climate change education have been fundamentally ineffectual in changing students' attitudes and behavior (Rousell & Cutter-Mackenzie-Knowles, 2020).

To pursue the advancement of SDGs under any category, humanity must preserve life on land and life under water. All of our regular functions as human beings within our societal spheres are dependent on nature. In an attempt to restore human–animal relationships, a study has used storytelling to raise awareness and responsibility toward wildlife among university students (Lin & Li, 2018). A responsible education system should provide individuals with the right skill sets and knowledge to promote ethical and responsible attitudes and creativity in problem-solving to preserve resources for the future.

Infrastructure Sphere

The third sphere is concerned with the steps that lead toward improved quality of life across nations through infrastructure and development. Poverty is a significant barrier to the quality of the education transmitted and received. Learners at all academic levels are harshly affected in resource-limited areas due to the lack of access to the digital infrastructure and networks (SDG 9), and insufficient digital literacy and skills. Poverty makes a strong link with SDG4 as digital exclusion is a clear facet of the profound inequalities (SDG 10) that are affecting millions of learners around the world (Cambridge, https://www.cam.ac.uk/stories/digitaldivide). Alongside poverty, Zero Hunger is one of the highest priorities of humanity and is a goal that has been carried forward from the MDGs to the SDGs. Students who suffer from malnutrition are 79% less likely to perform at the expected level when compared to students in a nutritionally supportive environment. Learners with an under-weight status are 37% less likely to perform well compared with their counterparts (Asmare, Taddele, Berihun, & Wagnew, 2018). Increasing attention must be given to sustainable rural development, pursuing synergies that bridge between progress factors across energy (SDG 7), health

(SDG 3), education (SDG 4), water (SDG 6), food (SDG 2), gender (SDG 5), and economic growth (SDG 8) (United Nations, 2021). Similarly, access to clean water and sanitation (SDG 6) directly impacts health and well-being (SDG 3) and consequently affects the quality of education (SDG 4). UNICEF has warned that many schools located in resource-limited areas lack access to clean water and sanitation, claiming lives and negatively affecting educational outcomes (United Nations, 2010). To close the education and skills gap across nations, new paradigms for clean water access should be developed and practiced to reverse these trends (United Nations, 2010). Another point stressed by UNICEF states that "Children living in electrified households spend an average of 274 more days at school than those living in households without electricity". (UNICEF, 2020), referring to SDG 7. Impacting SDG 5 (Gender Equality), having "electricity in the home also helps reduce gender inequalities by providing girls, who are traditionally more engaged in housework than boys, opportunities to study after sunset". (UNICEF, 2020). Ensuring universal access to affordable, reliable, and modern energy services, particularly for use in computer network operations and digital infrastructures (SDG 9) in rural or marginalized areas will impact the lifestyles and opportunities for millions of learners across the planet. Moreover, access to affordable and clean energy will diminish the digital divide between urban and rural populations, improving the availability of digital technologies for higher education in the rural context.

In accordance with the FAIR educational model, it is crucial to reimagine education to leave no one behind, and to provide an inclusive access model of sustained education for new and emerging tools and technologies across all demographics. Moreover, the role of digital technologies seems crucial since more higher education institutions are located within urban settings and thus access to online and remote means of learning can facilitate continuous education for learners in rural settings. Industrial innovation and infrastructures in rural settings which offer sustainable and reliable digital solutions (e.g., satellite-based distance learning) would promote quality education and accessibility (Krithivasan, Baru, & Iyer, 2005). During the COVID pandemic over the past couple of years, multiple studies report students being "anxious, stressed, overwhelmed, tired, and depressed", while 14% of students under lockdown have requested professional help in regulating their emotions (Camacho-Zuñiga et al., 2021). The continuous learning innovations and coping mechanisms, in addition to various strategies developed by higher education institutions in providing timely and adequate information, online social activities and events, and helplines to reach out to those in need of professional assistance, have played a vital role in ameliorating and recovering from this crisis and restoring good health and well-being (Camacho-Zuñiga, Pego, Escamilla, & Hosseini, 2021).

Even though the actions taken thus far are remarkable, it is evident that continuous effort from all nations, specifically the most developed nations, is required to prevent a global collapse. Even progress among the priorities of the

17 SDGs plays a vital role. The lack of parallel advancement is likely to result in inefficient implementation or failure to fulfill the high-reaching ambitions of the 2030 Agenda [18]. This objective can be met through Partnership for the Goals. In the case of education, partnerships among educators, researchers, government, policymakers, and the industrial sectors promote coordinated and innovative actions that are aimed to unlock solutions to enhance the goals and ambitions of the global education community.

Conclusions

Economies, societies, families, and individuals globally are being disrupted by a number of factors including AI, new demographic trends, and more recently, the economic and social impact brought about by the coronavirus disease (COVID-19) pandemic. All these factors have profound implications for the future of work and learning.

In the wake of these challenges, governments in both advanced and developing nations stand at a crossroads in terms of the future of learning and work. Only carefully crafted, well-coordinated policies can ignite national movements to provide all citizens— not just elite groups, with the opportunities to develop to their fullest potential throughout life through skills mastery and lifelong learning. Such policies require the coordination and co-creation across multiple stakeholders, including employers, industry associations, education institutions, trade unions, and nonprofits, together with the government to ensure meaningful, sustainable economies and lives.

In developing countries, the urgency is even greater, with many of the 17 Sustainable Development Goals holistically hinging on SDG 4, Quality Education. Through reimagined education, not only can societies create better future livelihoods, but also many SDGs can be achieved in terms of better health, well-being, equality, and sustainability.

References

Anne, B. (2017). Gender biases in student evaluations of teachers. *Journal of Public Economics, 145*, 27–41.

Asatani, K., Takeda, H., Yamano, H., & Sakata, I. (2020). Scientific attention to sustainability and SDGs: Meta-analysis of academic papers. *Energies, 13*(4), 975.

Asmare, B., Taddele, M., Berihun, S., & Wagnew, F. (2018). Nutritional status and correlation with academic performance among primary school children, northwest Ethiopia. *BMC Research Notes, 11*(1), 1–6.

Bulle, J. J. (2021). From students to learners: Tecmilenio's educational transition. *Observatory of Educational Innovation*.

Camacho-Zuñiga, C., Pego, L., Escamilla, J., & Hosseini, S. (2021). The impact of the COVID-19 pandemic on students' feelings at high school, undergraduate, and postgraduate levels. *Heliyon, 7*(3), e06465.

Casanova, A. M., Caballero, A., Kandri, S. E., Kerr, T., & Sterlin, E. (2019). Breaking paradigms to develop leaders for the 21st century. Tec de Monterrey: How a Top University in Mexico Radically Overhauled its Educational Model. *International Finance Corporation.* https://www.ifc.org/wps/wcm/connect/06d96e58-6aa1-4317-8ce3-87fb60b86cd1/IFC-TechMontereyCaseStudy-final-3.pdf?MOD=AJPERES&CVID=m-x1B1Z

Chen, L., Chen, P., & Lin, Z. (2020). Artificial intelligence in education: A review. *IEEE Access, 8*, 75264–75278.

Dang, H.-A. H., & Serajuddin, U. (2020). Tracking the sustainable development goals: Emerging measurement challenges and further reflections. *World Development, 127*, 104570.

Forum, W. E. (2020). These are the top 10 job skills of tomorrow – and how long it takes to learn them. https://www.weforum.org/agenda/2020/10/top-10-work-skills-of-tomorrow-how-long-it-takes-to-learn-them/

Fox, O., & Stoett, P. (2016). Citizen participation in the UN Sustainable Development Goals consultation process: Toward global democratic governance. *Global Governance, 22*, 555.

Fraisl, D., Campbell, J., & See, L. (2020). Mapping citizen science contributions to the UN sustainable development goals. *Sustain. Sci. 15*(6), 1735–1751.

Fung, M. (2020a). Developing a Robust System for Upskilling and Reskilling the Workforce: Lessons from the SkillsFuture Movement in Singapore. In *Anticipating and Preparing for Emerging Skills and Jobs*, Brajesh Panth & Rupert Maclean, ed. (pp. 321–327). Singapore: Springer.

Fung, M. (2020b, September 9). Laying the foundations for Asia's digital workforce. *The Business Times.* https://www.businesstimes.com.sg/opinion/laying-the-foundations-for-asias-digital-workforce

Fung, M., Lim, F. S. H. (2019). Fourth industrial revolution: New paradigm for education and training. *Proceedings, Fourth Annual Public Policy Conference* (pp. 103–110). Manila, Philippines: Philippine Institute for Development Studies.

Fung, M., Taal, R., & Sim, W. (2021). SkillsFuture: The Roles of Public and Private Sectors in Developing a Learning Society in Singapore. In *Powering a Learning Society During an Age of Disruption*, Sungsup Ra, Shanti Jagannathan, & Rupert Maclean, ed. (pp. 195–208). Singapore: Springer.

Gratton, L., & Scott, A. J. . (2016). *The 100-Year Life: Living and Working in an Age of Longevity.* Bloomsbury Publishing.

Guemouria, Y., Acebo, I., Rosales-Lopez, M. J., & Hosseini, S. (2021). Does Gender Gap in Confidence Explain Gender Gap in Academic Achievement? Paper presented at the *International Conference on Interactive Collaborative Learning.*

Hernandez-de-Menendez, M., Morales-Menendez, R., Escobar, C. A., & Arinez, J. (2021). Biometric applications in education. *International Journal on Interactive Design and Manufacturing (IJIDeM), 15*(2), 365–380.

Kaliampos, J., & Kohl, M. (2020). "I Think They Are Irresponsible": Teaching Sustainability with (Counter) Narratives in the EFL Classroom.

Kickbusch, I., & Hanefeld, J. (2017). Role for academic institutions and think tanks in speeding progress on sustainable development goals. *BMJ, 358*, j3519.

Krithivasan, S., Baru, M., & Iyer, S. (2005). Satellite based Interactive Distance Education: A Scalable and quality learning model. *Malaysian Journal of Distance Education, 7*(2), 1–20.

Laufer, M., Leiser, A., Deacon, B., Perrin de Brichambaut, P., Fecher, B., Kobsda, C., & Hesse, F. (2021). Digital higher education: a divider or bridge builder? Leadership perspectives on edtech in a COVID-19 reality. *International Journal of Educational Technology in Higher Education*, 18(1), 1–17.

lideresdelmanana. (2020). http://lideresdelmanana.itesm.mx/content/resultados-de-egresados-al-2020-version-en-ingles

Lin, C.-I., & Li, Y.-Y. (2018). Protecting life on land and below water: Using storytelling to promote undergraduate students' attitudes toward animals. *Sustainability*, 10(7), 2479.

Liu, Y., Du, J., Wang, Y., Cui, X., Dong, J., Hao, Y., ... Hu, Y. (2021). Evenness is important in assessing progress toward sustainable development goals. *National science review*, 8(8), nwaa238.

Lopez-Tapia, D., Sosa-Flores, A., Palestino-Diaz, I., Acosta-Soto, L., Hosseini, S. . (2022). one planet, one nation: an analysis of the actions taken in response to the seventeen sustainable development goals on the 2030 agenda of the United Nations. *Volume 253 of WIT Transactions on Ecology and the Environment (Electronic ISSN: 1743-3541)*.

Marron, R. K., Naughton, D., & Oaks, S. (2019). Monitoring Progress Toward SDG Target 4.7 in Europe: Proposed Framework and Tools.

Martínez, G. O., Leal, M. O. C., Alvarado, J. C. O., Soto, L. F. A., Sanabria, D. M. B., Armas, G. G. D., ... Moreno, M. A. R. (2021). Detection of Engineering Interest in Children Through an Intelligent System Using Biometric Signals. *Proceedings of the International Conference on Industrial Engineering and Operations Management Monterrey, Mexico, November 3-5, 2021*.

Maurice, J. (2016). Measuring progress toward the SDGs—A new vital science. *The lancet*, 388(10053), 1455–1458.

MOOCS (Massive Online Open Access course). (n.d.). http://mooctec.com.mx/

Mount, F. (2008). Five Types of Inequality. In *Contemporary Social Evils*.

Mourshed, M., & Fung, M. (2021, May 28). A new way to close Asia's digital skills gap. *Fortune*. https://fortune.com/2021/05/27/asia-digital-skills-gap-singapore-training/

Nagy, J. A., Benedek, J., & Ivan, K. (2018). Measuring sustainable development goals at a local level: A case of a metropolitan area in Romania. *Sustainability*, 10(11), 3962.

Olivares, S. L. O., Islas, J. R. L., Garín, M. J. P., Chapa, J. A. R., Hernández, C. H. A., & Ortega, L. O. P. . (2021). Tec21 educational model: Challenges for a transformative experience. *Editorial Digital del Tecnológico de Monterrey*.

Platform, S. D. G.-K. (n.d.). Information for integrated decision-making & participation. https://sustainabledevelopment.un.org/topics/information-integrated-decision-making-and-participation

Rousell, D., & Cutter-Mackenzie-Knowles, A. (2020). A systematic review of climate change education: Giving children and young people a 'voice'and a 'hand'in redressing climate change. *Children's Geographies*, 18(2), 191–208.

Sachs, J. D. (2012). From millennium development goals to sustainable development goals. *The lancet*, 379(9832), 2206–2211.

Silander, D. (2021). EU and agenda 2030–Peace, justice & strong institutions. *Journal of Geography, Politics and Society*, 11(4), 18–28.

Stoian, D., Monterroso, I., & Current, D. (2019). SDG 8: Decent Work and Economic Growth–Potential Impacts on Forests and Forest-Dependent Livelihoods. In *Sustainable Development Goals: Their Impact on Forests and People* (pp. 237–278).

TPrize. (n.d.). http://tprize.mx/en/

Tucker, M. S. (2019). *Vocational Education and Training for a Global Economy: Lessons from Four Countries*. ERIC.

UNESCO. (2018). *Preparing Teachers for Global Citizenship Education: A Template*. Paris: UNESCO.
UNESCO. (n.d.-a) https://en.unesco.org/artificial-intelligence/education
UNESCO. (n.d.-b). Education for sustainable cities. https://en.unesco.org/unesco-for-sustainable-cities/education-for-sustainable-cities
UNESCO. (n.d.-c). SDG resources for educators - Responsible consumption and production. https://en.unesco.org/themes/education/sdgs/material/12
UNICEF. (2019). *It is Getting Hot: Call for Education System to Repsond to the Climate Crisis*.
UNICEF. (2020). *Key Asks for 2020 SDG Voluntary National Reviews*.
United Nations. (2010). *Lack of clean water impacts children's learning and health, UNICEF warns*.
United Nations. (2015). *The Millennium Development Goals Report*. p. 72, 2015, doi: 978-92-1-101320-7.
United Nations. (2021). *Rural development | Department of Economic and Social Affairs*. https://sdgs.un.org/topics/rural-development
University of Cambridge. (n.d.). *"Pay the wi-fi or feed the children": Coronavirus has intensified the UK's digital divide*. https://www.cam.ac.uk/stories/digitaldivide
Wampfler, R., Klingler, S., Solenthaler, B., Schinazi, V., & Gross, M. (2019). Affective state prediction in a mobile setting using wearable biometric sensors and stylus. Paper presented at the *Proceedings of the 12th International Conference on Educational Data Mining, EDM 2019*, Montréal, Canada, July 2–5, 2019. International Educational Data Mining Society (IEDMS).
Xu, Z., Chau, S. N., Chen, X., Zhang, J., Li, Y., Dietz, T., …Huang, B. (2020). Assessing progress toward sustainable development over space and time. *Nature, 577*(7788), 74–78.
Yangsheng, Z. (2021). An AI based design of student performance prediction and evaluation system in college physical education. *Journal of Intelligent & Fuzzy Systems, 40*(2), 3271–3279.

3
THE BIO REVOLUTION

Innovations Transforming Economies, Societies, and Our Lives

Michael Chui, Matthias Evers, James Manyika, Alice Zheng, and Travers Nisbet

3.1 Introduction

Nearly seven decades after the double helix structure of a DNA molecule was discovered, the world of biology appears to have reached a new phase of growth. A flurry of recent innovations—such as CRISPR-Cas9 to edit genes and stem cell advances to reprogram cells—are providing new understanding, new materials, and new tools, as well as lower costs. The science is so advanced, for example, that in 2016, a Human Cell Atlas project was kicked off to create comprehensive reference maps of all human cells as a basis for research, diagnosis, monitoring, and treatment. Moreover, as a result of scientific advances, a growing number of applications are emerging from the lab and being put to commercial use.[1]

The potential for beneficial economic and social impact seems enormous. As much as 60 percent of the physical inputs to the global economy could, in principle, be produced biologically. Our analysis suggests that around one-third of these inputs are biological materials, such as wood, cotton, and animals bred for food. For these materials, innovations can improve upon existing production processes. For instance, squalene, a moisturizer used in skin-care products, is traditionally derived from shark liver oil and can now be produced more sustainably through the fermentation of genetically engineered yeast. The remaining two-thirds are not biological materials—examples include plastics and aviation fuels—but could, in principle, be produced using innovative biological processes or be replaced with substitutes using bio innovations. For example, nylon is already being made using genetically engineered microorganisms instead of petrochemicals. To be clear, reaching the full potential to produce these inputs biologically is a long way off, but even modest progress toward it could transform supply and demand and economics of, and participants in, the provision

DOI: 10.4324/9781003230762-5

of physical inputs. Biology has the potential in the future to determine what we eat, what we wear, the products we put on our skin, and the way we build our physical world.

Human health is one of the most significant domains where biological advances are being applied. Biology is already helping save lives through innovative treatments tailored to our genomes and microbiomes. In the future, we estimate that almost half of the global disease burden could be addressed through applications that are scientifically conceivable today. Moreover, many of the innovations born of these bio innovations contributed to the global response to the SARS-CoV-2 pandemic in early 2020 (see Box E1, "An April 2020 snapshot of early contributions by bio innovations in the fight against COVID-19", at the end of this executive summary). Many other domains, from agriculture to energy, could also benefit from biological processes and products. Biology could even be deployed to mitigate climate change, by helping reduce net man-made greenhouse gas (GHG) emissions.

However, the risks from these innovations are profound and unique. Biological systems self-replicate, are self-sustaining, and are highly interconnected; changes to one part of a system can have cascading effects and unintended consequences across an entire ecosystem or species. Accidents can have major consequences—and, especially if used unethically or maliciously, manipulating biology could become a Pandora's box that, once opened, unleashes lasting damage to the health of humans, ecosystems, or both. The risks are particularly acute because many of the materials and tools are relatively cheap and accessible. Moreover, tackling these risks is complicated by a multiplicity of jurisdictional and cultural value systems, which makes collaboration and coordination across countries difficult.

This report, which draws on a wealth of academic and technical research, takes a detailed look at how advances in biological science and their practical application could transform our economy and society. By our estimate, more than two-thirds of the total impact could hinge on consumer, societal, and regulatory acceptance of these applications.

A new era is dawning that we refer to as the Bio Revolution. Like all periods of economic and technological disruption, it is an era of both great opportunity and considerable uncertainty.

3.1.1 Bio Innovation is Occurring in Four Key Arenas

A wave of innovation is being enabled by advances in biological sciences accelerated by developments in computing, data analytics, machine learning, AI, and biological engineering. We group innovations into four arenas: Biomolecules, biosystems, biomachine interfaces, and biocomputing (Figure 3.1).

Major breakthroughs in each of the four arenas are reinforcing one another. In biomolecules and biosystems, advances in omics and molecular technologies—the

	 **Biomolecules**	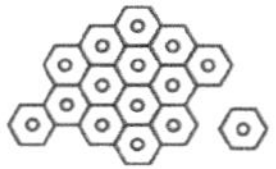 **Biosystems**	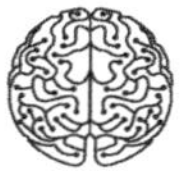 **Biomachine interfaces**	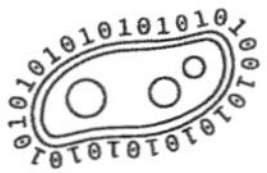 **Biocomputing**
Definitions				
Mapping	Cellular processes and functions via measuring intracellular molecules (e.g., DNA, RNA, proteins) in the study of omics	Complex biological organizations and processes, and interactions between cells	The structure and function of nervous systems of living organisms	Intracellular pathways or networks of cells to return outputs based on specific conditions (for computation)
Engineering[1]	Intracellular molecules (e.g., via genome editing)	Cells, tissues, and organs, including stem cell technologies and transplantation	Hybrid systems that connect nervous systems of living organisms to machines	Cells and cellular components for computational processes (storing, retrieving, processing data)
Examples	Gene therapy for monogenic diseases	Cultured meat grown in a lab	Neuroprosthetics for motor control (implant or external headset) of human or robotic limb	Data storage in strands of DNA

1. Design, de novo synthesis, or modification.

FIGURE 3.1 Bio innovation is occurring in four key arenas.

mapping and measuring of molecules and pathways within cells, and engineering them—are enhancing our understanding of biological processes, as well as enabling us to engineer biology.[2] For example, CRISPR technology allows scientists to edit genes more quickly and precisely than previous techniques. Advances in biomachines and biocomputing involve deep interaction between biology and machines; it is becoming increasingly possible to measure neural signals and power precise neuroprosthetics.[3] It is now also possible to store the world's wealth of data using DNA—by some measures, one kilogram of DNA could hypothetically store all current data in the world (Extance, 2016; Seffers, 2019).

Worldwide DNA sequencing now creates huge volumes of biological data every year (Hayden, 2015). These technical advances, such as lower-cost sequencing or high-throughput screening, have helped lower the costs of entry, accelerate the pace of experimentation, and generate new forms of data to help us better understand biology. Advances at the single-cell level, such as single-cell imaging tools and single-cell ribonucleic acid (RNA) sequencing, are allowing scientists to build increasingly high-resolution maps of cells, which can be a basis for research, diagnosis, and treatment. Increasingly, the ability to understand and engineer biological processes exists across a variety of dimensions.

Mapping the genome is a foundational building block. This dates to the Human Genome Project, a 13-year, $3 billion journey to map the entire genetic makeup of humans, that began in 1990. Accordingly, genomics is the most technologically advanced branch of omics, and has the most related applications either in development or already in use.[4] But other omics are necessary complements, and work on them is increasing. However, the power of the map of the human genome began to materialize only when sequencing DNA became cheaper and faster. The cost of DNA sequencing is now decreasing at a rate faster than Moore's Law (Figure 3.2).[5] In 2003, mapping the human genome cost about $3 billion; by 2019, it was less than $1,000. Within a decade or even sooner, the cost could be less than $100 (Brown, 2019; Regalado, 2020).

3.1.2 New Biological Capabilities Could Bring About Transformational Change in Economies, Societies, and Our Lives

New biological capabilities have the potential to bring sweeping change to economies and societies. The effects will be felt across value chains, from how R&D is conducted to the physical inputs in manufacturing to the way medicines and consumer products are delivered and consumed. These capabilities include the following:

- **Biological means** could be used to produce a large share of the global economy's physical materials, potentially with improved performance and sustainability. Significant potential exists to improve the characteristics of

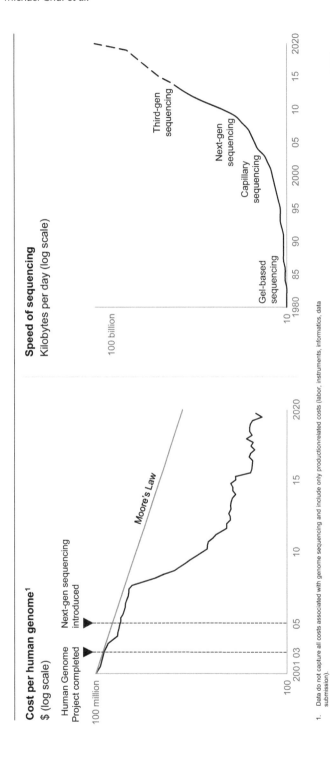

FIGURE 3.2 Rapid advances in computing, bioinformatics, and AI are enabling the analysis of omics data.

materials, reduce the emissions profile of manufacturing and processing, and shorten value chains. Fermentation, for centuries used to make bread and brew beer, is now being used to create fabrics such as artificial spider silk. Biology is increasingly being used to create novel materials that can raise quality, introduce entirely new capabilities, be biodegradable, and be produced in a way that generates significantly fewer carbon emissions. Mushroom roots rather than animal hides can be used to make leather (Crow, 2019; Anzilotti, 2018). Plastics can be made with yeast instead of petrochemicals.

- **Increased control and precision in methodology** are occurring across the value chain, from delivery to development and consumption with more personalization. Advances in biological sciences have made R&D and delivery processes more precise and predictable; the character of R&D is shifting from discovery by accident to rational design. Increasing knowledge of human genomes and the links between certain genes and diseases is enabling the spread of personalized or precision medicine, which can be more effective than the one-size-fits-all therapies of the past.[6] Precision also applies to agriculture, where insights from a plant or soil's microbiome increasingly can be used to optimize yield as well as to offer consumers with, for instance, personalized nutrition plans based on genetic tests (Sergaki et al., 2018; Kolodziejczyk et al., 2019; Reinagel, 2019; Vesnina et al., 2020).

- **The capability to engineer and reprogram human and nonhuman organisms is increasing**. Gene therapies could offer complete cures of some diseases for the first time. The same technological advances that are driving capabilities that improve human health can be used to introduce valuable new traits that, for instance, improve the output or yield of nonhuman organisms like microbes, plants, and animals. Crops can be genetically engineered to produce higher yields and be more heat- or drought-resistant, for instance. By permanently genetically altering the vectors spreading disease (such as mosquitoes), gene drives could be used to prevent vector-borne diseases, including malaria, dengue fever, schistosomiasis, and Lyme disease, although they also come with ecological risks.[7]

- **New methodologies using automation**, machine learning, and proliferating biological data are enhancing discovery, throughput, and productivity in R&D. Biology and computing together are accelerating R&D, thereby addressing a productivity challenge. McKinsey analysis in 2017 found that the ratio of revenue to R&D spending in the biopharmaceutical industry hit a low point in productivity between 2008 and 2011 (Chilukuri et al., 2017). An explosion of biological data due to cheaper sequencing can be used by biotech companies and research institutes that increasingly are using robotic automation and sensors in labs that could increase throughput up to ten times (de Almeida, 2018). Further, advanced analytics, more

powerful computational techniques, and AI can be leveraged to provide better insights during the R&D process.
- **Potential is growing for interfaces between biological systems and computers**. A new generation of biomachine interfaces relies on close interaction between humans and computers. Such interfaces include neuroprosthetics that restore lost sensory functions (bionic vision) or enable signals from the brain to control physical movement of prosthetic or paralyzed limbs. Biocomputers that employ biology to mimic silicon, including the use of DNA to store data, are being researched. DNA is about one million times denser than hard-disk storage; technically, one kilogram of DNA could store the entirety of the world's data (as of 2016).[8]

While these are early days, the scope and scale of these emerging capabilities could have a broad impact on economies and societies, touching multiple domains both directly and indirectly. These applications may change everything from the food we consume to textiles to the types of health treatments we receive and how we build our physical world. The potential value is vast. As noted, as much as 60 percent of the physical inputs to the global economy could be produced biologically, and even modest progress toward that 60 percent number could be transformative.

Beyond the physical world, innovations could transform the prevention, diagnostics, and treatment of disease. At least 45 percent of the global disease burden could be addressed with capabilities that are scientifically conceivable today, according to our analysis.

Bio innovations, such as high-throughput screening, CRISPR, and machine learning for analyzing large and complex biological data, have also begun to shape R&D. We estimate that roughly 30 percent of private-sector R&D in major economies is in industries where biological data, biological inputs, or biological means of production could be used (Figure 3.3).[9]

3.2 A Visible Pipeline of Applications Can Deliver Profound Impact across a Wide Range of Domains in the Next Two Decades

To examine a wide range of applications, we compiled a library of about 400 use cases. They constitute an already-visible pipeline for the years ahead. We estimated the direct impact by sizing four value gain drivers: Reduced disease burden, improved quality, cost productivity, and environmental benefit. These estimates of potential value did not include knock-on effects. Using expert input and historical analogs, we then extrapolated our assessed impact to different time horizons by estimating the level and pace of adoption, as discussed below.[10]

Over the next 10–20 years, we estimate that these applications alone could have a direct economic impact of between $2 trillion and $4 trillion globally per

Scope and factors in our assessment	Included	Excluded
Technology Applicability	• Mapping and engineering of biomolecules, biosystems, biomachine interfaces, and biocomputing	• Mature technologies out of scope (e.g., small molecules, biologics, genetically modified crops)
Development phase Maturity of use cases	• Scientifically conceivable today and plausibly commercialized by 2050 (e.g., CAR-T therapies for solid tumors) • Use cases that are not yet scientifically feasible and are still in research phases (e.g., microbiome-based skin-care products)	• Not yet scientifically conceivable today (e.g., production via biological means) • Unlikely to have material economic impact by 2050 (e.g., biology-based parallel computing)
Domains Cluster of sectors	• Direct biology-centric domains where core product or service could be inherently biological, such as the following sectors: Healthcare systems and services, pharmaceuticals and medical products, agriculture, consumer goods and services, basic materials manufacturing, and energy	• Other sectors not inherently biological that experience indirect impact (e.g., upstream, downstream, ancillary), including insurance, entertainment, finance

Impact Value gain drivers	• Value gain drivers of direct impact estimated
	  – Reduced disease burden translated to economic productivity
	  – Improved quality, measured by greater willingness to pay
	  – Cost productivity (e.g., incremental cost saving to produce product)
	  – Environmental benefit (from reduced greenhouse gas emissions)
		• Knock-on effects, such as reduced agricultural land use from shifting to alternative proteins or changes to life insurance from longer life spans
		• Broader societal impact, such as effects on inequality or population phenotype

FIGURE 3.3 Overview of methodology for estimating direct economic impacts.

Source: McKinsey Global institute.

year (Exhibit 4). Whether the impact is toward the bottom or top of that range will depend on how and when innovations are adopted. As we discuss below, significant uncertainty surrounds both scientific feasibility and commercial availability. The potential could be significantly higher if downstream and secondary effects are taken into account, as discussed in the next section.

Human health and performance have the most scientific advances and the clearest pipeline from research to application. Science is advanced, and the market is generally accepting of innovations. However, based on our use cases, the impact could be more broad-based; in the next 10–20 years, more than half of the direct impact is likely to be outside health, primarily in agriculture and consumer products (Figure 3.4).

Our library of use cases suggests that most value in the next one to two decades will come in four domains, or clusters of sectors where applications are emerging from bio innovation. Here we summarize use cases in each of these key domains.[11]

- **Human health and performance.** A new wave of innovation is underway that includes cell, gene, RNA, and microbiome therapies to treat or prevent disease, innovations in reproductive medicine such as carrier screening, and improvements to drug development and delivery.[12] Many more options are being explored and becoming available to treat monogenic (caused by mutations in a single gene) diseases such as sickle cell anemia, polygenic diseases (caused by multiple genes) such as cardiovascular disease, and infectious diseases such as malaria.[13] We estimate between 1 and 3 percent of the total global burden of disease could be reduced in the next 10–20 years from these applications—roughly the equivalent of eliminating the global disease burden of lung cancer, breast cancer, and prostate cancer combined. Over time, if the full potential is captured, 45 percent of the global disease burden could be addressed using science that is conceivable today. The direct annual global potential impact in this domain is estimated at $500 billion to $1.3 trillion over the next 10–20 years, or 35 percent of the overall impact that we estimate for this period. The main capabilities enabling impact are the increased precision and personalization in the delivery of treatment and the accelerated pace and scope of R&D. In the longer term, innovations are likely to spread to more therapeutic areas such as cardiovascular and neurodegenerative diseases.
- **Agriculture, aquaculture, and food.** Applications such as low-cost, high-throughput microarrays have vastly increased the amount of plant and animal sequencing data, enabling lower-cost artificial selection of desirable traits based on genetic markers in both plants and animals.[14] This is known as marker-assisted breeding and is many times quicker than traditional selective breeding methods.[15] In addition, in the 1990s, genetic engineering emerged commercially to improve the traits of plants (such as yields

The Bio Revolution 57

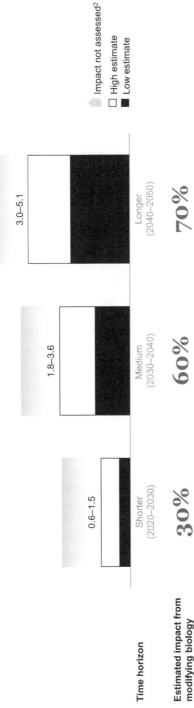

FIGURE 3.4 In 10–20 years, a visible pipeline of biological applications could create approximately $2 trillion to $4 trillion of direct annual economic impact.

and input productivity) beyond traditional breeding (National Academies of Sciences, Engineering, and Medicine, 2016). Historically, the first wave of genetically engineered crops has been referred to as genetically modified organisms (GMOs); these are organisms with foreign (transgenic) genetic material introduced.[16] Now, recent advances in genetic engineering (such as the emergence of CRISPR) have enabled highly specific cisgenic changes (using genes from sexually compatible plants) and intragenic changes (altering gene combinations and regulatory sequencings belonging to the recipient plant) (National Academies of Sciences, Engineering, and Medicine, 2016). Other innovations in this domain include using the microbiome of plants, soil, animals, and water to improve the quality and productivity of agricultural production; and the development of alternative proteins, including lab-grown meat, which could take pressure off the environment from traditional livestock and seafood. Direct annual impact from all applications in this domain could be between about $800 billion and $1.2 trillion over the next 10–20 years, or 36 percent of the total.

- **Consumer products and services**. Opportunities are opening up to use increasing volumes of biological data to offer consumers personalized products and services based on their biological makeup. Applications include direct-to-consumer (DTC) genetic testing, beauty and personal care based on microbiomes, and innovative approaches to wellness and fitness in both humans and pets. Some of these applications could have indirect impact on human health, such as wellness or fitness applications.[17] Annual direct economic impact over the next 10–20 years in this domain could be $200 billion to $800 billion, or 19 percent of the total. Roughly two-thirds of this may come from the capability to personalize.

- **Materials, chemicals, and energy**. New biological ways of making and processing materials, chemicals, and energy could transform many industries and our daily lives, although economics are challenging. Improved fermentation processes can increase the speed of production or quality of materials that are already created using fermentation (such as food and feed ingredients). Further, the creation of new bioroutes can enable the manufacture of more materials and chemicals biologically and the production of completely novel materials. Finally, advances are being made in energy, with greater use of biofuels, improving energy extraction, and improving energy storage. Applications include innovations related to production of materials such as improved fermentation processes, new bioroutes utilizing the ability to edit the DNA of microbes to develop novel materials with entirely new properties (self-repairing fabrics are one example), and building on advances in biofuels to innovate new forms of energy storage. Over the next 10–20 years, the direct annual global impact could be $200 billion to $300 billion a year, or 8 percent of the total. This is a conservative estimate given uncertainty about what novel materials may emerge and the historical challenges of scaling innovations in this domain. About three-quarters of this economic potential is related to improved resource efficiency from new methods of production.

3.3 The Total Economic Impact Will Likely Be Larger Than the Direct Impact of the Use Cases We Have Identified and Assessed

The direct potential impact estimated across the domains may be only a small portion of the potential scale of impact. Even in the near term, the impact could be larger, as new scientific breakthroughs emerge and as the direct impact we note above starts to have knock-on effects or spills over to other sectors. More broadly, the impact could radiate out to almost every sector of the economy, with effects on society and the environment. For instance, the visible pipeline of applications we sized in the human health domain is just a fraction of the full potential: As noted, between 1 and 3 percent of the current total global burden of disease could be reduced in the next 10–20 years from just the use cases we examined—roughly the size of eliminating the global disease burden of lung cancer, breast cancer, and prostate cancer combined. While this near-term impact is rather significant, it is only a fraction of the transformational change that may be achievable. Many factors will shape the full extent of impact and the ability to capture as much of the full potential as possible; they include funding for basic science and treatments that pass clinical trials and are commercially viable alternatives to existing therapies.

The total economic impact could be larger than our direct sizing for a number of reasons:

- **Unassessed use cases**. Our library of about 400 use cases, while extensive, is not exhaustive. We acknowledge that there are many use cases being developed in private labs or in the defense industry, where developments remain confidential for commercial or national security reasons.
- **Faster and higher adoption**. Several factors could accelerate adoption of scientific advances. Companies could help speed up time to market and adoption of some applications by working with the scientific community, for example focusing on scientific advances and technologies that are likely to have the most impact, investing in them, and partnering with innovative startups. In addition to adoption speed, adoption peaks could be higher due to factors such as shifting product features, customer preferences, and lower prices. One example of this potential is higher or faster adoption of currently expensive therapies (for instance, CAR T-cell therapy for cancer) due to broader insurance coverage or lower prices.[18]
- **Knock-on economic effects**. The impact of some applications could in turn have knock-on effects on the broader economy. For example, improved

health could mean that people lead longer and more productive lives; this in turn means that retirement ages may rise, demand for eldercare delivered in the home may rise, and social security and pensions may need to adapt. Alternative proteins are another example: if they replace some meat production, land now dedicated to grazing could be repurposed for conservation efforts or new commercial uses.

- **Impacts on upstream, downstream, and ancillary players.** After the first wave of change in the domains directly affected by bio innovations, a second wave may spill over to adjacent sectors or firms, transforming value chains and encouraging new business models and players. For example, applications in agriculture, aquaculture, and food could affect food retailing. Numerous fast-food chains have announced deals with plant-based meat-substitute producers to offer vegetarian and vegan versions of popular menu items. Logistics and transportation players may adapt to genetically engineered produce being able to be kept fresh for far longer even without being refrigerated, and to increased demand for alternative proteins.

- **Existing scientific breakthroughs spur more breakthroughs.** Some innovations have the ability to generate more breakthroughs, by helping to improve existing products and processes or by inventing and implementing new ones. For example, the Human Genome Project initially set out to determine a map of the human genome. In doing so, the project was instrumental in pushing the development of high-throughput technologies for preparing, mapping, and sequencing DNA. The improved ability to sequence DNA has, in turn, led to sequencing of the genomes of microbes, plants, and animals, which has advanced many fields of science, including microbiology, virology, infectious disease, and plant biology. In addition, new biology and new technologies brought about by the Human Genome Project have enabled many other large-scale research initiatives to go forward. Examples include the Encyclopedia of DNA Elements research consortium (ENCODE), International HapMap Project, 1000 Genomes, Cancer Genome Anatomy Project, Human Microbiome Project, and Roadmap Epigenomics Project (Hood and Rowen, 2013; "Spinoff projects", 1990–2003).[19]

- **More scientific breakthroughs enable more commercial applications.** Biology research is continually developing, and scientific breakthroughs we haven't yet contemplated could provide a foundation for downstream commercial applications that may become available in the next few decades. For example, before the Human Genome Project, researchers knew the genetic basis of tens of disorders. Today, they know the basis of thousands of conditions. Genomics is thus helping transform medicine. More than 100 different drugs approved by the US Food and Drug Administration (FDA) are now packaged with instructions that tell doctors to test their patients for genetic variants linked to efficacy, dosages, or risky side effects (Rojahn, 2013). Funding basic science or helping promising applications accelerate through research pipelines could directly influence the number of commercial applications in the future, beyond use cases we may have missed in our sizing.

In the longer term, every sector may be affected as bio innovation transforms profit pools, value chains, and business models. In the years ahead, if you are not using biology to make products, you will very likely be consuming products made that way. The impact could go much further, with biology potentially being used to address some of the great challenges of our time.

As an example, climate change is a key area in which biology could play a role. By 2040–2050, the direct applications we sized could reduce annual average man-made GHG emissions by 7–9 percent from 2018 emissions levels. This is the equivalent of up to eight times the total carbon dioxide (CO_2) emissions of the global airline industry in 2018. [20] Applications such as a shift toward bioroutes for production and alternative proteins would be important contributors to reduced emissions. The knock-on effects could alleviate pressure on cropland and reduce deforestation.

Biology could also make a significant contribution to efforts to increase food security around the world, addressing hunger and malnutrition. The Bill & Melinda Gates Foundation, for example, suggests that by using improved fertilizer and more productive crops such as genetically engineered varieties, African farmers could theoretically double their yields (Lopatto, 2015).

However, for all this potential, biological applications will not likely be a panacea for societal ills and challenges. In many ways, their societal effects proceed unevenly, in part driven by level of access to these innovations across socioeconomic groups or nations. And, critically, the risks of biology will need to be addressed and satisfactorily mitigated if biology is to realize its potential.

3.4 Bio Innovation Carries Profound and Unique Risks and Issues

Profound risks accompany this surge of innovation in biology. Get it right and the benefits could be significant; get it wrong and disastrous consequences could ensue at the population level. These risks introduce a unique set of considerations which, if not managed properly, could potentially outweigh the promised benefits:

- **Biology is self-replicating, self-sustaining, and does not respect jurisdictional boundaries**. For example, new genetically engineered gene drives applied to the vectors that spread disease (mosquitoes in the case of malaria) could have enormous health benefits, but they can be difficult to control and can potentially do permanent damage to ecosystems. There are also no boundaries for the spread of unintended consequences.

- **The interconnected nature of biology can increase the potential for unintended consequences**. Biology is highly interconnected; changes to one part of a system can have cascading effects and unintended consequences across entire ecosystems or species. Examples include planting a genetically engineered crop that could result in unintended effects on the species or broader ecosystem. Gene editing could also have unintended or "off target" effects. For instance, even in successful gene editing, "offtarget" mutations beyond those intended have been observed for all classes of genome editing tools used to date, including CRISPR (Cheng and Tsai, 2018; Carroll, 2019; Nature Medicine, 2018).
- **Low barriers to entry open the door to potential misuse with potentially fatal consequences**. Unlike nuclear materials, some biological technologies are relatively cheap and accessible. A thriving community of "biohackers" practices gene editing today in community labs or even at home. Commercial kits to perform CRISPR gene editing are sold on the internet. This activity might affect only the individuals biohacking their own bodies, but there are broader risks, for example, if individuals are able to create and unleash a virus. Beyond such risks, we could see increased competition between companies, particularly in consumer applications, which could lead to overhyped marketing. Competition to bring biologically based products and services to market in some cases has led to commercialization before the relevant science is fully tested and established, which could mislead consumers, erode trust, or even compromise health and safety.
- **Differing value systems make it hard to forge consensus, including on life-and-death issues**. At the heart of many of these risks is the challenge of coordination across value systems—at the individual, cultural, and national levels. Technical and scientific issues, such as embryo editing, quickly become moral questions, and often, decisions are expressions of one's value system. Beyond the many risks are significant ethical questions that exceed the scope of this report. Is the ability to edit out disabilities before birth "playing God"? Is it acceptable to edit an embryo to prevent sickle cell anemia, but wrong to choose a baby's skin or eye color? Sustained efforts and new approaches to engagement, oversight, regulation, and safeguarding are needed to manage such risks. These will need to take into account societal norms and acceptance that are often shaped by religious, cultural, and historical values and can vary widely between countries. The challenge of cooperation and coordination of value systems across cultures and jurisdictions is no easy task, particularly when advances in these scientific domains could be seen as a unique competitive advantage for businesses or economies.
- **Privacy and consent issues are fundamental**. Concerns about personal privacy and consent are rife, given that the cornerstone of biological advances is data mined from our bodies and brains. In the United States,

using the results of only 1.28 million DTC genetic tests, it was possible to access material from open databases and identify about 60 percent of Americans with European ancestry from a DNA sample as of late 2018, prompting some DTC companies to tighten up the availability of such data (Erlich et al., 2018). As applications of biomachine interfaces and, in particular, brain-machine interfaces spread, the amount of data harvested from brains will most likely increase. When and how do individuals give consent to what data are gathered and how they are used? Is the science available that can differentiate between thoughts that an individual wants and does not want to share?

- **Unequal access could perpetuate socioeconomic disparity, with potentially regressive effects.** Biological advances and their commercial applications may not be accessible to all in equal measure, thereby exacerbating socioeconomic disparity. At the country level, developments are advancing quickest and most broadly in relatively rich nations. Our analysis finds that countries with high rankings on the Institute for Health Metrics and Evaluation's (IHME) socio-demographic index account for roughly 30 percent of today's global disease burden but could gain about 70 percent of the total share of reduction in the global disease burden from bio innovations.[21] Within countries, access to some beneficial biological applications may be cost-prohibitive and thus available only to the wealthy, like cellular and gene therapies today. Furthermore, the very nature of these applications to edit "less desirable" traits could lead to outcomes that are regressive and disenfranchise marginalized groups. Examples of this could include genome editing for traits related to blindness or dwarfism, which are tied to the ongoing discussion of so-called ableism—that is, whether the aim of restoring a sense inherently marginalizes communities that do not see the lack of that sense as a disability.

These risks demand a considered response and potentially new approaches. In past waves of technological change, regulation has emerged in response to innovations; in biology, there is a strong argument for a proactive approach. As far back as 1975, prominent scientists, lawyers, and medics gathered in California to draw up voluntary guidelines to ensure the safety of recombinant DNA technology.[22] The scientific communities in other fields, such as nuclear physics and AI, are also grappling with analogous issues, and there could be room for cross-disciplinary collaboration. Regulation will be important, but so too will oversight and monitoring of science even as it develops, as well as safeguards that scientists build into new biological technologies.

National responses will not be sufficient, because biology doesn't respect borders—as the world experienced firsthand with the rapid spread of the COVID-19 infection around the globe. Moreover, we can already see very different regulatory responses reflecting a world with many different value systems. Some countries take a cautious view of frontier innovation, including embryo editing and genetic engineering of food crops; others take a permissive view. Lighter-touch regulation may deliver—or be seen to deliver—competitive advantage compared with a more restrictive approach. Global cooperation and coordination could help level the playing field but will be difficult to achieve when disparate value systems exist.

3.5 Science is the Starting Point—Applications Need to be Commercialized and Diffused Responsibly to Deliver Beneficial Impact at Scale

The journey from the lab to adoption has three broad stages—scientific research, commercialization, and diffusion—that bleed into each other in a continuous evolution. For biological applications to diffuse and deliver beneficial impact responsibly and at scale, six factors are relevant that determine whether adoption occurs and how long that takes. The first— investing in scientific research— is germane in the first stage. Four factors— value propositions, business models, go-to-market, and operational scalability—are key for the second and third stages, commercialization and diffusion. The sixth relates to risk and mechanisms for governing the use of applications; this is vital in all three stages:

- **Investment in scientific research.** Funding, tools, talent, and access to data are necessary and powerful elements of the investment needed to enable scientists to be successful. It tends to take years of research and sizable investment in these capabilities to get an idea to the point at which a product or service is scientifically feasible.[23] To give an idea of the financial investment needed, the Human Genome Project involved $3 billion in investment. Applications are moving along fastest in higher-income economies where investment money is available. The development of new tools and technologies in biological sciences has extended the capabilities of research. For instance, CRISPR was a major leap forward in the ability to edit genes. Expanding and ever-cheaper computing power has enabled the rapid development of bioinformatics.[24] Ensuring that sufficient numbers of skilled scientists are trained is vital. Finally, investment to ensure that scientists have access to the data on which advances depend is crucial. The development of annotated and accessible databases such as the Human Genome Project, GenBank, and UniProt has played a significant enabling role in biological advances.
- **Four factors play a role in commercialization and diffusion.** Once an application is scientifically feasible, other factors will determine the journey from lab to market to wide adoption and diffusion. We have identified four key factors, the first of which is whether a new biology-based product or service offers a value proposition to potential end users. Innovations need to compete with existing products not only on cost but also by offering higher

quality or new properties or, indeed, by meeting a need not fulfilled by existing offerings. Creating a value proposition is not easy. Many potential buyers of biology-based products are in industries with low margins such as energy and agriculture, and established products or methods of production have had years to develop ways to improve efficiency. Even when they start diffusing, some biology-based innovations remain costly. Although the cost is now falling rapidly, the cost to produce the first lab-grown hamburger was more than $300,000.

(Stephens et al., 2019; Arshad et al., 2017)

The second factor is whether business models are suitable in what may be a fast-changing landscape, as in most waves of innovation. New models, such as bionative companies that combine expertise in biology, chemistry, data science, and automation, may be needed. The third factor is ensuring that a new product or service effectively hits the right potential customers, with go-to-market elements, including pricing, sales, and marketing. A fourth vital factor is an ability to scale up operations; necessary aspects include having the right infrastructure, processes, supply chain, and talent. New biobased fermentation techniques can build on considerable existing fermentation capacity, but more will be needed. Healthcare capacity will need to adapt and grow to disseminate medical innovations. For instance, with CAR T-cells now being administered to a growing number of patients in hospitals and treatment centers, sufficient infrastructure for manufacturing and delivering the cells is necessary (Bell, 2018). Again, sufficient talent is needed. Genetic counselors to help patients and the public understand and interpret the results of genetic tests are already in short supply (Hoskovec, 2018). In the United States, for instance, there were approximately 5,000 certified genetic counselors in 2019 (*Genetic counselor*). Yet 26 million consumers have taken an at-home genetic test.

- **Risk and mechanisms governing use**. Given the profound and unique risks accompanying bio innovation, mechanisms governing use, including broad acceptance from society and regulation, are key both in the first stage and also as the science commercializes and diffuses. Even if an application is scientifically feasible and the economics are favorable, end users and other stakeholders must want to use it, sometimes accepting some risk. As an illustration, it took nearly 20 years from the production of the first strain of Golden Rice—fortified with vitamin A—to be approved for use in 2019 in the Philippines, the first country with many people suffering from vitamin A deficiency to approve Golden Rice.[25] Regulators delayed in the face of persistent opposition to GMOs (Hirsch, 2013). Our research finds that about 70 percent of the total potential impact could hinge on consumer, societal, and regulatory acceptance, based on an analysis of areas where regulations exist today in major economies.[26]

3.6 The Pace and Extent of Adoption of Bio Innovations Vary Significantly Depending on the Application

The pace and extent of adoption will vary enormously depending on the application and the domain (Figure 3.5). Some applications, including using new bioroutes to manufacture drugs, are already showing robust signs of early commercial adoption. Others such as CAR T-cell therapy for cancer have recently become commercially viable at the time of writing in 2020, meaning adoption is at an early stage and could increase rapidly over the coming decade. Still others, such as using genetically engineered plants to sequester CO_2, show promise in scientific research, but commercial viability and adoption by farmers or other buyers are likely to further out.

3.6.1 Innovators, Businesses, Governments, and Individuals Need to Strike a Balance that Enables Potential to be Captured While Managing Risks

Innovators, businesses, governments, and individuals need to become literate in biology, cognizant of the benefits of innovations as well as their risks, and how to strike the right balance between the two. The choices made today, and in the years ahead, will influence not only the path of biological science, but also the size and scope of its benefits for economies, societies, and the planet.

- **Innovators**. The scientists and researchers pioneering biological breakthroughs, and the developers and innovators who turn feasible science into commercially viable products, need to consider the opportunities and risks associated with their work. Peer review is a powerful internal governing mechanism to ensure that research is accurate and well grounded, but scientists cannot operate in a vacuum. Rather, they need to play a consistent and effective oversight role. They have a long track record of doing so. In 1975, prominent scientists, lawyers, and medical professionals gathered at the Asilomar Conference in California to draw up voluntary guidelines to ensure the safety of recombinant DNA technology, for instance.[27]
- **Businesses**. Businesses should consider how to take advantage of bio innovation, including adapting strategies. Companies operating in virtually every sector of the economy could be affected by bio innovations as applications in one domain have knock-on effects on upstream, downstream, and adjacent sectors. In the case of applications in agriculture, aquaculture, and food, there will be spillover into food retailing and transportation, for instance. Moreover, entire value chains could be transformed. In the case of materials, for instance, with a shift from plastic to bio-based plastic packaging increasingly desired by consumers, the packaging industry could look very different. The meat value chain is another case in point. In the traditional

The Bio Revolution 67

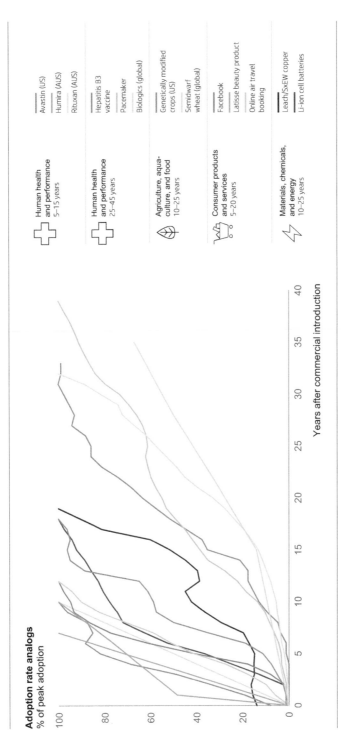

FIGURE 3.5 (a) Analogs suggest adoption rates for new technologies will vary by domain.

(*Continued*)

Estimated time horizon of acceleration point of use cases across domains
The acceleration point is when adoption starts to experience rapid growth[1]

Example use cases	Existing Before 2020	Short term 2020–2030	Medium term 2030–2040	Long term Beyond 2040
Materials, chemicals, and energy[5]	New bioroutes for drug manufacturing (e.g., peptides)	Novel materials—biopesticides/biofertilizers (e.g., RNAi pesticides) Improved existing fermentation processes—food and feed ingredients (e.g., amino acids, organic acids)	Novel materials—biopolymers (e.g., PLA, PET)	Biosolar cells and biobatteries
Other applications	DNA sequencing for forensics		Biosequestration of CO_2 Bioremediation for pollution	

Not exhaustive

1. The point at which adoption accelerates. We characterize this as the max of the second derivative of the adoption curve—see our technical appendix for more detail. Adoption level and timing for each use case depend on many variables, including commercial availability, regulation, and public acceptance. These estimates are not fully risk- or probability-adjusted. | 2. Applications in the human health and performance domain include innovations to reduce disease burden at the individual and population levels, anti-aging treatments that extend life span, reproductive health (e.g., carrier screening) applications, and innovations in drug development and manufacturing. See chapter 6.1 for the full list of applications that we sized in this domain. | 3. Applications in the agriculture, aquaculture, and food domain include applications related to plants and animals for food purposes, food production, food transportation, and food storage. See chapter 6.2 for the full list of applications that we sized in this domain. | 4. Applications in the consumer products and services domain include direct-to-consumer genetic testing, beauty and personal care, wellness (e.g., fitness), and pets. We categorize wellness, nutrition, and fitness under consumer rather than health, because they do not directly alleviate the global disease burden or are elective or for adult enhancement, such as hair loss or cosmetics. While some of these applications could have indirect impact on the disease burden, such as fitness wearables, they are not direct treatments or therapies. See chapter 6.3 for the full list of applications that we sized in this domain. | 5. Applications in the materials, chemicals, and energy domain include innovations related to production of materials (e.g., improved fermentation process, new bio-routes, or novel materials), and energy production and storage. See chapter 6.4 for the full list of applications that we sized in this domain.

FIGURE 3.5 (CONTINUED) (b) Among applications assessed, adoption timing varies.

meat production value chain, animals are bred, fed, slaughtered (fished), and processed prior to distribution, while the value chain for cultured meat is highly compressed, involving only tissue sampling, media production, and live-tissue cultivation of cells into meat—often done by the same company.[28]

Many companies will likely need to adapt their business strategies. Given the uncertainty and evidently varied timing of adoption for different applications, companies should consider a portfolio-based approach toward investments in bio innovation that embraces applications that could become commercially viable in the relatively short term, and those that could deliver impact further out. By its nature, bio innovation is cross-discipline—embracing not only biological science, but also computing, AI, data analytics, and engineering. As such, it is unlikely that any business existing today can go it alone.

3.7 Civil Society, Governments, and Policy Makers Need to Inform Themselves about Biological Advances and to Provide Thoughtful Guidance

Several governments, including those of China, the United Kingdom, and the United States, published strategic plans and goals intended to catalyze innovation and capture its benefits. However, innovation needs to be balanced by mechanisms to govern use and misuse; whether existing professional and regulatory mechanisms are fit for purpose must be considered. This analysis suggests that in the next decade, more than 50 percent of the total potential impact could hinge on consumer, societal, and regulatory acceptance, rising to about 70 percent over the next two decades.[29] Effective mechanisms to govern the use, such as societal norms or regulations, will be needed to persuade society that innovations that bring benefits but may be risky and cause discomfort are being pursued safely. Today, policies to govern use vary significantly among countries with different value systems. Cross-jurisdictional cooperation is not extensive, as observed in the largely national (and sub-national) responses in the spring of 2020 to the COVID-19 pandemic.

- **Individuals and consumers** may be pivotal to the adoption path of biological advances. As observed, individual attitudes toward different types of bio innovation can shape the public dialogue, societal norms, regulation, and therefore the pace and extent of adoption. To contribute effectively to what can be controversial debates (consider embryo editing as an example), individuals need to seek to understand the benefits versus the risks. They also need to appreciate that there are personal trade-offs. DTC testing, for instance, provides individuals with potentially valuable insights into the probability of contracting certain diseases, but mining that information may compromise their privacy.

The current wave of innovation in biological sciences, combined with advances in data, analytics, and digitization, has been decades in the making. It builds on 50 years or more of scientific breakthroughs). The Bio Revolution goes far beyond treating disease and into virtually every sector of the economy. Scientists in conjunction with forward-thinking companies are now harnessing the power of nature to solve pressing problems in medicine and agriculture, and, in some areas, forging innovative solutions that could mitigate pressure on the environment and help tackle climate change. The serious, and potentially irreversible, risks inherent in biology need to be fully acknowledged and directly addressed. The choices stakeholders make today and in the years ahead will determine whether what is shaping up as a Bio Revolution delivers on its considerable promise—and in a way that is safe and equitable for humanity and sustainable for the planet.

Notes

1. DNA is short for deoxyribonucleic acid, an organic chemical found in all cells and in many viruses. DNA acts as the main carrier for genetic information. CRISPR-Cas9 stands for clustered regularly interspaced short palindromic repeats and CRISPR-associated protein 9. This tool uses a small piece of ribonucleic acid (RNA) with a short "guide" sequence that attaches to a target sequence of DNA and to the Cas9 enzyme. The Cas9 enzyme cuts the targeted DNA at the targeted location, which enables genetic material to be added or deleted. In the rest of this report, we refer to the tool as CRISPR. RNA is a biopolymer consisting of ribose nucleotides (nitrogenous bases appended to a ribose sugar molecule) connected and forming strands of varying lengths. Unlike most DNA molecules composed of two biopolymer strands, RNA typically is a single-stranded biopolymer. RNA molecules play essential biological roles, from translating genetic information encoded in DNA molecules into the cellular structures and molecular machines (that is, proteins) to regulating the activities of genes. A stem cell is a type of cell in a multicellular organism that has two capabilities: self-renewal by producing indefinitely more cells of the same type, and the ability to give rise to many other kinds of cells in the body by differentiation.
2. Omics is a collective term for technologies that allow the comprehensive identification and quantification of the complete set of molecules (for instance, proteins, carbohydrates, and lipids) of a biological system (cell, tissue, organ, biological fluid, or organism) at a specific point in time. Omics and molecular technologies is defined to cover the study of omics as well as technologies to engineer (design, synthesize, or modify) the same "omes".
3. Neuroprosthetics are hybrid bionic systems that link the human nervous system to computers, thereby providing motor control and restoring lost sensory function of artificial limbs.
4. Genomics is the study of genes and their functions, and techniques related to them. The genome consists of the full genetic complement of an organism—its DNA.
5. Moore's Law refers to the perception that the number of transistors on a microchip doubles every two years even while the cost of computers halves. See Gordon Moore, "Cramming more components onto integrated circuits", originally in *Electronics*, April 19, 1965, Volume 38, Number 8.
6. For a fuller description, see, for example, *The Precision Medicine Initiative*, obamawhitehouse.archives.gov/precision-medicine.

7   A gene drive is a technology that uses genetic engineering to enable a specific genetic variant to be passed from parent to child at a higher-than-normal rate (up to 100 percent).
8   Andy Extance, "How DNA could store all the world's data", *Nature*, September 2, 2016.
9   R&D funded by business enterprise sector across major regions such as China, the EU, and the United States. Analysis is based on data from EU Industrial R&D Investment Scoreboard (2019).
10 For more on the methodology, please see chapter 4 and the technical appendix.
11 For an in-depth discussion of applications across domains studied in this research, see chapter 6.
12 Carrier screening is a genetic test used to determine if a healthy person is a carrier of a recessive genetic disease. It provides life-lasting information about an individual's reproductive risk and their chances of having a child with a genetic disease.
13 Polygenic diseases are caused by more than one gene. Examples of polygenic conditions include hypertension, diabetes, and coronary heart disease. There are often many environmental factors, too, making it more difficult to discern to what degree a disease is genetic even when the multiple genes are identified.
14 A microarray is a high-throughput screening method where the DNA sequences representing the large number of genes of an organism, arranged in a grid pattern for detection in genetic testing.
15 Marker-assisted breeding uses DNA markers associated with desirable traits to enable breeders to select a trait of interest without using transgenic approaches. Therefore, marker-assisted breeding doesn't produce genetically engineered organisms.
16 A GMO is an organism whose genetic material has been altered or modified. In GM crops, DNA from foreign organisms such as bacteria are introduced. See Kaare M. Nielsen, "Transgenic organisms—time for conceptual diversification?", *Nature Biotechnology*, March 2003, Volume 21, Issue 3.
17 We include wellness, nutrition, and fitness in consumer products and services rather than health because they tend to be consumed directly by individuals rather than mediated by healthcare professionals, offer more consumer choice compared to traditional health applications, and in some cases, such as fitness, require a significant change in consumer behavior to realize positive impact. This domain also includes beauty/enhancement use cases.
18 CAR T-cell (chimeric antigen receptor T-cell). CAR T-cells are genetically engineered T-cells that express artificial chimeric antigen receptors on their surface. These engineered T-cells enable a patient's own immune system to identify and destroy targeted cells.
19 Epigenomics is the study of the epigenome, specifically epigenetic modifications that affect gene expression such as DNA methylation and histone modification. This can direct such actions as turning genes on or off, and controlling the production of proteins in particular cells.
20 Total GHG emissions, including from land use, land-use change, and forestry, were 75.9 $GtCO_2e$ in 2018, according to the UN's *Emissions gap report 2019*. For the purposes of policy discussion and target setting, greenhouse gases are generally quantified by global warming potential (GWP), a measure of how much energy the emissions of one ton of gas will absorb during a given period, relative to the emissions of one ton of carbon dioxide. GWP is calculated for a specific time span, most commonly 100 years. But the lifetime for each greenhouse gas is different. Methane lasts in the atmosphere only for approximately 12 years, so its GWP will differ depending on a given time span. One ton of methane has 28 times the effect of one ton of carbon dioxide when measured at a 100-year GWP but 84 times the effect at a 20-year GWP. Given the importance of action and the short-term potential gain of reducing agriculture's methane emissions, our primary analysis is based on 20-year GWP

values. The global CO_2 emissions of the airline industry were about 0.9 gigaton in 2018. *ICAO global environmental trends – present and future aircraft noise and emissions*, International Civil Aviation Organization working paper number 54, May 7, 2019. Also see *Understanding global warming potentials*, US Environmental Protection Agency; and *Climate change 2013: The physical science basis*, Intergovernmental Panel on Climate Change, 2013.

21 The socio-demographic index is a development classification system specific to the Institute for Health Metrics and Evaluation (IHME) based on metrics such as per capita income and average years of schooling. Figures given are based on the IHME Global Burden of Disease 2017.

22 Recombinant DNA molecules are formed by combining genetic material from multiple sources to create sequences not found in the genome (molecular cloning, for instance). See Paul Berg et al., "Summary statement of the Asilomar Conference on recombinant DNA molecules", *Proceedings of the National Academy of Sciences*, June 1975, Volume 72, Number 6.

23 We define scientific feasibility as experimental success in the target population (for instance, in the case of human health, success in humans rather than mice models). For applications where we could not identify proof of concept in academia or industry, we assessed feasibility using sector-specific analogs and expert interviews that estimate how far away scientific feasibility might be.

24 This is a hybrid science that links biological data with techniques for information storage, distribution, and analysis to support multiple areas of research, including biomedicine.

25 Prior to approval in Philippines, Golden Rice was registered as safe in Australia, Canada, New Zealand, and the United States, all countries with few vitamin A deficiency problems. See Michael Le Page, "GM golden rice gets landmark safety approval in the Philippines", *New Scientist*, December 31, 2019. This is based on World Health Organization data on the prevalence of vitamin-A deficiency in pregnant women and preschool-age children from 1995 to 2005. See WHO, *Global prevalence of vitamin A deficiency in populations at risk 1995–2005*, WHO Global Database on Vitamin A Deficiency, 2009.

26 We examined existing regulations and their applicability to sized applications. Applications were also considered at stake if they relate to highly sensitive topics in academic circles, such as embryo editing and bioweapons. Our analysis is as of September 2019.

27 Recombinant DNA molecules are formed by combining genetic material from multiple sources to create sequences not found in the genome (molecular cloning, for instance). See Paul Berg et al., "Summary statement of the Asilomar Conference on recombinant DNA molecules", *Proceedings of the National Academy of Sciences*, June 1975, Volume 72, Number 6.

28 Cultured meat is produced by the in vitro cultivation of animal cells.

29 Analysis includes examination of existing regulations in the different countries and their applicability to sized applications. Applications are also considered at stake if they are related to highly sensitive topics in academic circles, such as embryo editing and bioweapons. Analysis of existing regulations as of September 2019.

References

Anzilotti, E. (2018, April). *This very realistic fake leather is made from mushrooms, not cows.* Fast Company.

Arshad, M.S., Javed, M., Sohaib, M., Saeed, F., Imran, A., and Amjad, Z. (2017). Tissue engineering approaches to develop cultured meat from cells: A mini review. *Cogent Food & Agriculture* Volume 3 (1), 1320814.

BASF and NRGene. (2019, October 29). BASF reference is from a press release, see https://www.basf.com/global/en/media/news-releases/2019/10/p-19-372.html.

Bell, J. (2018, April 23). Car-T ups challenges in pharma supply chain. *Biopharma Dive*.

Brown, K.V. (2019, February 27). A $100 genome is within reach, Illumina CEO asks if world is ready.

Carroll, D. (2019, June). Collateral damage: Benchmarking off-target effects in genome editing. *Genome Biology* Volume 20. DOI: 10.1186/s13059-019-1725-0

Cheng, Y. and Tsai, S.Q. (2018, December). Illuminating the genome-wide activity of genome editors for safe and effective therapeutics. *Genome Biology* Volume 19, pp. 226.

Chilukuri, S., Fleming, E., and Westra, A. (2017, December). *Digital in R&D: The $100 billion opportunity*. McKinsey & Company.

Crow, T. (2019, April). *Mushroom leather: The key to sustainable fashion?* Particle.

de Almeida, M. (2018, November 14). *Taking biotech to the next level with laboratory automation*. Labiotech.

Editorial: Keep Off-Target Effects in Focus. (2018). *Nature Medicine* Volume 24, 1081.

Erlich, Y., Shor, T., Pe'er, I., and Carmi, S. (2018, November). Identity inference of genomic data using long-range familial searches. *Science* Volume 362(6415), 690–694.

Extance, A. (2016, September 2). How DNA could store all the world's data. *Nature* Volume 537, 22–24.

Hayden, E.C. (2015, July 1). Genome researchers raise alarm over big data. *Nature* Volume 7. DOI: 10.1038/nature.2015.17912

Hirsch, J. (2013, August 27). Golden Rice: A brief timeline of the world's most controversial grain. *Modern Farmer*.

Hood, L. and Rowen, L. (2013, September). The human genome project: Big science transforms biology and medicine. *Genome Medicine* Volume 5(9), 1–8.

Hoskovec, J.M., et al. (2018, February). Projecting the supply and demand for certified genetic counselors: A workforce study. *Journal of Genetic Counseling* Volume 27, 16–20.

Human Genome Project Information Archive. (1990–2003). https://web.ornl.gov/sci/techresources/Human_Genome/index.shtml

International Rice Institute Research. (2018). "Philippines approves Golden Rice for direct use as food and feed, or for processing," available online at https://www.irri.org/news-and-events/news/philippines-approves-golden-rice-direct-use-food-and-feed-or-processing

Kolodziejczyk, A.A., Zheng, D., and Eran, E. (2019, December). Diet-microbiota interactions and personalized nutrition. *Nature Reviews Microbiology* Volume 17(12), 742–753.

Lopatto, E. (2015, February). Can GMOs end hunger in Africa? *The Verge*.

National Academies of Sciences, Engineering, and Medicine. (2016). *Genetically engineered crops: Experiences and prospects*. Washington, DC: The National Academies Press.

Partnership on AI. (n.d.) Zymergen Case Studies. https://partnershiponai.org/case-study/zymergen/

Regalado, A. (2020, February 26). China's BGI says it can sequence a genome for just $100. *MIT Technology Review*.

Reinagel, M. (2019, September 27). Personalized nutrition: The latest on DNA-based diets. *Scientific American*.

Rojahn, S.Y. (2013, April 12). A decade of advances since the Human Genome Project. *MIT Technology Review*.

Seffers, G.I.(2019, September 1). Scientists race toward DNA-based data storage. *Signal*.
Sergaki, C., Lagunas, B., Lidbury, I., Gifford, M.L., and Schäfer, P. (2018). Challenges and approaches in microbiome research: From fundamental to applied. *Frontiers in Plant Science* Volume 9, 1205.
Spinoff Projects Related to the Human Genome Project. (1990–2003). Human Genome Project Information Archive. https://web.ornl.gov/sci/techresources/Human_Genome/research/spinoffs.shtml
Stephens, N., Sexton, A.E., and Driessen, C. (2019, July 10). Making sense of making meat: Key moments on the first 20 years of tissue engineering muscle to make food. *Frontiers in Sustainable Food Systems* Volume 45.
Vesnina, A., Prosekov, A., Kozlova, O., and Atuchin, V. (2020). Genes and eating preferences, their roles in personalized *Nutrition* Volume 11(4), 357.

4
HELP WANTED IN SPACE

The Impact of Artificial Intelligence on Employment in the Cosmos Economy

Jack Gregg

4.1 Background

The era of the space economy is already here. Business activities that were once monopolized by a few governments have become a diversified, growing, and scalable industrial ecosystem. In particular, current launch costs of $1,500 per kilogram ($1,500/kg) are less than 4% of NASA's Space Shuttle launch expense in 1981. Further developments in Artificial Intelligence (AI) and robotics, new fuel systems, reusable rockets, and launch vehicles, will continue to drive these operating costs even lower. Some suggest launch costs could decline to $100/kg by 2040, perhaps as low as $33/kg in some optimistic projections (Citigroup, 2022). Falling costs could help propel current $370 billion annual space business revenues in 2020 (Citigroup, 2022) to $3 trillion by 2040 (Office of Space Commerce, 2019).

Most private space companies today focus on immediate returns from activities in low Earth orbit (LEO) with investments in communications satellites, reusable rockets, visual and telemetric data acquisition, AI applied analytics, mission control services, insurance, rocket payload brokers, and commercial start-ups peculiar to the new space economy. Investments in future opportunities beyond LEO like human settlements, space infrastructure buildout, extensive space industrialization, space-based trade and commerce, mineral mining and refining, and solar energy generation, are already taking shape. As more of these activities enter the mainstream the need for qualified talent, both technical and managerial, will—pardon the pun—skyrocket.

The burgeoning space economy, industrialization and eventual human settlement in our solar system, will alter traditional notions of commerce with economic impacts similar to changes caused by the Agricultural and Industrial

Revolutions. While this will certainly take time to fully mature, perhaps generations, it will encompass a wide range of economic activities in exploring, settling, and leveraging the potential riches and resources of the solar system.

4.1.1 The Problem

The road to building the space economy is facing a dire dilemma. And if small entrepreneurial space startups and large aerospace prime contractors can't solve this huge looming challenge, then the forward momentum may slow down and stall out. The problem isn't investment funding: Billions of dollars are pouring into space startups. The problem isn't public acceptance: Space-related launches and marquee projects have captured the attention of the entire world. The problem isn't technology: Engineers are already solving most of the critical technical problems about living and working in space. And the problem isn't customer demand: revenue from space ventures is experiencing rapid and continued growth. The problem is as simple as it is fixable; it is the enormous lack of professional *human* talent.

To be sure the problem can be fixed if the thousands of qualified and self-motivated career-seekers will step forward to be part of the hundreds of space companies around the world. But it turns out that most of today's talented workforce just doesn't know much about the new space sector, the above-average salaries, or how to connect with the many professional opportunities in space's commercialization.

4.2 A Global Endeavor

For much of the last seven decades space activities were largely confined to the US and Soviet Russian governments. Today this burgeoning field, what I call the "Cosmos Economy", includes dozens of countries and countless public and private sector actors. The sector has already attracted billions of investment dollars from sovereign states, venture capital firms (VCs), private equity investors, new entrepreneurs, and established corporate players.

To date, more than 80 countries have launched and currently operate at least one satellite in space, including some developing countries like Ghana, Mongolia, and Bangladesh. Women and men from more than 40 countries have flown into space, with ten countries having independently launched satellites into orbit successfully with their own launch vehicles: United States, Russia, France, UK, China, India, Japan, Israel, Iran, and North Korea.

4.2.1 A Wide Range of Commercial Activities

The bulk of space activities today are privately financed. This is a dramatic shift from the earlier model of government underwriting space-related projects.

Today it is less about how much money supports space activities; rather, the focus is on who gets to set the goals and define mission success. An example of the new paradigm is SpaceX becoming the first private company outside of NASA to send Americans into space in 2019, marking a pivotal moment in the new space economy.

Currently, governments comprise approximately 23% of space spending (mostly military/ defense), and the remaining 77% from the private sector. There is every indication that private space investments will continue to grow and dominate in years to come. As of early 2022, 550 of 624 satellites launched (88.1%) were from the commercial sector, far outpacing academic (6.4%), government (3.5%), and military (1.9%) satellites (Bryce Tech, 2022.)

As of early 2022, at least 1,694 unique space companies came online in the past ten years and VCs have invested $17.1 billion in 328 space companies in 2021 alone, accounting for 3% of total global venture capital flows (Space Foundation, 2022). So, where is all this investment going? The burgeoning cosmos economy is focused on several key activities, some of which are interrelated. The following is a short list of some leading space-related commercial sectors that will demand an infusion of talent. Some of these examples focus on current, short term, space activities, while others take a longer horizon and focus on the development of a broader economic ecosystem. Bear in mind that the Cosmos Economy is not yet mature, it is vibrant and growing. Assumptions are constantly being amended as new developments enable new enterprise and career opportunities. As the commercial space economy finds broader adoption this list will grow.

Payload Launch: One of the largest sectors, payload launch involves technology and infrastructure to send satellites to near space and low Earth orbit. The Soviet Union launched Sputnik in 1957, and for the next five decades there was a slow and steady growth in satellites with roughly 60 to 100 satellites launched yearly until the early 2010s. As rocket launches became cheaper and satellites became smaller, it was not uncommon to see 100+ launches each year putting more than 1000 satellites in orbit. It used to be that private companies had to contract with NASA to launch satellites. Now the roles are reversed with many launches utilizing the rockets and resources of private companies such as SpaceX. Launch facilities are now spread across the globe from French Guiana to New Zealand, and strategic partnerships include cross-border combinations such as the United Arab Emirates (UAE) teamed with Japan and a top US university for scientific research activities.

Satellite Communications and Internet: Satellites are used primarily for Earth observation, communications, and internet with such commercial applications as improving connectivity, wireless broadband, optical communications, and other technologies. The economic possibilities linked to these activities are enormous, especially downstream data analytics. More than 2.5 billion people do not have access to the internet, and private companies like Elon Musk's

Starlink by SpaceX, UK-based OneWeb, and Amazon's Project Kuiper are planning to launch almost 50,000 satellites in the coming years to create "mega-constellations" in low Earth orbit. This will not only provide new access for billions of people, but also help dramatically bring down the cost of data for all industries and create new applications that rely on cheap data, such as autonomous driving.

Earth Observation: Earth observation involves imaging, tracking, and analytics technology for scientific, commercial, and military applications. Space-based sensors monitor the weather, climate, maritime positioning data, military movements, GPS technology, and more. Planet Labs, based in San Francisco, California, has developed the capability of capturing images with up to 30 cm (one foot) resolution. This area's growth helps support many other sectors by providing daily updated data. For example, this capability can help reduce road traffic and accidents, and help logistics companies better manage delivery algorithms. Satellite data helps farmers map crop yields on a pixel-by-pixel basis, improving efficiency on water and fertilizer use, and helps schedule optimal harvests to boost food production with increased cost efficiency. Satellites also monitor global ocean and freshwater resources to help identify problems and manage usage. Earth-observation satellites provide data for early warning systems that monitor political and military treaty compliance and violations. Such technologies, for example, have been used to detect troop build-ups in places such as North Korea and Russia's tactical positioning before and during its 2022 invasion of Ukraine.

Lunar and Planetary Landing: Many nations plan to explore celestial bodies like our Moon, various planets and their moons, and resource-rich asteroids. Several companies are currently planning to design, construct, and deliver critical infrastructure for such activities. In late 2021, for example, NASA selected five American companies to develop landers to return astronauts to the Moon under its new Artemis program including SpaceX, Blue Origin, Dynetics, Lockheed Martin, and Northrop Grumman. These private companies are designing and building hardware and software applications such as landing processes, mission modeling, risk-reduction activities, and are preparing and testing other requirements for human lunar missions. China plans to send humans to the far side of the Moon in the mid-2020s and its first crewed mission to Mars in 2033 with eventual plans to build a permanent base there. The European Union, India, South Korea, and Japan are also planning manned space missions.

Space Mining and Manufacturing: Our solar system's resources offer the opportunity to extract water, rare minerals, and other industrial metals. It is now generally accepted that in situ resource utilization (ISRU), which posits that raw materials to support living and working in space should be harvested from space instead of ferried from Earth, is the optimal approach to building space living and manufacturing infrastructure. Water, which is abundant in our solar system, maybe the most attractive resource in the near-term, not only for human life support but also because water may be split into hydrogen and oxygen to make rocket fuel. Another opportunity on Earth is "rare earth" metal acquisition which is in high industrial demand. Today, these critical minerals are concentrated in China and mined at great environmental cost to the planet. They are used in products like rechargeable batteries for electric and hybrid cars, advanced ceramics, computers, wind turbines, video monitors, fiber optics, superconductors, and even glass polishing. They are also essential for military equipment including jet engines and missile guidance systems, among others. As such, space mining has long been considered a major investment opportunity. An example is 16 Psyche, a tuber-shaped asteroid located between Mars and Jupiter, with an average diameter of about 140 miles (226 kilometers), or roughly one-sixteenth that of the Moon. Scientists estimate its platinum, iron, and nickel deposits may be worth $10,000 quadrillion—or many millions of times the value of our current global economy. While theoretical, the result of an unlimited supply of otherwise rare materials remarkably could bring the commercial cost of many nearly to zero (Carter, 2022).

Solar Energy: With some new technology around the corner, the Earth's orbit can become a solar farm that will send energy directly to communities on our planet. In space the sun never sets, and clouds never form thus boosting capture efficiency exponentially from current ground-based solar methods. Energy generated from space may circumvent the need for costly and unsafe transmission lines and can deliver power to remote emerging economies without the need for building and maintaining expensive local infrastructure. Further, it has been posited that an army on the move, a ship at sea, or even an airplane in flight, may receive power directly from sophisticated space-based energy infrastructure controlled by AI algorithms. The prospect of such pinpoint energy delivery will have a significant impact on commercial and military logistics, as well as reducing our reliance on fossil fuels.

Space Debris Removal and Mitigation: When a satellite is obliterated in orbit, thousands of pieces of space trash, almost too tiny to track, continue to circle the planet at over seventeen thousand miles per hour as lethal projectiles and can wreak havoc on other viable space hardware. The International Space Station (ISS) has repeatedly warned of space debris that endangers orbiting equipment and humans on board. Of increasing concern is that all these satellite pieces could trigger the onset of the Kessler syndrome, a phenomenon where colliding fragments impact one another in a never-ending escalating mele of cascading satellite destruction. The challenge of cleaning up LEO space is a persistent topic of discussion at global space conferences today with the universal agreement that space debris needs to be monitored and eventually removed. Unfortunately, there is no manageable (i.e., profitable) solution on the immediate horizon. As our planet becomes girded with more functioning satellites—and more space junk—the need for a debris solution becomes more acute.

Space Tourism: Sending paying passengers to space, either for a brief trip to LEO, a longer stay at the International Space Station, or eventually to a commercial resort, are already being planned. Like early 20th-century barnstorming today's recreational rides to space have successfully raised awareness and popular acceptance about the viability of human access to space. But there is more to space tourism than media coverage and celebrity endorsements. Carnival Cruise Lines, for example, is developing plans for their customers who wish to vacation in space. Other firms like SpaceX, Blue Origin, and Virgin Galactic have their sights set on creating a new transportation option for people and for express cargo payloads. For example, analysts believe that conventional long-haul airplane flights may potentially be supplemented by point-to-point rockets flights; SpaceX's planned Starship could transport 100 paying passengers from New York to Tokyo in roughly 40 minutes versus 15 hours in conventional aircraft.

Deep Space Exploration: The prospect of humans beyond the asteroid belt, Mars, or other outer planets, remains a technical challenge. Capabilities are not yet developed that will enable humans to safely reach the far reaches of our solar system in reasonable time. In the near term, unmanned space missions will continue using AI to explore deep space and gather data that will help facilitate human settlement development. Information collected from these missions has been and will be critical in designing future space exploration activities. Some academics prefer to eschew human participation in space exploration altogether. As discussed in *The End of Astronauts* (Goldsmith & Rees, 2022), robotic exploration of space is far cheaper and safer—at least for the foreseeable future. But we can dream a little: One can easily see how robotics and AI could augment the human ability to explore and settle deep space.

Research and Technological Spinoffs: Many products, materials, and processes developed specifically for the US space program in the 1960s and 1970s eventually found their way to commercial applications. Since the mid-1970s, the NASA Technology Transfer Program led to many consumer products such as memory foam; freeze-dried food; airplane cabin pressure systems; emergency silver heat-retaining blankets; the portable DustBuster® vacuums; and cochlear implants are among countless other commercial product applications. There are also obscure materials such as nitinol, a specialized alloy developed to allow flexible satellites to spring open origami style after being folded into a rocket faring. This presents potent opportunities for entrepreneurs, and it is likely the new space economy will continue to produce more discoveries that will migrate to Earth's industrial sectors as well as to new applications in the growing space economy.

Big Data Analytics: Satellite proliferation has generated the key ingredient for the digital economy and AI; big data. New datasets are only commercially useful if they can be analyzed and parsed for practical meaning quickly to serve customer needs. Satellites generate huge amounts of data that require analysis on a constant basis and there is growing demand for software companies that provide downstream analytic applications. These providers take raw data generated from satellite sensors and convert the data into useful information that fulfills a market demand and generates profitable revenues. According to Matt Perkins, head of Oxford University Innovation, "space rockets aren't the [only] way you make money from space…[a] way you make money is in the downstream end by using all this information coming from space. As this becomes cheaper that's going to open commercial opportunities with data being used in ways that people haven't yet thought of" (Bowler, 2018). With increasing Internet of Things (IoT) connectivity for smart cities and autonomous mobility systems, the unifying element will be a reliance on the increasing network of satellites orbiting the globe and collecting data. For example, Elon Musk's Starlink system of satellites promises to enable space-based internet communications for first-world and remote communities alike.

These examples, along with countless others, offer entrepreneurs, students, and career seekers a future filled with endless possibilities in the Cosmos Economy.

4.3 Career Opportunities

With nearly 1700 private companies actively involved with developing, marketing, and executing their space-related products and services, there is tremendous sustainable demand for qualified workers across many disciplines in burgeoning space sectors. Demand for space talent should continue for the next several decades as more enterprises enter the marketplace with new technologies and brand extensions of existing products.

According to the US Bureau of Labor Statistics, there will be a need for skilled scientists, engineers, technicians, and media/communications professionals—not to mention a whole host of non-STEM, (i.e., nontechnical) professionals in management, finance, marketing, logistics, sales, and other traditional business fields. The following examples provide just a glimpse of job categories that are likely to remain in high demand (Angeles & Vilorio, 2016):

Scientists: The range of scientists needed for commercializing space includes almost all disciplines. For example, astronomers do not only observe space objects but they also analyze data captured in space; astrophysicists use methods and tools from chemistry and physics to study the interaction between the sun, Earth, and other planets; and even meteorologists analyze data to improve space-weather forecasts, which may help to protect satellites, power transmissions, and transportation communication systems. Of critical importance are those scientists who can envision research opportunities and design research programs to test their theories about space. These principal investigators (PIs) have been at the forefront of discoveries about our place in the solar system and in the cosmos at large since the beginning of the space age. Many highly trained scientists in a variety of disciplines are employed by the private commercial space sector.

Engineers in a Range of Disciplines: Space companies will require thousands of engineers with different specializations in everything from hardware and software design to developing living and working environments. Some marquee engineer categories include:

Aerospace engineers: These engineers design, construct, and test space vehicles. In their designs, aerospace engineers must consider each environment's limitations. Engineers who focus on human space systems will be in high demand.

Computer Software and Hardware engineers: Hardware engineers research, design, develop, and test computer systems and equipment that are used to measure activity in outer space or on Earth. Software engineers analyze problems and processes and create user interface with hardware that enables a successful outcome based on project requirements. Those most in demand will be able to manage complex software design and implementation.

Electronics engineers: Electronics engineers focus on specific equipment, such as the instrument panels, life support systems, communications, navigation, and a broad range of critical mission infrastructure.

Mechanical engineers: These engineers often partner with other workers to create products—including sensors, tools, engines, or other devices that support space missions. For example, mechanical engineers may collaborate with aerospace engineers to develop the design of rocket nozzles, life support systems, or other critical components.

Civil engineers: Practitioners of this discipline will be needed to design and develop space-based outposts, settlements, and other large-scale constructions as commercial space activities expand in the solar system. Some of these construction projects will be in free space and others will likely be located on a celestial body (e.g., an asteroid, moon, or planet).

Systems engineers: The complexity of space equipment demands a comprehensive, strategic rather than tactical, and integrative approach to program design, execution, and accountability. The systems approach is interdisciplinary and is employed to reduce the likelihood of conflicting different engineering disciplines that may inadvertently impede the overall success of complex systems development. Space engineering is often described as a system of systems and the systems engineer who can successfully navigate the demands of different technical platforms is in high demand.

4.3.1 Finding Talent

Unfortunately, there aren't enough people prepared for these opportunities. One solution is, of course, to encourage students to pursue these areas before they enter the workforce. But what about those already working? Qualified talent may be hiding in plain sight.

When SpaceX went looking for people to build their rockets, they quickly realized that there were not many rocket-makers available in the labor market, so they had to get creative. They analyzed their production process and realized that many of the skills needed to fabricate their Falcon rockets were the same as those used by automobile production workers. Their successful solution was to recruit talent from the automotive industry and turn auto assemblers into rocket nerds. (Pop quiz: Where do you think Elon Musk found a ready supply of auto workers to transform into rocket professionals?)

A common assumption is that the only people who will find work in the space economy are those trained technically in such areas as computing and engineering, etc. This is a narrow view. Demand will also be for people who can manage people, projects, budgets, or programs and for leaders who can set the vision and metrics for success and make things happen. Indeed, the most needed talent will be those who can build relationships, manage the technicians, lead organizations with executable visions and corporate missions, and set the tone for the values of the firm. If these activities sound familiar they should; they are timeless business skills and there are plenty of people who have them today. And for those who may not be driven by space's glamour, just follow the money: the Space Foundation (2022) states the average US private sector space salary was $125,214 per year which is *double* the average US private sector salary of just $62,247.

4.4 AI and Robotics as Enablers

While many are concerned that new technologies like AI may eliminate future jobs, an alternate view is that AI and related innovations will usher in a new definition of work: A technology-empowered workforce. Martin Ford, the author of *Rule of the Robots: How Artificial Intelligence Will Transform Everything* (2021), supports the idea that the future roles of human workers in an economy dominated by AI are in areas that require problem-solving skills, professional communications, relationship management, business development, team management, supply chain control, product and organizational branding, systems analysis, customer relations, government policy and regulatory liaison, finance, and a wide range of other un-technical skills. These roles will focus on defining and nurturing the organization's success by achieving a long-term, sustainable, competitive advantage in the space market sector.

Building the new space economy will require a mix of human strategic oversight and automated industrial capabilities for such initial areas as infrastructure construction, raw resource mining and refining, solar energy generation, deep space transportation and logistics, large-scale agri-business to feed people on Earth as well as in space, and a full array of commercial activities that will come online as space settlement and commercial activities will repeatedly move from one new frontier to the next across the continuously developing solar system.

4.4.1 AI

Rather than thinking about AI as a single technology, instead it should be viewed as a constellation of science and engineering disciplines that infuse technology with intelligence. For the space economy to advance, AI will be needed for many applications. At its core, AI leverages computer systems to perform tasks that typically require human intelligence including visual perception, speech recognition, decision-making, and language translation, among others. With AI, technology can be substituted for humans to gather, process, and analyze huge amounts of data that might be impossible for humans to do alone, or in a practical amount of time. The following is a brief list of examples of artificial intelligence applications in the new space economy and brings focus to the need for engineers, analysts, and others to help analyze needs, define requirements, develop AI systems, implement the AI solution, and evaluate the success of the product or process. These examples are listed without priority.

AI Personal Assistants in Space: Space travelers on a long-duration mission will encounter communication delays preventing mission control from providing immediate support for emergencies or day-to-day mission-related activities. AI can provide an onboard assist, like Siri or Alexa in space, both of which were inspired by science fiction's HAL (**H**euristically programmed **Al**gorithmic), the artificial intelligence computer in Arthur C. Clarke's 1968 novel *A Space Odyssey*. IBM, in partnership with German space agency DLR and Airbus, created an AI assistant called Crew Interactive Mobile Companion (CIMON) for this purpose. For example, a deep space asteroid mining operation may encounter an unforeseen problem or emergency that needs immediate resolution. Instead of calling home to Mars or some other distant base and waiting hours or days for a reply, the company's on-board AI capability may be able to resolve the problem immediately in real-time. Some systems are designed to understand human speech and are equipped with facial recognition technology which allows for more perceptual interactions.

AI to Process Satellite Images: As mentioned earlier, the amount of data produced by Earth satellites is enormous and will only grow over time. AI tools are used to analyze data taken from space telescopes to discover new stars that may better explain the origin of our galaxy. Before AI and machine learning techniques were used to study the data, scientists could only identify about one hundred special infant galaxy-forming protostars. By employing AI technology, researchers can now identify over 2,000 protostars.

Satellite imagery of our planet alone offers an endless number of possibilities for using artificial intelligence. Space-based sensors produce many images of the Earth which are used for creating information about weather conditions, military movements, and other applications. Without AI algorithms, technicians have to process data manually, which will likely result in less accurate information. The use of artificial intelligence embedded directly on board a satellite further removes the additional communication time lag between ground and space stations. This challenge speaks directly to the need for AI engineers, analysts, and other problem solvers.

The power of machine learning algorithms lies in their ability to study millions of images in a matter of moments and register any changes as they occur such as troop movements or changes in weather conditions. This is especially important when tracking natural disasters. By automating various processes with the help of AI, the satellite will independently start taking images if the sensors register certain signals, such as critical differences in pressure or temperature of air streams. In addition, such satellites can be part of disaster warning systems. AI algorithms can calculate the likelihood of a phenomenon as well as the path of its development and probable consequences.

AI for System Monitoring: Like other complex systems, satellites and spacecraft require a lot of system monitoring. AI systems continuously monitor the performance of all kinds of sensors, not only notifying ground controls about any problems but also solving them independently. For example, SpaceX has equipped its satellites with a system of sensors and maneuvering mechanisms that can track the position of the object and adjust it to avoid collisions with other objects; something akin to a driverless spaceship operating in four dimensions.

AI for Mission Design, Planning, Compliance, and Space Assistance: Planning a mission to the Moon, Mars, or beyond is complex. AI makes it easier and improves chances for success. Space missions are knowledge-intensive, requiring as much technical data as possible gathered from multiple sources. Like Alexa or Siri, *Daphne* was developed at the Jet Propulsion Laboratory in Pasadena, California for systems engineers in satellite design teams. By providing access to relevant information including feedback as well as answers to specific queries, Daphne employs design automation and conceptual design tools to help aerospace engineers design better missions faster than humans without AI.

AI and Preventing Potential Space Debris: More satellites mean more potential problems with space debris. There are already AI-linked solutions, such as designing satellites to re-enter Earth's atmosphere in ways that allow them to disintegrate completely in a controlled manner. AI may also be used to potentially help detect and avoid possible collisions in space, preventing the creation of more debris.

Intelligent Navigation Systems: One important application of AI navigation for NASA is the development of autonomous rovers that navigate the surface of other planets like Mars. Autonomous robots are required to make decisions and avoid obstacles on a rough surface while determining the best route without reliance on specific commands from the mission control. Rover autonomous decisions have been credited with enabling some of the scientific breakthroughs on Mars.

AI for Training Systems: Simulation training on Earth for activities in space reduces cost, risk, and increases mission assurance because AI relies upon very large datasets and evaluates training success in real-time. With the help of AI simulations, researchers can create a great many training datasets and come up with innovative models before final product release. The entire AI training process can occur during the simulation process and be implemented without needing to go through the process of live data collection that is both difficult and expensive for applications in space.

The above examples of how AI may be employed in the new space economy demonstrate a wide range of employment opportunities for engineers, entrepreneurs, and business professionals who wish to be part of the new space economy. AI skills are highly transferable and attractive to hiring managers across a broad terrain of technical and non-technical employers.

4.4.2 Robotics

Today, the challenges for humans in the space environment provide at least some of the inspiration for the concept of autonomous operation; put simply, if a system can make its own decisions, without human intervention, it will benefit by helping to avoid placing human lives in danger.

4.4.2.1 Humans vs. Machines

Acquiring, training, retaining, and potentially replacing a human worker is a very expensive and lengthy process. Humans are quirky, and often display very individualistic behaviors that may not always fit neatly with their team or the greater organization's mission They need constant feedback and attention, and expect efforts to be rewarded with more money, a better job title, or even a bit of respect from their boss. Unlike humans, robots are easily obtained, reprogrammed, maintained, and replaced if their capabilities no longer match company production expectations. As a capital asset, they can be depreciated on the company balance sheet, they do not require a pension, a suite of benefits, or even an annual pro forma birthday party in the break room.

Participants in the future workforce, sentient or not, each have advantages and disadvantages. At least for the time being.

- **The advantages of robots**: They include 168-hour workweek with no overtime, no need for vacations, sick days, or mental health respites, no pension plan and no collective bargaining rules. They also include no arguments about doing the job, showing up late, taking long lunches, or inattention to detail. Furthermore, robots do not need air, food, sleep, coffee breaks, a fancy title, respect from their boss, or contentious meetings about attitude adjustments.
- **The advantages of people**: Qualified workers add value because of their ability to see how various elements of the work setting are integrated. They can independently and creatively adjust activities to improve processes. They can build and maintain critical relationships internally with other company employees and with external non-company constituents. They can recognize and employ *informal* influence structures to expedite the work process.
- **The new hybrid workforce**: What has come to be called *cobots*, humans working in close concert with robots, maybe the new industrial norm in space. Determining the best preference for optimizing production may not always be an easy decision. Sometimes it may be best to structure a blend of sentient and robotic capabilities in a hybrid workplace. This concept has yet to become a fully matured model, one advantage is the flexibility it creates, especially in a setting where critical decisions must be made about quality or customization.

The role of robots will be even more vital as the space economy builds out. Robots already execute scientific experiments where humans cannot physically be present, and they may be remotely controlled to complete more difficult or risky tasks, especially in dangerous settings. Robots are more reliable than human beings when it comes to completing repetitive tasks with precise accuracy, which is vital for many aspects of space-based manufacturing. Robots are expected to make exploration safer and more accessible for humans. The need to design robotic systems to solve problems and generate new solutions will create a substantial opportunity for employment in the new space economy. As humanity expands its reach within and across space, the ability to robotically assemble, service, and manufacture equipment, products, habitat, transport vehicles, and even food and energy in space will be essential for safety and sustainability.

4.5 Summary and Conclusion

The Cosmos Economy is not tomorrow's science fiction fantasy; it is *today's* economic fact. Current studies estimate annual space activities to reach as much as $3 trillion by the mid-2040s with dynamic growth expected to continue through the 21st century and beyond. Eventually, we should see widespread human settlements and interconnected space-based industrial activities supported by both private investors and national interests.

AI will help to enable and advance commercial space activities. Rather than replacing humans, the technology will buttress humanity's presence in space by performing tasks that we are simply not capable of doing on our own. Instead of dreading the power of AI, we are well advised to embrace the opportunity to achieve new things that have not been possible before. The potential for new industries, new careers, new opportunities for success, and for new solutions to many human and Earthbound problems may come from our journey to settle and develop the new space economy. In brief:

- Space exploration is no longer controlled or dominated by any one nation. Non-US global space participation is increasing as spaceports and other space-related business ventures spring up across the globe.
- Private space firms now exceed government space investments. The old business model where government contracts dictated commercial space activities has been eclipsed by private enterprises responding to market forces.
- Venture capital for space sector is increasing. Monies are flowing to both established and startup enterprises.
- Non-space companies are becoming increasingly active in new space business markets. These firms are entering the Cosmos Economy with both brand extensions and new business models.
- Our solar system has near-limitless mineral resources, including water. This immeasurable abundance has the potential to end scarcity, recalibrate economic systems for humanity, reduce commodity market volatility, and conceivably eliminate social and economic disparity.
- AI and robotic automation enhances, not eliminates, human labor for space. The most efficient workforce is a partnership between humans and automation. The synergies between the two far outperform that of any single workforce platform. The raw space environment, especially during the early phases of development, will rely heavily upon AI robotics to build a beachhead for future settlements and industrial installations.
- The demand for talent in the space sector will fuel career and investment opportunities for decades, across multiple fields for both traditional and new skillsets.

The challenge of writing and forecasting the future is that whatever you write is merely a best guess at that moment in time. We simply don't know what we don't know. But for those who grasp the enormous potential of the Cosmos Economy, we are encouraged to follow the prescient advice of Dr. Peter Drucker: "The best way to predict the future is to create it". Fortune has always favored bold visionaries, and the economic development of space offers unprecedented opportunities for those willing to embrace its potential.

References

Angeles, D. & Vilorio, D. (2016). *Space Careers: A Universe of Options*. U.S. Bureau of Labor Statistics.

Bowler, T. R. (2018). A New Space Race. In *Deep Space Commodities* (pp. 13–19). Palgrave Macmillan, Cham.

Bryce Tech (2022). *Bryce Briefing Q122*. Bryce Tech.

Carter, J. (2022). "Scientists Probe Huge Crater on 'Psyche,' the Massive Metal Asteroid Worth More Than Our Global Economy," *Forbes*.

Citigroup (2022). *SPACE: The Dawn of a New Age*. Citigroup.

Ford, M. (2021). *Rule of the Robots: How Artificial Intelligence Will Transform Everything*. Basic Books.

Goldsmith, D., & Rees, M. (2022). *The End of Astronauts. In the End of Astronauts*. Harvard University Press.

Office of Space Commerce (2019). "O'Connell Remarks to U.S. Chamber of Commerce," Office of Space Commerce, U.S. Department of Commerce.

Space Foundation (2022). *The Space Report*. Space Foundation.

5
THE 21ST-CENTURY IMPERATIVE FOR UNIVERSITIES

Redesigning Higher Education for the Climate Problem

Ruth DeFries

5.1 Introduction

Higher education's core mission is to transform lives for the benefit of individuals and society. Over the last 150 years, the buildup of greenhouse gases has turned climate change from a scientific to a societal problem. People living in places affected by wildfires, coastal flooding, storms, droughts, and other impacts are particularly at risk, with repercussions that ricochet globally into food prices, supply chains, and exacerbated inequities. Universities are beginning to respond to these challenges as they did to other societal challenges in prior eras. In the 19th century, American universities rose to the challenges of industrialization and a growing population by creating academic and professional fields in engineering, mining, and agriculture. In the early 20th century, urbanization gave birth to the field of social work to respond to growing urban poverty and the field of public health responded to the spread of disease. University efforts to address climate as a societal problem are in their infancy. This multidisciplinary field will evolve with future technologies that help monitor, analyze, and ameliorate climate change's numerous impacts. The main goal is to train professionals to incorporate climate as essential elements of finance, artificial intelligence (AI) and data analytics, disaster response and preparation, land use planning and architecture, health, and public administration, among other topics. Key competencies within all of these areas include: Systems approach to assess interactions between climate and society; the ability to collaborate to solve problems; depth of knowledge within a specific area to contribute to problem-solving collaborations; and a sensitivity to justice and equity concerns that permeate the climate problem.

5.2 The Climate Problem

From one perspective, climate change is remarkably simple. The basic physics was clear over 150 years ago when the scientist and inventor Eunice Newton Foote discovered that the sun's rays passing through carbon dioxide "would give to our Earth a high temperature" (Bell, 2021). Physicist and chemist Svante Arrhenius further identified that coal burning emits carbon dioxide into the atmosphere and increases temperatures. Ironically, he predicted that the impact on societies would be positive. Writing in 1896, he looked forward to "more equable and better climate especially as regards the colder regions of the earth. Ages when the earth will bring forth much more abundant crops than at present, for the benefit of rapidly propagating mankind" (Arrhenius, 1896).

The fundamental principle of the greenhouse effect—that greenhouse gases, predominantly carbon dioxide, allow incoming solar radiation to pass through the atmosphere but trap outgoing infrared radiation emitted from the Earth's surface—remains undisputed. But decades of research on the intricate workings of the planet's atmosphere, biosphere, and oceans raise more complex, yet-to-be-answered questions. At what point does incremental buildup of greenhouse gases lead to tipping points in ocean circulation or melting ice sheets that cascade into irreversible climate change? When and where will an overheated planet spur more intense storms and extreme droughts? Will forests become burning tinder boxes that release even more carbon dioxide and no longer sequester it from the atmosphere? Can the ocean continue to absorb excess carbon dioxide entering the atmosphere from humanity's dependence on fossil fuels?

While scientific uncertainties about the Earth systems' biogeochemical responses to increasing greenhouse gases remain, these uncertainties pale in comparison to those related to the human aspects of the Earth system. The greatest uncertainty in projecting future climate change arises from the timeline for transition to low greenhouse gas economies, a moving target depending on lifestyle changes, technological advances, and policy decisions. As the climate moves outside the envelope of human experience, will societies be able to cope with rising seas, fires, storms, and other impacts from climate change? Will governments, civil society, and the private sector alleviate the disproportionate effects on vulnerable populations, or will climate impacts exacerbate existing inequalities? Will countries of the world join together to reduce emissions and adapt to the impacts, or will global cooperation remain a mirage? Will corporations and governments implement sophisticated technologies and artificial intelligence to mitigate and adapt to climate change, or will these capabilities be co-opted to enhance profits from tragedies?

From a social perspective, climate change is an incredibly complex problem; taking action goes against human nature to respond to immediate, visible problems. Direct cause-and-effect linkages are difficult to distinguish against natural variability, which hinders public awareness of the problem. Moreover, greenhouse gases are invisible and the public cannot visualize the damage. Most critically, the root causes of climate change—fossil fuel burning and land use—have provided convenient, cheap energy and inexpensive food for decades. Reducing emissions from these many and varied sources will affect nearly every aspect of the global economy. Strong vested interests hinder change.

Greenhouse gas emissions have created market failures for multiple reasons: Emissions generally do not impact those actors generating the problem; there are few incentives to reduce emissions; the gases mix in the atmosphere, so that emissions in one place cascade into droughts and storms at distant locations, often affecting less powerful, vulnerable populations; and the burden of emissions will fall on future generations. In the meantime, political and commercial decisions to mitigate and adapt to climate change require long-term investments that might not bear fruit within politicians' terms in office or a corporate CEO's tenure.

Established governance systems have effectively addressed many environmental problems in the past, such as regulations to reduce local air and water pollution or global agreements to replace an industrial chemical responsible for stratospheric ozone depletion. Expertise in engineering, policy, and economics were all relevant to resolving these problems.

Similarly, climate change requires expertise from multiple disciplines to understand and manage the problem. But it is a much more difficult challenge than previous environmental problems. Climate change is neither locally visible, like air and water pollution, nor are the many sources of emissions easy to replace, like stratospheric ozone. Reducing emissions from burning fossil fuels which power the modern economy requires a transformation of energy sources that support civilization. Changes in land use, the second most significant source of emissions, require different paradigms for modern agriculture and people's diets. Moreover, the inequities from climate impacts that affect people and places that did not historically contribute to the problem raise difficult questions about who holds the responsibility to address the problem. Climate change is perhaps the most complex and existential problem that humanity has collectively faced.

Humans are entering uncharted territory by increasing greenhouse gases in the atmosphere beyond levels not experienced for millions of years (Foster, Royer, & Lunt, 2017). Societies constructed infrastructure, cities, agriculture, and all the fundamental support systems for modern civilization based on the expectations of a stable and predictable climate similar to the past. Societies need new kinds of institutions to navigate through this uncharted territory, among them new capabilities in universities to carry out research and train leaders and a workforce for the future.

5.2.1 Climate as a Societal Problem

Manifestations of climate change permeate many aspects of society. Increase in fires in some parts of the world, intensity of storms, droughts, heat waves, and sea-level rise can be attributed to the incremental build-up of greenhouse gases in the atmosphere. People living in affected areas are faced with the need to adapt to these changes. Issues of equity and justice rise to the fore as less economically advantaged populations often live in the places most vulnerable to these impacts and have fewer resources to buffer the impacts for their communities and households (Byers et al., 2018).

Climate mitigation to reduce emissions of greenhouse gases or sequester them from the atmosphere also raises fundamental concerns for society. A transition away from fossil fuels and other sources of emissions involves fundamental shifts in how people live, travel, and work as well as their diets and consumption habits. Issues of equity are also paramount in climate mitigation. For the developing world, where per capita energy consumption is a fraction of that in the industrialized world, realistic development pathways that do not depend on fossil fuels are not in hand. Moreover, the decades of international negotiations for a globally collective effort to reduce emissions continue to stumble on the basic question of which countries are responsible for reducing emissions—the countries that have benefited from fossil fuels and industrial agriculture and are responsible for the vast majority of historical emissions, or the countries whose emissions are on an upward trajectory?

Climate change raises a vast range of questions for disaster preparedness, institutions for international governance, health, agriculture, urban planning, and environmental justice, among others. At different times in history, other complex societal needs have come to the fore. At those times, universities established new fields and professional schools to carry out applied research and train a workforce with appropriate skills.

During the Industrial Revolution, the Morrill Act of 1862 was a US government response to expand higher education "related to agriculture and the mechanic arts". The result was the formation of land-grant colleges which addressed society's need for engineers and agricultural specialists to accommodate and accelerate the expansion of the country, its growing population, and the maturation of its economy. The Act initially created 15 new schools that offered engineering courses, which increased from six and grew to dozens over time.

The School of Mines of Columbia University, founded in 1864, is the precursor to the university's current school of engineering. It was the first mining and metallurgy school in the United States, Columbia's response to develop technologies that provided the growing material needs of American society. Fifty years after the Morrill Act, some 38,000 citizens had graduated with engineering degrees. Today approximately 130 US institutions award more than 130,000 engineering degrees each year (Roy, 2019).

Increasing urban poverty in the late 19th century in industrializing cities of Europe and North America gave birth to the field of social work. The paradox of growing poverty amidst increasingly productive and prosperous economies motivated charitable organizations to address the social ills of crime, neglected and abandoned children, unemployment, chronic disability, and various deprivations. Voluntary efforts emerged to intervene to help poor families, especially children, in the face of these problems. Universities ultimately responded to this social need by establishing schools of social work.

Public health is another example of a field shaped by universities to address a societal problem. Public health aims to promote and protect the health of people and communities in the places where they live, work, and play. The field's focus is to identify and implement population-level interventions such as vaccines and encouragement of healthy behaviors. Public health professionals view health as the combined outcome of an individual's social and economic environment, physical environment, and individual characteristics and behavior.

Public health interventions to prevent disease and secure health date back to ancient times with water supply, latrines, and sewers. Quarantines to attempt to curb the spread of disease, culling animals presumed to be disease vectors, and other public health practices were prevalent in medieval times. Later, epidemiology began with the mid-18th-century discovery that lack of fruits and vegetables causes scurvy, followed by discoveries of vaccines and identification of contaminated water as a source of infectious disease. These epidemiological observations laid the groundwork for public health interventions. In 1872, as growing cities became hotbeds of disease and pestilence, the American Public Health Association was established to serve as a professional educational and lobbying group to promote the interests of public health in the United States. During the second half of the 19th and the first half of the 20th centuries, municipal governments established local public health offices for water sanitation, waste removal, and food control. In this period, around the time of the 1918 influenza pandemic, Johns Hopkins and Harvard Universities established the first schools of public health (Tulchinsky, Varavikova, & Last, 2014).

Today, there are over a hundred accredited public health programs in the United States, which train a workforce for government, state and community public health agencies, hospitals, international and national health organizations, research institutions, and a wide range of other institutions. An established curriculum centers on environmental health science, health policy and management, social and behavioral sciences, epidemiology, and biostatistics (Calhoun, Ramiah, Weist, & Shortell, 2008).

Universities established schools of social work and public health in the early 20th century as societal problems of urban poverty and disease created the need for research and training. Both fields emphasize a systems approach for a holistic understanding of the causes of poverty and health. Similarly, identification and implementation of interventions to reduce concentrations of atmospheric greenhouse gases and adapt to climate change require a systems approach based on the complex interactions among human societies, the atmosphere, oceans, and biosphere. As universities established engineering, social work, and public health schools in response to societal needs in previous centuries, universities are beginning to respond to the need for research and training for climate experts to guide interventions based on a systems approach.

5.2.2 The Role of Universities in Addressing the Climate Problem

Research at universities has been pivotal to advancing understanding of the climate system and impacts of climate change for societies. A key focus has been forecasting future climate with increases in atmospheric greenhouse gases. As climate results from the interactions between the atmosphere, biosphere, oceans, and social components, no single discipline can successfully pursue this goal without working with scientists in other disciplines. A holistic approach to climate is the essence of the young and still emerging field of Earth System Science (ESS), and this field will continue to evolve as new technologies ranging from AI computing to robotics continue to advance.

Earth System Science had its roots in geophysics in the middle of the 20th century. The early focus was instrumentation, such as the well-known measurements by Charles Keeling to monitor atmospheric carbon dioxide at Mauna Loa, Hawaii, and numerical modeling to capture the physics of the greenhouse effect. With attention to stratospheric ozone and other environmental problems in the 1960s and 1970s and advancement in ecosystem ecology, a more holistic view of the planet emerged beyond a purely geophysical approach. A new scientific endeavor to understand the planet as interacting exchanges of gases and energy among the biosphere, atmosphere, oceans, and solid earth traces its origin to the 1983 NASA Earth System Science Committee (Steffen et al., 2020). This conception transcends disciplinary boundaries of chemistry, physics, biology, oceanography, and other traditional structures of universities.

A handful of universities organized programs and interdisciplinary working environments around ESS in the 1990s, such as the University of California at Irvine and the Potsdam Institute. However, as British ecologist Sir John Lawton wrote in 2001, "in the main we lack the organizations to nurture this new discipline" and "funding agencies, compartmentalized into traditional disciplines, are ill-equipped to rise to the new challenges posed by ESS" (Lawton, 2001). Twenty years later, a range of research centers and universities have programs in Earth System Science. Yet, despite the urgency and popular attention on climate, universities are still struggling with the institutional structures for degree programs and research collaborations to embrace the reality that the workings of the planet do not neatly subdivide and compartmentalize into separate disciplines.

Early conceptions of ESS largely focused on biological, physical, and chemical aspects of exchanges of gases and energy between the ocean, atmosphere, and biosphere. Earth system scientists depicted the "human" component as part of the system purely as a forcing factor on other components of the system through emissions of carbon dioxide and other pollutants and land use (National Research Council, 1986). Today, Earth system scientists recognize that the human component of the system is dynamic, both driving and reacting to changes in the Earth system. As the largest uncertainty in predicting climate is the future trajectory of emissions, rather than the biogeophysical response of the climate system, incorporating the human component is the most critical need for improving projections of climate change, understanding which segments of society will be affected, and preparing for and adapting to change. Economics, values, governance, social organization, and justice—topics in the realm of social sciences and humanities—are all extremely relevant to universities' contributions to addressing the climate problem. Institutional structures in universities are even less amenable to incorporating social sciences and humanities within the overall endeavor to understand our changing planet than they are for the natural sciences.

In tandem with the development of Earth System Science in the 20th century, sustainability science emerged as an academic pursuit. Sustainability science aims to develop an understanding of nature-society interactions and to contribute to the practice of sustainable development, an ambition agreed upon by 193 countries in 2015 and codified in 17 sustainable development goals (Costanza, Fioramonti, & Kubiszewski, 2016). Driven by two seemingly contradictory global trends of rapidly increasing environmental degradation and substantial improvements in material well-being of many people around the world (as measured by life expectancy, infant mortality, literacy, and other dimensions), sustainability science examines the interactions between nature and society as a globally interconnected, complex adaptive system. This understanding guides pathways for societies to address inequities, improve human well-being, and adapt to surprises and shocks while reducing emissions and other environmentally damaging trends. Governance arrangements, innovation, processes to engage local stakeholders to link knowledge with action, identification of leverage points, and assessments of vulnerability are some of the focal points for sustainability science to support interventions by governments, communities, and civil society to foster sustainable development (Clark & Harley, 2020). For example, topics relevant to sustainability science include the identification of unintended social and environmental consequences from interventions (e.g. effect of biofuels on food prices) and analyses of emissions trading or carbon taxation schemes across dimensions of efficacy and equity (Pauliuk, 2020).

Sustainability science is inherently interdisciplinary, ranging across natural sciences, economics, political science, and anthropology among other disciplines. Individualistic modes of research, hyper-specialization, lack of rewards in academia to contribute to applied solutions, and insufficient funding particularly in low-income countries hamper the ability of sustainability science to help address climate and other environmental and social problems (Messerli et al., 2019). The traditional disciplinary structure in universities for hiring faculty and designing innovative curricula inhibits programs that train students to address problems from a holistic, solutions-oriented perspective.

Earth System Science and sustainability science generally exist in universities as niche activities in which groups of scholars attempt to circumvent the barriers to collaborations across traditional disciplinary boundaries. These activities, in addition to the realization by ordinary citizens that climate change is affecting their everyday lives, are leading university leadership to recognize that academic institutions have a role in addressing the problem.

5.2.3 New Technologies to Address the Climate Problem

Universities have always been pioneers in technological advancement, and certainly, they will continue to deliver new discoveries and innovations to solve the climate problem. In the area of computing and AI, technologies are already being used to generate, process, and analyze data gathered from space and the planet in ways that could not have been imagined a generation ago. According to one recent study, using AI technologies today could reduce greenhouse gas emissions by 4%, boost global GDP by up to US$ 5 trillion, and create 38 million jobs by 2030 (Price Waterhouse Cooper & Microsoft Corp, 2019).

Over time, constellations of technologies can be combined to address problems across disciplines. For example, researchers can use AI and machine learning to integrate satellite imagery with household survey data for more granular poverty information and new policy solutions (Steele et al., 2017). In agriculture, food systems can be strengthened as farmers use AI to improve crop health, identify harmful weather patterns and plant diseases, and understand what will sell in markets at what price. In short, universities can help not only discover new technologies but also design commercial systems and public policies using such AI-driven innovations to help solve the climate problem.

5.2.4 Professional Fields to Address the Climate Problem

The buildup of greenhouse gases in the atmosphere has made climate change a societal problem rather than purely a scientific investigation. The implications reach far and wide into many sectors, including insurance, architecture, emergency response, international diplomacy, and local government, among many others. A new workforce is needed to fill these needs in addition to scientists and engineers, one that will understand how to use the current and future technologies and be comfortable working across several cognitive domains.

The many areas that will require a workforce with training in climate include:

- *Data analytics and artificial intelligence*: As mentioned above, the ability to process large amounts of data and apply machine learning techniques creates many opportunities for addressing climate change. Helping households minimize energy use, utilities optimize energy deployment, authorities send disaster alerts, and corporations track deforestation in their supply chains are a few such applications. A skilled workforce with quantitative and technical skills in data science is needed to develop these applications.
- *Disaster preparation and response*: The most obvious and detrimental impact of climate change on communities is the increase in severity of storms, droughts, and other extreme events. Expertise is needed to help communities improve resilience to these events, ranging from early warning systems using AI to recovery plans.
- *Land use planning and architecture*: On one hand, land use is a contributor to climate change through greenhouse gas emissions from transport, agriculture, and forest management. "Smart agriculture", energy-saving buildings, and land use planning for public transport can contribute to the goal of net-zero. On the other hand, land use planning and architecture can help people adapt to climate change through, for example, promotion of drought-resistant crops and building materials and design appropriate for future climate. Green infrastructure, such as wetlands and reefs to buttress protection against storm surges, urban green spaces to provide cooling, and stormwater runoff to improve drainage to reduce flooding, require expertise to assess their effectiveness and appropriate use in different situations.
- *Climate finance*: Mitigation and adaptation to climate change require large amounts of financing for large-scale investments. A range of mechanisms, such as voluntary and compliant carbon markets, are rapidly developing tools to mobilize financing. People who can apply financial mechanisms and have skills in carbon accounting will be needed for the rapidly expanding number of start-ups that are developing in response to demand for carbon credits.
- *Health*: One of the most detrimental impacts of climate change is on human health. Heat waves and extreme climate events have killed thousands of people in the last few decades (Beniston, 2004). Food security and spread of infectious diseases are sensitive to climate, as are supply chains to deliver health services and medication. Those working in the health sector need to incorporate climate risks in the planning for many different aspects ranging from healthcare delivery to individual behavior to minimize risk.
- *Public administration*: The climate problem may be one of the greatest market failures of all time and new public policies will be needed to address the myriad challenges that humanity faces. Governments at the supranational, national, and local levels will need to identify economic or environmental

externalities that markets fail to capture and develop effective regulatory or market mechanisms to address them. Governments also may be required to catalyze solutions by providing early-stage risk capital to support breakthrough innovations and encourage lifestyle changes to help solve the climate problem.

Currently, these capabilities do not exist in government bodies, corporations, and other institutions analogous to public health professionals and social workers. As the climate problem worsens, it is likely that national, state, and local governments will have expertise to carry out functions such as assessing risk from climate predictions, preparing communities to adapt to climate extremes, and incorporating climate projects into land use and infrastructure plans and regulations. Climate-affected corporations, some of which already have sustainability offices, will also likely expand their demand for people with climate expertise.

Regardless of the specialization, several competencies are critical for climate professionals to effectively address the complex problem. These competencies include:

- *Systems and multidisciplinary approach*: Climate and social systems interact with complex, nonlinear feedbacks. As many examples illustrate, such as the impact on food prices of biofuels (Naylor et al., 2007), seemingly useful policies or interventions can have unintended consequences that are difficult to predict. Professionals working on different aspects of climate need a comprehensive view of the complex system to anticipate unintended consequences of their decisions and to identify leverage points.
- *Collaboration*: No single individual can be conversant with the range of knowledge required to address the complex climate problem. People with different expertise need to collaborate to develop solutions. Educational programs in climate need to be structured to promote collaborations and provide experience with working in collaborative teams.
- *Depth of knowledge*: Complementing the need for education programs to enable students to work in collaborative teams, programs also need to provide depth of knowledge in specific areas so students can contribute to collaborations. The adage to "bring a brick not a cathedral" applies. Solutions to the climate problem, whether policies to reduce emissions or approaches to help communities build resilience to climate change, require multiple "bricks" from professionals trained with deep expertise in particular topics.
- *Justice and equity sensitivity*: The climate problem raises many issues of justice and equity at many scales. Within communities, vulnerable, marginalized populations are often located in more hazardous climate conditions with less access to resources. In international climate negotiations, industrialized countries historically contributed the bulk of greenhouse gases to the

atmosphere and are rightfully responsible for providing resources for less developed countries to adapt to climate change (Shukla, 2019). Across generations, questions of equity arise about the responsibilities of the current generation to future, unborn generations. An educational program needs to embed these questions of equity and justice across the entire curriculum to enable students to appreciate the many aspects of justice and equity.

5.2.5 Redesigning Higher Education for the Climate Problem

Universities' ability to conduct research and train workforces to help society avert and manage climate change requires nontraditional institutional arrangements. Universities recognized that complex problems such as social work and public health do not fit within the bounds of traditional disciplines. Similarly, education and research programs for climate require a structure for a holistic, systems perspective. Currently, major universities, such as Columbia and Stanford, have established schools to address climate as a societal problem.

More schools focused on addressing the climate problem need to be structured to meet the purpose. Hiring and evaluation criteria that are aligned with the needs of society are a critical element of schools focused on climate, just as engineering, social work, and public health schools were aligned with the needs of society at their respective times. Climate schools need to be multidisciplinary; social sciences, including economics, behavioral and political science, and business administration need to be equal partners to the natural sciences. Teaching needs to be grounded in real-world experiences with practical training. A diversity of researchers, instructors, and students across nationalities, races, socio-economic backgrounds, and other dimensions is critical to developing a workforce to address the range of needs across societies.

5.3 Conclusion

Universities have always played an important role as research and learning institutions to provide new knowledge, change paradigms, and meet society's new challenges as they evolve. The far-ranging global problem of climate change, like many challenges and opportunities of the past, requires that universities establish institutional structures to train a workforce and carry out research. At this time, government entities and corporations do not generally have established units to adequately address climate change.

Climate expertise is needed in a large range of applications across scales, from international policy at a global scale to finance, health, and disaster response at national and local scales. Universities need to not only develop technological tools to deal with climate change but also train people to work in a wide range of fields. Training needs to convey a systems view of climate with cascading, sometimes unpredictable impacts across different segments of society.

The analogies with engineering, public health, and social work—fields established from complex, societal problems of their days—suggests that over time a "climate worker" might be a recognized expert in governments, civil society, and corporations to foster abilities of communities, individuals, and organizations to minimize harm from climate change. Universities are in the early stages of developing structures to identify society's needs and train a workforce for the climate problem, and there is little time to waste in the race to combat one of the most pressing issues of the 21st century.

References

Arrhenius, S. (1896). XXXI. On the influence of carbonic acid in the air on the temperature on the ground. *London, Edinburgh, and Dublin Philosophical Magazine and the Journal of Science, 41*(251), 237–276.

Bell, A. (2021). *Our biggest experiment: An epic history of the climate crisis.* Berkeley, CA: Counterpoint Press.

Beniston, M. (2004). The 2003 heat wave in Europe: A shape of things to come? An analysis based on Swiss climatological data and model simulations. *Geophysical Research Letters, 31*(2).

Byers, E., Gidden, M., Leclère, D., Balkovic, J., Burek, P., Ebi, K., …Hillers, A. (2018). Global exposure and vulnerability to multi-sector development and climate change hotspots. *Environmental Research Letters, 13*(5), 055012.

Calhoun, J. G., Ramiah, K., Weist, E. M., & Shortell, S. M. (2008). Development of a core competency model for the master of public health degree. *American Journal of Public Health, 98*(9), 1598–1607.

Clark, W. C., & Harley, A. G. (2020). Sustainability science: Toward a synthesis. *Annual Review of Environment and Resources, 45,* 331–386.

Costanza, R., Fioramonti, L., & Kubiszewski, I. (2016). The UN sustainable development goals and the dynamics of well-being. *Frontiers in Ecology and the Environment, 14*(2), 59–59.

Foster, G. L., Royer, D. L., & Lunt, D. J. (2017). Future climate forcing potentially without precedent in the last 420 million years. *Nature Communications, 8*(1), 1–8.

Lawton, J. (2001). Earth system science. *Science, 292*(5524), 1965–1965.

Messerli, P., Kim, E. M., Lutz, W., Moatti, J.-P., Richardson, K., Saidam, M., …Glassman, A. (2019). Expansion of sustainability science needed for the SDGs. *Nature Sustainability, 2*(10), 892–894.

National Research Council. (1986). *Earth system science. Overview: A program for global change.* Retrieved from Washington, DC.

Naylor, R. L., Liska, A. J., Burke, M. B., Falcon, W. P., Gaskell, J. C., Rozelle, S. D., & Cassman, K. G. (2007). The ripple effect: biofuels, food security, and the environment. *Environment: Science and Policy for Sustainable Development, 49*(9), 30–43.

Pauliuk, S. (2020). Making sustainability science a cumulative effort. *Nature Sustainability, 3*(1), 2–4.

Price Waterhouse Cooper, & Microsoft Corp. (2019). *How AI can enable a sustainable future.* Retrieved from UK: https://www.pwc.com/gx/en/news-room/press-releases/2019/ai-realise-gains-environment.html

Roy, J. (2019). *Engineering by the numbers*. Retrieved from https://ira.asee.org/wp-content/uploads/2019/07/2018-Engineering-by-Numbers-Engineering-Statistics-UPDATED-15-July-2019.pdf

Shukla, P. R. (2019). Justice, equity and efficiency in climate change: a developing country perspective. In *Fair weather?* (pp. 145–159). Oxford, UK: Routledge.

Steele, J. E., Sundsøy, P. R., Pezzulo, C., Alegana, V. A., Bird, T. J., Blumenstock, J., …Iqbal, A. M. (2017). Mapping poverty using mobile phone and satellite data. *Journal of The Royal Society Interface, 14*(127), 20160690.

Steffen, W., Richardson, K., Rockström, J., Schellnhuber, H. J., Dube, O. P., Dutreuil, S., …Lubchenco, J. (2020). The emergence and evolution of Earth System Science. *Nature Reviews Earth & Environment, 1*(1), 54–63.

Tulchinsky, T. H., Varavikova, E. A., & Last, J. (2014). *A history of public health. The new public health*. London, UK: Academic Press, Elsevier.

6

THE TURING TRAP

The Promise & Peril of Human-Like Artificial Intelligence

Erik Brynjolfsson

Alan Turing was far from the first to imagine human-like machines.[1] According to legend, 3,500 years ago, Dædalus constructed humanoid statues that were so lifelike that they moved and spoke by themselves (Price, 2019). Nearly every culture has its own stories of human-like machines, from Yanshi's leather man described in the ancient Chinese *Liezi* text to the bronze Talus of the Argonautica and the towering clay *Mokkerkalfe* of Norse mythology. The word robot first appeared in Karel Čapek's influential play *Rossum's Universal Robots* and derives from the Czech word *robota*, meaning servitude or work. In fact, in the first drafts of his play, Čapek named them *labori* until his brother Josef suggested substituting the word robot ("The Origin", 2011).

Of course, it is one thing to tell tales about humanoid machines. It is something else to create robots that do real work. For all our ancestors' inspiring stories, we are the first generation to build and deploy real robots in large numbers.[2] Dozens of companies are working on robots as human-like, if not more so, than those described in the ancient texts. One might say that technology has advanced sufficiently to become indistinguishable from mythology.[3]

The breakthroughs in robotics depend not merely on more dexterous mechanical hands and legs, and more perceptive synthetic eyes and ears, but also on increasingly human-like artificial intelligence (HLAI). Powerful AI systems are crossing key thresholds: Matching humans in a growing number of fundamental tasks such as image recognition and speech recognition, with applications from autonomous vehicles and medical diagnosis to inventory management and product recommendations.[4]

These breakthroughs are both fascinating and exhilarating. They also have profound economic implications. Just as earlier general-purpose technologies

DOI: 10.4324/9781003230762-8

like the steam engine and electricity catalyzed a restructuring of the economy, our own economy is increasingly transformed by AI. A good case can be made that AI is the most general of all general-purpose technologies. After all, if we can solve the puzzle of intelligence, it would help solve many of the other problems in the world. And we are making remarkable progress. In the coming decade, machine intelligence will become increasingly powerful and pervasive. We can expect record wealth creation as a result.

Replicating human capabilities is valuable not only because of its practical potential for reducing the need for human labor but also because it can help us build more robust and flexible forms of intelligence. Whereas domain-specific technologies can often make rapid progress on narrow tasks, they founder when unexpected problems or unusual circumstances arise. That is where human-like intelligence excels. In addition, HLAI could help us understand more about ourselves. We appreciate and comprehend the human mind better when we work to create an artificial one.

These are all important opportunities, but in this essay, I will focus on the ways that HLAI could lead to a realignment of economic and political power.

The distributive effects of AI depend on whether it is primarily used to augment human labor or automate it. When AI augments human capabilities, enabling people to do things they never could before, then humans and machines are complements. Complementarity implies that people remain indispensable for value creation and retain bargaining power in labor markets and in political decision-making. In contrast, when AI replicates and automates existing human capabilities, machines become better substitutes for human labor and workers lose economic and political bargaining power. Entrepreneurs and executives who have access to machines with capabilities that replicate those of humans for a given task can and often will replace humans in those tasks.

Automation increases productivity. Moreover, many tasks are dangerous, dull, or dirty, and those are often the first to be automated. As more tasks are automated, a fully automated economy could, in principle, be structured to redistribute the benefits from production widely, even to those people who are no longer strictly necessary for value creation. However, the beneficiaries would be in a weak bargaining position to prevent a change in the distribution that left them with little or nothing. Their incomes would depend on the decisions of those in control of the technology. This opens the door to increased concentration of wealth and power.

This highlights the promise and the peril of achieving HLAI: Building machines designed to pass the Turing Test and other, more sophisticated metrics of human-like intelligence.[5] On the one hand, it is a path to unprecedented wealth, increased leisure, robust intelligence, and even a better understanding of ourselves. On the other hand, if HLAI leads machines to automate rather than augment human labor, it creates the risk of concentrating wealth and power. And with that concentration comes the peril of being trapped in an equilibrium in which those without power have no way to improve their outcomes, a situation I call the *Turing Trap*.

The grand challenge of the coming era will be to reap the unprecedented benefits of AI, including its human-like manifestations while avoiding the Turing Trap. Succeeding in this task requires an understanding of how technological progress affects productivity and inequality, why the Turing Trap is so tempting to different groups, and a vision of how we can do better.

———

Artificial intelligence pioneer Nils Nilsson noted that "achieving real human-level AI would necessarily imply that most of the tasks that humans perform for pay could be automated" (Nilsson, 2005). In the same article, he called for a focused effort to create such machines, writing that "achieving human-level AI or 'strong AI' remains the ultimate goal for some researchers" and he contrasted this with "weak AI", which seeks to "build machines that help humans". [6] Not surprisingly, given these monikers, work toward "strong AI" attracted many of the best and brightest minds to the quest of—implicitly or explicitly—fully automating human labor, rather than assisting or augmenting it.

For the purposes of this essay, rather than strong versus weak AI, let us use the terms *automation* versus *augmentation*. In addition, I will use HLAI to mean human-*like* artificial intelligence, not human-*level* AI, because the latter mistakenly implies that intelligence falls on a single dimension, and perhaps even that humans are at the apex of that metric. In reality, intelligence is multidimensional: A 1970s' pocket calculator surpasses the most intelligent human in some ways (such as for multiplication), as does a chimpanzee (short-term memory). At the same time, machines and animals are inferior to human intelligence on myriad other dimensions. The term "artificial general intelligence" (AGI) is often used as a synonym for HLAI. However, taken literally, it is the union of all types of intelligences, able to solve types of problems that are solvable by any existing human, animal, or machine. That suggests that AGI is not human-like.

The good news is that both automation and augmentation can boost labor productivity; that is, the ratio of value-added output to labor-hours worked. As productivity increases, so do average incomes and living standards, as do our capabilities for addressing challenges from climate change and poverty to health care and longevity. Mathematically, if the human labor used for a given output declines toward zero, then labor productivity would grow to infinity. [7]

The bad news is that no economic law ensures everyone will share this growing pie. Although pioneering models of economic growth assumed that technological change was neutral, [8] in practice, technological change can disproportionately help or hurt some groups, even if it is beneficial on average. [9]

In particular, the way the benefits of technology are distributed depends to a great extent on how the technology is deployed and the economic rules and norms that govern the equilibrium allocation of goods, services, and incomes. When technologies automate human labor, they tend to reduce the marginal value of workers' contributions, and more of the gains go to the owners, entrepreneurs, inventors, and architects of the new systems. In contrast, when technologies augment human capabilities, more of the gains go to human workers. [10]

A common fallacy is to assume that all or most productivity-enhancing innovations belong in the first category: automation. However, the second category, augmentation, has been far more important throughout most of the past two centuries. One metric of this is the economic value of an hour of human labor. Its market price as measured by median wages has grown more than tenfold since 1820. [11] An entrepreneur is willing to pay much more for a worker whose capabilities are amplified by a bulldozer than one who can only work with a shovel, let alone with bare hands.

In many cases, not only wages but also employment grow with the introduction of new technologies. With the invention of the airplane, a new job category was born: pilots. With the invention of jet engines, pilot productivity (in passenger-miles per pilot-hour) grew immensely. Rather than reducing the number of employed pilots, the technology spurred demand for air travel so much that the number of pilots grew. Although this pattern is comforting, past performance does not guarantee future results. Modern technologies—and, more important, the ones under development—are different from those that were important in the past. [12]

In recent years, we have seen growing evidence that not only is the labor share of the economy declining, but even among workers, some groups are beginning to fall even further behind (Karabarbounis and Neiman, 2014; Autor, 2019). [13] Over the past 40 years, the numbers of millionaires and billionaires grew while the average real wages for Americans with only a high school education fell (Acemoglu and Autor, 2011). Alhough many phenomena contributed to this, including new patterns of global trade, changes in technology deployment are the single biggest explanation.

If capital in the form of AI can perform more tasks, those with unique assets, talents, or skills that are *not* easily replaced with technology stand to benefit disproportionately. [14] The result has been greater wealth concentration (Tambe et al., 2021).

Ultimately, a focus on more human-like AI can make technology a better substitute for the many non-superstar workers, driving down their market wages, even as it amplifies the market power of a few. [15] This has created a growing fear that AI and related advances will lead to a burgeoning class of unemployable or "zero marginal product" people. [16]

As noted above, both automation and augmentation can increase productivity and wealth. However, an unfettered market is likely to create socially excessive incentives for innovations that automate human labor and provide too weak incentives for technology that augments humans. The first fundamental welfare theorem of economics states that under a particular set of conditions, market prices lead to a *pareto optimal* outcome, that is, one where no one can be made better off without making someone else worse off. But we should not take too much comfort in that. The theorem does not hold when there are innovations that change the production possibilities set or externalities that affect people who are not part of the market (Korinek and Stiglitz, 2019).

Both innovations and externalities are of central importance to the economic effects of AI since AI is not only an innovation itself but also one that triggers cascades of complementary innovations, from new products to new production systems (Brynjolfsson and McAfee, 2017). Furthermore, the effects of AI, particularly on work, are rife with externalities. When a worker loses opportunities to earn labor income, the costs go beyond the newly unemployed to affect many others in their community and in the broader society. With fading opportunities often come the dark horses of alcoholism, crime, and opioid abuse. Recently, the United States has experienced the first decline in life expectancies in its recorded history, a result of increasing deaths from suicide, drug overdose, and alcoholism, which economists Anne Case and Angus Deaton call "deaths of despair". [17]

This spiral of marginalization can grow because concentration of economic power often begets concentration of political power. In the words attributed to Louis Brandeis: "We may have democracy, or we may have wealth concentrated in the hands of a few, but we can't have both". In contrast, when humans are indispensable to value creation, economic power will tend to be more decentralized. Historically, most economically valuable knowledge—what economist Simon Kuznets called "useful knowledge"—resided within human brains (Kuznets, 1965). But no human brain can contain even a small fraction of the useful knowledge needed to run even a medium-sized business, let alone a whole industry or economy, so knowledge had to be distributed and decentralized (Hayek, 1945). The decentralization of useful knowledge, in turn, decentralizes economic and political power.

Unlike nonhuman assets such as property and machinery, much of a person's knowledge is inalienable, both in the practical sense that no one person can know everything that another person knows and in the legal sense that its ownership cannot be legally transferred (Brynjolfsson, 1994). In contrast, when knowledge becomes codified and digitized, it can be owned, transferred, and concentrated very easily. Thus, when knowledge shifts from humans to machines, it opens the possibility of concentration of power. When historians look back on the first two decades of the 21st century, they will note the striking growth in the digitization and codification of information and knowledge. [18] In parallel, machine learning models are becoming larger, with hundreds of billions of parameters, using more data and getting more accurate results (Ng, 2015).

More formally, incomplete contracts theory shows how ownership of key assets provides bargaining power in relationships between economic agents (such as employers and employees, or business owners and subcontractors) (Grossman and Hart, 1986; Hart and Moore, 1990). To the extent that a person controls an indispensable asset (like useful knowledge) needed to create and deliver a company's products and services, that person can command not only higher income but also a voice in decision-making. When useful knowledge is inalienably locked in human brains, so too is the power it confers. But when it is made alienable, it enables (though does not demand) greater concentration of decision-making and power (Brynjolfsson and Ng, 2021).

The risks of the Turing Trap are amplified because three groups of people—technologists, businesspeople, and policy-makers—each find automation alluring. Technologists have sought to replicate human intelligence for decades to address the recurring challenge of what computers could not do. The invention of computers and the birth of the term "electronic brain" were the latest fuel for the ongoing battle between technologists and humanist philosophers ("Simon Electric", 2021). The philosophers posited a long list of ordinary and lofty human capacities that computers would never be able to do. No machine could play checkers, master chess, read printed words, recognize speech, translate between human languages, distinguish images, climb stairs, win at Jeopardy or Go, write poems, and so forth.

For professors, it is tempting to assign such projects to their graduate students. Devising challenges that are new, useful, and achievable can be as difficult as solving them. Rather than specify a task that neither humans nor machines have ever done before, why not ask the research team to design a machine that replicates an existing human capability? Unlike more ambitious goals, replication has an existence proof that such tasks are, in principle, feasible and useful.

While the appeal of human-like systems is clear, the paradoxical reality is that HLAI can be more difficult and less valuable than systems that achieve superhuman performance.

In 1988, robotics researcher Hans Moravec noted that "it is comparatively easy to make computers exhibit adult level performance on intelligence tests or playing checkers, and difficult or impossible to give them the skills of a one-year-old when it comes to perception and mobility" (Moravec, 1988). But I would argue that in many domains, Moravec was not nearly ambitious enough. It is often comparatively easier for a machine to achieve *superhuman* performance in new domains than to match ordinary humans in the tasks they do regularly.

Humans have evolved over millions of years to be able to comfort a baby, navigate a cluttered forest, or pluck the ripest blueberry from a bush. These tasks are difficult if not impossible for current machines. But machines excel when it comes to seeing X-rays, etching millions of transistors on a fragment of silicon, or scanning billions of webpages to find the most relevant one. Imagine how feeble and limited our technology would be if past engineers set their sights on merely matching human-levels of perception, actuation, and cognition.

Augmenting humans with technology opens an endless frontier of new abilities and opportunities. The set of tasks that humans and machines can do

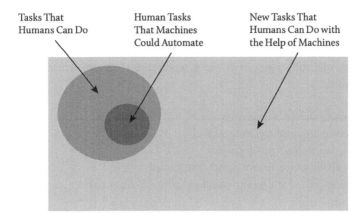

FIGURE 6.1 Opportunities for augmenting humans are far greater than opportunities to automate existing tasks.

together is undoubtedly much larger than those humans can do alone (Figure 6.1). Machines can perceive things that are imperceptible to humans, they can act on objects in ways that no human can, and, most intriguingly, they can comprehend things that are incomprehensible to the human brain. As Demis Hassabis, CEO of DeepMind, put it, the AI system "doesn't play like a human, and it doesn't play like a program. It plays in a third, almost alien, way ... it's like chess from another dimension" (Knight, 2017). Computer scientist Jonathan Schaeffer explains the source of its superiority: "I'm absolutely convinced it's because it hasn't learned from humans" (Waters, 2018). More fundamentally, inventing tools that augment the process of invention itself promises to expand not only our collective abilities but to accelerate the rate of expansion of those abilities.

What about business people? They often find that substituting machinery for human labor is the low-hanging fruit of innovation. The simplest approach is to implement plug-and-play automation: Swap in a piece of machinery for each task a human is currently doing. That mindset reduces the need for more radical changes to business processes (Beane and Brynjolfsson, 2020). Task-level automation reduces the need to understand subtle interdependencies and creates easy A-B tests, by focusing on a known task with easily measurable performance improvement.

Similarly, because labor costs are the biggest line item in almost every company's budget, automating jobs is a popular strategy for managers. Cutting costs, which can be an internally coordinated effort, is often easier than expanding markets. Moreover, many investors prefer "scalable" business models, which is often a synonym for a business that can grow without hiring and the complexities that entails.

But here again, when businesspeople focus on automation, they often set out to achieve a task that is both less ambitious and more difficult than it needs to be.

To understand the limits of substitution-oriented automation, consider a thought experiment. Imagine that our old friend Dædalus had at his disposal an extremely talented team of engineers 3,500 years ago and built human-like machines that fully automated every work-related task that his fellow Greeks were doing.

- Herding sheep? Automated
- Making clay pottery? Automated
- Weaving tunics? Automated
- Repairing horse-drawn carts? Automated
- Incense and chanting for victims of disease? Automated

The good news is that labor productivity would soar, freeing the ancient Greeks for a life of leisure. The bad news is that their living standards and health outcomes would come nowhere near matching ours. After all, there is only so much value one can get from clay pots and horse-drawn carts, even with unlimited quantities and zero prices.

In contrast, most of the value that our economy has created since ancient times comes from new goods and services that not even the kings of ancient empires had, not from cheaper versions of existing goods (Bresnahan and Gordon, 1996). In turn, myriad new tasks are required: Fully 60 percent of people are now employed in occupations that did not exist in 1940 (Autor et al., 2021). In short, automating labor ultimately unlocks less value than augmenting it to create something new.

At the same time, automating a whole job is often brutally difficult. Every job involves multiple different tasks, including some that are extremely challenging to automate, even with the cleverest technologies. For example, AI may be able to read mammograms better than a human radiologist, but it is not very good at the other twenty-six tasks associated with the job, according to O-NET, such as comforting a concerned patient or coordinating on a care plan with other doctors (Killock, 2020). My work with Tom Mitchell and Daniel Rock on the suitability for machine learning analyzed 950 distinct occupations. We found that machines could perform at least some tasks in most occupations, but zero in which machine learning could do 100 percent of the tasks (Brynjolfsson et al., 2018).

The same principle applies to the more complex production systems that involve multiple people working together (Brynjolfsson et al., 2019). To be successful, firms typically need to adopt a new technology as part of a system of mutually reinforcing organizational changes (Milgrom and Roberts, 1990). Consider another thought experiment: Imagine if Jeff Bezos had "automated" existing bookstores by simply replacing all the human cashiers with robot cashiers. That might have cut costs a bit, but the total impact would have been muted. Instead, Amazon reinvented the concept of a bookstore by combining humans and machines in a novel way. As a result, they offer vastly greater product selection, ratings, reviews, and advice, and enable 24/7 retail access from the comfort of customers' homes. The power of the technology was not in automating the work of humans in the existing retail bookstore concept but in reinventing and augmenting how customers find, assess, purchase, and receive books and, in turn, other retail goods.

Third, policy-makers have also often tilted the playing field toward automating human labor rather than augmenting it. For instance, the US Tax Code currently encourages capital investment over investment in labor through effective tax rates that are much higher on labor than on plants and equipment. [19]

Consider a third thought experiment: Two potential ventures each use AI to create $1 billion in profits. If one of them achieves this by augmenting and employing a thousand workers, the firm will owe corporate and payroll taxes, while the employees will pay income taxes, payroll taxes, and other taxes. If the second business has no employees, the government may collect the same corporate taxes, but no payroll taxes and no taxes paid by workers. As a result, the second business model pays far less in total taxes.

This disparity is amplified because the tax code treats labor income more harshly than capital income. In 1986, top tax rates on capital income and labor income were equalized in the United States, but since then, successive changes have created a large disparity, with the 2021 top marginal federal tax rates on labor income of 37 percent, while long capital gains have a variety of favorable rules, including a lower statutory tax rate of 20 percent, the deferral of taxes until capital gains are realized, and the "step-up basis" rule that resets capital gains to zero, wiping out the associated taxes, when assets are inherited.

The first rule of tax policy is simple: You tend to get less of whatever you tax. Thus, a tax code that treats income that uses labor less favorably than income derived from capital will favor automation over augmentation. Treating both business models equally would lead to more balanced incentives. In fact, given the positive externalities of more widely shared prosperity, a case could be made for treating wage income *more* favorably than capital income, for instance by expanding the earned income tax credit. [20] It is unlikely that any government official can define in advance exactly which technologies and innovations augment humans rather than merely substitute for them; indeed, most technologies have elements of each and the outcome depends a great deal on how they are deployed. Thus, rather than prescribe or proscribe specific technologies, a broad-based set of incentives can gently nudge technologists and managers toward augmentation on the margin, much as carbon taxes encourage myriad types of cleaner energy or research and development tax credits to encourage greater investments in research.

Government policy in other areas could also do more to steer the economy clear of the Turing Trap. The growing use of AI, even if only for complementing workers, and the further reinvention of organizations around this new general-purpose technology imply a great need for worker training or retraining. In fact, for each dollar spent on machine learning technology, companies may need to spend nine dollars on intangible human capital (Tambe et al., 2021). However, education and training suffer from a serious externality issue: Companies that incur the costs to train or retrain workers may reap only a fraction of the benefits of those investments, with the rest potentially going to other companies, including competitors, as these workers are free to bring their skills to their new employers. At the same time, workers are often cash- and credit-constrained, limiting their ability to invest in their own skills development (Newman, 2006). This implies that government policy should directly provide education and training or provide incentives for corporate training that offset the externalities created by labor mobility. [21]

In sum, the risks of the Turing Trap are increased not by just one group in our society, but by the misaligned incentives of technologists, businesspeople, and policy-makers.

The future is not preordained. We control the extent to which AI either expands human opportunity through augmentation or replaces humans through automation. We can work on challenges that are easy for machines and hard for humans, rather than hard for machines and easy for humans. The first option offers the opportunity of growing and sharing the economic pie by augmenting the workforce with tools and platforms. The second option risks dividing the economic pie among an ever-smaller number of people by creating automation that displaces ever-more types of workers.

While both approaches can and do contribute to productivity and progress, technologists, businesspeople, and policy-makers have each been putting a finger on the scales in favor of replacement. Moreover, the tendency of a greater concentration of technological and economic power to beget a greater concentration of political power risks trapping a powerless majority into an unhappy equilibrium: The Turing Trap.

The backlash against free trade offers a cautionary tale. Economists have long argued that free trade and globalization tend to grow the economic pie through the power of comparative advantage and specialization. They have also acknowledged that market forces alone do not ensure that every person in every country will come out ahead. So they proposed a grand bargain: Maximize free trade to maximize wealth creation and then distribute the benefits broadly to compensate any injured occupations, industries, and regions. It has not worked as they had hoped. As the economic winners gained power, they reneged on the second part of the bargain, leaving many workers worse off than before. [22] The result helped fuel a populist backlash that led to import tariffs and other barriers to free trade. Economists wept.

Some of the same dynamics are already underway with AI. More and more Americans, and indeed workers around the world, believe that while the technology may be creating a new billionaire class, it is not working for them. The more technology is used to replace rather than augment labor, the worse the disparity may become, and the greater the resentments that feed destructive political instincts and actions. More fundamentally, the moral imperative of treating people as ends, and not merely as means, calls for everyone to share in the gains of automation.

The solution is not to slow down technology, but rather to eliminate or reverse the excess incentives for automation over augmentation. A good start would be to replace the Turing Test, and the mindset it embodies, with a new set of practical benchmarks that steer progress toward AI-powered systems that exceed anything that could be done by humans alone. In concert, we must build political and economic institutions that are robust in the face of the growing power of AI. We can reverse the growing tech backlash by creating the kind of prosperous society that inspires discovery, boosts living standards, and offers political inclusion for everyone. By redirecting our efforts, we can avoid the Turing Trap and create prosperity for the many, not just a few.

Author's Note

The core ideas in this essay were inspired by a series of conversations with James Manyika and Andrew McAfee. I am grateful for valuable comments and suggestions on this work from Matt Beane, Seth Benzell, Avi Goldfarb, Katya Klinova, Alena Kykalova, Gary Marcus, Andrea Meyer, Dana Meyer, and numerous participants at seminars at the Stanford Digital Economy Lab and the University of Toronto Creative Destruction Lab, but they should not be held responsible for any errors or opinions in the essay.

Notes

1 An earlier articulation of this test comes from Descartes in *The Discourse*, in which he wrote,
    If there were machines which bore a resemblance to our bodies and imitated our actions as closely as possible for all practical purposes, we should still have two very certain means of recognizing that they were not real men. The first is that they could never use words, or put together signs, as we do in order to declare our thoughts to others ... Second, even though some machines might do some things as well as we do them, or perhaps even better, they would inevitably fail in others, which would reveal that they are acting not from understanding.
2 Millions of people are now working alongside robots. For a recent survey on the diffusion of robots, AI, and other advanced technologies in the United States, see Nikolas Zolas, Zachary Kroff, Erik Brynjolfsson, et al., "Advanced Technologies Adoption and Use by United States Firms: Evidence from the Annual Business Survey", NBER Working Paper No. 28290 (Cambridge, Mass.: National Bureau of Economic Research, 2020).
3 Apologies to Arthur C. Clarke.

4 See, for example, Daniel Zhang, Saurabh Mishra, Erik Brynjolfsson, et al., "The AI Index 2021 Annual Report", arXiv (2021), esp. chap. 2, https://arxiv.org/abs/2103.06312. In regard to image recognition, see, for instance, the success of image recognition systems in Olga Russakovsky, Jia Deng, Hao Su, et al., "Imagenet Large Scale Visual Recognition Challenge", *International Journal of Computer Vision* 115 (3) (2015): 211–252. A broad array of business application is discussed in Erik Brynjolfsson and Andrew McAfee, "The Business of Artificial Intelligence", *Harvard Business Review* (2017): 3–11.

5 See, for example, Hubert Dreyfus, *What Computers Can't Do* (Cambridge, Mass.: MIT Press, 1972); Nils J. Nilsson, "Human-Level Artificial Intelligence? Be Serious!" *AI Magazine* 26 (4) (2005): 68; and Gary Marcus, Francesca Rossi, and Manuela Veloso, "Beyond the Turing Test", *AI Magazine* 37 (1) (2016): 3–4.

6 John Searle was the first to use the terms strong AI and weak AI, writing that with weak AI, "the principal value of the computer … is that it gives us a very powerful tool", while strong AI "really is a mind". Ed Feigenbaum has argued that creating such intelligence is the "manifest destiny" of computer science. John R. Searle, "Minds, Brains, and Programs", *Behavioral and Brain Sciences* 3 (3) (1980): 417–457.

7 However, this does not necessarily mean living standards would rise without bound. In fact, if working hours fall faster than productivity rises, it is theoretically possible, though empirically unlikely, that output and consumption (other than leisure time) would fall.

8 See, for example, Robert M. Solow, "A Contribution to the Theory of Economic Growth", *The Quarterly Journal of Economics* 70 (1) (1956): 65–94.

9 See, for example, Daron Acemoglu, "Directed Technical Change", *Review of Economic Studies* 69 (4) (2002): 781–809.

10 See, for instance, Erik Brynjolfsson and Andrew McAfee, *Race Against the Machine: How the Digital Revolution Is Accelerating Innovation, Driving Productivity, and Irreversibly Transforming Employment and the Economy* (Lexington, Mass.: Digital Frontier Press, 2011); and Daron Acemoglu and Pascual Restrepo, "The Race Between Machine and Man: Implications of Technology for Growth, Factor Shares, and Employment", *American Economic Review* 108 (6) (2018): 1488–1542.

11 For instance, the real wage of a building laborer in Great Britain is estimated to have grown from sixteen times the amount needed for subsistence in 1820 to 167 times that level by the year 2000, according to Jan Luiten Van Zanden, Joerg Baten, Marco Mira d'Ercole, et al., eds., *How Was Life? Global Well-Being since 1820* (Paris: OECD Publishing, 2014).

12 For instance, a majority of aircraft on United States Navy aircraft carriers are likely to be unmanned. See Oriana Pawlyk, "Future Navy Carriers Could Have More Drones Than Manned Aircraft, Admiral Says", Military.com, March 30, 2021. Similarly, companies like Kittyhawk have developed pilotless aircraft ("flying cars") for civilian passengers.

13 For a broader survey, see Morgan R. Frank, David Autor, James E. Bessen, et al., "Toward Understanding the Impact of Artificial Intelligence on Labor", *Proceedings of the National Academy of Sciences* 116 (14) (2019): 6531–6539.

14 Seth G. Benzell and Erik Brynjolfsson, "Digital Abundance and Scarce Architects: Implications for Wages, Interest Rates, and Growth", NBER Working Paper No. 25585 (Cambridge, Mass.: National Bureau of Economic Research, 2021).

15 There is some evidence that capital is already becoming an increasingly good substitute for labor. See, for instance, the discussion in Michael Knoblach and Fabian Stöckl, "What Determines the Elasticity of Substitution between Capital and Labor? A Literature Review", *Journal of Economic Surveys* 34 (4) (2020): 852.

16 See, for example, Tyler Cowen, *Average Is Over: Powering America beyond the Age of the Great Stagnation* (New York: Penguin, 2013). Or more provocatively, Yuval Noah Harari, "The Rise of the Useless Class", Ted Talk, February 24, 2017, https://ideas.ted.com/the-rise-of-the-useless-class/.
17 Robert D. Putnam, *Our Kids: The American Dream in Crisis* (New York: Simon and Schuster, 2016) describes the negative effects of joblessness, while Anne Case and Angus Deaton, *Deaths of Despair and the Future of Capitalism* (Princeton, N.J.: Princeton University Press, 2021) documents the sharp decline in life expectancy among many of the same people.
18 For instance, in the year 2000, an estimated 85 billion (mostly analog) photos were taken, but by 2020, that had grown nearly twenty-fold to 1.4 trillion (almost all digital) photos.
19 See Daron Acemoglu, Andrea Manera, and Pascual Restrepo, "Does the United States Tax Code Favor Automation?" *Brookings Papers on Economic Activity* (Spring 2020); and Daron Acemoglu, ed., *Redesigning AI* (Cambridge, Mass.: MIT Press, 2021).
20 This reverses the classic result suggesting that taxes on capital should be lower than taxes on labor. Christophe Chamley, "Optimal Taxation of Capital Income in General Equilibrium with Infinite Lives", *Econometrica* 54 (3) (1986): 607–622; and Kenneth L. Judd, "Redistributive Taxation in a Simple Perfect Foresight Model", *Journal of Public Economics* 28 (1) (1985): 59–83.
21 While the distinction between complements and substitutes is clear in economic theory, it can be trickier in practice. Part of the appeal of broad training and/or tax incentives, rather than specific technology mandates or prohibitions, is that they allow technologies, entrepreneurs, and, ultimately, the market to reward approaches that augment labor rather than replace it.
22 See David H. Autor, David Dorn, and Gordon H. Hanson, "The China Shock: Learning from Labor-Market Adjustment to Large Changes in Trade", *Annual Review of Economics* 8 (2016): 205–240.

References

Acemoglu, D. and Autor, D. (2011). Skills, Tasks and Technologies: Implications for Employment and Earnings. *Handbook of Labor Economics*. 4: 1043–1171.

Autor, D. (2019). Work of the Past, Work of the Future. *NBER Working Paper No. 25588*.

Autor, D., Salomons, A., and Seegmiller, B. (2021, July 26). New Frontiers: The Origins and Content of New Work, 1940–2018. NBER Preprint.

Beane, M. and Brynjolfsson, E. (2020). Working with Robots in a Post-Pandemic World. *MIT Sloan Management Review* 62(1): 1–5.

Bresnahan, T. and Gordon, R.J. (1996). Introduction. *The Economics of New Goods*. Chicago: University of Chicago Press.

Brynjolfsson, E. (1994). Information Assets, Technology and Organization. *Management Science* 40(12): 1645–1662. https://doi.org/10.1287/mnsc.40.12.1645

Brynjolfsson, E. and McAfee, A. (2017, August 7). Artificial Intelligence, for Real. *Harvard Business Review* 1: 1–31.

Brynjolfsson, E. and Ng, A. (2021). Big AI Can Centralize Decisionmaking and Power. And That's a Problem. *MILA-UNESCO Working Paper*. Montreal: MILA-UNESCO.

Brynjolfsson, E., Mitchell, T., and Rock, D. (2018). What Can Machines Learn, and What Does It Mean for Occupations and the Economy? *AEA Papers and Proceedings*, 43–47.

Brynjolfsson, E., Rock, D., and Tambe, P. (2019). How Will Machine Learning Transform the Labor Market? *Governance in an Emerging New World* (619). https://www.hoover.org/research/how-will-machine-learning-transform-labor-market

Grossman, S.J. and Hart, O.D. (1986). The Costs and Benefits of Ownership: A Theory of Vertical and Lateral Integration. *Journal of Political Economy* 94(4): 691–719.

Hart, O.D. and Moore, J. (1990). Property Rights and the Nature of the Firm. *Journal of Political Economy* 98 6): 1119–1158.

Hayek, F.A. (1945). The Use of Knowledge in Society. *The American Economic Review* 35(4): 519–530.

Karabarbounis, L. and Neiman, B. (2014). The Global Decline of the Labor Share. *The Quarterly Journal of Economics* 129 (1): 61–103.

Killock, D. (2020). AI Outperforms Radiologists in Mammographic Screening. *Nature Reviews Clinical Oncology* 17 (134). https://doi.org/10.1038/s41571-020-0329-7

Knight, W. (2017, December). Alpha Zero's 'Alien' Chess Shows the Power, and the Peculiarity, of AI. *Technology Review*.

Korinek, A. and Stiglitz, J.E. (2019). Artificial Intelligence and Its Implications for Income Distribution and Unemployment. *The Economics of Artificial Intelligence* 349–390. https://doi.org/10.3386/w24174

Kuznets, S.S. (1965). *Economic Growth and Structure: Selected Essays*. New York: W. W. Norton & Co.

Milgrom, P. and Roberts, J. (1990). The Economics of Modern Manufacturing: Technology, Strategy, and Organization. *American Economic Review* 80(3): 511–528.

Moravec, H. (1988). *Mind Children: The Future of Robot and Human Intelligence*. Cambridge, MA: Harvard University Press.

Newman, K.S. (2006). *Chutes and Ladders: Navigating the Low-Wage Labor Market*. Cambridge, MA: Harvard University Press.

Nilsson, N.J. (2005). Human-Level Artificial Intelligence? Be Serious!. *AI Magazine*, 26 (4): 68. https://doi.org/10.1609/aimag.v26i4.1850

Ng, A. (2015, November 24). "What Data Scientists Should Know about Deep Learning", speech presented at Extract Data Conference.

Price, C. (2019, June 19) Plato, Opinions and the Statues of Daedalus. *OpenLearn*.

Simon Electronic Brain–Complete History of the Simon Computer. (2021, January 4). *History Computer*. https://history-computer.com/simon-electronic-brain-complete-history-of-the-simon-computer/

Tambe, P., Hitt, L., Rock, D., and Brynjolfsson, E. (2021). Digital Capital and Superstar Firms. *Hutchins Center Working Paper #73*. Washington, DC: Hutchins Center at Brookings. https://www.brookings.edu/research/digital-capital-and-superstar-firms

Waters, R. (2018, January 12). Techmate: How AI Rewrote the Rules of Chess. *Financial Times*.

PART II

Augmented Learning in the Global Age

7
AI AND EDUCATION
Will the Promise be Fulfilled?

Alexandros Papaspyridis and Jason La Greca

7.1 Artificial Intelligence (AI)

The term *Artificial Intelligence* (AI) was first coined by John McCarthy in 1956. In fact, AI formed the central topic of the Dartmouth Conference of that year (Papaspyridis, 2019). For this reason, McCarthy is often considered by many as the father of AI (Childs, 2011) with the Dartmouth Conference signifying first large-scale event devoted to the subject (AAAI, 2005).

McCarthy first defined AI as "the science and engineering of making intelligent machines, especially intelligent computer programs" where "intelligence is the computational part of the ability to achieve goals in the world" (Knight, 2006). To classify a machine as having artificial intelligence, it needs to act and think both rationally, and like a human. These behaviors are often evaluated by the *Turing Test*.

AI has progressed significantly since McCarthy and his contemporary's early explorations. Deep learning, reinforcement learning, and more recently transformer models and neural networks with billions of parameters are now able to surpass human accuracy in vision, speech, and translation skills.

7.1.1 Terminology

In this chapter, we will use AI as an umbrella term that includes subsets of machine learning (ML) or deep learning (DL).

7.1.2 AI Advances

With the advancement of deep learning (LeCun, Bengio, & Hinton, 2015), significant acheivements in visual object recognition, object detection, speech recognition, and natural language processing have also emerged. In 2016, (He, Zhang, Ren, & Sun, 2016) we first reached human parity in the task of object recognition (computer vision). In 2017, Microsoft researchers achieved human parity in the switchboard speech recognition test (5.1% error rate), which, in 2018, was followed by machine translation (69.9%) and machine reading comprehension (88.5%) using the SQuAD reading comprehension test. More recently in 2020, Microsoft researchers successfully completed an artificial intelligence system capable of generating captions for images that are in many cases more accurate than those authored by humans when measured by the NOCAPS benchmark.

Reinforcement Learning (Sutton & Barto, 2018) has been another transformational AI approach that was used in the development of Alpha Go (Silver, et al., 2016), by DeepMind, an Alphabet subsidiary. Alpha Go is a computer program that played the boardgame Go and went on to beat the incumbent human world champion in 2016. In late 2017, DeepMind introduced AlphaZero, a single system that taught itself— that is, without a pre-existing schema or pre-programmed model— how to master the three very different games of chess, shogi, and Go. In doing so, AlphaZero eventually beat each of the prior world-champion computer programs dedicated to each game. In 2016 DeepMind turned what they had learned into to a new AI system called AlphaFold, which is now capable of predicting the three-dimensional structure of a protein from the sequence of amino acids (Jumper, et al., 2021), and was named method of the year 2021 by the journal, *Nature*.

The next evolution of Natural Language Processing (NLP) involves the use of Transformers Language Models. These models are sophisticated enough to consist of up to 530 billion parameters (Naik, 2021), which in turn allows AI applications to not only comprehend written texts but also to author them in ways that often are almost indistinguishable from humans. These large foundation models, such as OpenAI's GPT-3, are poised to usher in a new era of tools to help creative activities (The Economist-Leaders, 2022), such as writing and coding (GitHub, n.d.).

7.1.3 IT & AI in Education

One of the key goals of the use of information technology (IT) in Higher Education has been to empower learners through structured flexibility and to scaffold good practices that lead to time-saving for educators during the emergence of computer-based learning. While the kernel for modern learning management systems and IT in Higher Education started back in the 1920s, with Pressey's invention of the teaching machine, it was in the early 1960s that research publications on the intersection of IT and education emerged with notable theorists such as James Finn, Norman Crowder, and Gordon Pask helping to define the future fields of instructional design and eLearning cited in (Seels, 1989).

In 1970, Ceylin Büyüksoy (1970) first discussed applying AI to both determine and uncover new learning techniques, and Jaime Carbonell created the intelligent tutoring systems, under which for the first-time computers were used to directly assist learning. It was not until 1993, however, that the first World Conference on Artificial Intelligence in Education was held in Edinburgh, UK (Deloitte, 2019). It is interesting to note that many of the questions asked during this forum remain a common point of contention today; notably, how tasks should be structured for students, how student actions should be tracked, and when and how the educator should intervene (Hill, 2003). Indeed, entirely new areas of the debate on AI and education have since emerged for each of these questions, some – like ethical AI will be covered in more depth later in this chapter. With the explosive growth in technology adoption and the emergence of AI techniques and tools, the consultancy and market analysis firm HolonIQ, has forecast that

> AI adoption in education will explode over the next five years and is expected to reach global expenditure of $6 billion by 2025. Much of the growth will come from China followed by the USA, together accounting for over half of global AI education spend.
> (HolonIQ, 2019)

While China's recent crackdowns on EdTech are due to both perceived and real educational inequalities (Lee, 2021), the COVID-19 pandemic has accelerated adoption in many other parts of the world. While it is too early to tell if HolonIQ's predictions are accurate, the rate at which universities seek to drive transformation and develop AI models to support the classroom of the future, enhance line of business processes, and proactively incorporate industry skills into their teaching programs has only increased. This is further evidenced by emerging uses of AI to promote a holistic engagement model for students from outreach, acquisition, retention, and proactive support through to assessment, learning, employability, and eventually job placement. No longer are the ideas for AI implementation bound to support discrete skills acquisition, but rather how we can augment the HyFlex (Papaspyridis & La Greca, 2022) classroom experiences to provide an engaging digital campus with transferable real-world skills while minimizing costs through process automation and simplification.

7.2 Frameworks for AI in Education

In discussing the applications of AI in Education (AIED, or AIEd), it is useful to develop a defining framework and taxonomy. Wang and Cheng (2022) identified three areas in this regard: Learning from AI, learning about AI, and learning with AI. While Feng & Law (2021) identified two sustained themes: intelligent tutoring systems and massive open online courses.

In an earlier publication, Papaspyridis (2020) used Microsoft's Education Transformation Framework (ETF) for Higher Education as the key taxonomy. The Higher Education ETF, is structured in four pillars:

- **Student Success**: Attract students, drive student outcomes, and connect with students in lifelong relationships.
- **Teaching & Learning**: Build an environment that empowers academics to do their best work with personalized learning systems and collaborative spaces that empower students to reach their full potential.
- **Academic Research**: Empower all researchers with a powerful and flexible computing environment to perform their research without constraints from the underlying infrastructure and collaborate with other researchers across the world.
- **Secure & Connected Campus**: Reimagine how to configure, optimize, and manage campus resources by connecting the physical infrastructure with digital technology to deliver a seamless and modern campus experience.

For K-12, we can adopt a similar framework (Microsoft Education, n.d.).

An alternative approach is to leverage the cognitive services being used, such as vision (image detection, object recognition, handwriting-to-text), speech (speech-to-text, text-to-speech), and natural language processing (e.g., Q+A bots). It is important to note that AI can be explicit or implicit. By explicit, we refer to systems that are powered by AI, such as decision-making software. By implicit, we refer to AI systems used in a specific function of a bigger system, such as the recommendation engine of a learning content management platform. As AI tools continue to become more pervasive, almost all systems will require some form of AI to implement specific functions, the sophistication of which will also increase alongside the evolution of the underlying models and technologies.

Below we will examine multiple AI applications in higher education. Through these, we will demonstrate that while AI has already become pervasive (Newton, 2021), there are still challenges to overcome in how these technologies are being used. A recent informal survey (Williamson, 2021) on key reasons for using AI in education included "[to] help address rising costs of public ed", "data analytics for learning feedback loops to inform teachers", and "analysis of experiments in pedagogy".

7.3 Teaching and Learning: Embracing the Shift to Hybrid

Perhaps the biggest promise of AI has been in the promotion and realization of *personalized learning experiences*. By aligning learning outcomes, graduate attributes, and emerging industry skills, universities have worked for years to envision intelligently tailored learning experiences that help learners not only improve their knowledge but ultimately prepare each for their chosen career. Bloom (1984) observes that the average student tutored one-to-one using mastery learning techniques performed two standard deviations better than students educated in a classroom environment with one teacher to 30 students. With or without mastery learning, AIED has promised to deliver a powerful, yet affordable one-on-one tutoring solution. Early work in AIED identified four key elements: Domain expertise (domain model); teaching expertise (pedagogical model); student (learner) model; and user interface (Kay, 2015). Researchers have also developed models that represent the social, emotional, and metacognitive aspects of learning (Luckin, Holmes, Griffiths, & Forcier, 2016).

Examples of AIED in tutoring include the use of reinforcement learning (the technology we saw earlier that has been deployed to play Go). This has been particularly common in language studies, as either a way to prepare students for English-language proficiency tests, or in self-paced language learning apps (Smith, 2019). Similarly, enterprise and professional development tools such as LinkedIn and Pluralsight are increasing their use of AI to personalize recommendations and learning pathways for higher education students, professionals, and those looking for new careers. Universities themselves are looking for ways to borrow from some of these ideas, notably in making intelligent, personalized recommendations for students. The true challenge for universities then is to consolidate their myriad upstream data sources into a unified data estate, thus allowing for AI models to be more insightful and capable of meaningful suggestions.

In parallel, *chat bots* and student concierge experiences are now commonplace across the sector. Serving as both the interface for and connective tissue of a tightly integrated digital campus experience, humanlike AI chat interfaces are now capable of more than simply answering mundane questions from a prefilled question-answer database. In many cases, chat bots can join multiple systems together, which subsequently allows for immediate responses to an increasingly broad range of student asks, and/or proactive nudges from any number of trigger points. In a complicated environment, such as a modern university, the ability for students to access a single place to ask, update, or trigger workflows is truly timesaving and engaging. Being able to receive actionable insights, recommendations, and/or insights based on an array of interconnected upstream systems is transformational.

AI chat bots, automation and workflow are most effective when explicitly designed with humans-in-the-loop, and/or when other students are empowered to help one another. As a tool to augment classroom engagement, educator-in-the-loop question bots coordinate the exchange of ideas and ensure that each question is answered timely and accurately. As the bot is aware of both the topic and the most appropriate teaching team member by skill or relationship to the student, it can loop in the best person, at the right time, to make sure no student is left behind. Critically, educator-in-the-loop bots are not intended, or capable of replacing human teachers, but instead act to extend their capacity.

Through the adoption of an AI-moderated student-to-student community bot, educators are freed from mundane questions and general triage, empowering them to engage in higher-order practices. The experience for students is also enhanced, as not only are their questions responded to either immediately, or much sooner than before, but they are thrust into an immersive community of learning, where they build stronger personal bonds with their peers. Their interactions with human educators are similarly enriched, and course delivery is holistically uplifted.

The use of AI in assessment tools is also increasing. Janison (Janison, n.d.), a Microsoft partner, for example, has developed solutions for marking low-stakes scenarios with a human as the ultimate reviewer, codifying answers according to standard taxonomies, checking proctoring video feeds for possible violations of exam integrity and referring them to human proctors, and recommendation of content pathways based on results and the candidate's profiles.

Learning analytics is an area that continues to attract attention, especially post-pandemic. With the need to better engage, motivate, and retain learners and talent, universities now more than ever are seeking efficient, easy-to-implement tools that either act to augment existing feedback loops, or otherwise enhance an educator's ability to support students' development across a broad range of skills. Providing timely feedback to large cohorts has been difficult historically, but with the increasing volume and quality of data made available through HyFlex learning environments, universities and even individual educators are now exploring how AI can be used to better understand and support learners. We are now much closer to developing models and tools that provide a holistic view of each individual learner, which in turn changes how we, as educators, teach,

Dr. Kellermann at the University of New South Wales, Australia is now using machine learning to predict the success or failure of individual students within the first 2 weeks of the semester. He in turn uses this data to proactively reach out to students to offer support, thus resulting in significantly higher retention and student satisfaction than in previous iterations of the course (Microsoft, 2019). The Question Bot (QBot) responds to questions that students raise in Microsoft Teams. QBot is available as open source (Antares Solutions n.d.). Without AI, however, a single academic's ability to capture, analyze, and decide on appropriate actions from raw engagement data, results, answer choices, attendance, and online communication patterns are simply not scalable or even feasible. One could even argue that without the use of AI, the very human relationship between academics and students cannot be scaled to the same quality. And it is only with AI that we can continue to evolve from the impersonal, where the lecturer would seldom know the names of those who sat in front of them, to now having direct meaningful, timely, and data-driven conversations with individual learners—without a significant impact on workload.

AI-augmented Learning Analytics has also been implemented to support the development of important graduate attributes and skills. Specifically, universities with the help of Microsoft Partners like Antares and Discourse Analytics are increasingly using communication insights to understand group dynamics and to identify which groupings are most likely to succeed in complex tasks. As the educator, placing students into high-performing and supportive groupings promotes collaboration, peer feedback, and improved outcomes.

AI technology is instrumental in enhancing accessibility and inclusivity in education. AI has been used to power Azure Immersive Reader (Microsoft, n.d.-a–k). It implements proven techniques to improve reading comprehension for new readers, language learners, and people with learning differences such as dyslexia by helping them with features like reading aloud, translating languages, and focusing attention through highlighting and other design elements (Microsoft, 2022). Immersive Reader has been integrated into the Microsoft Office suite (Microsoft, n.d.-a–k). The Rochester Institute of Technology uses Microsoft Translator's speech recognition to convert spoken language into fluent, punctuated text to help students with hearing impairments (Roach, 2018).

7.4 Connected Campus and Student Success: Modernize Experiences

Another area that seems to be amenable to AI is that *predictive analytics*. Using disparate data sources, such as grades, timing of assignment submissions, as well as Wi-Fi usage and use of university resources (library, canteens, etc.), an institution can identify students at risk and provide suitable interventions. The Association for Institutional Research (AIR), EDUCAUSE, and the National Association of College and University Business Officers (NACUBO) (collectively serving nearly 2,500 institutions and representing over 80% of postsecondary students in the United States (22 million students) issued a joint statement to reaffirm higher education's commitment to the use of data and analytics to support students and help institutions take better decisions (The Association for Institutional Research (AIR), EDUCAUSE, the National Association of College and University Business Officers (NACUBO), 2020). The report clearly states the benefits as

> We strongly believe that using data to better understand our students and our own operations paves the way to developing new, innovative approaches for improved student recruiting, better student outcomes, greater institutional efficiency, and cost-containment, and much more. Data are an institutional strategic asset and should be used as such.

Discourse Analytics (Discourse Analytics, n.d.) has built a platform that leverages student mindsets, and not their demographics, to prescriptively nudge students across their entire learner journey. Nudging provides appropriately modulated messages via existing communication channels (e.g., student Customer Relationship Management: CRM), at the right time to achieve specific student outcomes such as enrollment, recruitment, melt, financial aid, and student success. By leveraging existing data from across university software platforms (Student Information System (SIS), Learning Management System (LMS), Enterprise Resource Planning system (ERP), CRM, etc.) the platform builds individualized learner profiles that focus on noncognitive aspects of the learner (financial comfort, self-awareness, resilience, curiosity) that are then clustered using a patented Think-Alike Clustering algorithm. Discourse Analytics uses these profiles to create prescriptive nudges to drive improved outcomes across enrollment, recruitment, financial aid, and student success. The results transform outcomes and include retention lift of 22%, increase in enrollment yield of 63%, and accelerating mastery by 25%.

In 2020, (Papaspyridis, 2020), we addressed how we can modernize experiences for higher education constituents using bots, for students to get their questions answered, or for suppliers to have answers to POs. Like chat bots being used in teaching and learning scenarios, the user of these services can have their questions answered by a human. Chat bots are therefore being used as 24 × 7 available first-level assistants that can progressively get better at addressing end-user questions, by enriching the Q+A database and through improvements in conversational AI (Microsoft, n.d.-a–k). In collaboration with MIP Politecnico di Milano Graduate School of Business, FLEXA is a learning platform (Frattini, 2021) that allows any user to decide where and how to access their personalized learning path from anywhere in the world and with any device. The Beacon bot at the Staffordshire University has been designed to help ease the stress and anxiety that many students experience in their first year at university (Courtois, 2019).

7.5 Academic Research: Cloud-Powered Academic Research

AI is an increasingly important domain in Computer Science (CS) departments. These advancements relied on the availability of powerful computational infrastructure that has been doubling every 3.4 months (OpenAI, 2018. Bigger is better seems to be a trend supported in the transformer models, with the 1.6 trillion parameters being the largest one (Wiggers, 2021). The infrastructure needed to train these models is phenomenal, with the 0.5 billion models requiring over 4,000 Graphics Processing Units (GPUs) and is estimated to cost over $85 million (Quach, 2021).

AI is increasingly becoming an important tool in academic research outside CS, in bioinformatics (Jumper, et al., 2021), medicine (Liu et al., 2021), physics (RoboticsBiz, 2021; Physics Meets ML, n.d.), materials (Na, Jang, & Chang, 2021), and mathematics (University of Sydney, 2021) to social sciences (Robila & Robila, 2020). AI has been used to predict the future impact of scientific research (Ham, 2021).

Therefore, it is apparent that no domain has been left untouched, and therefore it is important to facilitate cross-pollination between domains and AI researchers, as well as to ensure that AI is part of the curriculum of all disciplines. Universities that want to excel in AI research should think of the cloud as the only way to ensure that they can have scalable computational resources. In the latest TOP500 supercomputer list rankings, Microsoft Azure has joined the Top 10 club at 30.05 Petaflops (Raines, 2021). Every researcher can benefit from Azure Cognitive Services (Microsoft, n.d.-a–k) which provides a powerful way to incorporate pre-trained ML models for speech, language, vision, and decision as well as powerful foundation models (Bommasani & Liang, 2021) from OpenAI.

Project Malmo is an AI research platform based on the game Minecraft (Linn, 2016). This has allowed researchers to test different algorithms, such as Deep Q Learning (Bhagat, 2021) or General-Purpose AI agents that can achieve open-ended goals (Potapov, 2022).

7.6 Challenges and Controversies

During the COVID-19 pandemic, the International Baccalaureate Organization (IBO) used an AI system to determine final grades as high-school exams were canceled. The system used students' past grades and schools' data to determine final grades. The results created a furor as some deviated significantly from the students' predicted grades. There was no appeal process for the AI assessment, as the usual appeal in previous years was about re-marking specific exam papers (Evgeniou, Hardoon, & Ovchinnikov, 2020). The authors conclude that:

> Including AI in the decision-making process without carefully thinking through an appeals process and linking the appeals process to the algorithm design itself will likely end not only with new crises but potentially with a rejection of AI-enabled solutions in general. And that deprives us of the potential for AI, when combined with humans, to dramatically improve the quality of decision-making.

In the United Kingdom, an algorithm was employed to assign GCSE and A-level marks (Richardson, 2020). Smith (2020) has a great description of the objective and challenge of this algorithm. The UK exam regulator Ofqual had announced its intention to study the potential to use AI in marking (Black, 2020), however, it has been unspecified whether the algorithm used in determining 2020 results employed AI. It did result in a similar outcry to the IB ones and a U-turn on how grades were computed.

In the following section, we will examine the principles that should govern AI development for sensitive use cases, such as the one here which results in a student being granted or denied a place in higher education.

7.7 Capability Maturity and Data Management

AI/ML systems require data and are inextricably connected with data. From data to decisions and actions with AI, we consider evolution in four stages:

- *Descriptive*: Reports that detail *what* happened
- *Diagnostic*: Interactive dashboards, such as based on Power BI that provide insights as to *why* did things happen?
- *Predictive*: Using Machine Learning to predict *what will* happen
- *Prescriptive*: Using AI to provide recommendations on *what* course of action to take

This taxonomy is useful to gradually evolve the capabilities through data analytics. All these capabilities depend on data. All kinds of data are being generated internally within the institution by machines (e.g., access cards, Wi-Fi logins), people (LMS, SIS, CRM), and externally in social networks, and external databases, which may be relational or not. In this collection of disparate data, the data estate must be managed and curated, to be available for reporting, visualization in dashboards, or building ML models. The data assets must be unified and secured, apply data governance to ensure privacy and compliance before allowing to build of intelligent insights (Microsoft, n.d.-a–k). When talking about data repositories, data warehouses have now been enhanced with data lakes and lakehouses that hold a wide variety of data types, from structured to semi-structured to unstructured, at any scale (Microsoft, n.d.-a–k).

7.8 Governance and Ethics

Some key concerns on the use of AI have been around introducing and reproducing historical biases in a sense by providing an algorithmic predetermination of students' achievement, progress, and futures based on historic performance of socioeconomic groups. Does belonging to a racial/gender group make you a priori a potential failure for a specific class? How can we deal with and mitigate race, gender, and socioeconomic biases? AI can introduce biases, and, very importantly, puts a magnifying glass on our own existing biases. This human bias should not be an excuse to not look at the biases of an AI system but is an opportunity to address human biases as well.

An informal survey on reasons to question the use of AI in education included "bias being reproduced through algorithmic black boxes", "environmental consequences of increasing digitalization" and "algorithmic predetermination of students' achievement, progress and futures" (Williamson, 2021).

First, we need to realize that **it starts with data**. As previously discussed, AI/ML systems require data and are inextricably connected with data. Therefore, whatever issues, challenges, and policies we discuss about AI/ML, we should first start with data. Data needs to be accurate, to be protected as may include

Personally Identifiable Information (PII) and be subject to pertinent regulations, such as European Union's (EU) General Data Protection Regulation (GDPR), or the California Privacy Rights Act (CPRA). There is a compliance risk as well as the need to avoid data loss by ensuring correct labeling and authorized access only (Microsoft, n.d.-a–k). Moreover, the data lifecycle must be actively managed, while in research the FAIR data are data that meet the principles of *findability, accessibility, interoperability,* and *reusability* (GOFAIR, n.d.).

The importance of data in an educational institution has led to the rise of the Chief Data Officer, but at the same time has given rise to the need to establish a data-driven decision-making culture as well as to the need to establish why privacy is everyone's responsibility. This is in line with a Microsoft Asia and IDC Asia/Pacific study (Microsoft Stories Asia, 2019) that the educational sector is currently lagging primarily in *Data* and *Culture*.

Beyond data, there is an increasing emphasis on the ethical use of AI. Since 2018, Microsoft's President Brad Smith advocated for ensuring that AI is designed and used responsibly, establishing ethical principles to protect people, govern AI's use and assess how AI will impact employment and jobs. (Smith & Shum, 2021).

Microsoft has established six principles for Responsible AI: *Fairness; Inclusiveness; Reliability & Safety; Transparency; Privacy & Security; Accountability* (Microsoft, n.d.-a–k).

Let's dig deeper into each of these six principles:

- **Fairness** is a complex and contextual issue that includes the equitable allocation of resources, opportunities, or information, denigrating people/reinforce stereotypes, or underrepresented groups.
- **Inclusiveness** is about being intentionally inclusive and diverse groups from design up, including accessibility guidelines.
- **Reliability and safety** to ensure that do not create harm and has well-understood risks and harms
- **Transparency and interpretability/intelligibility**: InterpretML is an open-source package used for training interpretable glass box machine learning models and explaining black box systems.
- **Privacy & Security**: In collaboration with Harvard University, we have shared a series of findings that can protect AI services with guidance materials for modeling, detecting, and mitigating security risks and ethics issues. *Differential privacy* (DP) adds a carefully tuned amount of statistical noise to sensitive data, helping to protect data used in AI systems by preventing re-identification and we have introduced an open-source (OS) toolkit and an OS library for data protection and anonymization for text and images. Additional work on tools for *confidential computing for ML* and *homomorphic encryption*.
- **Accountability** includes principles for the use of facial recognition and ensuring all principles are followed across the development lifecycle.

To operationalize these principles, we have established the Office of Responsible AI (ORA), the Responsible AI Strategy in Engineering (RAISE), and the Aether committee that advises our leadership on the challenges and opportunities presented by AI innovations. Key is our effort to review sensitive use cases to help ensure that Microsoft AI principles are upheld, for our own tools as well as those we work on alongside our customers and partners.

Customers, such as Higher Education institutions that would like to benefit from Microsoft's experience and can leverage a vast assortment of online materials at the AI Business School (Microsoft, n.d.-a–k), the AI business school for education learning path (Microsoft, n.d.-a–k) and the Responsible AI resources (Microsoft, n.d.-a–k).

At a global level, UNESCO is working on "The Artificial Intelligence and the Futures of Learning" project that includes a guidance on ethical principles on the use of AI in education that builds on the "Recommendation on the Ethics of Artificial Intelligence" (UNESCO, n.d.). The Organisation for Economic Co-operation and Development (OECD) AI Policy Observatory has put together AI principles "that are innovative and trustworthy and that respects human rights and democratic values. Adopted in May 2019, they set standards for AI that are practical and flexible enough to stand the test of time" (OECD.AI Policy Observatory, n.d.).

7.9 Future Opportunities and Challenges

7.9.1 Delivering System Impact

In looking at how to deliver the promise of AIED, Luckin, Holmes, Griffiths, & Forcier, (2016) stress the three forces from the work of Michael Fullan and Katelyn Donnelly: Pedagogy, technology, and system change. In this chapter, we have identified efforts in both technology and pedagogy, but only as they pertain to individual applications. We have not addressed systemic change in any depth, but outlined in Section 7.6, the shortcomings of the introduction of AI/algorithmic approaches to IB and A-level university exams.

EdTech companies and pioneering educators have seen success within a direct-to-educational consumer (parents as buyers, and students as users) paradigm. They have not yet had their platforms or ideas integrated or elevated as part of the core educational experience, or beyond their faculty/subject. The focus now needs to be on how to scale these innovative pilots and how to create synergies between the teacher's instruction in the class and technologies being implemented. To be successful, universities need to invest heavily in teaching and learning, change management, and faculty development (Papaspyridis & La Greca, 2022). They need to revisit the academic promotions and career roadmaps, which historically bind academics to a publish-or-perish mentality and not student experience OKRs. Universities need to hire staff based on their desire to teach, while also uplifting those who are more focused on research.

IT teams need to be enablers while working across the university to bring their data estate in order. EdTech and Big Tech need to work together to ensure that data formats & APIs are standardized and that data security, governance, and privacy, are kept paramount. EdTech and Big Tech need to work together to both demonstrate and agree upon standards of data collection that benefit the teacher, student outcomes, and support HyFlex instruction.

7.9.2 Technology

AIED is progressing and most EdTech companies are now integrating AI into their products. And natural language interfaces have made bots and voice navigation a reality for consumers, but the promise of intelligent tutoring has not yet been generalized. Luckin, Holmes, Griffiths, & Forcier (2016) advocate for an education DARPA to promote addressing these grand challenges. Singapore National AI Strategy has identified education as one of the seven areas it will prioritize (Smart Nation Singapore, n.d.) focusing on personalized education through adaptive learning and assessment.

What will be the impact of emerging AI challenges, such as deep fakes and AI essay mills in education (Ryder, 2019)? It is certain that academic integrity will continue to be a cat-and-mouse game that will need to evolve beyond antiplagiarism (Bailey, 2021). Are there assessment approaches that embrace these technologies, or are there methods that can detect AI-authored works, or predict and proactively support students who are more susceptible to engaging in dishonest behaviors? These are all areas that education leaders, researchers, and classroom teachers will need to address sooner rather than later.

What will be the role of reinforcement learning in overcoming bias? Will we allow AI to run experiments and be positively/negatively rewarded based on successes or failures? It seems highly unlikely that our society can allow AI systems to run experiments in such sensitive use cases. Humans should be in control and accountable. However, it is important to surface human biases and build a culture of transparency where these biases can be assessed and mitigated.

7.10 Final Thoughts

AI technology has come of age in and through advances in Foundation Models, it will have an increasing impact on creative activities. Already, uses of AIED are omnipresent in higher education, in teaching and learning to embrace the shift to hybrid; to modernize experiences; and to cloud-power academic research as well as EdTech. This work covered several different use cases and presented a capability maturity model progressing from reporting to prediction. To ensure data is useful, it is important to put in place a modern data estate with appropriate data governance processes, including security, access, privacy, and lifecycle policies.

The rather hasty (due to the urgency) introduction of AI and algorithmic approaches in IB and A-level assessment was ill-fated due to, among other reasons, removing the human from the loop. This leads to the importance of adopting a governance and ethics framework for the development of AIED, starting from data, prior to embarking on such a project.

AIED can deliver its promise of personalized learning experiences that lead to significantly better student performance at a system level. For this to be achieved, institutions need to prioritize investments in teaching and learning, change management, and faculty capacity; build a data-driven decision-making culture; and ensure governance and ethics are put in place.

References

AAAI. (2005). *A Brief History of AI*. Retrieved August 4, 2018, from https://aitopics.org/misc/brief-history

Antares Solutions. (n.d.). *Question Bot – Plugin for Microsoft Teams*. Retrieved from GitHub: https://github.com/unsw-edu-au/QBot

Bailey, J. (2021, February 22). *Using a Free AI to Write an Essay*. Retrieved from PlagiarismToday: https://www.plagiarismtoday.com/2021/02/22/using-a-free-ai-to-write-an-essay/

Bhagat, R. (2021, June 3). *MineRL*. Retrieved from GitHub: https://github.com/rishavb123/MineRL

Black, B. (2020, January 9). *Exploring the Potential Use of AI in Marking*. Retrieved from Ofqual blog: https://ofqual.blog.gov.uk/2020/01/09/exploring-the-potential-use-of-ai-in-marking/

Bloom, B. S. (1984, June–July). The 2 sigma problem: The search for methods of group instruction as effective as one-to-one tutoring. *Educational Researcher, 13*(6), 4–16. doi:10.2307/1175554

Bommasani, R., & Liang, P. (2021, October 18). *Reflections on Foundation Models*. Retrieved from Stanford University HAI: https://hai.stanford.edu/news/reflections-foundation-models

Ceylin Büyüksoy, Z. T. (1970). Determining learning techniques by using artificial intelligence and observing the impacts of differentiated education model. *European Journal of Teaching and Education, 2*, 122–130.

Childs, M. (2011). *John McCarthy: Computer Scientist Known as the Father of AI*. Retrieved from https://www.independent.co.uk/news/obituaries/john-mccarthy-computer-scientist-known-as-the-father-of-ai-6255307.html

Courtois, J.-P. (2019, October 7). *How AI is Transforming Education and Skills Development*. Retrieved from Official Microsoft Blog: https://blogs.microsoft.com/blog/2019/10/07/how-ai-is-transforming-education-and-skills-development/

Deloitte. (2019). *Global Development of AI-Based Education*. Retrieved 12 27, 2021, from https://www2.deloitte.com/content/dam/Deloitte/cn/Documents/technology-media-telecommunications/deloitte-cn-tmt-global-development-of-ai-based-education-en-191108.pdf

Discourse Analytics. (n.d.). Retrieved from Discourse Analytics – Nudging for Better Outcomes: https://www.discourseanalytics.com/

Evgeniou, T., Hardoon, D. R., & Ovchinnikov, A. (2020, August 13). *What Happens When AI is Used to Set Grades?* Retrieved from Harvard Business Review: https://hbr.org/2020/08/what-happens-when-ai-is-used-to-set-grades

Feng, S., & Law, N. (2021, March 15). Mapping artificial intelligence in education research: A network-based keyword analysis. *International Journal of Artificial Intelligence in Education, 31*, 277–303. doi:10.1007/s40593-021-00244-4

Frattini, F. (2021, July 5). *Created in Collaboration with Microsoft, the AI-Powered Continuous Learning Platform "FLEXA" by MIP Politecnico di Milano is an Answer to an Increasing Need for Lifelong Learning Services.* Retrieved from Global Banking and Finance Review: https://www.globalbankingandfinance.com/created-in-collaboration-with-microsoft-the-ai-powered-continuous-learning-platform-flexa-by-mip-politecnico-di-milano-is-an-answer-to-an-increasing-need-for-lifelong-learning-servi/amp/

GitHub. (n.d.). *Your AI Pair Programmer.* Retrieved from GitHub Copilot: https://copilot.github.com/

GOFAIR. (n.d.). *FAIR Principles.* Retrieved from https://www.go-fair.org/fair-principles/

Ham, B. (2021, May 17). *Using Machine Learning to Predict High-Impact Research.* Retrieved from MIT News: https://news.mit.edu/2021/using-machine-learning-predict-high-impact-research-0517

He, K., Zhang, X., Ren, S., & Sun, J. (2016). Deep residual learning for image recognition. *Proceedings of the IEEE conference on computer vision and pattern recognition* (pp. 770–778). Retrieved from https://openaccess.thecvf.com/content_cvpr_2016/papers/He_Deep_Residual_Learning_CVPR_2016_paper.pdf

Hill, J. R. (2003). *Proceedings of the World Conference on Artificial Intelligence in Education, Edinburgh, Scotland, 1993.*

HolonIQ. (2019, May 24). *2019 Artificial Intelligence & Global Education Report.* Retrieved from HolonIQ: https://www.holoniq.com/notes/2019-artificial-intelligence-global-education-report/

Janison. (n.d.). Retrieved from Online Assessment & Learning Solutions: https://www.janison.com/

Jumper, J., Evans, R., Pritzel, A., Tim Green, M. F., Ronneberger, O., & Tunyasuvunakoo, K. (2021). Highly accurate protein structure prediction with AlphaFold. *Nature, 596*(7873), 583–589.

Kay, J. (2015). Whither or wither the AI of AIED? *Seventeenth International Conference on 2015 Workshop Proceedings*, (pp. 1–10). Madrid.

Knight, H. (2006). *Early Artificial Intelligence Projects A student's perspective.* Retrieved August 4, 2018, from https://projects.csail.mit.edu/films/aifilms/AIFilms.html

LeCun, Y., Bengio, Y., & Hinton, G. (2015, May 27). Deep learning. *Nature, 521*, 436–444. doi:10.1038/nature14539

Lee, L. C. (2021, August 5). *Why Did China Crack Down on Its Ed-Tech Industry?* Retrieved from The Diplomat: https://thediplomat.com/2021/08/why-did-china-crack-down-on-its-ed-tech-industry/

Linn, A. (2016, March 13). *Project Malmo: Using Minecraft to build more intelligent technology.* Retrieved from Microsoft | The AI Blog: https://blogs.microsoft.com/ai/project-malmo-using-minecraft-build-intelligent-technology/

Liu, P. R., Lu, L., Zhang, J. Y., Huo, T. T., Liu, S. X., & Ye, Z. W. (2021). Application of artificial intelligence in medicine: An overview. *Current Medical Science, 41*(6), 1105–1115. doi:10.1007/s11596-021-2474-3

Luckin, R., Holmes, W., Griffiths, M., & Forcier, L. B. (2016). *Intelligence Unleashed: An Argument for AI in Education*. Retrieved from Open Research Online: http://oro.open.ac.uk/50104/1/Luckin%20et%20al.%20-%202016%20-%20Intelligence%20Unleashed.%20An%20argument%20for%20AI%20in%20Educ.pdf

Microsoft. (2019, July 19). Demo: Teams in the classroom at microsoft inspire 2019. Retrieved from https://www.youtube.com/watch?v=NcbQ2UK69Tc

Microsoft. (2022, February 9). *What is Azure Immersive Reader?* Retrieved from Microsoft Docs: https://docs.microsoft.com/en-us/azure/applied-ai-services/immersive-reader/overview

Microsoft. (n.d.-a). *AI Business School for Education*. Retrieved from Microsoft Docs: https://docs.microsoft.com/en-us/learn/paths/ai-business-school-education/?WT.mc_id=sitertzn_homepage_mslearn-card-aibusinessschool

Microsoft. (n.d.-b). *Azure Cognitive Services - Add cognitive capabilities to apps with APIs and AI services*. Retrieved from Azure: https://azure.microsoft.com/en-us/services/cognitive-services/#overview`

Microsoft. (n.d.-c). *Azure Immersive Reader*. Retrieved from Microsoft Azure: https://azure.microsoft.com/en-us/services/immersive-reader/

Microsoft. (n.d.-d). *Conversational AI | Microsoft Power Virtual Agents*. Retrieved from Power Virtual Agents: https://powervirtualagents.microsoft.com/en-us/conversational-ai/

Microsoft. (n.d.-e). *Data Estate Modernization*. Retrieved from Microsoft - Industry Solutions: https://www.microsoft.com/en-us/industrysolutions/solutions/data-estate-modernization

Microsoft. (n.d.-f). *Immersive Reader - Microsoft Learning Tools*. Retrieved from https://www.onenote.com/learningtools

Microsoft. (n.d.-g). *Microsoft Purview: Govern, Protect, and Manage Your Data Estate*. Retrieved from Microsoft Azure: https://azure.microsoft.com/en-us/services/purview/#overview

Microsoft. (n.d.-h). *Put AI into action with AI Business School*. Retrieved from Microsoft AI: https://www.microsoft.com/en-us/ai/ai-business-school

Microsoft. (n.d.-i). *Responsible AI*. Retrieved April 21, 2022, from AI: https://www.microsoft.com/en-us/ai/responsible-ai?activetab=pivot1%3aprimaryr6

Microsoft. (n.d.-j). *Responsible AI Resources*. Retrieved from Microsoft AI: https://www.microsoft.com/en-us/ai/responsible-ai-resources

Microsoft. (n.d.-k). *What is Data Lake*. Retrieved from Microsoft Azure: https://azure.microsoft.com/en-us/overview/what-is-a-data-lake/#what-is-a-data-lake

Microsoft Education. (n.d.). *Microsoft K-12 Education Transformation Framework*. Retrieved December 27, 2021, from: https://www.microsoft.com/en-us/education/school-leaders/k-12-microsoft-education-transformation-framework

Microsoft Stories Asia. (2019, September 23). *Higher Education Institutions in Asia Pacific Stand to Double the Rate of Innovation with Artificial Intelligence*. Retrieved from Microsoft: https://news.microsoft.com/apac/2019/09/23/higher-education-institutions-in-asia-pacific-stand-to-double-the-rate-of-innovation-with-artificial-intelligence/

Na, G. S., Jang, S., & Chang, H. (2021, July 14). Predicting thermoelectric properties from chemical formula with explicitly identifying dopant effects. *NPJ Computational Materials, 7*. doi:10.1038/s41524-021-00564-y

Naik, A. R. (2021). *NVIDIA, Microsoft Introduce New Language Model MT-NLG With 530 Billion Parameters, Leaves GPT-3 Behind*. Retrieved December 26, 2021, from: https://analyticsindiamag.com/nvidia-microsoft-introduce-new-language-model-mt-nlg-with-530-billion-parameters-leaves-gpt-3-behind/#:~:text=Earlier%20this%20week%2C%20in%20partnership%20with%20Microsoft%2C%20NVIDIA,is%20powered%20by%20DeepSpeed%20and%20Me

Newton, D. (2021, May 26). *Artificial INTELLIGENCE Grading Your 'Neuroticism'? Welcome to Colleges' New Frontier*. Retrieved from USA TODAY: https://www.usatoday.com/story/news/education/2021/04/26/ai-infiltrating-college-admissions-teaching-grading/7348128002/

OECD.AI Policy Observatory. (n.d.). *OECD AI Principles Overview*. Retrieved from OECD AI: https://oecd.ai/en/ai-principles

OpenAI. (2018, May 16). *AI and Compute*. Retrieved from OpenAI: https://openai.com/blog/ai-and-compute/

Papaspyridis, A. (2020). *AI in Higher Education: Opportunities and Considerations*. Retrieved December 27, 2021, from: https://news.microsoft.com/apac/2020/03/26/ai-in-higher-education-opportunities-and-considerations/

Papaspyridis, A., & La Greca, J. (2022). *Never Let a Good Crisis Go to Waste: The New Normal is Hybrid and Flexible*. Retrieved from Global Learning Council.

Papaspyridis, A. (2019). *What Is problem solving by searching in AI and how do different techniques for solving a classical AI search problem compare in terms of efficiency?* Singapore: Tanglin Trust School. PM: MOVE UP, AUTHOR INITIAL WAS INCORRECT

Physics Meets ML. (n.d.). Retrieved from Physics Meets ML: http://www.physicsmeetsml.org/

Potapov, A. (2022, February 11). *Towards General-Purpose Minecraft AI Agents*. Retrieved from SingularityNET: https://blog.singularitynet.io/towards-general-purpose-minecraft-ai-agents-41fe415d6dd

Quach, K. (2021, October 12). *Behold the Megatron: Microsoft and Nvidia Build Massive Language Processor*. Retrieved from The Register: https://www.theregister.com/2021/10/12/nvidia_microsoft_mtnlg/#:~:text=Nvidia%20and%20Microsoft%20announced%20their%20largest%20monolithic%20transformer,together%2C%20named%20the%20Megatron-Turing%20Natural%20Language%20Generation%20model

Raines, K. (2021, November 15). *Microsoft Announces new NDm A100 v4 Public AI Supercomputers and Achieves Top 10 Ranking in TOP500*. Retrieved from Azure Compute Blog: https://techcommunity.microsoft.com/t5/azure-compute-blog/microsoft-announces-new-ndm-a100-v4-public-ai-supercomputers-and/ba-p/2966848

Richardson, H. (2020, August 25). *Ofqual Chief Sally Collier Steps Down after Exams Chaos*. Retrieved from BBC News: https://www.bbc.com/news/education-53909487

Roach, J. (2018, April 5). *AI Technology Helps Students Who Are Deaf Learn*. Retrieved from Microsoft / The AI Blog: https://blogs.microsoft.com/ai/ai-powered-captioning/

Robila, M., & Robila, S. A. (2020). Applications of artificial intelligence methodologies to behavioral and social sciences. *Journal of Child and Family Studies*, 2954–2966. doi:10.1007/s10826-019-01689-x

RoboticsBiz. (2021, May 1). *Machine Learning in Physics – The Power and Promise*. Retrieved from rb: https://roboticsbiz.com/machine-learning-in-physics-the-power-and-promise/

Ryder, M. J. (2019, April 18). *If AI Can Write News Items, They Can Write Essays Too*. Retrieved from MJRyder.net: https://mjryder.net/ai-essay-mills/

Seels, B. (1989). *The Instructional Design Movement in Educational Technology*. Educational Technology.

Silver, D., Huang, A., Maddison, C. J., Guez, A., Sifre, L., Driessche, G. V., & Schrittwieser, J. (2016). Mastering the game of Go with deep neural networks and tree search. *Nature, 529*(7587), 484–489.

Smart Nation Singapore. (n.d.). *National AI Strategy*. Retrieved May 31, 2022, from Smart Nation Singapore: https://www.smartnation.gov.sg/initiatives/artificial-intelligence

Smith, B., & Shum, H. (2021, January 17). *The Future Computed: Artificial Intelligence and Its Role in Society*. Retrieved from Official Microsoft Blog: https://blogs.microsoft.com/blog/2018/01/17/future-computed-artificial-intelligence-role-society/

Smith, C. S. (2019). *The Machines are Learning, and So are the Students*. Retrieved December 27, 2021, from: https://www.nytimes.com/2019/12/18/education/artificial-intelligence-tutors-teachers.html

Smith, G. (2020, August 19). *Don't Blame AI for the British A-Level Test Scandal*. Retrieved from Mind Matters: https://mindmatters.ai/2020/08/dont-blame-ai-for-the-british-a-level-test-scandal/

Sutton, R. S., & Barto, A. G. (2018). *Reinforcement learning: An introduction*. Cambridge, MA: MIT Press.

The Association for Institutional Research (AIR), EDUCAUSE, the National Association of College and University Business Officers (NACUBO). (2020, 2). *Analytics Can Save Higher Education. Really*. Retrieved December 27, 2021, from: https://changewithanalytics.com/wp-content/uploads/2020/02/Joint_Analytics_Statement_2020.pdf

The Economist-Leaders. (2022, August 09). Foundation models: How smarter AI will change creativity. *The Economist*. Retrieved from https://www.economist.com/leaders/2022/06/09/artificial-intelligences-new-frontier

UNESCO. (n.d.). *Artificial Intelligence in Education*. Retrieved May 31, 2022, from UNESCO: https://en.unesco.org/artificial-intelligence/education

University of Sydney. (2021, December 1). *Maths Researchers Hail Breakthrough in Applications of Artificial Intelligence*. Retrieved from Phys.org: https://phys.org/news/2021-12-maths-hail-breakthrough-applications-artificial.html

Wang, T., & Cheng, E. C. (2022). Towards a tripartite research agenda: A scoping review of artificial intelligence in education research. In E. Cheng, R. Koul, T. Wang, & X. Yu (Eds.), *Artificial intelligence in education: Emerging technologies, models and applications. Lecture Notes on Data Engineering and Communications Technologies*, (Vol. 104, pp. 3–24). Springer. doi:10.1007/978-981-16-7527-0_1

Wiggers, K. (2021, January 12). *Google Trained a Trillion-Parameter AI Language Model*. Retrieved from VentureBeat: https://venturebeat.com/2021/01/12/google-trained-a-trillion-parameter-ai-language-model/

Williamson, B. (2021, November 13). Retrieved from Twitter: https://twitter.com/BenPatrickWill/status/1459623228947771399?t=Tr51hk-en5J95nzRZLXtfg&s=09

8
PROCEED WITH CAUTION
The Pitfalls and Potential of AI and Education

Kelly Shiohira and Wayne Holmes

8.1 Introduction

The arguments for the integration of AI into education are multiple and multifaceted. AI has permeated everyday life, and there is a growing number of AI-assisted educational technologies being implemented in classrooms worldwide. Like any tool, AI can be used to improve or to harm society. From a humanistic perspective, citizens need to understand their roles and rights with respect to AI, recognize when they are unfairly disadvantaged by AI and know the avenues of recourse, and above all become conscientious users of AI products—particularly AI products designed for education.

At the same time, calls to skill or upskill individuals in topics such as big data, the data value chain (the process of data creation and use from first identifying a need for data to its final use and possible reuse), and cloud storage are coming from academia and industry, with some companies substantially invested in training partnerships with universities and other educational institutions, as well as the development of their own platforms and courses.[1] The preoccupation with data is nearly universal: Customers are themselves the product for a number of big corporations, which include not only social media platforms but also less conspicuous companies that typically exploit data such as supermarkets and health insurers. Accordingly, the demand for data scientists and engineers has risen sharply in recent years and shows no sign of slowing down. Education is expected to deliver this expertise.

AI is also frequently hailed as a "solution" to core problems in education, including a lack of qualified teachers, poor learning outcomes, and the need to manage achievement gaps (Davies et al., 2020; OECD, 2021b; Seldon & Abidoye, 2018). A multitude of products have been developed and billions of dollars invested in AI for education, and some studies show promising results for content knowledge gains (e.g., Major et al., 2021). However, wide-scale implementation and testing have yet to occur, even as a range of claims are being made without robust evidence (Miao and Holmes, 2021; Bryant et al., 2020).

At the same time as it is being integrated into education, the practicalities of many types of AI conflict with a fundamental education philosophy that education is, as Nelson Mandela noted, "the most powerful weapon that you can use to change the world". The Declaration on the Rights of the Child calls education an "amplifier of all other rights". Education is also often cited as a tool to break cycles of poverty (e.g., Conchas, 2008). While the success of education in these areas may be up for debate, underlying all of these assertions is a belief that education can change the future of an individual, regardless of current circumstances.

However, the AI systems being introduced into education are built on statistical models. Predictions are extrapolations based on trends or patterns derived from previous data. Learners are clustered based on their common attributes and treated commonly. In short, there is a set model to be followed, and each person can be plotted along it, defined by the average experience. At the very least, the dichotomy between education as an enabler of the extraordinary and AI as reliant on the predictable must be acknowledged. This conversation begins by considering the current and potential uses of AI in classrooms and other learning environments; the limitations of learning *with*, *through* and *about* AI; and more broadly what the role of AI *should* be—the types of problems it is best suited to addressing and what exchanges are made in its implementation.

However, first, we need to be clear about what we mean by AI, which is actually notoriously difficult to define. One helpful definition is given by UNICEF (2021):

> Machine-based systems that can, given a set of human-defined objectives, make predictions, recommendations, or decisions that influence real or virtual environments. AI systems interact with us and act on our environment, either directly or indirectly. Often, they appear to operate autonomously, and can adapt their behaviour by learning about the context.

It is important to reiterate that AI is not a machine that thinks independently. AI is merely a set of human-created algorithms that aim to mimic some human thought processes, such as decision-making. They do so to a greater or lesser extent, using a range of database techniques (machine learning approaches such as supervised, unsupervised, reinforcement and deep learning, all of which depend on huge amounts of data) and knowledge-based techniques (e.g., model-based expert systems) (Holmes et al., 2019).

All of these techniques raise ethical issues, about which there is no universal consensus, although many sets of principles (Jobin et al., 2019). Meanwhile, international organizations have begun to publish normative instruments such as the Recommendation on the Ethics of Artificial Intelligence (UNESCO, 2021). Drawing on these and related sources, the key terms employed in discussions of AI ethics are:

- **Accuracy**: Potential and actual sources of error or bias must be identified, recorded, and addressed.
- **Bias**: Cases in which an algorithm discriminates based on gender, race, ability, or other characteristics.
- **Transparency**: The possibilities to (i) access, review, monitor and criticize algorithms (*auditability*) and (ii) understand the outputs of an algorithm (*explainability*).
- **Fairness**: Ensuring that algorithms and their outputs do not lead to discrimination, while everyone has equal access to AI and its benefits.
- **Privacy**: The right of individuals to understand and control the use of their data (text, sound, image), and protect it from exposure to risks such as identity theft or misuse.
- **Responsibility** or **human oversight**: Human agents must be able to change or reform an algorithm and make timely redress in the case of adverse effects.
- **Safety** and **security**: AI must not cause harm, such as discrimination, violation of privacy, and bodily harm, or have negative psychological, social, economic, and emotional effects.
- **AI for the Public Good**: AI should be used for public, societal, individual, and/or economic good.

8.2 Implementing AI in Education

AI is being implemented in education in three main ways: Through learning *about* AI, or programs of study concerned with teaching AI as a subject; learning *with* AI, or applications of AI to the learning of other subject areas; and preparing *for* AI, or the education necessary to understand the current and future impact of AI on society, individuals, work and the environment.

8.2.1 Learning with AI

"Learning with AI", or using AI tools to support teaching and learning in other subjects, also known as "AI in Education" or AIED, may be further categorized as system-supporting, student-supporting, and educator-supporting.

8.2.1.1 System-Supporting AI

System-supporting AI includes AI tools designed to help with student recruitment, timetabling, finances, and other back-end administrative tasks required of educational institutions. Some innovative system-supporting AI applications are currently being explored, for example, the Skills-OVATE[2] portal in Europe, which uses data scraping of online job adverts and AI to reveal competencies required by businesses in order to enable closer matches between skills offerings and skills demand, and the PSET CLOUD[3] in South Africa, which seeks to leverage interoperability of existing government data systems, big data and AI to support improved decision-making by government, educational institutions and citizens through an analysis of skills supply and demand in the country.

8.2.1.2 Student-Supporting AI

Student-supporting AI has been developed over the last 40 years and is now offered by a wide range of "EdTech" corporations. Covid-19 also triggered a new round of corporate investment in AI EdTech, with the global corporate investment in AI EdTech quintupling between 2019 and 2020, launching education applications into the top three AI investment areas that year (Zhang et al., 2022).

The most prominent type of student-supporting AI is the so-called "intelligent tutoring systems" or "personalized learning platforms". These screen-based systems provide some information, an activity, and possibly a quiz, and as the student engages, they collect back-end information such as performance, time on task, and type of error. These inputs are used to direct further learning, so students follow their own adapted but still mostly rote-learning pathways. Most of these platforms focus on primary and secondary school learners, for example, ASSISTments[4] or Byjus,[5] but there are some examples of government systems focused on adult learning such as the FutureSkills[6] initiative in India. Some platforms such as the ViLLE[7] learning platform from Finland enable learners to choose difficulty levels and engage from multiple locations (UNESCO, 2022).

Other student-supporting AI includes dialogue-based tutoring systems which use a dialogic Socratic approach to teaching and learning; chatbots (an example is Genie, Deakin University, 2018), which leverage natural language processing; augmented reality (e.g., Vulcan[8] uses augmented reality and sensor information to provide immediate feedback on simulated tasks such as welding, carpentry, and painting); automatic writing evaluation tools; and exploratory learning environments.

Automatic writing evaluation tools seek to evaluate long-form text with a similar aim to that achieved by computer-graded multiple-choice tests. They typically evaluate an input such as a paragraph or an essay against a database of graded standardized essays, for example, those submitted for national assessments. These systems can provide immediate feedback but they are not without issues (e.g., Feathers, 2019). For example, automated writing assessment can be completely fooled by nonsensical but lyrical prose, and forces conformity to a majority-based writing style, "unable to accept effective rhetorical and stylistic uses of language from alternative traditions derived from class or race" (Hockly, 2019: 84).

In exploratory learning environments, students engage practically to modify or build and then test components of a computer simulation or model. For example, open-source physics enables students to build computer-based representations of physics models, such as throwing a ball with different amounts of force to see the various results.[9] Similarly, FractionsLab provides virtual manipulatives that allow students to explore foundational fractions concepts and processes (Mavrikis et al., 2022). Despite their flexibility, exploratory learning environments are not unstructured, but have set learning outcomes and intended learning processes (de Jong, 1991). However, unlike intelligent tutoring systems, exploratory learning environments accommodate open-ended tasks and focus on the process of learning as well as content knowledge (Lameras & Arnab, 2021). Critics of exploratory learning environments cite poor learning outcomes due to cognitive overload, but AI-assisted exploratory learning applications may provide automatic guidance and feedback to help learners navigate the intended learning processes, achieve the prespecified outcomes, and avoid becoming stuck in unproductive learning cul-de-sacs (Holmes et al., 2019; Fratamico et al., 2017).

8.2.1.3 Educator-Supporting AI

According to a recent survey (Bryant et al., 2020), teachers work an average of 50 hours per week, with about half of that time allocated to direct student interactions. The rest is allocated to preparation, administration, professional development, and evaluation and feedback. The report speculates that 11 of these administrative hours and two direct contact hours per week could be eliminated through the use of artificial intelligence. In fact, most student-supporting AI tools do replace some teacher functions, and thus presumably do reduce some demand on teacher time, which certainly sounds like a benefit. However, what is lost in the process is also a discussion worth having. What do teachers learn about individual students during their marking and assessment? What does the reduction of this time yield in practice? These are questions that have not yet been properly explored, much less answered.

However, there are glimmers of AI tools designed specifically to directly support teachers, for example, Graide[10] and X5GON.[11] Graide supports teachers while they are grading assignments but, unlike with automatic writing evaluation, it is the teacher who does the grading, not the AI. Meanwhile, X5GON enables teachers to identify open educational resources from across the internet to help them with their specific teaching requirements.

8.2.2 Learning about AI

Students and adult learners "learn about AI" techniques and technologies, through traditional as well as informal and non-formal learning opportunities. In traditional learning environments, AI is treated as a course, subject or part of an existing subject, and a curriculum is developed with accompanying learning outcomes and assessment frameworks. However, a review of 148 UNESCO member states in 2022 found that only 21 governments have developed curricula for AI as a mandatory and/or elective subject, while only 27 have developed AI as a component of an existing ICT or IT curriculum, suggesting that this space is still very much in development. At the primary level, students typically learn to recognize examples of AI and engage with coding; while at the secondary school level, students deal with data, coding, and the integration of AI into society. At both levels, students are expected to know the definitions and features of AI, how to apply AI to solve problems or perform tasks, and how to self-advocate if their rights are violated (Miao and Shiohira, 2022). At the tertiary level, universities internationally offer degrees, modules and short courses in a range of AI subjects, including data analytics, machine learning, neural networks, big data, and so on, culminating in anything from a course certificate to a postgraduate qualification. Meanwhile, non-formal learning opportunities[12] include a wide range of AI courses and tutorials available for students aged 8 and up (though it must be noted a majority require Internet access and so are inaccessible to millions of young people worldwide) as well as "hackathons" or similar initiatives which can be run by government, industry or the third sector. Informal or unstructured learning opportunities include participation in groups such as school or community clubs invested in AI and related topics.

8.2.3 Preparing for AI

There is no doubt that AI is having a significant impact on the lives of the half of the world's population currently connected to the Internet. It is impossible to go online and not somehow be affected by data harvesting, targeted advertising or personalized recommendations. Even offline, AI is everywhere from setting traffic light intervals to making decisions about financial loans, credit card limits, and visa applications. One type of AI, known as "Generative Adversarial Networks" (GANs), can even be used to create fake but plausible photographs of people. It has also been predicted that half of the current human job tasks could be automated (Manyika et al., 2017; Shiohira, 2021).

There is, therefore, an urgent need for all "learning about AI" to include preparing for life with AI as an integral part of the course of study—and yet, these aspects are all too often ignored (Miao and Shiohira, 2022). Other than one excellent example that invests heavily in understanding the role of AI in everyday life (the MIT "Middle School AI Ethics Curriculum"), most of the courses just mentioned typically invest almost exclusively in the technological dimension of AI, learning what AI is, how it works, and its various capabilities. Few curricula pay significant attention to the human dimension of AI, for example, the positive as well as negative aspects of its integration into everyday life. Ethics, where they are addressed, are primarily based on data challenges, with little reflection on social effects, environmental impact, or the protection of human rights.

However, the latest version of the EU's DigComp Digital Competency Framework (2.2) does specifically look at the impact of AI on humans and the competencies that all citizens should have to enable them to deal with the growing issues, with a focus on misinformation and disinformation in social media and news sites, the exploitation of personal data, data protection, privacy and AI ethics. The Council of Europe is also investigating the impact of AI and education on human rights, democracy and the rule of law (due 2022). In addition, the EU established an expert group[13] that aimed to apply the EU's Ethics Guidelines for Trustworthy AI to education and training. These Guidelines focus on issues such as respect for human autonomy, prevention of harm, fairness, and explicability (European Commission, 2019). However, while these European initiatives are important, they are not well-known. Nonetheless, everyone, from school-aged children to the adult population, requires opportunities to gain the AI knowledge, skills and attitudes recommended by DigComp 2.2, and to become familiar with the issues identified by the EU's expert group.

8.3 Ethics of AI&ED

Readers will have already noticed a number of ethical challenges to the application and teaching of AI in education, such as whether the pedagogical approaches used by a majority of AI are sound, whether the AI applied is effective at improving learning outcomes, and whether sufficient attention is paid to "preparing for AI", the fundamental education needed by everyone to successfully navigate life in an AI world. This section presents a few additional areas in which current practices in AI&ED may be less than ethically robust.

8.3.1 AI&ED and Human Rights

Human rights are universal freedoms and protections that all people are entitled to, regardless of origin, race, gender, ethnicity, or ability. Examples of human rights include the right to life, freedom, and security and the right to a fair trial (UDHR: UN, 1948; ECHR: Council of Europe, 1953). The United Nations Convention on the Rights of the Child (UNCRC: UN, 1989) further details the rights of children, to include, among many others, the right to education, protection from economic exploitation, and privacy.

AI is often declared an instrument to ensure access to quality education, and has been proposed as a "solution" to both the global teacher shortage and the scarcity of teachers in high-risk environments like conflict areas, refugee camps, and remote rural areas.[14] However, AI cannot replace human teachers (Kolchenko, 2018). These contradictory arguments reveal one of two disquieting truths. Either the intention *is* to create AI that replaces teachers, and test this on our most vulnerable populations; or we are content to accept "good enough" for the world's most marginalized and disadvantaged learners by providing technology as a substitute for human teachers.

Another human right is the right to effectively contest decisions, and for decisions with a significant impact on an individual's life not to be made solely by automated processing. The decisions involved in AI programs such as classifying learners by ability certainly have a significant impact on a student's life, and predictive or summative uses of AI such as the now-infamous and disastrous use of algorithms to predict final examination grades in the UK are clearly problematic (Quinn, 2020). The implications are that AI must always be subjected to human oversight, and the final responsibility for decisions made should be held by people. Additionally, avenues of redress or complaint must be defined in the AI&ED space. Due to a lack of transparency around how decisions are made and a conflation of roles between teachers and some AI products, complaints, queries, or other concerns about outcomes remain unresolved.

8.3.2 The Effectiveness of AI in Education

This chapter has mentioned a small number of the AI tools currently in use in education, for all of which there is limited evidence of their effectiveness. And while some metanalyses of "personalized learning" tools show moderate content learning gains (e.g., Zheng et al., 2021), they are based on a small number of studies conducted across a wide range of contexts and technologies, at times sponsored by the companies who developed the technology in question. One unintentional but revealing statistic is the tiny fraction of relevant studies that meet the rigor criteria for a metanalysis. For example, an initial search by Major et al. (2021) returned 198 potential studies after title screening. However, only fifteen met the criteria (appropriate research design, validity, and reliability). Another challenge is the amount of AI research funded by AI companies. An investigation into tenure-track academics at four universities found that over half had received funding from technology companies (Abdalla & Abdalla, 2021).

For the last 50 years, education research has emphasized the importance of learner agency and learner-centric approaches to teaching and learning (Williams, 2017; Hildebrand, 2018). However, there is little evidence of learner-centric approaches in AI in education, despite the frequent references to so-called "personalized-learning". In fact, learners using AI tools may have less control over their learning, certainly have less control over their data contributions to the education system, and may have less ownership of their own learning outcomes than they would be using traditional paper-based learning methods (Lupton & Williamson, 2017).

At the same time, most student-supporting AI tools adopt a behaviorist or instructional approach to teaching and learning that involves direct instruction or "spoon feeding" information. This type of learning prioritizes remembering over thinking, facts over critical engagement, and undermines what is known today about robust learning as well *as* some of the most cited "transversal" or "soft" skills required for life and work in the 21st century, sometimes abbreviated to the "4Cs": Creativity, Collaboration, Communication, and Critical Thinking.[15] And in so doing, these AI applications can also disempower educators, turning them into mere technology facilitators. It is also unclear whether AI could ever provide the type of time-sensitive responsive education that considers not just academic needs but socio-emotional context, personal interests, and the interpersonal dynamics of teaching and learning. It is important to recognize the amazing skills that human educators bring to the classroom, which no AI tool can replicate.

While the link between AI and personalized learning is often overstated, a link between AI and competency-based education (CBE) is often understated. CBE is a model of education increasingly making its way from the Technical and Vocational Education and Training (TVET) sector into higher education and primary and secondary curriculum design, and in fact CBE is now the dominant form of education globally (Tan et al., 2018). CBE seeks a "fixed learning, flexible time" approach, and requires students to demonstrate the application of knowledge, skills, and values gained during programs to applicable contexts through assessment. In TVET, the assessment criteria are closely linked to industry standards, either through the co-creation of the curriculum and learning outcomes or through the development of criteria based on industry research (Keevy et al., 2021; Johnstone & Leasure, 2015). Whether industry standards should be similarly used in the education of children, which is increasingly happening, is a contentious issue that warrants much more debate.

8.3.3 Personalized Learning

The idea of giving each individual student exactly what they need when they need it is appealing. However, partly because "personalisation" has emerged from the marketing industry and Silicon Valley, there are questions around the extent to which AI can actually achieve personalization and whether it is as good as it might at first appear (Watters, 2021). The first confounding factor is that learning and education are primarily social activities, while the pedagogy adopted by most AI applications is individual and even isolated. The second point is that, even if personal, AI-assisted educational tools typically only provide learners with their own individual pathway through a predefined set of materials, while leading to the same fixed outcomes as everyone else (Holmes et al., 2019, 2022).

The third point is that while a teacher can frame learning for individual students based on their shared experiences and knowledge of the student, AI tools can only provide content based on a common cluster. In other words, AI will provide exactly what the learner needs—as long as exactly what they need is aligned to the common or average needs of other learners deemed similar by whatever parameters are built into the algorithm. In any case, the vast majority of these tools ultimately undermine student agency rather than contribute to it. The student has no choice but to do what the AI requires, meaning that there's no opportunity for them to develop self-regulation skills or to self-actualize in the classroom.

8.3.4 Data Ownership

Education has always been in the business of collecting and analyzing student data, generally with no more than a consent inferred from enrolment. What data is collected and how it is used is not always a transparent process even before AI gets involved, and very little control over their data is granted to students. In fact, databases of student examination data have been used to develop some automated writing evaluation systems (e.g., Letrus[16]), likely unbeknownst to and certainly of no direct benefit to those who have already completed their examinations.

What distinguishes the use of AI in classrooms is scale. Using an AI platform, a single student can generate more than 5 million digital traces in a single day (Ferreira, 2012). This can include both intentionally generated data, such as responses to questions on a platform, and unintentionally generated data, such as facial expression, number of clicks, and seconds per page. Digital traces are one type of data exhaust, or data generated as a by-product of people's online engagements (Digital Element, 2018), the type of data most open to exploitation or resale by companies because users often don't even know they are generating it. This sort of "liquid surveillance" (Bauman and Lyon, 2013) or "surveillance capitalism" (Zuboff, 2019) have only recently begun to be challenged by, for example, the EU General Data Protection Regulation and the US Federal Trade Commission (FTC). The FTC recently announced it would closely monitor online education companies to ensure that children's rights to online privacy are not violated, important given that digital education is dominated by companies operating on corporate surveillance business models (FTC, 2022).

In education, the academic field known as Learning Analytics seeks to use education data to better understand the learning process and improve learning outcomes and environments (du Boulay et al., 2018), as well as to create new AI products for education. However, a critical question educators and education researchers must ask themselves is the same question currently being asked of corporates: To what extent can good intentions for outcomes justify the intentional violation of individual privacy? If we hold such high standards for ethical research, particularly with children, why should students and their parents not have the right to informed consent before this data is used for anything other than their individual report cards?

In higher education, the potential for exploitation is just as great. AI technologies have enabled everything from location-based tracking to engagement determinations based on facial expressions. During the 2020 Virtual Conference on AI in Education and Training (Shiohira and Keevy, 2020), one institution proudly proclaimed that they used AI to track everything from what meals students ate to how long they spent in their dorm rooms. The institution aimed to improve services, a laudable intention, but the methods eliminated any semblance of privacy students may have had. The idea of a "smart campus" in which all interactions are online, recorded, and used for decision-making seems as inevitable as it is disquieting (Stokel-Walker, 2020).

8.3.5 Proprietary Content and Transparency

A vast majority of AIED operating today is corporate or "social enterprise" owned. While these two types of organizations may be fundamentally different (the former prioritizing maximum profits for shareholders, the latter social change), they usually share one important common feature: Proprietary and protected intellectual property. This inevitably raises tensions between the modus operandi of the company and the need for transparency, including auditability or the ability of third parties to review, monitor and criticize algorithms, and explainability or the ability of people engaging with the algorithm to understand its determinations. As noted, transparency is tied to a fundamental human right, the right of individuals to contest decisions. As systems grapple with these sorts of fundamental questions different mechanisms are beginning to emerge. For example, China has outlawed proprietary and closed AI systems from operating in its schools (McMorrow et al., 2021).

8.4 Ethics by Design

The purpose of this chapter is to outline the current state of play of AI and Education, and to raise the ethical and humanistic challenges which at times are overlooked in the enthusiasm for a new approach. However, this does not mean we don't think the ethical and pedagogically sound application of AI to education is impossible. This section outlines some key recommendations to help ensure that going forward AI&ED is ethical and effective.

8.4.1 Don't Ignore "Preparing for AI"

Learning about the impact of AI in society and every day should receive proper weight and attention, rather than being considered an add-on to the technical skills required to develop AI. In fact, in K-12 the ethics and social impact of AI are allocated fewer hours than either the foundations of AI (data literacy, coding, algorithms) or developing AI (Miao and Shiohira, 2022). One way of addressing this is by ensuring that AI curricula and courses focus on both the human and technological dimensions of AI, intertwined throughout. For example, when learning about AI-assisted facial recognition students should be exposed both to how facial recognition systems work and what their potential impact is on society.

8.4.2 Innovate Around Data Privacy

The European Commission has identified AI systems that are used for student assessment, to deliver so-called personalized education, to perform evaluations, or to potentially impact cognitive or emotional development as "high risk", emphasizing the importance of privacy and data governance, transparency, human oversight, accuracy and security (European Commission, 2021). Even those tools that do not fit this description are often using data for purposes that may include comparison to stereotypes or average profiles (Chrysafiadi & Virvou, 2013), and anyone with a basic understanding of statistics (which certainly should include AI developers) can tell immediately how flawed and dangerous that approach can be. Even the best statistical model is open to some possibility of type 1 error (in layman's terms drawing the wrong conclusion from the evidence). The algorithms that underpin AI are also subject to these sorts of mathematical limitations, and this approach can lead to discrimination, particularly in underrepresented populations (Sapiezynski et al., 2019).

All is not lost, however, and ensuring that ethical principles are embedded by design, particularly transparency and human oversight might mitigate the risk. While society and governments seem to be a long way from developing the type of oversight agencies that could ensure the safety and reliability of AIED, researchers are beginning to pay attention (e.g., Miao et al. 2021, Holmes & Porayska-Pomsta, 2022) and there is at least one international commercially backed association, EdSafe AI,[17] invested in guiding institutions, individuals and governments how to implement accountable, fair and ethical AI in education.

The second good practice is to prioritize human oversight and promote teacher agency. AI must be a tool of the teacher and not the other way around. Teachers must be given opportunities to train in the use of AI technologies for teaching and learning, both in initial teacher education and in-service training, and should have ultimate decision-making authority on which AI is used and how it is integrated into their classrooms. Teachers are the fail-safe that will catch the errors AI makes.

A final point is that data must be collected and used ethically. In 2021, the OECD published a series of ethical principles for data in government (OECD, 2021a), but they universally apply. Paraphrased, they are:

- Act with integrity: Do not access, share, or use data for personal profit or goals that do not serve the public interest.
- Ensure trustworthy data access, sharing, and use.
- Incorporate data ethics into planning, funding, and contracts related to data and its management.
- Monitor and retain control over data inputs. Human oversight must always be preserved.
- Ensure that there is a legitimate reason for collecting and using data. being specific about the purpose.
- Place the needs of users (i.e., teachers and learners) at the center of data activities.
- Ensure data is representative and fit for purpose.
- Collect only the minimum amount of data necessary for the defined purpose.
- Define boundaries for data collection, access, sharing, and use.
- Be transparent about what data is collected, when and how it is collected, and for what purpose.
- Ensure data literacy among the (users) so that they may understand the implications of data use.
- Make data and source code open, to support socio-economic benefits, foster citizen engagement and ensure transparency, accountability, and public scrutiny of decisions and outcomes.
- Ensure no personally identifiable information is made public, but recognize that anonymized data can be de-anonymized.
- Broaden human control over their data, including the right to withdraw consent for its use.

This last point in particular links to the principles of self-sovereign identity, a growing movement toward ensuring that the creators of data are the controllers of that data. For example, advocates have recently challenged universities' control over the qualifications earned and paid for by individuals (Dale-Jones and Keevy, 2021), with some innovative solutions, such as DigiLocker in India, being developed (Molokwane & Shiohira, in press). The developers and managers of AIED tools should be equally concerned with the ownership of the data they are collecting and exploiting, and recognize that data does not, as some seem to believe, belong to the developer of the system that collected it, but rather to the individual who generated it.

8.4.3 Facilitate Robust Research

Teaching is fundamentally a research-based science, and when it comes to the use of AI in the classroom the fundamentals do not shift. If an AI application does not have *sufficient independent evidence of its efficacy*, ideally through independent research undertaken by qualified personnel using experimental or robust quasi-experimental designs, it should not be integrated into schools or other educational settings. Governments, businesses and social enterprises invested in AIED should make the additional investment to support independent research from trusted education research institutions. While a few have done so, mostly in the USA, most have not, and few robust large-scale studies are available (Bryant et al., 2020).

However, process and outcome evaluations are as necessary as impact evaluations. An AI product may be effective at, for example, improving learner outcomes in mathematics, but under what conditions, with what additional supports, and with what trade-offs? The unforeseen consequences of AI implementation need investigation as much as the learning outcomes do (Holmes et al., 2021). The obvious effects to be investigated center on students; for example, the long-term effects of learner classification on learners of different ability levels, or the effects of AI use on transversal skills such as communication or collaboration—but there are likely other effects on teacher quality, motivation, and engagement. AI tools may potentially affect even the system level, for example, funding decisions and allocation or curriculum design.

8.4.4 Create AI Programs That Support Innovative Pedagogies

Much has been written about "21st Century Skills", the definition of which shifts as rapidly as does technology. The "knowledge economy" is giving way to the "innovation economy", an age characterized by rapid innovation, shifting technologies, lifelong learning, and the need for meta-skills such as "learning to learn" and the application of skills in new contexts. It is unlikely that traditional rote learning as implemented in most current AIED applications (despite their claims to the contrary) can address these needs. While mathematics and language are a foundation for advanced skills such as communication and critical thinking, the role of memorization and drilling is limited in an education system built for the innovation economy. More robust pedagogies focus on socio-emotional learning, self-actualization, collaboration, and critical thinking.

While few current AI-assisted applications support these pedagogies, some individuals and organizations have looked at how AI might drive new pedagogical approaches better suited to life and work in the innovation age. Some existing AI curricula do attempt to leverage pedagogical theories such as constructivism (Piaget, 1972) and/or constructionism (Papert and Harel, 1991), computational thinking, and design thinking (Razzouk and Shute, 2012), mainly in the form of project-based learning. In some examples, students engage in identifying a social problem or market need and developing an AI-assisted solution, often through the construction of an app. AI concepts are introduced along the way. A few curricula engaging in these sorts of methods are government-led, but far more are industry-created, including offerings from IBM, Intel and Microsoft, or driven by the civil society sector, for example, the offerings of Technovation Girls[18] or the International Society for Technology in Education.[19]

Exploratory learning environments, in play-based learning, activity-based learning, and collaborative group work, offer another avenue for AI to be used to meaningfully enhance pedagogy. In these environments, AI might be used to help students achieve the intended learning outcomes, offering guidance and feedback based on open-ended activities. In this case, the AI essentially functions similarly to a non-player character in a video game, an adaptive agent that points the way toward challenges and offers support when the student is not progressing toward the activity goals. In this context, AI offers benefits such as immediate and adaptive feedback, while open-ended activities mean that the learning process as well as content outcomes are supported. The variability in the program or simulation can give learners AI-supported choices about what and how to engage, preserving more of their autonomy.

8.5 Concluding Comments

As this chapter has discussed, the connections between AI and education (AIED) are growing rapidly. On the one hand, we have the teaching of AI, what has been called "AI literacy", which in turn comprises its technological dimension (how it works and how to create it) and its human dimension (its impact on all people, society and the planet). We have argued that, in any serious attempt to teach about AI, the technological and human dimensions of AI should be given broadly equal emphasis and should be intertwined throughout, rather than a token discussion of ethics being tagged on at the end of a course. We have also noted that, so far, this rarely happens. In fact, exploring the human impact should always have been integral to the teaching of technology. However, with AI, we are talking about a technology with an impact that is more hidden, potentially more powerful and impactful on humans, and at a massively greater scale than anything before. Given the increasingly integral role that AI is playing in everyday life, we argue that the teaching of AI's human and technological dimensions to all citizens, young and old, in developed and developing countries alike, is now critical.

On the other hand, we have taught with AI-assisted applications, in order to support students, educators, and institutions (AIED). Again, as we have noted, many of the existing AI tools that have been developed for use in classrooms to support the teaching and learning of other subjects, raise important challenges that are only now beginning to be considered. For example, to date, few of the available applications have been independently or robustly evaluated, and those have only demonstrated their efficacy in limited contexts and for narrow learning outcomes. Second, most of the existing AI-assisted educational technologies perpetuate poor pedagogic practices, with a tendency to embody an outmoded behaviorist pedagogy of drill-and-practice, albeit sometimes with a few extras.

These applications of AI ultimately undermine both teacher and student agency, as choices are limited and machine-made decisions on learning pathways and content difficult to understand, let alone challenge. Third, the most easily available AIED tools have been developed by commercial organizations, which raises issues of both the commercialization of education and, at times, questionable business practices without clear consent or boundaries. Some business models even depend on capturing, analyzing, and exploiting or selling the data generated by thousands of students whose schools are paying for their access to the platform, usually without genuinely informed consent. Apart from the impact on data privacy, security and ownership, building education's dependence on commercial offerings can be risky. What happens when the company chooses to stop making a particular proprietary tool available?

We could continue to identify multiple other ways in which the application of AI in education should be considered carefully. However, to be clear, we are not arguing that AI has no place in education, but rather that we need to identify the *right kind* of AI and apply it in the *right way* (in particular, with an eye on human rights) if we are to leverage for the common good what AI technologies make possible. Robust debate over the content of AI curricula and the role of AI-assisted applications in classrooms is necessary. On the curriculum side, stakeholders should be consulted to ensure human, social and economic needs are all met, and that the technological and humanistic dimensions are equally valued. In classrooms, rather than starting from the technologies, we should start with the genuine education grand challenges, which educators are usually best placed to identify. Which of these is AI suited to address, and which are social problems that require social solutions? What exchanges and compromises will be made in the implementation of AI-assisted technologies?

Artificial Intelligence, currently in the guise of data-hungry machine learning, is the most powerful technology of our day. It has the potential to inform new approaches to education and new pedagogies, but can also perpetuate or even exacerbate current limitations. Unfortunately, most of the uses of AI in education today do the latter. Hopefully, this chapter will encourage more scholars and educators to consider both the potential and the challenges of AI, to think more seriously about how the benefits of AI can be safely, ethically, and effectively leveraged in classrooms, and ultimately to help ensure that AI&ED is implemented in ways that are genuinely and demonstrably beneficial for the whole of humanity.

Notes

1 For example, see IBM SkillsBuild at https://skillsbuild.org
2 See https://www.cedefop.europa.eu/en/tools/skills-online-vacancies
3 See https://psetcloud.org.za
4 See https://new.assistments.org

5 See https://byjus.com/global
6 See https://futureskillsprime.in
7 See https://www.oppimisanalytiikka.fi/ville
8 See https://www.vulcan-edu.com/en/home/
9 See https://www.compadre.org/osp
10 See https://www.graide.co.uk
11 See https://www.x5gon.org
12 Non-formal learning opportunities are structured learning programmes delivered by trained personnel that take place outside of the traditional classroom or the formal education system.
13 See https://www.pubaffairsbruxelles.eu/education-commission-launches-expert-group-to-develop-ethical-guidelines-on-artificial-intelligence-and-data-for-educators-eu-commission-press
14 For example, see "Can't Wait to Learn": https://www.warchildholland.org/news/artificial-intelligence-learning/
15 The "4Cs" terminology was coined by the Partnership for 21st Century Skills. https://www.battelleforkids.org/networks/p21
16 See https://www.letrus.com
17 See https://www.edsafeai.org
18 See https://technovationchallenge.org
19 See https://www.iste.org

References

Abdalla, M., & Abdalla, M. (2021). The Grey Hoodie Project: Big Tobacco, Big Tech, and the Threat on Academic Integrity. *AIES '21: Proceedings of the 2021 AAAI/ACM Conference on AI, Ethics, and Society July 2021*, 287–297. https://doi.org/10.1145/3461702.3462563

Bauman, Z., & Lyon, D. (2013). *Liquid surveillance: A conversation*. Polity Press. ISBN: 978-0-745-66282-4

Bryant, J., Heitz, C., Sanghvi, S., & Wagle, D. (2020). *Artificial intelligence in education: How will it impact K-12 teachers*. McKinsey Global Institute. https://www.mckinsey.com/industries/education/our-insights/how-artificial-intelligence-will-impact-k-12-teachers

Chrysafiadi, K., & Virvou, M. (2013). Student modeling approaches: A literature review for the last decade. *Expert Systems with Applications*, 40(11), 4715–4729.

Conchas, G. (2008). Cited in Teachers College Columbia University. Education as a Tool for Breaking the Cycles of Poverty. https://www.tc.columbia.edu/articles/2008/november/education-as-a-tool-for-breaking-the-cycles-of-poverty

Dale-Jones, B., & Keevy, J. (2021). Digital credentials: Discussions on fluency, data privacy and the recognition of learning in higher education beyond COVID-19. In M. Venter, and S. Hattingh (Eds.), *Learning for a better future: Perspectives on higher education, cities, business & civil society*. AOSIS Publishing.

Davies, H. C., Eynon, R., & Salveson, C. (2020). The mobilisation of AI in education: A bourdieusean field analysis. *Sociology*, 55(3), 539–560. https://doi.org/10.1177/0038038520967888

De Jong, T. (1991). Learning and instruction with computer simulations. *Education and Computing*, 6(3–4), 217–229.

Deakin University. (2018). Meet genie, the new smartphone app for deakin students. *Deakin Life*. https://blogs.deakin.edu.au/deakinlife/2018/07/13/meet-genie-the-new-smartphone-app-for-deakin-students/

Digital Element. (2018). *Digital data exhaust report 2018.* LBMA. https://www.digitalelement.com/wp-content/uploads/2018/10/Digital-Data-Exhaust-Survey-Report-2018.pdf

du Boulay, B., Poulovassilis, A., Holmes, W., & Mavrikis, M. (2018). What does the research say about how artificial intelligence and big data can close the achievement gap? In R. Luckin (Ed.), *Enhancing learning and teaching with technology* (pp. 256–285). Institute of Education Press.

European Commission. (2021). Proposal for a regulation of the european parliament and of the council laying down harmonised rules on artificial intelligence (artificial intelligence act) and amending certain union legislative acts. https://eur-lex.europa.eu/legal-content/EN/TXT/HTML/?uri=CELEX:52021PC0206&from=EN

European Commission. Directorate General for Communications Networks, Content and Technology. & High Level Expert Group on Artificial Intelligence. (2019). *Ethics guidelines for trustworthy AI.* Publications Office. https://data.europa.eu/doi/10.2759/346720

Feathers, T. (2019). Flawed algorithms are grading millions of students' essays. *Vice.* https://www.vice.com/en_us/article/pa7dj9/flawed-algorithms-are-grading-millions-of-students-essays

Ferreira, J. (2012). Video: CEO of Knewton, an ITS company, talking at the Office of Ed Tech at the White House Education Datapalooza Event. https://www.youtube.com/watch?v=GeajedxpWJA

Fratamico, L., Conati, C., Kardan, S. et al. (2017). Applying a framework for student modeling in exploratory learning environments: Comparing data representation granularity to handle environment complexity. *International Journal of Artificial Intelligence in Education, 27,* 320–352. https://doi.org/10.1007/s40593-016-0131-y

FTC. (2022). *FTC to Crack Down on Companies that Illegally Surveil Children Learning Online* [Press release]. https://www.ftc.gov/news-events/news/press-releases/2022/05/ftc-crack-down-companies-illegally-surveil-children-learning-online (Accessed 30 May 2022).

Hildebrand, D. (2018). Experience is not the whole story: The integral role of the situation in Dewey's democracy and education. *Journal of Philosophy of Education, 52*(2), 287–300.

Hockly, N. (2019). Automated writing evaluation. *ELT Journal 73,* 82–88. https://doi.org/10.1093/elt/ccy044

Holmes, W., Bialik, M., & Fadel, C. (2019). *Artificial intelligence in education. Promises and implications for teaching and learning.* Boston, MA: Center for Curriculum Redesign. https://drive.google.com/file/d/1lmzlbhKvYyRB6J0USCndqXitmVgsfTbI/view

Holmes, W., Persson, J., Chounta, I-A., Wasson, B. & Dimitrova, V., (2022). *Artificial intelligence and education. A critical view through the lens of human rights, democracy, and the rule of law.* Strasbourg, France: The Council of Europe.

Holmes, W. & Porayska-Pomsta, K. (2022). *The ethics of artificial intelligence in education. Practices, challenges, and debates.* New York: Routledge.

Jobin, A., Ienca, M. & Vayena, E. (2019). The global landscape of AI ethics guidelines. *Nature Machine Intelligence, 1,* 389–399.

Johnstone, S., & Leasure, D. (2015). How competency-based education can fulfill the promise of educational technology. *Lecture Notes in Computer Science, 9177*(3), 127–136. Springer, 2015.

Keevy, J., Shiohira, K., Matlala, R., & Molokwane, P. (2021). *New qualifications and competencies for future-oriented TVET: TVET delivery, Providing innovative solutions Volume 3*. UNEVOC.

Kolchenko, V. (2018). Can modern AI replace teachers? Not so fast! Artificial intelligence and adaptive learning: Personalized education in the AI age. *HAPS Educator, 22*(3), 249–252. doi:https://doi.org/10.21692/haps.2018.032

Lameras, P., & Arnab, S. (2021). Power to the teachers: An exploratory review on artificial intelligence in education. *Information, 13*(1), 14.

Lupton, D., & Williamson, B. (2017). The datafied child: The dataveillance of children and implications for their rights. *New Media & Society, 19*(5), 780–794. https://doi.org/10.1177/1461444816686328

Major, L., Francis, G., &Tsapali, M. (2021). The effectiveness of technology-supported personalised learning in low- and middle income countries: A meta-analysis. *British Journal of Educational Technology*. https://doi.org/10.1111/bjet.13116

Manyika, J., Lund, S., Chui, M., et.al. (2017). *Jobs lost, jobs gained: Workforce transitions in a time of automation*. McKinsey Global Institute.

Mavrikis, M., Rummel, N., Wiedmann, M., Loibl, K., & Holmes, W. (2022). *Combining exploratory learning with structured practice educational technologies to foster both conceptual and procedural fractions knowledge*. Educational Technology Research and Development. https://doi.org/10.1007/s11423-022-10104-0

McMorrow, R., Yu, S., Kinder, T., & Hale, T. (2021, July 26). China's education sector crackdown hits foreign investors. *Financial Times*. https://www.ft.com/content/dfae3282-e14e-4fea-aa5f-c2e914444fb8

Miao, F., Holmes, W., Huang, R., & Zhang, H. (2021). *AI and education: A guidance for policymakers*. UNESCO Publishing.

Miao, F., & Shiohira, K. (2022). *K-12 AI curricula. A mapping of government-endorsed AI curricula*. UNESCO. https://unesdoc.unesco.org/ark:/48223/pf0000380602

Molokwane, P., & Shiohira, K. (in press). *The african continental qualification framework: Innovation and technology training module*. Addis Ababa: African Union.

OECD. (2021a). *Good practice principles for data governance in the public sector*. Paris: OECD. https://www.oecd.org/gov/digital-government/good-practice-principles-for-data-ethics-in-the-public-sector.pdf

OECD. (2021b). *OECD digital education outlook 2021: Pushing the frontiers with artificial intelligence, blockchain and robots*. OECD. https://doi.org/10.1787/589b283f-en

Papert, S., & Harel, I. (1991). *Constructionism*. Ablex Publishing Corporation.

Piaget, J. (1972). *The principles of genetic epistemology*. Routledge & Kegan Paul.

Quinn, B. (2020). UK exams debacle: How did this year's results end up in chaos? *The Guardian*. http://www.theguardian.com/education/2020/aug/17/uk-exams-debacle-how-did-results-end-up-chaos

Razzouk, R., & Shute, V. (2012). What is design thinking and why is it important?. *Review of Educational Research, 82*(3), 330–348.

Sapiezynski, P., Ghosh, A., Kaplan, L., Mislove, A., & Rieke, A. (2019). Algorithms that "Don't See Color": Comparing Biases in Lookalike and Special Ad Audiences. *Proceedings of the 2022 AAAI/ACM Conference on AI, Ethics, and Society*. https://doi.org/10.1145/3514094.3534135

Seldon, A., & Abidoye, O. (2018). *The fourth education revolution: Will artificial intelligence liberate or infantilise humanity?* The University of Buckingham Press.

Shiohira, K. (2021). *Understanding the impact of artificial intelligence on skills development*. UNESCO-UNEVOC International Centre for Technical and Vocational Education and Training. https://unevoc.unesco.org/pub/understanding_the_impact_of_ai_on_skills_development.pdf

Shiohira, K., & Keevy, J. (2020). *Virtual conference on artificial intelligence in education and training: Virtual conference report*. UNESCO-UNEVOC TVeT Forum, 11 to 15 November 2019. https://unevoc.unesco.org/home/UNEVOC+Publications/lang=en/akt=detail/qs=6295

Stokel-Walker, C. (2020). Universities are using surveillance software to spy on students. *Wired UK*. https://www.wired.co.uk/article/university-covid-learning-student-monitoring

Tan, K., Chong, M. C., Subramaniam, P., & Wong, L. P. (2018). The effectiveness of outcome based education on the competencies of nursing students: A systematic review. *Nurse Education Today*, *64*, 180–189.

UNESCO. (2021). Recommendation on the Ethics of Artificial Intelligence. https://unesdoc.unesco.org/ark:/48223/pf0000381137

UNESCO. (2022). *UNESCO international literacy prizes 2021: Inclusive distance and digital literacy learning, trend analysis of nominated applications*. Paris: UNESCO. Available at: https://unesdoc.unesco.org/ark:/48223/pf0000380601/PDF/380601eng.pdf.multi (Accessed 16 May 2022).

UNICEF. (2021). Policy guidance on AI for children. https://www.unicef.org/globalinsight/media/2356/file/UNICEF-Global-Insight-policy-guidance-AI-children-2.0-2021.pdf.pdf

Watters, A. (2021). *Teaching machines*. Boston, MA: The MIT Press.

Williams, M. (2017). John Dewey in the 21st Century. *Journal of Inquiry & Action in Education*, *9*(1). 91–102. https://files.eric.ed.gov/fulltext/EJ1158258.pdf

Zhang, D., Maslej, N., Brynjolfsson, E., et al. (2022). *The AI index 2022 annual report*. Stanford, CA: The Stanford Institute for Human-Centered AI. https://hai-annual-report.stanford.edu

Zheng, L., Niu, J., Zhong, L., & Gyasi, J. (2021). The effectiveness of artificial intelligence on learning achievement and learning perception: A meta-analysis. *Interactive Learning Environments*. Online. https://doi.org/10.1080/10494820.2021.2015693

Zuboff, S. (2019). *The age of surveillance capitalism: The fight for a human future at the new frontier of power*. London: Profile Books.

9
EXTENDING BIOLOGICAL INTELLIGENCE

The Imperative of Thinking Outside Our Brains in a World of Artificial Intelligence

Annie Murphy Paul

The future of learning and work will be shaped by advances in artificial intelligence. That much appears certain. But what role will be played by *natural* intelligence—the capacities of our biological brains? Surely the most impressive results in both schools and workplaces will come about through a partnership of digital smarts and human smarts. For such a partnership to succeed, however, we must understand what is distinctive and unique about the human brain's biological intelligence. Moreover, we need to know how to cultivate its particular strengths and compensate for its specific weaknesses—traits that emerged not from the deliberate designs of a computer scientist, but from the urgent imperatives of evolution.

It is the contention of this chapter that human intelligence is distinctive in that it is *embodied, situated,* and *socially distributed*. Understanding its nature thus requires us to range across a number of related disciplines. Embodied cognition explores the role of the body in our thinking; for example, how making hand gestures increases the fluency of speech and deepens our understanding of abstract concepts. Situated cognition examines the influence of place on our thinking: for instance, how environmental cues that convey a sense of belonging enhance our performance in that space. Socially distributed cognition probes the effects of thinking with others—such as how people working in groups can coordinate their individual areas of expertise ("transactive memory"), and how groups can work together to produce results that exceed their members' individual contributions ("collective intelligence").

The embodied, situated, and socially distributed aspects of biological intelligence render it very different from its artificial cousin. A reminder of this fact is necessary because we have so often compared our human intelligence to computer intelligence. Since the advent of the cognitive revolution some seven decades ago, the brain-as-computer metaphor has come to pervade our language and our thinking. In order for our brains to team up effectively with computers, we have to stop thinking of them as being *like* computers. A new metaphor is needed. One possibility is the brain as a magpie.

Magpies—members of the corvid family, including crows, jays, and ravens—are well known for making their nests out of whatever is available in the environment. The birds have been observed using an astonishing array of materials: not only twigs, string, and moss, but also dental floss, chopsticks, shoelaces, eyeglass frames, and croquet wickets. During the American Dust Bowl of the 1930s, which eliminated vegetation from huge swaths of the West, magpies' corvid cousins made nests out of barbed wire.

The magpie provides a felicitous analogy for the way the mind works. Our brains, it might be said, are like magpies, fashioning their finished products from the materials around them, weaving the bits and pieces they find into their trains of thought. Set beside the brain-as-computer metaphor, it's apparent that the brain as magpie is a very different kind of analogy, with very different implications for how mental processes operate.

For one thing, thought happens not only inside the skull but out in the world, too; it's an act of continuous assembly and reassembly that draws on resources external to the brain. For another, the kinds of materials available to "think with" affect the nature and quality of the thought that can be produced. Finally, the capacity to think well is not a fixed property of the individual but rather a shifting state that is dependent on access to extra-neural resources and the knowledge of how to use them.

This is, admittedly, a radically new way of thinking about thinking. It may not feel easy or natural to adopt. But a growing mass of evidence generated within several scientific disciplines suggests that it's a much more accurate rendering of how human cognition actually works.

The Extended Mind

To optimize the pairing of artificial and natural intelligence, we need more than a metaphor. Fortunately, a theoretical framework that can accommodate and organize the distinctive features of human intelligence is available: The theory of the extended mind, first introduced in the journal *Analysis* in 1998 (Clark and Chalmers, 1998). Philosophers Andy Clark and David Chalmers opened their article with a deceptively simple question: "Where does the mind stop and the rest of the world begin"? Clark and Chalmers noted that we have traditionally assumed that the mind is contained within the head—but, they argued, "there is nothing sacred about skull and skin". Elements of the world outside may effectively act as mental "extensions", allowing us to think in ways our brains could not manage on their own.

Clark and Chalmers initially focused their analysis on the way technology can extend the mind—a proposal that quickly made the leap from risibly preposterous to self-evidently obvious, once their readers acquired smartphones and began offloading large chunks of their memories onto their new devices. Yet as early as that original paper, Clark hinted that other kinds of extensions were possible. "What about socially extended cognition?" he and Chalmers asked. "Could my mental states be partly constituted by the states of other thinkers? We see no reason why not". In the years that followed, Clark continued to enlarge his conception of the kinds of entities that could serve as extensions of the mind. He observed that our physical movements and gestures play "an important role in an extended neural-bodily cognitive economy"; he noted that humans are inclined to create "designer environments"—carefully appointed spaces "that alter and simplify the computational tasks which our brains must perform in order to solve complex problems".

Over the course of many more published papers and books, Clark mounted a broad and persuasive argument against what he called the "brainbound" perspective—the view that thinking happens only inside the brain—and in favor of what he called the "extended" perspective, in which the rich resources of our world can and do enter into our trains of thought. Clark's bold proposal is not the esoteric thought experiment of an ivory tower philosopher; it is a plainly practical invitation to think differently and better.

Research from many disciplines has now yielded dozens of techniques for thinking outside the brain. These include methods for sharpening our interoceptive sense, so as to use these internal signals to guide our decisions and manage our mental processes; they encompass guidelines for the use of specific types of gestures, or particular modes of physical activity, to enhance our memory and attention. This research offers instructions on using time in nature to restore our focus and increase our creativity, as well as directions for designing our learning and working spaces for greater productivity and performance. These studies describe structured forms of social interaction that allow other people's cognition to augment our own; they also supply guidance on how to offload, externalize, and dynamically interact with our thoughts.

Becoming acquainted with these techniques can be likened to acquiring a second education—one that is increasingly essential, but almost always overlooked in our focus on educating the brain. Over many years of elementary school, high school, and even college and graduate school, we're never explicitly taught to think outside the brain. Yet this instruction is available if we know where to look; our teachers are the artists, scientists, and authors who have figured out these methods for themselves, and the researchers who are, at last, making these methods the object of study.

The Limited Biological Brain

Extending the mind is necessary because of the built-in quirks and limits of the biological brain. The human brain is limited in its ability to pay attention, capacity to remember, facility with abstract concepts, and power to persist at a challenging task. Importantly, these limits apply to *everyone's* brain. It's not a matter of individual differences in intelligence, it's a matter of the biological nature and evolutionary history of the organ we all possess.

The brain *does* do a few things exquisitely well, like sensing and moving the body, navigating through space, and connecting with other humans. These activities can be managed fluently, and almost effortlessly. The same cannot be said of other important types of tasks: Accurately recalling complex information, engaging in rigorous logical reasoning, and grasping abstract or counterintuitive ideas. Here we arrive at a dilemma, one that we all share: The modern world is extraordinarily complex. Succeeding in this world thus requires focused attention, prodigious memory, sustained motivation, and proficiency with abstractions. The gap between what our biological brains are capable of, and what modern life demands, is getting larger each day.

The usual response to the cognitive challenges posed by contemporary life has been to double down on what Clark calls "brainbound" thinking. We urge ourselves and others to bear down, "just do it"—to *think harder*. But, as we often find to our frustration, the brain is made of stubborn and unyielding stuff, its vaunted plasticity notwithstanding. Confronted by its limits, we may conclude that we ourselves are simply not smart enough, or not "gritty" enough. In fact, it's the way we handle our mental shortcomings that is the problem. The smart move is not to lean ever harder on the brain, but to reach beyond it.

In order to get the most out of our biological intelligence—and to make it the best possible partner for artificial intelligence—we must skillfully employ mental extensions. To some extent, we are already thinking "outside the brain". Yet we often do it haphazardly, without much intention or skill. It's no wonder this is the case. Our efforts at education and training, as well as management and leadership, are aimed almost exclusively at promoting brainbound thinking. Beginning in elementary school, we are taught to sit still, work quietly, and think hard—a model for mental activity that will prevail during all the years that follow. The skills we develop and the techniques we are taught are those that involve using our heads: Committing information to memory, engaging in internal reasoning and deliberation, and endeavoring toward self-discipline and self-motivation.

The Intelligent Body

Meanwhile, there is no corresponding cultivation of our ability to think outside the brain—no instruction, for instance, on how to tune into the body's inner signals (a process called *interoception*). We're not trained to use bodily movements and gestures to understand highly conceptual subjects like science and mathematics, or to come up with novel and original ideas. Schools don't teach students how to restore their depleted attention with exposure to nature and the outdoors, or how to arrange their study spaces so that they extend intelligent thought. Teachers and managers don't demonstrate how abstract ideas can be turned into physical objects that can be manipulated and transformed in order to achieve insights and solve problems. Employees aren't shown how the social practices of imitation and vicarious learning can shortcut the process of acquiring expertise. Classroom groups and workplace teams aren't coached in scientifically validated methods of increasing the collective intelligence of their members. Our ability to think outside the brain has been left almost entirely uneducated and undeveloped.

This oversight is the regrettable result of what has been called our "neurocentric bias"—that is, our idealization and even fetishization of the brain—and our corresponding blind spot for all the ways cognition extends beyond the skull. (As the comedian Emo Philips has remarked: "I used to think that the brain was the most wonderful organ in my body. Then I realized who was telling me this"). Seen from another perspective, however, this near-universal neglect represents a thrilling opportunity of unrealized potential.

Until recently, science shared our culture's blind spot regarding thinking outside the brain. But this is no longer the case. Psychologists, cognitive scientists, and neuroscientists are now able to provide a clear picture of how the availability and application of extra-neural inputs shape the way we think. Even more exciting, they're able to offer practical guidelines for enhancing our thinking through the use of these outside-the-brain resources.

Such developments are unfolding against the backdrop of a much broader shift in how we view the mind. We've conventionally thought of the brain as a workhorse, driven to labor ever harder. But we might more fruitfully think of it as an orchestra conductor. Instead of doing so much in our heads, we can seek out ways to shift mental work onto the world around us and to supplement our limited neural resources with extraneural ones.

How to Extend the Brain

Mental extensions fall into four categories, the first and most obvious being our tools. Technology is designed to fulfill just this function, and we're accustomed to using our devices to both unburden the mind and augment its capacity.

There are other resources that we often overlook, for example, our bodies. The burgeoning field of embodied cognition has demonstrated that the body plays an integral role in the thought processes that we usually associate with the brain. The body is especially adept at alerting us to patterns of events and experience, patterns that are too complex to be held in the conscious mind.

When a scenario we encountered before crops up again, the body gives us a nudge: Communicating with a shiver or a sigh, a quickening of the breath, or a tensing of the muscles. Those who are attuned to such cues can use them to make more-informed decisions. A study led by a team of economists and neuroscientists in Britain, for instance, reported that financial traders who were better at detecting their heartbeats made more profitable investments and lasted longer in that notoriously volatile profession.

The body is also uniquely capable of grounding abstract concepts in the concrete terms that the brain understands best. Abstract concepts are the order of the day in physics class; conventional modes of instruction, like lectures and textbooks, often fail to convey them effectively. Some studies in the field of physics education found that students' understanding of the subject is less accurate after an introductory college physics course. What makes a difference is offering students a bodily experience of the topic they're learning about. They might encounter torque, for example, by holding an axle on which two bicycle wheels have been mounted. When the wheels are spun and the axle is tilted from horizontal to vertical, the student handling it feels the resistive force that causes objects to rotate. Such exposures produce a deeper level of comprehension, psychological research has found, leading to higher test scores, especially on more challenging theoretical questions.

Another extraneural resource available for our use is physical space. Moving mental contents out of our heads and onto the space of a sketch pad or whiteboard allows us to inspect it with our senses, a cognitive bonus that the psychologist Daniel Reisberg calls "the detachment gain". That gain was evident in a study published in 2016, in which experimenters asked seventh- and eighth-grade students to illustrate with drawings the operation of a mechanical system and a chemical system. Without any further instruction, these students sketched their way to a more accurate understanding of the systems they drew. Turning a mental representation into shapes and lines on a page helped them to elucidate more fully what they already knew while revealing with ruthless rigor what they did not yet comprehend.

Three-dimensional space offers additional opportunities for offloading mental work and enhancing the brain's powers. When we turn a problem to be solved into a physical object that we can interact with, we activate the robust spatial abilities that allow us to navigate through real-world landscapes. This suite of human strengths, honed over eons of evolution, is wasted when we sit still and think.

This holds true for a wide variety of problem types, including basic arithmetic, complex reasoning, and challenges that require creative insight. People who are permitted to manipulate concrete tokens representing elements of the problem to be solved bear less of a cognitive load and enjoy increased working memory. They learn more and are better able to transfer their learning to new situations. They are more motivated and engaged and experience less anxiety. They even arrive at correct answers more quickly.

One last resource for augmenting our minds can be found in other people's minds. We are fundamentally social creatures, oriented toward thinking with others. Problems arise when we do our thinking alone, for example, the well-documented phenomenon of confirmation bias. According to the argumentative theory of reasoning, advanced by the cognitive scientists Hugo Mercier and Dan Sperber, this bias is accentuated when we reason in solitude. Humans' evolved faculty for reasoning is not aimed at arriving at objective truth, Mercier and Sperber point out; it is aimed at defending our arguments and scrutinizing others'. Vigorous debates, engaged with an open mind, are the solution. "When people who disagree but have a common interest in finding the truth or the solution to a problem exchange arguments with each other, the best idea tends to win", they write, citing evidence from studies of students, forecasters, and jury members.

The minds of other people can also supplement our limited individual memory. Daniel Wegner, a psychologist at Harvard, named this collective remembering "transactive memory". As he explained it, "Nobody remembers everything. Instead, each of us in a couple or group remembers some things personally — and then can remember much more by knowing who else might know what we don't". A transactive memory system can effectively multiply the amount of information to which an individual has access. Organizational research has found that groups that build a strong transactive memory structure perform better than groups for which that structure is less defined. Linda Argote, a professor of organizational behavior and theory at Carnegie Mellon University, reported that results from an observational study showed that when a trauma resuscitation team developed a robust shared memory system and used it to direct tasks to the team members most qualified to take them on, their patients had shorter hospital stays (Argote, 2012).

All four of these extraneural resources—technology, the body, physical space, and social interaction—can be understood as mental extensions that allow the brain to accomplish far more than it could on its own. Evidence suggests that extensions are most powerful when they are employed in combination, and incorporated into mental routines that draw on the full range of extra-neural resources available to us.

Principles of Brain Extension

The skilled use of extensions is a proficiency that has gone largely unrecognized and uncultivated by our schools and workplaces, and it was long ignored by researchers in psychology, education, and management. But some general principles of effective extending are *now clearly discernible. Let's take up, in turn, three sets of such principles.*

Principle 1: Offloading

The first set of principles lays out some habits of mind we would do well to adopt, starting with this one: Whenever possible, we should *offload* information by moving it out of our heads and into the world. Offloading has many benefits. It relieves us of the burden of keeping a host of details "in mind", thereby freeing up mental resources for more demanding tasks, like problem-solving and idea generation. It also produces for us the "detachment gain", whereby we can inspect with our senses, and often perceive anew, an image or idea that once existed only in the imagination.

In its most straightforward form, offloading is the simple act of putting our thoughts down on paper. A habit of *continuous* offloading, through the use of a daily journal or field notebook, can extend our ability to make fresh observations and synthesize new ideas. Likewise, offloading information onto a space that's big enough for us to *physically* navigate (wall-sized outlines, oversized concept maps, multiple-monitor workstations) allows us to apply to that material our powers of spatial reasoning and spatial memory.

Externalizing information can also take a more involved form: It may entail carefully designing a task such that one part of the task is offloaded, even as another part absorbs our full attention. This was the practice adopted by law professor Monte Smith, who had his students offload the task of structuring a legal memo onto a model while they focused their efforts on understanding and articulating their newly acquired knowledge of the law. Offloading need not require written language, either. At times, offloading may be *embodied*: When we gesture, for example, we permit our hands to "hold" some of the thoughts we would otherwise have to maintain in our heads. Likewise, when we use our hands to move objects around, we offload the task of visualizing new configurations onto the world itself, where those configurations take tangible shape before our eyes.

At other times, offloading may be *social*: For example, engaging in argument allows us to distribute among human debaters the task of tallying points for and against a given proposition; constructing a transactive memory system offloads onto our colleagues the task of monitoring and remembering incoming information. Offloading also occurs in an interpersonal context when we externalize "traces" of our own thinking processes for the benefit of our teammates; in this case, we're offloading not to unburden our own minds, but to facilitate collaboration with others.

Principle Two: Making It Real

The second principle is: Whenever possible, we should endeavor to transform information into an artifact, to make data into something *real*—and then proceed to interact with it through labeling, mapping, feeling, tweaking, and showing it to others. Humans evolved to handle the concrete, not to contemplate the abstract. We extend our intelligence when we give our minds something to grab onto, such as when we turn a foreign-language vocabulary word into a gesture we can see, sense, and demonstrate to others. Vague impressions of what constitutes "excellent work" can usefully take form as a display of actual models to aspire to; dry intellectual deliberations can acquire a rooted, embodied dimension when we closely attend to, and label and track, the internal sensations that arise from the interoceptive system. Our days are now spent processing an endless stream of symbols; with a bit of ingenuity, we can find ways to turn these abstract symbols into tangible objects and sensory experiences and thereby think about them in new ways.

Principle Three: Altering Our Mental State

The third principle: Whenever possible, we should seek to productively alter *our own state* when engaging in mental labor. The limits of the brain-as-computer metaphor here become clearly visible. When fed a chunk of information, a computer processes it in the same way on each occasion—whether it's been at work for five minutes or five hours, located in a fluorescent-lit office or positioned next to a sunny window, near other computers or the only computer in the room. This is how computers operate, but the same doesn't hold for human beings. The way we're able to think about information is dramatically affected by the state we're in when we encounter it.

Effective mental extension, then, requires us to think carefully about inducing in ourselves the state that is best suited for the task at hand. We might engage in a bout of brisk exercise before sitting down to learn something new; for example, we might seek out an opportunity to engage in group synchrony and shared physical arousal (spicy food, anyone?) when we're expected to work together as a team. We might get up from our desks and get our hands and bodies moving when we're seeking to understand a spatial concept; we might plan a trip into the wilderness when we're in need of a creative boost. Deliberately altering our own state could entail taking a walk in a nearby park when our frazzled attention requires restoration or seeking out a sparring partner with whom to argue when we want to make sure our ideas are sound. Instead of heedlessly driving the brain like a machine, we'll think more intelligently when we treat it as the context-sensitive organ it is.

The second set of principles offers a higher-level view of how mental extension works, based on an understanding of what the brain evolved to do. The brain is well-adapted to sensing and moving the body, navigating through physical space, and interacting with other members of our species. On top of this basic suite of human competencies, civilization has built a vast edifice of abstraction, engaging our brains in acts of symbolic processing and conceptual cognition that don't come nearly as naturally. These abstractions have, of course, allowed us to exponentially expand our powers—but now, paradoxically, further progress may depend on running this process in reverse. In order to succeed at the increasingly complex thinking demanded by modern life, we will find ourselves needing to translate abstractions *back into* the corporeal, spatial, and social forms from which they sprang.

Principle Four: Re-embody

We can begin to understand what this means by taking up the fourth principle: Whenever possible, we should take measures to *re-embody* the information we think about. The pursuit of knowledge has frequently sought to disengage thinking from the body, to elevate ideas to a cerebral sphere separate from our grubby animal anatomy. Research on the extended mind counsels the opposite approach: We should be seeking to draw the body back into the thinking process. That may take the form of allowing our choices to be influenced by our interoceptive signals. It might take the form of enacting, with bodily movements, the academic concepts that have become abstracted, detached from their origin in the physical world. Or it might take the form of attending to our own and others' gestures, turning back to what was humanity's first language. As research on embodied cognition has demonstrated, at a deep level the brain still understands abstract concepts in terms of physical action, a fact reflected in the words we use ("reaching for a goal", "running behind schedule"); we can give the brain an assist in its efforts by bringing the literal body back into the act of thinking.

Principle Five: Re-Spatialize

The fifth principle emphasizes another human strength: Whenever possible, we should take measures to *re-spatialize* the information we think about. We inherited a brain that was built to pick a path through a landscape and to find the way back home. Research from neuroscience indicates that our brains process and store information in the form of mental maps. We can work in concert with the brain's natural spatial orientation by placing the information we encounter into expressly spatial formats: Creating memory palaces, for example, or designing concept maps. In the realm of education research, experts now speak of "spatializing the curriculum" by employing spatial language and gestures, engaging in sketching and map-making, and learning to interpret and create charts, tables, and diagrams. The spatialized curriculum has obvious applications to subjects like geometry, but researchers report that learning in a spatial mode can also help students think in more advanced ways about topics including chemistry, biology, and history. Nor should spatial reasoning be restricted to schools; the workplace offers abundant opportunities for reconceiving information in spatial terms.

Principle Six: Re-socialize

The sixth principle rounds out the roster of our innate aptitudes: Whenever possible, we should take measures to *re-socialize* the information we think about. Linguists believe that the continual pattern we carry on in our heads is in fact a kind of internalized conversation. Likewise, many of the written forms we encounter at school and at work, such as exams, evaluations, case studies, essays, and proposals, are really social exchanges put on paper and addressed to some imagined listener or interlocutor. There are significant advantages to turning such interactions-at-a-remove back into actual social encounters. Abundant research demonstrates that the brain processes the "same" information differently, and often more effectively when other human beings are involved. We are inherently social creatures, and our thinking benefits from bringing other people into our train of thought.

Principle Seven: Generate Cognitive Loops

The third and final set of principles of mental extension steps back for a still-wider view, taking up a rather profound question: What *kind* of creatures are we? We can't design effective protocols for extension without a nuanced understanding of our highly particular, intriguingly eccentric human nature. A clear-eyed acknowledgment of our quirks can lead us to create new kinds of mental routines, such as the one encapsulated in the seventh principle: Whenever possible, we should manage our thinking by *generating cognitive loops*.

As Clark has pointed out, when computer scientists develop artificial intelligence systems, they don't design machines that compute for a while, print out the results, inspect what they have produced, add some marks in the margin, circulate copies among colleagues, and then start the process again. That's not how computers work, but it is how *we* work; we are "intrinsically loopy creatures", as Clark likes to say. Something about our biological intelligence benefits from being rotated in and out of internal and external modes of cognition, from being passed among the brain, body, and world. This means we should resist the urge to shunt our thinking along the linear path appropriate to a computer—input, output, done—and instead allow it to take a more winding route.

We can pass our thoughts through the portal of our bodies: Seeking the verdict of our interoception, seeing what our gestures have to show us, acting out our ideas in movement, and observing the inspirations that arise during or after vigorous exercise. We can spread out our thoughts in space, treating the contents of the mind as a territory to be mapped and navigated, surveyed, and explored. And we can run our thoughts through the brains of the people we know, gathering from the lot of them the insights no single mind could generate. Most felicitous of all, we can loop our thoughts through all three of these realms. What we *shouldn't* do is keep our thoughts inside our heads, inert, unchanged by encounters with the world beyond the skull.

Principle Eight: Create Cognitively Congenial Situations

We are situationally sensitive creatures, responsive to the immediate conditions and circumstances in which we find ourselves. Hence, the eighth principle: Whenever possible, we should manage our thinking by *creating cognitively congenial situations*. We often regard the brain as an organ of awesome and almost unfathomable power. But we're also apt to treat it with high-handed imperiousness, expecting it to do our bidding as if it were a docile servant. Pay attention to *this*, we tell it, to remember *that*, buckle down *now* and get the job done. Alas, we often find that the brain is an unreliable and even impertinent attendant: fickle in its focus, porous in its memory, and inconstant in its efforts. The problem lies in our attempt to command it. We'll elicit improved performance from the brain when we approach it with the aim, not of issuing orders, but of creating situations that draw out the desired result.

Instead of dictating to a student the information she needs to learn, for example, have her explain it in front of a group of her peers; the gestures she makes will generate a deeper level of understanding. Instead of handing an employee a manual packed with guidelines, create spaces and occasions where stories—full of the tacit knowledge manuals can't convey—will get told by his coworkers. Instead of instructing a team to cooperate and work together, plan an event where synchronized movement and mutual physiological arousal are bound to take place. The art of creating intelligence-extending situations is one that every parent, teacher, and manager needs to master.

Principle Nine: Embedding Extensions

The final principle of extension doubles back on itself with a self-referential observation. What kind of creatures are we? The kind who *extend*, eagerly and energetically, when given the chance. Research from neuroscience and cognitive psychology indicates that when we begin using a tool, our "body schema"—our sense of the body's shape, size, and position—rapidly expands to encompass it as if the tool we're grasping in our hand has effectively become an extension of our arm. Something similar occurs in the case of mental extensions. As long as extensions are available, we humans will incorporate them into our thinking. Accordingly, the ninth principle: Whenever possible, we should manage our thinking by *embedding extensions* in our everyday environments.

Such embedded extensions might take the form of cues of belonging and identity, for example, that bolster our motivation and improve our performance when displayed in our study and work spaces. They might be represented by the transactive memory system we construct with a group of colleagues over time, in which the burden of attending to and remembering information is distributed across group members. They could even be present as the indoor plants and "green" walls and roofs that help restore our attention by providing regular glimpses of nature. Once securely embedded, such extensions can function as seamless adjuncts to our neural capacity, supporting and augmenting our ability to think intelligently.

It's worth noting that this principle bears a bias toward stability: Enduring cues of belonging and identity are hard to sustain in an office where "hot-desking", or unassigned workspace, is the norm; a transactive memory system is difficult to build in a work environment where turnover is high or team composition is constantly changing. In a dynamic and fast-changing society where novelty and flexibility are celebrated, the maintenance and preservation of valued mental extensions also deserve our respect. We may not know how much they bolster our intelligence until they're gone.

A Future Curriculum?

This nested set of principles, what we might call a "curriculum of the extended mind", is not currently taught in any school or addressed in any workplace training. That ought to change and learning to extend the mind should be an element of everyone's education. At present, to the degree that people know how to extend their minds, it's something they've figured out on their own.

Strikingly, we now have evidence that individuals do differ in how fully they have developed their capacity to extend. Furthermore, scientists have found that this competence can be accurately and precisely measured, using a variation on conventional IQ tests. Most intriguing, results from these studies show that skill at employing extensions, as assessed by a test, corresponds to real-world performance; individuals who can extend their minds more fully can solve problems more effectively in everyday life.

In February 2019, a group of psychologists from the Netherlands published a study in the journal *Nature Human Behaviour*. The researchers set out "to quantitatively assess a powerful, although understudied, feature of human intelligence: our ability to use external objects, props and aids to solve complex problems". They started with a conventional test of intelligence, the Raven Advanced Progressive Matrices. This IQ test presents users with a series of geometric puzzles, each of which is missing a piece. Test-takers are asked to select, from a number of options provided, the piece that correctly completes each pattern. In the standard version, test takers are expected to carry out the required operations in their heads, imagining how each potential choice might or might not fit. The rules of the test don't permit them to extend their minds with extra-neural resources; they must rely on their internal reasoning processes alone. In the version of the test designed by Clark and his colleagues, by contrast, test takers are able to digitally manipulate the potential solution pieces, moving them around the screen to create new configurations.

To assess the validity of the new test they had created, the researchers recruited 495 students from the Netherlands' Leiden University and Erasmus University.

Half the students were randomly assigned to take the conventional version; the other half were given the extended-mind variant of the test. In the case of the second group, the researchers monitored how actively test-takers engaged in manipulating the layout on the screen.

A suggestive finding soon surfaced: Test-takers who took full advantage of the new interactive feature were often able to identify patterns that had not been apparent to them before they began shifting the pieces around. An analysis of the moves they made while taking the test showed that these active extenders seemed to be running their thinking processes through successive loops—switching between external actions, which altered the problem-solving space in helpful ways, and internal evaluations of the new configurations thus created. "Our study showed very clearly the relationship between the amount of interaction participants engaged in and how well they solved the problems", says Bruno Bocanegra, an assistant professor of psychology at Erasmus University and the lead author of the paper. "We saw people interacting with the pieces, reflecting on the new configurations, reassessing their strategy, and then reaching out to interact again. These loops are what allowed them to solve the problems effectively" (Bocanegra, et al., 2019).

Final results demonstrated that the more test-takers extended their minds using the moveable pieces, the more successful they were at solving the complex visual puzzles. What's more, the extended-mind version of the test was better than the standard, "static" Raven at predicting students' intellectual performance outside the lab. The test that measured the students' skill at mental extension, the authors wrote, "might be tapping into an additional behavioral aspect of intelligence that is not currently measured" by conventional IQ tests.

Bocanegra's publication is just a start, but it's easy to envision a broad expansion of similar efforts. Imagine a test that would evaluate how well an individual is able to use interoception, movement, and gesture to think; how adept she is at soaking up natural settings, designing built environments, and exploiting the space of ideas to enhance her cognition; how skillfully she manages thinking with experts, peers, and groups. Such an assessment could represent a new kind of IQ test, measuring a new sort of intelligence. Of course, it's possible that such a test would be misused, as IQ tests often have been: Employed to rank, divide, and exclude individuals, instead of helping them to develop. But such misuse need not be inevitable. Once we make mental extensions visible, what we do with that awareness is up to us.

One of the most important things we can do with an awareness of mental extensions is to think carefully about how they can be integrated with the growing presence of artificial intelligence in our schools and workplaces. In the fast-approaching future, the smartest students and workers will be those who can most effectively combine the dazzling innovations of AI with the intelligence that is deeply rooted in our human nature.

References

Argote, L. (2012). *Organizational learning: Creating, retaining and transferring knowledge.* Springer Science & Business Media.

Bocanegra, B. R., Poletiek, F. H., Ftitache, B., & Clark, A. (2019). Intelligent problem-solvers externalize cognitive operations. *Nature Human Behaviour, 3*(2), 136–142.

Clark, A., & Chalmers, D. (1998). The extended mind. *Analysis, 58*(1), 7–19.

10
EDUCATION FOR A POST-WORK SOCIETY

AI, the Liberal Arts and the Future of Leisure

Jon K. Burmeister

> We must consider, therefore, what we should do to occupy our leisure.... [T]here are some branches of education which ought to be studied with a view to living a life of leisure.
> ~ Aristotle, *Politics* 1337b40; 1338a9-10

Introduction

In the second half of the 21st century, educational systems around the world will face a challenge unparalleled in their history. Most of these systems have largely organized themselves around one main goal: preparing students for their future working lives. Yet this goal will become increasingly irrelevant as we approach the 22nd century for two reasons: Vast amounts of human labor will be automated by advances in artificial intelligence (AI), and—unlike in the past—fewer and fewer new jobs will be created along the way. It is not difficult to imagine a situation in which "only" half of a nation's population is unable to find full-time work by the end of this century, with their physical needs being taken care of by a universal basic income (UBI). If this comes to pass, and if our educational goals remain unchanged, the psychological and social results would be devastating, given that most schools—whether K-12 or in higher education—simply do not prepare people to find meaning and fulfillment from such a life. Humans who do not have work but are sustained by a UBI face the danger of becoming something like domestic house cats: creatures deprived of their freedoms and of their traditional life activities, due to the fact that all of their needs are met for them by others. Thus we see that a large amount of free time does not equate to a large amount of freedom. Without the right educational systems in place, there could well be an inverse relation between free time and freedom.

It is essential, therefore, to consider what the *new* goals of education might be for such an AI-driven society, and what sort of pedagogical structures might help us achieve those goals. To do this we must ask ourselves what sorts of activities humans could do in their lives of free time that would help them reach a state of both individual and communal well-being. I argue that a liberal arts education will be the best foundation for preparing people to live fulfilling lives of leisure. While the terms "liberal arts" and "liberal education" (herein used interchangeably) usually refer only to higher education, the core ideas of this form of education apply equally well to K-12 schooling. A liberal education develops traits that are crucial for a life well-lived in any century, and those traits will become even more crucial for flourishing in the highly automated, information-soaked societies of the future.

My first section investigates some recent advances in AI and computing research to provide a sense of both their astonishing speed and the threat they pose to traditional forms of human work and future job creation. In the second section, I explore what humans might do with their newly freed time by framing the issue in terms of different kinds of *freedoms*. A liberal education, ideally given from elementary school onward, can prepare people to realize those freedoms by cultivating traits such as intellectual humility, self-knowledge, curiosity, and creativity. The first kind of freedom I discuss is "freedom from Big Tech", that is, freedom from the exploitation of our attention and our less healthy desires by platforms such as Facebook, Instagram, and TikTok, with the liberal arts fostering the required traits of self-knowledge and self-regulation.[1] The second sort of freedom cultivated by the liberal arts is Aristotle's idea of a "freedom for *a-telic* activities"—that is, the capacity to engage in undertakings that are done for their *own* sake and which are the essential stuff of human happiness. My overall argument is that a genuine liberal arts education—one that instills the ability to be deeply curious, to think synthetically, to understand the workings of one's own mind, and to make judgments critically and independently—will be the best preparation for a life of freedom and fulfillment in a post-work society.

I Artificial Intelligence and Technological Unemployment

The kind of job displacement that my argument is concerned with is not "the automation of jobs." The automation of jobs has been occurring beneficially for hundreds of years, as farmers and later factory workers fell from a large to a very small percentage of the workforce, and the freshly unemployed stepped into newly created lines of work (such as office workers and therapists). The automation of jobs is only a serious problem if it occurs without the accompanying creation of enough jobs to replace those that were lost. This phenomenon is what John Maynard Keynes refers to as "technological unemployment," the situation in which technologically based reductions in the workforce outstrip the number of new jobs that the economy is able to create (Keynes, 1932).

The skeptic might respond that, even if we do see significant technological unemployment by the late 21st century, this will surely not lead to the destruction of all or even most human jobs. But societies do not need total unemployment to be severely upended; at the height of the Great Depression, unemployment stood "only" at 24.9% (Martin, n.d.). For our purposes, the phrase "post-work society," will mean one in which a large fraction of a society's population is no longer working full-time.

To make the case that technological unemployment will be a major feature of the second half of the 21st century, I will mention just a few recent advances in AI and computing. Because these fields are developing so rapidly, the advances mentioned will appear comically outdated in just a few years' time, but my argument as a whole will remain relevant regardless of what the latest computing advances happen to be.

Stanford University's "AI Index Report for 2021" addresses recent progress in machine vision and natural language processing. Machine vision (the ability to visually identify objects) is an ability that a computer gains after an image classifier system is trained on a large set of images. According to Stanford, the average time to train such a system to recognize objects such as dogs and cars fell from 6.2 minutes in 2018 to a mere 47 seconds in 2020 (Zhang et al. 2021, p. 48). Machine vision's cost and accessibility have fallen even more dramatically: the cost to train an image classifier system in 2017 was $1,100, but by 2021 it had fallen to $7.43 (Zhang et al. 2021, p. 49). Equally impressive is the acceleration of computers' abilities to comprehend human language. In 2016, natural language processing systems that took a reading comprehension test scored 67%, but just four years later the systems score rose to 95% (Zhang et al. 2021, p. 63), besting the reading comprehension skills of the average American high schooler.

A common response to these sorts of advances is that computers are still not able to learn in a truly *flexible* way, much less be creative in their application of ideas. But recent developments in computational flexibility call many of our intuitions about computers' abilities into question. Consider the program AlphaZero created by DeepMind (a subsidiary of Google's parent company), which, in 2018, was able to achieve superhuman mastery of the games of chess, shogi, and Go (Silver et al., 2018, p. 1140). The first point that is striking about AlphaZero is that—unlike most game-playing programs—it was taught no strategies at all, only the basic rules of each of the three games. This means that it engaged in "blank-slate" learning by acquiring winning strategies completely on its own, including some that the programmers themselves did not know. We should mark the significance of a moment in history when a machine possesses a practical understanding of a topic that went beyond the comprehension of its creators.

Another remarkable point about AlphaZero is that the game Go is often described as one requiring intuition and creativity. This is because the size of the

Education for a Post-Work Society   **175**

board and the rules of the game prevent the kind of brute-force computation which can be used in chess to defeat human chess players, such as when Deep Blue beat Gary Kasparov in 1997. There are nonetheless many Go strategies, developed over 3,000 years of human play, that can be hand-coded into software. Such was the case with a simpler program called AlphaGo, which in 2016 defeated the human world champion Go player. This was impressive enough, but just one year later the newer program AlphaZero, possessing no knowledge of Go strategies whatsoever, needed only 30 hours of unsupervised reinforcement learning before it was able to beat AlphaGo (Silver et al., 2018, p. 1143). This means that an intelligent machine was able to acquire and surpass 3,000 years of human learning in just 30 hours of unsupervised training, a fact that hints at the possibilities of AI for discovery and creativity in the real-world.

Recall that AlphaZero's capacity for blank-slate learning and "creative" gameplay applies not only to the game of Go but also to the games of chess and shogi. Almost all current AI programs are forms of "artificial narrow intelligence (ANI)" because when placed in a context that is even slightly different they usually fail completely. By contrast, blank-slate machine learning that can flexibly adapt to *multiple* contexts with different rules is an advance that gives us a first glimpse of the holy grail of AI research: The creation of "artificial general intelligence" (AGI), which is a machine intelligence that is equivalent to human intelligence in its ability to learn and solve problems in a wide variety of different contexts.

To be sure, AlphaZero only operates in the clean and rule-based domain of digital games, but DeepMind and many other companies are already applying the techniques of deep reinforcement learning to real-world physical contexts such as robotics research and self-driving cars. As machine learning, computer vision, and the algorithmic control of actuators moves into the three-dimensional world, many more kinds of human work will be threatened.[2] It is also worth remembering that AI does not need to automate all or even close to all human work in order to radically destabilize our current modes of living and to overturn the traditional goals of our educational systems. These questions, therefore, demand serious consideration: What will people do with the free time that AI grants (or forces) upon them, and how should people be educated so that they are best prepared to spend their free time well?

II How to Be Free in Your Free Time

To consider how future humans might best spend their expanded leisure time, it is useful to frame the conversation in terms of different types of freedoms and different types of *threats* to freedom. Following Nietzsche (1982, p. 175), we can distinguish between "freedom *from*" (sometimes called "negative freedom") and "freedom *for*" (sometimes called "positive freedom"). Within that framework, there are at least four types of freedom necessary for human well-being: 1) freedom *from* natural threats (starvation, homelessness, etc.)—a freedom that can be granted to all those living in an AI-driven economy with a universal basic income, 2) freedom *from* bad political actors, 3) freedom *from* Big Tech (which seeks to capture our attention), and 4.) freedom *for* a-telic activities—that is, activities which we do for their own sake, and which embody the highest form of human flourishing. A liberal arts education cultivates the second, third, and fourth kind of freedom, but because much has already been written on the connections between the liberal arts and political self-rule, I will focus on the third and fourth kinds of freedom.

A. What Is a Liberal Arts Education?

Before elaborating on those freedoms, it is important to clarify my definition of a liberal arts education. Definitions of "the liberal arts" and "a liberal education" have been notoriously varied across the centuries and also amongst educators today. My definition is grounded in the etymology of the word "liberal," which comes from the Latin "*liber*" meaning "free." Historically, a liberal arts education was often conceived of as an education appropriate for a "free person," that is, a person who was not subjugated to continuous labor, who could develop their own mind in a free way, and who was a citizen with a voice in the political system. But the "*liber*" element of a "liberal education" is also sometimes conceived of in the sense of *liberating*, that is, helping to *make* someone free by endowing them with certain ideals, capacities, self-conceptions, and goals. As a first definition, then, a liberal education should be viewed as a *liberating* education that helps students achieve the three kinds of freedom mentioned above: political freedom, psychological freedom (in relation to Big Tech), and the freedom that comes with being able to pursue activities worth pursuing just for their own sake (such as the arts). To provide students with the best chance of achieving these freedoms, a liberal education must train their minds to think abstractly but apply those ideas concretely; to think critically and analytically, which is the capacity to logically assess evidence both for and against a position before making a judgment about it; to grasp the underlying connections between the different parts of reality; to feel both more deeply and more clearly; and to question both themselves and the world with more curiosity, more autonomy, and more creativity.

How would an education achieve such lofty goals? The chances of success certainly rise the earlier one starts cultivating the abilities mentioned above. The Montessori system of education (K-12) stands within the tradition of liberal education through its approach of "child-directed work," which foster within children traits such as intellectual curiosity and autonomy of learning (American Montessori Society, n.d.). A powerful predecessor of the Montessori system is presented by J.J. Rousseau in his 18th c. masterpiece *Emile*, which claims that the ideal education is one that requires children to learn how to learn *on their own*.

As Rousseau says about the child, "The goal is less to teach him a truth than to show him how he must always go about discovering the truth" (205). The liberal, that is, liberating, dimension to this sort of education is clear: the student learns how to think for themselves and develop their own faculties of reason, therefore enabling them to rely less on others. Rousseau (1979) describes such an education and such a student beautifully when he says, "Forced to learn by himself, he uses his reason and not another's" (207).

In higher education, a school that offers a liberal education typically provides a broad curriculum in disciplines such as philosophy, history, literature, mathematics, physics, psychology, etc. While a liberal education must include these subjects and many more, it is crucial to emphasize that many students who take classes in all of these disciplines do not actually receive a liberal education at all. The second essential element of a liberal education, and one significantly more difficult for a teacher to implement, is the one mentioned in the paragraph above: teaching students how to become independent learners, and how to rely on their own reason for their conclusions. These lofty goals for post-work education cannot be achieved through a system of mere "information transfer" in which students are passive receptacles. Rather, those goals can only be achieved through a specific classroom environment, one that includes intensive student participation, a modeling by the teacher of the spirit of Socratic perplexity and inquiry, a regular questioning of how the topics being discussed relates to seemingly unrelated disciplines (and therefore to the larger whole of reality), and a pedagogical space that is held open for students' own powers of mental inquiry to flower. The section below will discuss two different kinds of freedom, and expand on how a liberal education can help a person to develop each of those freedoms in turn.

B. Freedom from Big Tech

B.1 Freed by AI, and then Subjugated by It?

The emergence of Big Tech over the past two decades has brought with it an AI-driven "attention economy" in which technology corporations compete for the increasingly scarce resource of human attention. This results in a struggle to maintain control over our attention and therefore over our time. Yet this struggle is a deeply lopsided one, given that our adversaries are the most economically and psychologically powerful companies the world has ever known, and use the extraordinary powers of AI to try to capture and hold our attention. On the other hand, AI has and will increasingly bring the human race enormous benefits, including both economic abundance and freedom from many menial forms of work. Considering the growing dangers that Big Tech companies pose to our psychological well-being, one might say that "AI giveth and AI also taketh away".

To discuss "freedom from Big Tech" and "freedom of attention" in the context of copious leisure time, it is useful to look at the writings of Aldous Huxley. The driving question of Huxley's 1925 essay "Work and Leisure" is what humans would do, and should do, with a life of the technologically endowed free time. He reflects on a future in which all people will enjoy "an amount of leisure such as is enjoyed at the present day only by the privileged few" (Huxley, 2000, p. 411). While he is sympathetic to the social reformers who wish to hasten the coming of this future, he is doubtful that most people will spend their free time wisely. For example, he is skeptical of H.G. Wells' utopian novel *Men Like Gods* which depicts future humans as studying the natural sciences, philosophy, and the fine arts, living out their days in a noble pursuit of truth and beauty. Huxley bitingly remarks that Wells seems to believe that "these leisured masses [of the future]…will do all the things which our leisured classes of the present time so conspicuously fail to do" (Huxley, 2000, p. 411). What most of the leisured classes actually do, according to Huxley, is waste their time with love affairs and frivolous distractions in the desperate attempt to stave off boredom. Even working people, he says, spend their brief moments of leisure in thoughtless distractions, ones that are merely cheaper versions of those the rich pursue. Huxley argues that if a life of leisure were available to the mass of humanity, the result would be "an enormous increase in the demand for such time-killers and substitutes for thought as newspapers, films, fiction…and enormous numbers of people, hitherto immune from these mental and moral diseases, would be afflicted by ennui, depression and universal dissatisfaction" (Huxley, 2000, p. 414).

Huxley's analysis of a widespread life of leisure may seem overly grim, but what is undeniable is that when one compares the "time-killers and substitutes for thought" available in 1925 with those in the 21st century, the former stand to the latter as a candle to the sun. In early 2022, five of the top ten most valuable companies in the world by market capitalization (Johnston, 2022)—Apple, Microsoft, Alphabet (parent company of Google), Meta (formerly Facebook), and Amazon—are technology companies whose business models are either wholly or partially based on capturing human attention. This group of Big Tech companies, which collectively own services such as Instagram, YouTube, AppleTV+, Minecraft, Amazon Prime Video, and Twitch, make up the bulk of what is often called the "attention economy," and they provide nearly endless amounts of entertainment and distraction in order to capture and monetize eyeballs on the basis of highly targeted advertising. These companies accomplish this by using human attention, measured through clicks and views, to gather data on those humans for the purpose of creating detailed psychological profiles of them. This allows the companies not only to better advertise to their users but also to more successfully capture their attention in the future, by presenting content this is so precisely tailored to the individual viewer that it feels almost irresistible. How do these companies create such psychological profiles? They do it with the help of machine learning algorithms, which take the raw data of user inputs and translate it into generalized insights about the user.

In light of these developments, it is not an encouraging sign that in late 2021, the social video app TikTok overtook Google as the most visited web domain in the world (Cardita and Tomé, 2021). In other words, a service that primarily provides amusing 15-second videos has overtaken a service used to search and find information. This should not come as a surprise to anyone who has used TikTok and seen how quickly its algorithms hone in on a user's interests, presenting an unending stream of short videos on whatever topics were contained in the videos that the user previously stopped to watch, or even slightly paused to watch—information tracked and aggregated by TikTok's algorithms.

The art of algorithmically capturing human attention is only in its early stages, and is therefore a crude and primitive version of what we will see in the coming decades. We discussed above how artificial intelligence will bring about technological unemployment (displacing more jobs than are created), and by the time this starts to occur more dramatically, Big Tech's algorithms are likely to be far better at influencing and directing the attention of their users. With the growth of the "internet of things" (smart refrigerators, biometric devices, etc.) and VR/AR devices, the amount of data from which Big Tech can glean insights about us will balloon. It cannot be stressed enough that, in the year 2023, we have only seen a small fraction of the neuro-manipulative techniques that Big Tech will eventually bring to bear on us.

All of this leads to a troubling conclusion. At the point in the future when many humans will be handed enormous amounts of free time, Big Tech companies will be far more skillful at capturing our attention and, therefore, capturing our free time. We face a future in which, freed from the drudgery of work by advances in AI, the attention and free time of most people could be subjugated by those very same technological powers. In this scenario, our boundless free time would not actually be free time. In a very real sense, our free time would be *unfree*.

"Unfree" might strike some readers as too strong a word, but former Google employee and Oxford-trained philosopher James Williams does not think so. He uses similar language in his book *Stand Out of Our Light: Freedom and Resistance in the Attention Economy*, when he describes "the defining moral and political struggle of our time" as "the liberation of human attention" (Williams, 2018, xii). Williams speaks so dramatically about the topics of attention, "attention capture" and "attention liberation" due to a claim he makes in the very first words of his book: "In order to do anything that matters, we must first be able to give attention to things that matter" (Williams, 2018, xi). It is difficult to argue with this claim, or with its importance. Our ability to direct our attention toward objects of our own choosing, instead of objects chosen *for* us, is the precondition for achieving the goals we have for our lives. But according to Williams, our current information technologies, and especially social media, operate like a "faulty GPS": instead of helping us achieve the goals we have set for ourselves, they very often work directly against those goals and take us to an entirely different destination. This "faulty GPS" phenomena—the algorithmic hijacking of our attention, our time, and our goals—is a phenomenon experienced by anyone who has found themselves deep in a YouTube or Twitter rabbit hole in the midst of trying to make progress on some larger project. Because these platforms either auto-play the next video or automatically populate the feeds that we scroll, our use of their services represents a kind of *outsourcing* of our decision-making to an AI about how we will spend our time and attention.

Despite this bleak picture, and despite the extraordinary resources of these trillion-dollar corporations, James Williams argues that we can in fact wage a resistance. Much of the resistance, he claims, must operate at larger structural levels of society through collective and political action, but some of it must operate at the individual level of personal "self-rule" and "self-regulation." Williams explains the kind of self-rule he has in mind by drawing on J.J. Rousseau's famous definition of freedom as self-legislation: "To be driven by appetite alone is slavery, and obedience to the law one has prescribed for oneself is liberty" (Williams, 2018 p. 167). Setting boundaries for ourselves and for our appetites (e.g., the appetite for the pleasant distractions of short viral videos) and then sticking to those boundaries is essential, according to Williams, in order to avoid getting sucked into Big Tech's attention-capture machine.

Therefore, what I call "freedom from Big Tech" is one part of "freedom from one's lower appetites": quick, easy, short-term pleasures. These lower appetites are what many Big Tech companies, with the power of AI, are aiming to exploit for the sake of their profits. Tristan Harris, another ex-Googler and technology ethicist, put it this way in his testimony before the US Senate in 2019: "…in an attention economy, there's only so much attention, and the advertising business model always wants more. So it becomes a race to the bottom of the brain stem" (Harris, 2019, p. 1). As tremendously wealthy AI companies with armies of Ph.D.'s strategize to exploit our basic appetites to capture our attention, our chances of successfully resisting them, and of maintaining control over our attention and our time, seem slim so long as we are, quite literally, left to our own devices. Humans today, and those in the future with both more free time and more formidable algorithmic adversaries, can benefit from some assistance from the liberal arts.

B.2 The Liberal Arts and Freedom from Big Tech

How can a liberal arts education assist in developing this kind of self-regulation, the kind of "personal boundary setting" which can help us remain free from the temptations of Big Tech? One key tactic for resisting any kind of unhealthy desire is understanding how the desire operates, why it is attractive, and why it is unhealthy. Having such an understanding of attention-capture techniques requires the liberal arts skills already discussed, such as critical and abstract thinking, and the ability to see connections between seemingly disparate areas of reality—in this case, between machine learning algorithms, the economics of advertising, and the neuroscience of attention.

A second element of resisting an attractive but unhealthy desire is the ability to monitor one's own internal states in order to observe, in real-time, how one is being affected by the object of desire. In other words, resisting the wiles of Big Tech and retaining control of one's powers of attention requires a high degree of *self-knowledge*.[3] This ability is also one explicitly cultivated by a liberal arts education, not only in the sense that self-knowledge is one of the central Socratic virtues but also because a liberal education places a premium on introspection, and on the study of the human psyche more generally. Referring to Harvard's 1945 *General Education in Free Society*, the historian Willis Rudy says that its authors conceived of the liberally educated person as "one who was inwardly as well as outwardly 'free' because he could truly govern himself, was self-critical, and led a self-examined life." (Rudy, 1960, p. 134). In other words, *there is an intimate connection between self-knowledge and self-regulation*, and the better a person is at introspecting and understanding themselves—including their specific weaknesses—the less likely they are to fall prey to their unhealthy desires.

Of course, discussing the virtues of self-knowledge and self-regulation in a classroom setting by no means ensures that a student will automatically attain those virtues, or practice them in their everyday lives. But over the course of a four-year liberal arts education, a bulwark of ideas and goals can be cultivated in a student's mind which can alter both their motivations and the way they deal with their emotions. This was the finding of a group of psychologists in their four-year study of students entering and leaving a liberal arts college, a study which showed that their education had "motivational and emotional effects" on the students (Winter et al., 1982, p. 80). One conclusion of this study, which controlled for the normal processes of young adult maturation, showed that attending a four-year liberal arts college (vs. other types of colleges) led students to become "more integrated and instrumental in the emotional or 'psychological' sphere as well as the cognitive sphere" (Winter et al., 1982, p. 80). As the authors state,

> liberal education brings growth in a series of overlapping but distinct components, involving cognition, emotion, and motivation. Growth in these components is not a simple function of higher education in itself, but rather now can be linked to specific characteristics of a liberal arts college.
> (Winter et al., 1982, pp. 169–170)

In summary, a liberal education can help people live lives of free time that are free from a psychological indentured servitude to Big Tech's AI, by helping them develop the self-understanding and self-regulation needed to resist the invasive attempts to control their attention, their time, and their goals.

C. Freedom for A-Telic Activities

C.2 A-Telic Activities and the "Chief Good" for Humans

Even if humans of the future are able to establish their psychological freedom from technology corporations, their lives would still lack something significant. Freedom from Big Tech is simply a "negative freedom," a freedom *from* restrictive and damaging influences, and therefore it does not tell us how to actually live happy and meaningful lives. What would such a freedom be *for*? This problem is seen more clearly by thinking back to the bored aristocrats that Aldous Huxley laments. Analogically, we might also think of a person incarcerated for decades who is handed his freedom, along with an adequate living stipend, and then is at a loss as to how he should actually spend his days. Is there a way that those who do not need to work can avoid spending their days simply jumping from one frivolous and unfulfilling distraction to the next?

In *Nicomachean Ethics*, Aristotle presents a profound way of thinking through this question. He discusses the concept of activities done "for their own sake," which are sometimes referred to today as "a-telic" activities. To see why such activities are so crucial to human fulfillment, we must start where Aristotle starts, with foundational ideas about human motivation. As he says in the first lines of his book, humans do many things in life for the sake of some larger goal or "*telos*," such as working a job in order to receive a paycheck. In terms of activities done for the sake of something else, there is usually a long hierarchy of "stacked" goals. For example, most people work in order to make money, and they make money in order to buy things such as groceries, and they buy groceries in order to have the groceries in their kitchen, and they have groceries in their kitchen to eventually eat those groceries, etc. And yet, Aristotle continues, it would not make sense to do *everything* in life for the sake of some larger goal, since then the process would never end and we would never reach a stopping point with our goals, but be perpetually striving for something beyond our reach. He thus, introduces a conceptual distinction between what is desired "for the sake of something else" and what is desired "for its *own* sake." He sums up these ideas as follows:

> If there is some end [goal/*telos*] of the things we do, which we desire for its own sake (everything else being desired for the sake of this), and if we do not choose everything for the sake of something else (for at that rate the process would go on to infinity, so that our desire would be empty and vain), clearly this must be the good and the chief good. Will not the knowledge of it then have a great influence on life?
>
> (2009, p. 3)

But what is this "chief good" for humans, that which is desired for its own sake and not for the sake of anything else? Aristotle says that it is happiness ("*eudaimonia*"). By this term, he does not mean the transient pleasant moods often associated with the term "happy," but rather something like "human flourishing."[4] Yet he acknowledges that people conceive of happiness (*eudaimonia*) in very different ways, so he begins to chip away at a definition of *eudaimonia* by saying that it does not consist of gaining any particular possessions or honors, but rather the doing of certain *activities*. Which activities? This is where the category of "a-telic" activities comes in: activities that are worth doing "for their own sake." (The prefix "a-" means "not", and the root "telic" means "having some purpose or goal".) We can see how the concept of a-telic activities mirrors the structure of the "primary good" of happiness: both are desired not for some external goal but rather for their own sake. In other words, *a-telic activities are their own reward*.

Yet Aristotle argues that happiness does not come from just any a-telic activities, but rather from ones that make use of the human capacity of reasoning. Examples he gives are playing music, scientific and philosophical thinking, and the activity of conversation in a true friendship. These are a-telic activities that are reason-based because they are distinct from physical- or animal-based a-telic activities, such as sex, eating, and drinking. Therefore Aristotle is claiming that reason-based a-telic activities are the foundational stuff of human happiness and human flourishing. To engage in such activities is to fulfill our potential as rational creatures, and this is what it means to be in a state of *eudaimonia*. We do these activities for their own sake, just for the joy of doing them, and while we are doing them we are in the best and most fulfilling state that a human being can achieve.

Some people might think that, in a work-free existence, their primary a-telic activity would be some form of relaxation, such as lying on the beach. Yet Aristotle claims that relaxation is not an a-telic activity, since it is actually directed at a larger goal. The reason we want to relax is not simply to relax, he says, but rather because we are tired from some activity. As he puts it, "we need relaxation because we cannot work continuously. Relaxation is not an end; for it is taken for the sake of activity" (2009, p. 193). In other words, relaxation appears extremely appealing only to someone who is tired from some activity, and without the contrast to effortful activity, relaxation is not actually very appealing. The truth of this is clear from innumerable examples of working people who eagerly anticipate their retirement as a time of endless relaxation, but then, only months after retiring, grow bored with the life of mere relaxation and seek out some kind of activity to occupy their time. As the human race approaches its own "retirement" from its millennia of work, a real possibility exists that it too will fall prey to the speciously attractive idea of "endless days of relaxation." But the human race will need something more, and Aristotle would say that this is a-telic activities.

In contrast to the idea of relaxation, Aristotle reserves the word "leisure" (*schole* in Greek) to refer to reason-based a-telic activities. Political activity is "unleisurely", he says, since it is not done for its own sake; its goal is beyond itself in terms of the larger good of the whole community. But as he says in the *Politics*, leisure "involves pleasure, happiness [*eudaimonia*], and well-being. [...] Those who work do so with a view to some end, which they regard as still unattained. But happiness is an end…" (1998, p. 301). Clearly, Aristotle argues that a life of leisure—a life of rational, a-telic activities—is the most desirable sort of life. Yet the ability to engage in such activities is not something that humans possess by default. Rather, it is an ability that humans must acquire through the right kind of education.

C.2 The Liberal Arts and A-Telic Activities

With this definition of reason-based a-telic activities in mind, it becomes clear that a liberal education is an ideal way to prepare people to engage in these activities over the course of their lives. Aristotle claims that some types of education should be directed explicitly toward the goal of leisure when he says,

> It is clear therefore that there are some branches of learning and education which ought to be studied with a view to living a life of leisure. It is clear, too, that these forms of education and of learning are valued for their own sake, while those studied with a view to work should be regarded merely as matters of necessity and valued as means to other things.
>
> (1998, p. 301)

This quote is one of the foundational passages in western history for the distinction between a vocational education and a liberal education. As it turns out, a liberal arts course in music, philosophy, or mathematics *does* contribute to extrinsic goals such as a person's future career (some liberal arts skills are in fact hotly in demand today, under the term "soft skills"); yet, a slate of such courses is also extremely well suited to prepare people to spend their free time in truly pleasurable and meaningful a-telic activities. As Daniel Araya notes,

> Rather than understanding education in terms of fixed objects that are transferred from one generation to the next, we need to begin to design educational systems that support liberal notions of knowledge and learning linked to design and meaning making.
>
> (Araya, 2017, p. 191)

Aristotle makes the additional point that a liberal education is *itself* an a-telic activity. He speaks about this in the quote above when he says that there are "forms of education and learning valued for their own sake." That is, liberal arts courses not only prepare students to engage in certain a-telic activities in the future but also involve engaging in them in the *present*. This is why the Greek word for leisure, "*schole*," is the root of the English word "school." In Aristotle's view, a truly liberal education is one that requires real effort but is not onerous, tedious, or work-like.

Given that most forms of education today are, to use his words, "studied with a view to work" and "regarded merely as matters of necessity and valued as means to other things" (1998, p. 301), it is no wonder that so many students today find their college courses burdensome and deeply unpleasant—the opposite of something worth doing for the joy of it, for its own sake.

To conclude, I will mention a point especially relevant to finding fulfillment in a long life of unending free time. As mentioned earlier, a liberal education endows a student with a deep *curiosity* about the world. This curiosity may lead a person to take up various hobbies, but it is a curiosity that runs deeper than that. A truly curious person lives a life that goes beyond the stringing together of disconnected hobbies. As Miriam Joseph puts it, a liberal education gives a person an understanding of how the world fits together, for "the essential activity of the student is to relate the facts learned into a unified, organic whole, to assimilate them…as the rose assimilates food from the soil and increases in size, vitality, and beauty" (2002, p. 7). In this view, a flourishing human being is one who freely and passionately absorbs the world into themselves, synthesizing all that they learn into a larger whole. Former Yale president Alfred Griswold echoes this vision when he states, "The purpose of liberal education is to expand to the limit the individual's capacity – and desire – for self-improvement, for seeking and finding enjoyment and meaning in everything he does" (Griswold, 1959, p. vi). Such a life is only possible if it is filled with the a-telic activities mentioned above, activities that a liberal education is specifically designed to incorporate into students' lives.

III Conclusion

In the second half of the 21st century, humans without traditional working lives will face a crisis of freedom and a crisis of purpose. In order for people to live free, fulfilling, and flourishing lives in the AI-driven societies of the future, we must begin *now* to plan for a new model of kindergarten-through-college education, one explicitly designed to prepare people for lives of leisure. A liberal education, as described above, is just such a model. The fact that the liberal arts are currently in significant decline in higher education, both in terms of enrollment and in terms of funding, comes at the worst possible historical moment, since we are just on the cusp of needing them more than ever. While the traditional liberal education is no doubt incomplete and open to many improvements, it is the best starting point we have for designing the kind of universal education needed for a post-work society.

Notes

1 Another kind of freedom cultivated by the liberal arts – *political* freedom – is also needed both for freedom in general and for freedom from Big Tech, but there is not room in this essay to explore this crucial topic.

2   In the realm of computer hardware, there have been similarly stunning advances that promise to extend into the future. MIT professor and renowned robotics researchers Rodney Brooks points out that in 1959, the IBM 7090 mainframe computer was one of the world's fastest computers, and cost $20 million dollars in today's money. Yet this computer was 728 billion times slower than a 2021 laptop.

Addtionally, advances such as photonic computing, quantum computing, and the new sub-field of "quantum machine learning" indicate that the capacity of computers to replace human work will continue to accelerate over the coming decades.

3   Somatic practices such as mindfulness meditation are especially well suited for enabling a person to engage in the real-time monitoring of their internal states. While such practices are not part of a traditional liberal arts education, there is no reason that they could not be incorporated into it.

4   "Flourishing", rather than "happiness", is a better translation of the Greek word *"eudaimonia"* not just because *eudaimonia* goes beyond pleasant moods, but also because it possesses an objective dimension which the highly subjective English word "happiness" does not capture (as in the phrase, *"whatever* makes you happy"). For Aristotle, this objective dimension of *eudaimonia*/flourishing comes from the fact that certain activities cause a human being to flourish in life and others do not, regardless of what that person might subjectively think about the situation. For example, a well-supplied, well-cared-for crystal meth addict might have the subjective experience of enormous happiness, but we would not say that this person is objectively flourishing in his capacities and potential as a human being.

References

American Montessori Society. (n.d.). *5 Core Components of Montessori Education*. https://amshq.org/About-Montessori/What-Is-Montessori/Core-Components-of-Montessori

Araya, D. (2017). Liberal arts education in the age of machine intelligence. In D. Araya & P. Marber, Eds., *The Evolution of Liberal Arts in the Global Age* (pp. 185–193). Taylor & Francis.

Aristotle. (1998). *The politics*. Oxford World's Classics.

Aristotle. (2009). *Nicomachean ethics*. Oxford University Press.

Cardita, S. & Tomé, J. (2021, December 20). *In 2021, the internet went for TikTok, space and beyond*. Cloudflare. https://blog.cloudflare.com/popular-domains-year-in-review-2021/

Griswold, A.W. (1959). *Liberal education and the democratic ideal, and other essays*. Yale University Press.

Harris, T. (2019, June 25). Testimony at the U.S. Senate Sub-Committee Hearing "Optimizing for Engagement: Understanding the Use of Persuasive Technology on Internet Platforms" [Testimony transcript]. https://www.commerce.senate.gov/services/files/96E3A739-DC8D-45F1-87D7-EC70A368371D#

Huxley, A. (2000). "Work and leisure." In R.S. Baker & J. Sexton, Eds., *Aldous Huxley complete essays: Vol. 1*. Ivan R. Dee. (Original work published 1925.)

Johnston, M. (2022, May 4). *Biggest companies in the world by market cap*. Investopedia. https://www.investopedia.com/biggest-companies-in-the-world-by-market-cap-5212784

Joseph, M. (2002). *The trivium: The liberal arts of logic, grammar, and rhetoric: understanding the nature and function of language*. (M. McGlinn, Ed.). Paul Dry Books.

Keynes, J.M. (1932). "Economic possibilities for our grandchildren." In *Essays in persuasion* (pp. 358–373). Harcourt Brace and Co.

Martin, C.R. (n.d.). "WCP: How government statistics define the stories of the working class." Georgetown University's *Kalmanovitz Initiative for Labor and the Working Poor*. https://lwp.georgetown.edu/news/how-government-statistics-define-the-stories-of-the-working-class/

Nietzsche, F. (1982). Therefore spoke Zarathereforetra. In Walter Kaufmann, Ed., *The Portable Nietzsche*. Penguin Books. (Original work published 1883–1892.)

Rousseau, J.J. (1979). *Emile or on education*. Basic Books. (Original work published 1762.)

Rudy, W. (1960). *The evolving liberal arts curriculum: A historical review of basic themes*. Bureau of Publications, Teachers College, Columbia University.

Silver, D., Hubert, T., Schrittwieser, J., et.al. (2018). "A general reinforcement learning algorithm that masters chess, shogi, and Go through self-play." *Science*. Vol. 362, Issue 6419, p. 1140–1144.

Williams, J. (2018). *Stand out of our light: Freedom and resistance in the attention economy*. Cambridge University Press.

Winter, D.G., McClelland, D.C., & Stewart, A.J. (1982). *A new case for the liberal arts*. Jossey-Bass Publishers.

Zhang, D., Mishra, S., Brynjolfsson, E., Etchemendy, J., Ganguli, D., Grosz, B., Lyons, T., Manyika, J., Niebles, J.C., Sellitto, M., Shoham, Y., Clark, J., & Perrault, R. (2021). "The AI index 2021 annual report." AI Index Steering Committee, Human-Centered AI Institute, Stanford University. https://aiindex.stanford.edu/wp-content/uploads/2021/11/2021-AI-Index-Report_Master.pdf

11
THE MOST VALUABLE INTELLIGENCE IS NOT ARTIFICIAL

Great Books, Free Minds, and St. John's College*

Peter Marber

Life in the 21st century is remarkably different from that of a generation ago; it has been "disrupted", to borrow an overused word from Silicon Valley. With headlines warning us that automation and robotics associated with the Artificial Intelligence (AI) Revolution may change—or end—work as we know it, parents, students, companies, and universities are grappling with new questions: How do you educate for a world we can't even imagine? If you could design a curriculum and higher educational setting from a fresh start, what would college look like? Should it be designed around employment demands, personal happiness, or both?

For decades college students have been migrating pragmatically to computer science and other technical majors for better employment opportunities. But is this the right direction? From workplace surveys, critical thinking and problem-solving top the lists of skills that employers want and need for the future, encompassing self-management, active learning, resilience, stress tolerance, and flexibility (Whiting, 2020). Also in demand are innovation, change and time management, communication and storytelling, and a growth mindset (Udemy, 2020). Some suggest focusing on other very human capabilities—what machines can't yet easily replicate—including creativity, adaptability, and collaboration (Rainie & Anderson, 2017).

These surveys underscore the qualities that employers value. But what do workers want? Even before the COVID-19 pandemic, there was growing evidence that college graduates sought work that was personally more fulfilling

---

* Some of the material in this chapter can be found in my article published by *Quartz* in June 2017 titled "BACK TO THE FUTURE: The most forward-thinking, future-proof college in America teaches every student the exact same stuff".

rather than simply remunerative. Over the last two generations, the average American college graduate has changed jobs nearly a dozen times (US Bureau of Labor Statistics, 2021). Perhaps people jumped jobs for more money, but maybe there's more to the story. A Gallup/Bates College survey found that a remarkable 80% of recent college graduates said it's important to derive a sense of purpose from their work. The survey also found that only 38% strongly agreed that they have discovered work that was gratifying, and just 6% were thriving in their overall well-being. But graduates with high purpose in their work were ten times more likely to be personally thriving (Gallup, 2019). This trend seems to have accelerated during the recent pandemic as millions of Americans left their jobs in what's been called "The Great Resignation". They have rethought what work means to them, how they are valued by employers, and how they want to spend their time.

Surprisingly, workplace skill demands and individual happiness trends actually interrelate: Future work success and personal fulfillment are both tied to *free thinking*. Only by thinking freely can we nurture creative and critical minds, which is how we build our individual identities, as well as our expertise. It's how we cultivate our own unique intellect and values system instead of merely accepting whatever we're told—whether it's from a government, a church, or an AI app on our phones. This mindset is also the basis for a functioning democracy. The ancient Greeks understood the paramount importance for citizens to develop abilities to refute, debate, understand, and *freely* process information; democracy cannot exist if we accept what we're told without question. That's why the Greeks invented the liberal arts style of education, to prepare individuals to be active participants in civic life. Indeed, the phrase *liberal* arts can be traced back to the Latin word *liber* (meaning "free"), which is also the root of *liberty*.

But learning to think independently and freeing one's mind in the 21st century is easier said than done, particularly in a world increasingly dominated by AI and computers. Humans are not nearly as rational as we might like to think we are. In *Star Trek* parlance, we are much more Kirk than Spock; we tend to make decisions based on instinct, gut feel, and impulses rather than on any logical reasoning of risk and probability.

Profit-hungry corporations know this and, in fact, build business models to monetize our lack of rationality. With AI, merchants code software to exploit human instincts and compulsions for profit. They hijack our attention, make suggestions ("if you liked that, try this"), and narrow our decision options, leaving us in a restrictive loop of smaller and smaller individual choices. The results? A dumbed-down world, one that steers our desires in directions not always in our best interest and that quietly weakens our cognitive abilities.

In the face of AI's onslaught, as well as our workforce needs, let's remember what should be the ultimate goal of higher education: to train *human*s to think freely and independently, to help them *learn to learn*, to adapt, and to collaborate with others. This has been, and always will be, the best hedge against an uncertain future.

Heading in the Wrong Direction?

At a time when it's becoming more and more important to learn and think independently, many American college students may not be thinking or learning at all. In *Academically Adrift: Limited Learning on College Campuses*, Richard Arum and Jarip Roksa chronicled how few American students really improve cognitively–and learn to learn–during their undergraduate education (Arum & Roksa, 2011). Few bachelor's programs require sufficient amounts of the reading, writing, and discourse needed to develop critical thinking skills. In fact, more than one-third of American undergraduates now major in business and management-related subjects, reading mainly textbooks and short articles, and rarely writing a paper longer than three pages. Further, the social bonds and skills formed in college today often center on extracurriculars that have little connection to cognitive development and collaborative problem-solving.

This could reflect legitimate pocketbook concerns. As US higher education costs have outpaced inflation for decades, students have been shifting their college major focus toward more practical diplomas for jobs to pay off mounting student debt, now more than $1.7 trillion (Hanson, 2022). Skyrocketing costs may also be behind some of the recent findings of renowned scholar Howard Gardner and colleague Wendy Fischman. Of the 2,000 students interviewed for their book *The Real World of College: What Higher Education Is and What It Can Be*, most undergrads today approach college with a "transactional" perspective (Fischman & Gardner, 2022):

> They don't see value in what they are learning, nor do they understand why they take classes in different fields or read books that do not seem directly related to their major….their overarching goal is to build a résumé with stellar grades, which they believe will help them secure a job post-college… In short, they are more concerned with the pursuit of earning than the process of learning.

Their research confirms some observations in William Deresiewicz' *Excellent Sheep: The Miseducation of the American Elite and the Way to a Meaningful Life* in which he argues that even our nation's most elite students were failing to think critically and creatively—and lacked a sense of purpose (Deresiewicz, 2015).

It shouldn't surprise us, therefore, that fewer than 4.5% of undergraduate degrees now are earned in traditional humanities, down from a peak of 17.2% in 1967 (American Academy of Arts and Sciences, 2021). Cost-cutting measures driven by declining demand have led many small colleges and universities to cut back or eliminate programs in the liberal arts. These trends have been a death knell to many schools in recent years. From 2016–2021, 71 higher education institutions shuttered their doors; 85% were liberal arts colleges (Higher Ed Dive Team, 2022).

Back to the Future

Given automation and AI trends, many believe that higher education needs to be more tech-focused in order to better align with the future of work. But instead of investing scarce resources re-tooling schools with more technology that surely will become outdated, why not focus on what students really need by returning to the roots of liberal education? Free, independent thinking never grows obsolete.

Consider St. John's College, America's third oldest higher ed institution founded in 1696. With approximately 1000 students between two campuses in Annapolis and Santa Fe, St. John's remains one of the most idiosyncratic colleges in the world by maintaining a strict focus on handpicked classics—a philosophy wildly out of sync with today's academic trends and student demands.

Many American schools offer courses with similar readings to St. John's, and its two campuses look much like hundreds of other small colleges. So what makes St. John's so unique, what the *New York Times* called, "the most contrarian college in America"? (Bruni, 2018). It begins with St. John's strict adherence to its own curated curriculum and teaching methods, known simply as "The Program" based on the "Great Books"—foundational works of Western civilization in philosophy, literature, history, the sciences, music, and language, among other disciplines. But to dismiss the Program as antiquated and out of touch would be a huge mistake; St. John's curriculum and culture may just be a model for how to future-proof students in our century of rapid technological and lifestyle changes by freeing their minds and fostering individual purpose in life.

Note that the college didn't always offer the Program over its 300+ year history, and in fact was a military school for much of the 19th and early 20th centuries. During that period, American higher education was in transition. In the late 1800s a new specialized research model was emerging - led by Johns Hopkins in Baltimore - in an effort to produce greater scientific knowledge during the Industrial Revolution. The result of that movement was the modern hyper-specialized research university which defined academic departments and what we now call "majors".

The Great Books philosophy began as a backlash against the specialized research model (Menand, 2021). An early fan was Mortimer Adler, who introduced the approach while an undergraduate in John Erskine's General Honors course at Columbia University. So impressed, Adler took the idea to the University of Chicago in 1930 to reinvigorate liberal arts education there. He launched an undergraduate course that required students to read one Great Book per week for two years, and the idea caught on with other Chicago academics, including Stringfellow Barr and Scott Buchanan.

Enter St. John's College. Heavily in debt during the Depression, the school lost its accreditation in 1936 when its president, Amos Woodcock, pushed to graduate a student that the faculty had essentially flunked. The college's board of trustees fired Woodcock and made Buchanan and Barr the proverbial offer they couldn't refuse: Bring their new pedagogy from Chicago to Annapolis and rebuild St. John's College around their Great Books curriculum. With just 20 starting students and some skeptical faculty in the fall of 1937, Barr and Buchanan launched "The New Program" which consisted principally of reading and discussing 200 curated classics sequenced chronologically. With just a few changes over the decades, St. John's has stayed largely with Barr and Buchanan's original plan.

In contrast to some better-known American liberal arts institutions like Brown or Vassar that allow students to choose from a vast array of classes with few restrictions, St. John's offers only the Program; it's *prix fixe* in a higher education world of *a la carte*. Four years of literature, language, philosophy, political science and economy, and math. Three years of laboratory science, and two of music. That's it. No contemporary social studies. No accounting or finance. No computer classes. No distinct majors or minors.

The phrase "Great Books" may be a bit misleading; the college actually refers to its curriculum as "texts" which include musical compositions, scientific essays, short stories, and poems. More importantly, the texts flow in a highly structured sequence. Starting with the Greeks and working through the late 20th century, the list is altered with great scrutiny. The college adds only what it believes are seminal works, and often it takes decades to reach consensus on what may be worthy of inclusion. Juniors and seniors have electives and can suggest texts for a class or two. The sequencing of courses is very important to the St. John's method, with knowledge building over the semesters and years.

While some critics charge that Great Books curriculums promote sexist/elitist/racist biases of "dead white men", St. John's reading list is not etched in stone and has grown more inclusive. Over the decades, Latin and German were removed, and the Program has integrated voices of women (including Sappho, Virginia Woolf, and Sylvia Plath) and people of color (Toni Morrison, James Baldwin, and Jorge Luis Borges, among others; see Figure 1 for the full 4-year curriculum and sequence). The school also expanded its graduate offerings with a Masters in Eastern Classics that explores the philosophical, literary, and religious traditions of China, India, and Japan (requiring Sanskrit or Mandarin) and have plans for a degree in Middle Eastern classics (Table 11.1).

The aim of the Program is ambitious and deeply earnest, as the school proudly heralds:

> St. John's College is a community dedicated to liberal education. Liberally educated persons, the college believes, acquire a lifelong commitment to the pursuit of fundamental knowledge and to the search for unifying ideas. They are intelligently and critically appreciative of their common heritage and conscious of their social and moral obligations. They are well-equipped to master the specific skills of any calling, and they possess the means and the will to become free and responsible citizens.

TABLE 11.1 The Program's Undergraduate Sequence and Reading List

FRESHMAN YEAR
- HOMER: *Iliad, Odyssey*
- AESCHYLUS: *Agamemnon, Libation Bearers, Eumenides, Prometheus Bound*
- SOPHOCLES: *Oedipus Rex, Oedipus at Colonus, Antigone, Philoctetes, Ajax*
- THUCYDIDES: *Peloponnesian War*
- EURIPIDES: *Hippolytus, Bacchae*
- HERODOTUS: *Histories*
- ARISTOPHANES: *Clouds*
- PLATO: *Meno, Gorgias, Republic, Apology, Crito, Phaedo, Symposium, Parmenides, Theaetetus, Sophist, Timaeus, Phaedrus*
- ARISTOTLE: *Poetics, Physics, Metaphysics, Nicomachean Ethics, On Generation and Corruption, Politics, Parts of Animals, Generation of Animals*
- EUCLID: *Elements*
- LUCRETIUS: *On the Nature of Things*
- PLUTARCH: *Lycurgus, Solon*
- NICOMACHUS: *Arithmetic*
- LAVOISIER: *Elements of Chemistry*
- HARVEY: *Motion of the Heart and Blood*
- Essays by: Archimedes, Fahrenheit, Avogadro, Dalton, Cannizzaro, Virchow, Mariotte, Driesch, Gay-Lussac, Spemann, Stears, J.J. Thompson, Mendeleyev, Berthollet, J.L. Proust

SOPHOMORE YEAR
- THE OLD TESTAMENT
- THE NEW TESTAMENT
- ARISTOTLE: *De Anima, On Interpretation, Prior Analytics, Categories*
- APOLLONIUS: *Conics*
- VIRGIL: *Aeneid*
- PLUTARCH: "Caesar", "Cato the Younger", "Antony", "Brutus"
- EPICTETUS: *Discourses*, Manual
- TACITUS: *Annals*
- PTOLEMY: *Almagest*
- PLOTINUS: *The Enneads*
- AUGUSTINE: *Confessions*
- MAIMONIDES: *Guide for the Perplexed*
- ST. ANSELM: *Proslogium*
- AQUINAS: *Summa Theologica*
- DANTE: *Divine Comedy*
- CHAUCER: *Canterbury Tales*
- MACHIAVELLI: *The Prince, Discourses*
- KEPLER: *Epitome IV*
- RABELAIS: *Gargantua* and *Pantagruel*
- PALESTRINA: *Missa Papae Marcelli*
- MONTAIGNE: *Essays*
- VIETE: *Introduction to the Analytical Art*

(Continued)

TABLE 11.1 (Continued)

- BACON: *Novum Organum*
- SHAKESPEARE: *Richard II, Henry IV, The Tempest, As You Like It, Hamlet, Othello, Macbeth, King Lear, and Sonnets*
- POEMS BY: Marvell, Donne, and other 16th- and 17th-century poets
- DESCARTES: *Geometry, Discourse on Method*
- PASCAL: *Generation of Conic Sections*
- BACH: *St. Matthew Passion, Inventions*
- HAYDN: *Quartets*
- MOZART: *Operas*
- BEETHOVEN: *Third Symphony*
- SCHUBERT: Songs
- MONTEVERDI: *L'Orfeo*
- STRAVINSKY: *Symphony of Psalms*

JUNIOR YEAR
- CERVANTES: *Don Quixote*
- GALILEO: *Two New Sciences*
- HOBBES: *Leviathan*
- DESCARTES: *Meditations, Rules for the Direction of the Mind*
- MILTON: *Paradise Lost*
- LA ROCHEFOUCAULD: *Maximes*
- LA FONTAINE: *Fables*
- PASCAL: *Pensees*
- HUYGENS: *Treatise on Light, On the Movement of Bodies by Impact*
- ELIOT: *Middlemarch*
- SPINOZA: *Theological-Political Treatise*
- LOCKE: *Second Treatise of Government*
- RACINE: *Phaedre*
- NEWTON: *Principia Mathematica*
- KEPLER: *Epitome IV*
- LEIBNIZ: *Monadology, Discourse on Metaphysics, Essay On Dynamics, Philosophical Essays, Principles of Nature and Grace*
- SWIFT: *Gulliver's Travels*
- HUME: *Treatise of Human Nature*
- ROUSSEAU: *Social Contract, The Origin of Inequality*
- MOLIERE: *Le Misanthrope*
- ADAM SMITH: *Wealth of Nations*
- KANT: *Critique of Pure Reason, Foundations of the Metaphysics of Morals*
- MOZART: *Don Giovanni*
- JANE AUSTEN: *Pride and Prejudice*
- DEDEKIND: "Essay on the Theory of Numbers"
- "Articles of Confederation", "Declaration of Independence", "Constitution of the United States of America"
- HAMILTON, JAY, AND MADISON: *The Federalist*
- TWAIN: *The Adventures of Huckleberry Finn*

(Continued)

TABLE 11.1 (Continued)

- WORDSWORTH: *The Two Part Prelude of 1799*
- Essays by: Young, Taylor, Euler, D. Bernoulli, Orsted, Ampere, Faraday, Maxwell

<u>SENIOR YEAR</u>
- Supreme Court opinions
- GOETHE: *Faust*
- DARWIN: *Origin of Species*
- HEGEL: *Phenomenology of Mind*, "Logic" (from the Encyclopedia)
- LOBACHEVSKY: *Theory of Parallels*
- TOCQUEVILLE: *Democracy in America*
- LINCOLN: Selected Speeches
- FREDERICK DOUGLASS: Selected Speeches
- KIERKEGAARD: *Philosophical Fragments, Fear and Trembling*
- WAGNER: *Tristan and Isolde*
- MARX: *Capital, Political and Economic Manuscripts of 1844, The German Ideology*
- DOSTOEVSKI: *Brothers Karamazov*
- TOLSTOY: *War and Peace*
- MELVILLE: *Benito Cereno*
- O'CONNOR: Selected Stories
- WILLIAM JAMES; *Psychology, Briefer Course*
- NIETZSCHE: *Beyond Good and Evil*
- FREUD: Introductory Lectures on Psychoanalysis
- BOOKER T. WASHINGTON: Selected Writings
- DUBOIS: *The Souls of Black Folk*
- HUSSERL: *Crisis of the European Sciences*
- HEIDEGGER: *Basic Writings*
- EINSTEIN: Selected papers
- CONRAD: *Heart of Darkness*
- FAULKNER: *Go Down Moses*
- FLAUBERT: *Un Coeur Simple*
- WOOLF: *Mrs. Dalloway*
- Poems by: Yeats, T.S. Eliot, Wallace Stevens, Valery, Rimbaud
- Essays by: Faraday, J.J. Thomson, Millikan, Minkowski, Rutherford, Davisson, Schrodinger, Bohr, Maxwell, de Broglie, Heisenberg, Mendel, Boveri, Sutton, Morgan, Beadle & Tatum, Sussman, Watson & Crick, Jacob & Monod, Hardy

A defining feature of the Program is a resistance to placing texts in a political, social, or historic context for discussion. But St. John's is not a cloister, and students and faculty are well aware of the history and social settings of their studies. However, context is viewed as ideology, something that St. John's believes distorts true education and the ability to form one's own opinion. This is crucial to the school's philosophy; by freeing texts from context, St. John's claims it frees students' minds to ponder for themselves multiple possibilities and meanings. Those possibilities are then discussed and debated, and discarded when weak or specious, leaving better interpretations some space to surface. This creates what sociologist Alvin Gouldner called a "culture of critical discourse" (Gouldner, 1979), something sorely missing on many American campuses today.

Ultimately, this is what creates independent thinking. Anthony Kronman, former Dean of Yale Law School, argues in *Education's End: Why Our Colleges and Universities Have Given Up on the Meaning of Life*, that wrestling with Great Books can disrupt easy assumptions about purpose in life, and force students to think more and deeply articulate their personal beliefs. A St. John's-style of education to Kronman reveals a diversity of views and encourages a probing examination of the best way to live. He notes, engaging the texts "teach us that each of us can make, and wants to make, a life uniquely our own – a life that has no precise precedent in all the lives that have gone before and that can never be repeated exactly". (Kronman, 2008). This is what free minds and independent thinking are all about, isn't it?

With the Program, St. John's curriculum may seem limited compared to the telephone book-size course catalogs most colleges offer. But "Johnnies" (the colleges' nickname for students) and faculty would argue just the opposite. This curriculum is carefully designed not only to build knowledge but also to understand how knowledge is ultimately created; it is teaching students how to learn. In this respect, St. John's students *de facto* major in *epistemology*. And for those of us who never studied Ancient Greek (a St. John's requirement for two years), epistemology is the philosophy of knowledge or the investigation of what distinguishes substantiated and supportable belief from mere opinion.

Now *that* sounds like it could come in handy these days. We live in an age when more than 300 exabytes of data—the equivalent of one million Libraries of Congress—are created *every day*, with much being intentionally misleading, fake, or just plain wrong. What could be more valuable than developing an intellectual filter, honing the capacity to know what is important to know, distilling enormous amounts of information to form a rational position, or knowing how to listen and respond to—or perhaps integrate—someone else's point of view? In this vein, St. John's uses traditional texts taught in ancient methods to impart skills that have never been more crucial, particularly in our AI-driven age when so many forces try to steal our attention and undermine our abilities to form our own opinions.

The Program in Practice

You will not find 300-person lectures, teaching assistants, or multiple-choice tests at St. John's. Instead, classes are led by "tutors" who guide students through Socratic inquiry (and yes, students do read about the Socratic practice during freshman year in Plato's *Theaetetus)*. Despite its reputation as a sadistic exercise in student humiliation, the Socratic method actually is an interactive form of intellectual sandpapering that smooths out hypotheses and eliminates weak ideas through group discourse. Ben Baum, head of admissions at the college, notes that "the Socratic experience at St. John's is actually about listening to each other and, as a result, every voice is heard in a way that feels genuinely compassionate and collaborative – not combative". Tutors lead St. John's discussions but rarely dominate; they are more like conversation facilitators, believing that everyone in class is a teacher, everyone a learner. The tutors function as guides, more intent on listening to the students and working with them than imposing upon them their own understandings.

Faculty member Erica Beall elaborates:

> When a tutor walks into class, an intellectual effort begins that is wholly different from lecturing. We enter not as the expert, but as the most rigorously prepared student in the room. The 70 minutes guiding a tutorial reflect hours of careful reading, dwelling on details, puzzling over what is unobvious in the text, and reflecting on where one might direct students' attention to open up avenues for progress.

As one can imagine, you won't find a lot of Johnnies texting or surfing social media while in class; there is no place to hide in classrooms that range from small (seminars, 20 students led by two tutors) to smaller (tutorials, 10–15 students, one tutor) to smallest (preceptorials, three to eight students, one tutor).

There is a formality in a St. John's class—an un-ironic seriousness—that feels out of another era. Students and tutors address each other by "Mr." or "Ms." (or the gender-inclusive honorific of choice). Classrooms have a retro feel, with rectangular seminar tables and blackboards on surrounding walls, and science labs filled with analog instruments, wood and glass cabinets, and amusingly shaped beakers and test tubes.

You need to observe a few St. John's classes to get a sense of what's happening between and among the students and tutors. Discussions are often free-flowing, with students thinking out loud and talking to the ceiling; you can almost hear the gears turning in their brains. There are many "a-ha" moments in a St. John's classroom, sometimes coaxed out by tutors in Socratic fashion. But often they are triggered by students theorizing and responding among themselves.

In one class I attended, students were covering Ptolemy, the 2nd-century mathematician. Ptolemy believed that all the celestial bodies and sun revolved around the earth in a circle, and he based all his mathematical calculations on this perspective. Students were buzzing at the blackboard, working with a geometry sphere around the table, talking about diameters, meridians and equators, tilts, and horizons. Keep in mind this is all prep for what will be studied in a few months, when these Johnnies will learn that it would be another 1400 years before Copernicus proved Ptolemy's calculations correct but his conclusion wrong: The earth and planets actually revolve around the sun. These same students eventually will feel the excitement of learning of Kepler's conclusion 150 years later, that Copernicus was also right *and* wrong: Yes, the earth and planets revolved around the sun—but in an elliptical, not circular, orbit. This curricular layering is central to the St. John's Program. Later texts respond to and build upon previous texts. In essence, students intellectually follow modern thought as it has been built over the last 2000+ years instead of just memorizing the end results.

The cognitive rigor, immersion, and passion so present at St. John's are rare on American campuses these days. Johnnies read roughly 200 texts during their four years and write 25–30 papers that are more than 10 pages long. Seniors choose a writer or single text and do a deep-dive dissertation that typically runs 40–50 pages. Three tutors are then tasked with carefully reading the student's thesis, judging whether or not it is sufficient to complete the college requirement for graduation. Finally, a formal, public hour-long oral examination is held in which student discuss the essay—not unlike a doctoral defense. Here are a few of the senior capstone topics for a recent graduating class: The 19th-century English scientist Michael Faraday's heuristic description of electromagnetic phenomena; 17th-century mathematician Gottfried Wilhelm Leibniz's treatment of curvature in what's called the "chain line" problem; the use of Aristotelian terminology by 20th-century physicist Werner Heisenberg in describing quantum mechanics; and the possible revision of "space" from Immanuel Kant's *The Critique of Pure Reason* into a plurality of "spaces". Few college-educated outsiders have a clue what any of these papers are about, but they are not atypical of what's being studied, discussed, and written about at St. John's. And they represent the culmination of what might be the most valuable bachelor's degree in the world.

Life After College

While it's fair to say most liberal arts students live in a bubble cut off from reality, St. John's is unapologetic about, and in fact encourages, its four-year respite from the pressures and distractions of the outside world. Rather than being fixated on earning a living, most in the St. John's community would agree with Roosevelt Montas that its version of liberal education "instead asks what a living is for". (Montás, 2021).

But Johnnies seem to do just fine after graduation. About two-thirds go on for further degrees—including law school (a favorite), master's and doctoral programs (the school produces more graduates who go on to earn PhDs per capita than almost any other American college), and some to medical and business schools.

As mentioned earlier, many surveys about work in the future highlight the importance of uniquely human skills in the face of automation and AI including, among others: Persistence, motivation, and self-discipline; adeptness in communication, negotiation, collaboration, and team-building; and adaptability to changes in the external environment while maintaining what psychologist Albert

Bandura calls "self-efficacy"—an individual's belief in their ability to succeed in a particular situation (Bandura, 1977).

Perhaps because of the independent thinking and confidence strengthened by the Program, Johnnies wind-up with interesting life paths. In my research, I discovered many fascinating alumni for such a small school including Lydia Polgreen, former Editor-in-Chief of the *Huffington Post*; US Senator Ben Sasse from Nebraska; Kate Bennett, White House correspondent for CNN; and Jaq Holzman, founder of Elektra Record who signed dozens of seminal bands including The Doors and Queen.

Josh Rogers, Annapolis class of 1998, noted how St. John's boosted his "why not me" personality, and explained how it freed him to believe he could think up novel ideas like those that he read about. And he did. Within a few years of graduating St. John's, Rogers—with no formal coding or computer training—filed 16 patentable applications embedded in many popular websites. He then founded his own multibillion-dollar financial services company with more than 400 employees.

Ted Merz, an alumnus from the late 1980s, was one of the first fifteen employees at *Bloomberg News*. He went on to oversee operations in the Americas before heading-up strategic projects ranging from building news analytics to piping Twitter into Wall Street trading platforms. "Not a day goes by", Merz told me, "that I don't rely on the thought processes I developed at St. John's".

And don't forget the winemakers. Yes, Johnny winemakers, a fascinating story that could fill a book. Several alums have established and elevated America's global standing in wine, starting with 1952 alum Warren Winiarski. He is a Smithsonian award-winning pioneer in Napa who founded Stag's Leap Vineyards and won the 1976 "Judgement of Paris", beating some of the most famous French red wines in a now legendary blind test. For more than five decades Winiarski also has helped many in the St. John's community launch their own groundbreaking careers to define, refine, and redefine winemaking including alumni Larry Turley, his sister Helen Turley and brother-in-law John Wetlaufer, John and his son Alex Kongsgaard (an alum), and Abe Schoener, a former St. John's tutor, among many others.

Why wine and St. John's? Alum Zach Rasmusson, a former Winiarski apprentice and three-decade winemaker now with Duckhorn Vineyards, explains:

> With a fierce desire to express our individuality, winemaking is our chosen métier. It embodies the Greek ideal of areté, of achieving personal excellence. With the continuous unpredictable challenges of weather, winemaking creates an Odyssean test every year. It involves all the abilities and potentialities available to humans. We learn over time how to adapt to the changing elements, how to perfect our craft, but also realize that next year will test us again. It helps develop unrelenting resilience to what life throws at you.

Getting with the Program

Clearly, St. John's is not for everyone—prospective students and faculty included. First, to be a successful undergrad you need to be a voracious reader to cover the Program texts at a brisk pace. You also need the capacity for and love of writing because St. John's requires *a lot* of it. It helps to feel comfortable speaking in public, too, since so much of St. John's learning occurs out loud around a table with your classmates and tutors.

Quirky. Nerdy. Bookworms. These words may come to mind when thinking about what kind of high schoolers would pick St. John's versus other mainstream colleges. But not only straight-A achievers choose the Program (though there are plenty of them). Many Johnnies were outsiders who didn't necessarily fit into traditional high school cultures, nor did particularly well by typical high school metrics. There are a decent number of legacy students with parents or grandparents who've attended. Regardless of how they got there, successful Johnnies all share a sincere love of learning and a willingness to think *really* hard.

While many alumni claim they found their lost tribe at St. John's, around 20% of the freshman class leaves after their first year. Some find the curriculum too rigid and want to explore different things. Some complain of cabin fever; there are only around 100 students per graduating class in Santa Fe and Annapolis, and you get to know everyone—students, faculty, and staff—pretty quickly. Because of the staged coursework, students from each campus can escape for a semester or two on the other campus without interrupting the Program. While Johnnies can certainly use summer to travel and study overseas, unfortunately, the sequenced curriculum makes a Junior Year abroad difficult without taking off a full year from the Program. With that said, students in Annapolis can and do explore nearby cities (Washington DC, Baltimore, Philadelphia, New York), and Santa Fe does offer stunning scenery with world-class hiking, biking, and skiing.

There are no fraternities at St. John's (though plenty of parties); no rah-rah football games (unless you walk to the nearby Naval Academy in Annapolis); no food courts or swanky dorms. But the Johnnies who stay express heartfelt pleasure and pride in the idiosyncrasies of St. John's, such as the school's eccentric love of swing dancing and croquet.

If you think that the curriculum is unique for students, take a moment and think about the kind of person who wants to teach the Program. Being a tutor at St. John's is a truly singular experience, in many ways more akin to being a *sensei* at a hyperspecialized *dojo* than a traditional college professor. Sure, most liberal arts instructors develop and design curriculum to foster student learning and engage young minds. But that's where the similarities to St. John's faculty end.

Most tenure-tracked professors today specialize in a field, like literature, and often are expected to concentrate in arcane niches. Kidding aside, it wouldn't be unusual to peruse a college website and see a nano-focused faculty biography like this:

Professor Brown is a renowned expert on mid-18th century British elegies. Leveraging her scholarship on Thomas Gray, she has queried lament, grief and sorrow, the idealized dead, along with consolation and solace, in her award-winning volume, *Everyone Must Die: Welsh Requiems and Gravestones, 1747–1754*.

In addition to class lectures, such specialists are expected to research, publish, and speak publicly on their micro-expertise—often with job seniority, security, and mobility tied to such output. This would be typical for a small college professor, one at a larger state school, and certainly at an elite research university. But not at St. John's.

Erica Beall, who graduated from Annapolis and then earned her psychology doctorate at USC, highlights the differences:

> First, tutors don't lecture on autopilot, but rather focus intensely and lead probing discussions. They must be alive to the conversation, fully present at every moment. After class, most of what occupies the time and energy of the tutor has no place on a CV. These activities include dozens of hours each week meeting with students, thoughtfully commenting on their papers, preparing for upcoming classes, as well as studying texts outside the Program with our students and colleagues. There's little time for research, writing, and publishing.

Instead of specializing over time, St. John's curriculum often demands that faculty *generalize* and teach courses that are outside of their doctoral training. A tutor with an English Ph.D., for example, may be asked to teach science texts, while a STEM Ph.D. may lead readings in history. New tutors often apprentice with experienced ones like Eva Brann in Santa Fe, who started at St. John's in 1957 and has become one of the Program's *zen* masters. According to Beall, "It often takes a decade for a tutor to teach every class on the Program. Every tutor is expected to do this, for the sake of cultivating in themselves the intellectual breadth that is reflected in the program itself". It's clearly a unique faculty experience, one that certainly limits a tutor's mobility to more mainstream college lecturing.

Who Wants the Program?

The Program at St. John's may not sound like the model bachelor's curriculum for a future dominated by AI and technologies. Learning for the sake of learning is a beautiful thing, but given the costs of a private undergraduate degree, it's no wonder that most students want college to pay off in a more immediate, concrete way—like a six-figure job.

For many parents, St. John's may sound like four overindulgent years of naval-gazing banter. Similar to other liberal arts schools, the college struggled after the

Great Recession to attract students as shrunken savings and concerns about job security led to a plunge in applications. And those headwinds still remain, along with two structural problems in higher education: Rising costs and the "demographic cliff"—declining births tied to the 2008/9 recession which will reduce the number of traditional college applicants through the next decade or two.

Mark Roosevelt felt the headwinds when he was recruited as Santa Fe campus president in 2016 after reviving the famed but troubled Antioch College in Ohio. Since joining St. John's, Roosevelt is credited with making some tough decisions and getting the college on better financial footing while keeping the prized Program intact. When asked why he took on the challenge, Roosevelt quickly responds, "what St. John's does is unique and it does it better than any college in the world. That was and still is worth fighting for".

To broaden its applicant pool, the school has expanded a successful summer curriculum for high school juniors—a one-week Program taste-test. Moreover, sensing global demand for liberal arts education versus more dominant single-subject degrees, St. John's has pursued overseas applicants for its unique curriculum and built some strong secondary school pipelines around the world. Approximately 20% of recent classes have been filled by international students, adding a nice mix of cultural and racial diversity.

Admissions director Baum explains,

> St. John's broad liberal arts Program is certainly unique in the US but even more so compared to higher education options overseas, which tend to force students to concentrate in one subject and exclusively teach through large lectures and textbooks.

Asian universities, in particular, have been exploring ways to nurture the critical thinking skills embedded in American liberal arts degrees. In a fascinating 2021 study—and a testament to the Program—professors at Incheon National University in South Korea replicated St. John's curriculum with 120 students over two years. Compared to control groups, they found that the St. John's approach significantly improved group discussion efficacy, critical thinking skills, self-directed learning, a sense of belonging, and a degree of adaptability (Lee, Y. & Lee, Y., 2021) – echoing the qualities that so many recruiters have said they want in their employees.

Because of the low-tech, common curriculum and a lack of expensive infrastructure like professional-level sports stadiums and 5-star dorms, St. John's cost structure is remarkably low compared to many lesser institutions. As a result, Roosevelt urged the school to boldly reset tuition in 2018 to $35,000 when peers charged nearly $60,000.

Still expensive, such a level is comparable to nonresident state university tuition while offering a unique, boutique educational experience to a wider range of students. Roosevelt notes:

We are proud to spend our money on faculty salaries and small classes rather than fancy athletic facilities. Other colleges use those amenities to generate more net revenue by increasing class sizes and using adjunct professors. Our tuition reset was really about making the college more affordable and raising our profile so that more people would know about our low 7:1 student-to-faculty ratio.

To keep a further lid on tuition, he and the school also launched a successful $300 million capital campaign with funds coming largely from alumni, led by a $50 million challenge grant from winemaker Winiarski.

St. John's operates with two campus presidents, and when asked why she wanted to head Annapolis, Nora Demleitner responded:

> There are few places left in America where people focus on actively listening to one another and the institutional culture reinforces openness to new ideas and perspectives. Most rare is a place where one is academically respected for changing one's thinking in light of better arguments and reasoning. St. John's College gives me hope for a future in which real, deep, respectful dialogue can again play a central role in our pluralist democracy.

Still, some may question whether a St. John's bachelor's degree is worth it. To paraphrase Matt Damon in *Good Will Hunting*, why waste $150,000 on an education that you coulda got for $1.50 in late fees at the public library? True. Every text studied at St. John's *can* be found at a public library. But that's missing the point. As Shawn Watts, alum and district court judge for the native Prairie Band Potawatomi Nation in Kansas, told me,

> St. John's is less about the books than the process and the community. It trains your mind and frees it at the same time. This allows you to truly follow your own passions and interest in life without the subconscious impositions and prodding of our wired world.

In the face of a very uncertain future shaped by automation and AI, a St. John's education may be money very well spent.

Thinking Ahead

As the AI Revolution and other technologies have transformed all kinds of organizations, many companies and entire industries have died failing to adapt to the new world order. Equally daunting challenges confront colleges and universities, with predictions that half of America's institutions may close in the coming decades (Lederman, 2017). Some say that traditional bachelor's degrees will be less needed, replaced by cheaper, easy-to-understand micro-credentials and skill badges. Maybe higher education will be largely online and possibly free from quasi-schools like Khan Academy, and the monastic 4-year residential experience of American colleges like St. John's will be a rarified luxury.

Amid these trends, St. John's remains unruffled. As the school trumpets:

> knowledge advances and the fundamental outlook of humanity may change over the centuries, but [the skills we teach] remain in one form or another indispensable. They enable all human beings to know the world around them and to know themselves in this world, and to use that knowledge with wisdom. Under the guidance of these arts, they can free [students] from the constraint of prejudice and the narrowness of beaten paths....and students can acquire the habit of listening to reason. A genuinely conceived liberal arts curriculum cannot avoid aiming at these most far-reaching of all human goals.

The Program is also downright practical: It helps students free their minds, find purpose in life, and develop cognitive shields to protect their attention and decision-making abilities against the ruthless realities of AI.

If residential colleges do survive, they would be wise to emulate not only the goals of a St. John's education—cultivating independent, creative thinkers who excel at learning– but also its relatively lower cost, common curriculum, more collaborative experience, and the Program's emphasis on listening and making sense of multiple perspectives. Maybe this old-school approach is exactly how to produce the kind of innovative human intelligence that we'll need to navigate tomorrow's world of artificial intelligence.

Bibliography

American Academy of Arts & Sciences (2021). Bachelor's degrees in the humanities. Available at https://www.amacad.org/humanities-indicators/higher-education/bachelors-degrees-humanities#topII1

Arum, R., & Roksa, J. (2011). *Academically adrift: Limited learning on college campuses*. University of Chicago Press.

Bandura, A. (1977). Self-efficacy: Toward a unifying theory of behavioral change. *Psychological Review*, 84, 191–215.

Bruni, F. (2018). The most contrarian college in America. *The New York Times*, 11.

Deresiewicz, W. (2015). *Excellent sheep: The miseducation of the American elite and the way to a meaningful life*. Simon and Schuster.

Fischman, W., & Gardner, H. (2022). *The real world of college: What higher education is and what it can be*. MIT Press.

Gallup & Bates College (Lewiston, Me). (2019). Forging pathways to purposeful work: The role of higher education. Available at https://www.gallup.com/education/248222/gallup-bates-purposeful-work-2019.aspx

Gouldner, A. W. (1979). *Future of intellectuals and the rise of the new class*. Seabury Press.
Hanson, M. (2022). Student loan debt statistics. EducationData.org, May 30, 2022. Available at https://educationdata.org/student-loan-debt-statistics
Higher Ed Dive Team. (2022). A look at trends in college consolidation since 2016. Higher Ed Dive. Available at https://www.highereddive.com/news/how-many-colleges-and-universities-have-closed-since-2016/539379/
Kronman, A. T. (2008). *Education's end*. Yale University Press.
Lederman, D. (2017). *Clay christensen, doubling down*. Inside Higher Ed. Available at https://www.insidehighered.com/digital-learning/article/2017/04/28/clay-christensen-sticks-predictions-massive-college-closures
Lee, Y., & Lee, Y. (2021). The effectiveness of the classes adapting and utilizing discussion methods of St. John's college. *Korean Journal of General Education*, 15(2), 113–132.
Menand, L. (2021). What's so great about great-books courses? *The New Yorker*. Available at https://www.newyorker.com/magazine/2021/12/20/whats-so-great-about-great-books-courses-roosevelt-montas-rescuing-socrates
Montás, R. (2021). *Rescuing socrates: How the great books changed my Life and why they matter for a new generation*. Princeton University Press.
Rainie, L., & Anderson, J. (2017). *The future of jobs and jobs training*. Pew Research Center. Available at https://www.pewresearch.org/internet/2017/05/03/the-future-of-jobs-and-jobs-training/
Udemy. (2020). 2020 workplace learning trends report: The skills of the future. Available at https://business.udemy.com/resources/5-workplace-learning-trends-2020/
U.S. Bureau of Labor Statistics. (2021). Number of jobs, labor market experience, and earnings growth: Results from a national longitudinal survey. Available at https://www.bls.gov/news.release/nlsoy.nr0.htm
Whiting, K. (2020). These are the top 10 job skills of tomorrow—and how long it takes to learn them. *World Economic Forum* (Vol. 21). Available at https://www.weforum.org/agenda/2020/10/top-10-work-skills-of-tomorrow-how-long-it-takes-to-learn-them/

12
CHINESE GLOBALIZATION

BRI and the Future of Higher Education

Daniel Araya and Michael A. Peters

Since the end of World War II, the United States and its allies have overseen a global order built on trade liberalization and the development of a Western model of global integration. That order now appears to be winding down (Zakaria, 2011). Beyond the age of "Western hegemony", Asia is returning to the patterns of commerce and cultural exchange that thrived long before European colonialism and American predominance (Khanna, 2019). Underwriting Asia's resurgence is the return of Chinese leadership across an enormous Eurasian trading system (Jacques, 2009). Chinese President Xi Jinping's signature "Belt and Road Initiative" (BRI), stretches across Asia, the Middle East, Africa, Europe, and Latin America, representing the largest infrastructure project in history (Figure 12.1).

BRI forms a central component of Xi's "Major Country Diplomacy" (大国外交) strategy, underscoring China's broader leadership ambitions. Building on decades of domestic investments in ports, pipelines, rail, and telecommunications, China's expanding supply chain empire is now underwriting the emergence of a new global order. More than markets alone, BRI serves as a platform for global integration across 149 countries and a new phase in Chinese globalization. Taken to its logical conclusion, China's BRI reflects the rise of a new multipolar system and a post-American world order. One industry that could benefit immensely from BRI is higher education (HE).

This chapter considers the long-term impact of BRI on the changing landscape of HE with a particular focus on artificial intelligence (AI). We argue that China's HE planning marks a new stage in globalization. Across developing countries, the nexus of HE is shifting away from Western countries and toward China. Just as Anglo-American power has been ceding ground to China in terms of trade, investment, and technological innovation, so China's growing influence in education could represent a tipping point in the emergence of a new global order.

DOI: 10.4324/9781003230762-15

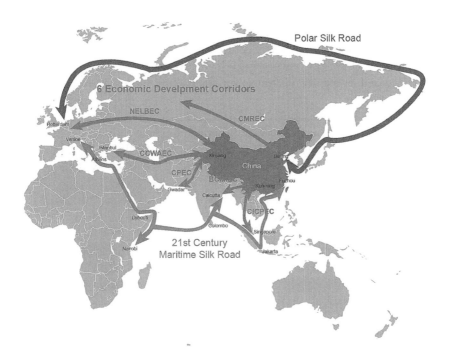

FIGURE 12.1 China's Belt and Road Initiative.

China Rising

China's economic expansion now exerts a gravitational pull on the world economy (Economist, 2018). Gathering emerging markets in its orbit, China's BRI reimagines the world as a single complex network of supply chains, trade arteries, and communication grids (Khanna, 2019). Building on its enormous supply-chain infrastructure, the country's immense capacity for steel, concrete, and iron now drive hundreds of infrastructure projects around the world.

First described as the "Silk Road Economic Belt", China's BRI projects represent the culmination of decades of domestic investment in the pursuit of Chinese modernization. Beginning as overland routes for road and rail transportation through landlocked Central Asia, BRI has since expanded to include vast swathes of infrastructure investment around the world.

This includes transport, energy, mining, information technology, and communications in the development of industrial parks, special economic zones (SEZ), and urban development projects.

The stated objective of BRI is to develop a transcontinental investment program that aims at combining infrastructure development with economic integration along the route of the historic Silk Road.[1] The "Belt" in BRI refers to the "Silk Road Economic Belt", while the "Road" refers to Indo-Pacific sea routes connecting China to Southeast Asia, South Asia, the Middle East, Europe, and Africa. BRI envisages developing six major economic cooperation corridors and several key maritime pivot points across Eurasia. More concretely, this includes:

1. The New Eurasian Land Bridge Economic Corridor (NELBEC)
2. China—Mongolia—Russia Economic Corridor (CMREC)
3. China—Central Asia—West Asia Economic Corridor (CCWAEC)
4. China—Indochina Peninsula Economic Corridor (CICPEC)
5. Bangladesh—China—India—Myanmar Economic Corridor (BCIMEC)
6. China—Pakistan Economic Corridor (CPEC)

More recently, China's State Council Information Office has published a 2018 white paper advancing the country's "Arctic Policy" with the aim of adding trade routes to BRI in the Arctic as well. BRI has no formal institutionalized body. Implementation is spread across a wide range of actors and stakeholders with the National Development and Reform Commission (NDRC) playing a guiding role.

Chinese Globalization

Critics of BRI suggest that the project is more aspirational than real. Building on accusations of "debt-trap diplomacy" and neocolonialism, the United States government has been particularly vocal in its criticism of BRI. However, research by Deborah Bräutigam (Bräutigam, 2010; Brautigam and Rithmire, 2021) at Johns Hopkins University, contests this view. Trade volume between China and its BRI participating countries was more than 6 trillion USD between 2013 and 2018. China's foreign direct investment (FDI) in these countries has exceeded 80 billion dollars.[2] In fact, China's import from and export to BRI participating countries totaled 300 billion dollars in the first quarter of 2019, up 7.8% year-on-year and occupying 28.6% of the country's total foreign trade volume.

Where the United States has largely prioritized security agreements and a vast military-industrial complex, "Chinese globalization" is increasingly clustered around an array of bilateral and multilateral trade agreements. Indeed, even as the United States seeks to bolster its influence in the Asian region through a series of security agreements (i.e., the Quadrilateral Security Dialogue, the Australia–UK–US Partnership, the Indo-Pacific Economic Framework for Prosperity), Asian economic integration is accelerating. Together, the Comprehensive and Progressive Agreement for Trans-Pacific Partnership (CPTPP) and the Regional Comprehensive Economic Partnership (RCEP) agreements reflect a changing global order. RCEP alone represents the world's largest trade agreement, integrating a third of the global economy ($29.7 trillion) and a third of the world's population (2.2 billion people) into the largest free trade bloc in history.

China as a Global Technology Leader

In addition to its importance as a global trade network for Chinese goods and services, BRI offers a platform for a long-term strategic shift around advanced Chinese technologies.[3] This includes electric vehicles (EV), telecommunications, robotics, AI, semiconductors, clean energy, technologies, advanced electrical equipment, rail infrastructure, and maritime engineering. China is spending billions of dollars on research in genomics, quantum computing, robotics, and advanced materials (Economist, 2019).

China's ambitious economic goals are directly tied to technological development and the development of high skill labor. Alongside its expanding influence across export and manufacturing, China is increasingly focused on domestic consumption and a long-term shift toward high-technology industries—especially AI. As part of "Made in China 2025" (published in 2015), the Chinese government has targeted ten advanced technology manufacturing industries, including advanced information technologies and robotics, aviation, maritime, rail, new energy vehicles, electrical generation, agricultural machinery, new materials, and pharmaceuticals.

China's government aims to make the country a "world-leader" in AI by 2025 with a core AI industry exceeding RMB 400 billion (USD 60.3 billion) and an AI-related industry exceeding RMB 5 trillion (USD 754.0 billion). In fact, China accounted for nearly one-fifth of global private investment funding in AI in 2021, attracting $17 billion for AI start-ups (Zhang et al., 2022). With some of the largest technology companies in the world (Alibaba, Baidu, ByteDance, Tencent), technological innovation has become an integral part of Beijing's broader strategic planning.

In fact, China has unique advantages in driving AI across two critical categories: (1) A huge population and therefore an enormous abundance of data; and (2) engineering talent. Building on massive quantities of data and ample venture funding, China is hoping to lead the world in AI over this decade with the COVID pandemic likely accelerating this process.

AI and Chinese Human Capital Development

Chinese planners are increasingly focused on bridging reskilling and lifelong learning through advancements in AI. Moving beyond an education system primarily focused on mass manufacturing, China's government has signaled the need to upgrade its enormous workforce in order to develop the strategic capabilities needed for high-technology industries. In conjunction with the internet and digital technologies more broadly, AI is expected to be integrated across a wide variety of educational resources and services. This includes using AI to promote lifelong learning in the context of digital transformation and the acceleration of smart technologies in education.

China's State Council's "New Generation Artificial Intelligence Development Plan" published in 2017 prioritizes the mass application of AI to industries across the country—particularly education. The plan calls for implementing AI training at every level of education. In fact, China has begun actively integrating AI education into student education, including software coding courses, and access to labs featuring robotics, drones, and 3D printing. According to the country's Minister of Education, Huai Jinpeng, AI will be deeply integrated into Chinese education.[4]

In 2019, the Chinese State Council published two significant plans to drive continued reform in China's education sector. These include, China's Education Modernization 2035[5] (2035 Plan) issued in February of 2019, and the Implementation Plan for Accelerating Education Modernisation (2018–2022)[6] (Implementation Plan). Aimed at modernizing China's education system, the plans aim to accelerate the digitalization of Chinese education, leveraging AI and other emerging technologies to modernize teaching and learning.

Together, government planning and tax incentives for AI ventures are expected to improve student learning while building out the Chinese technology industry as a whole. China produced around one-third of both AI journal papers and AI citations worldwide in 2021. In fact, China's global share of research papers in the field of AI has expanded dramatically from 4.26% (1,086) in 1997 to 27.68% in 2017 (37,343), surpassing the United States (China AI Development Report, 2018).

The expectation is that the application of AI to education could hold the potential to address teacher scarcity, offer alternative models of education, and potentially reshape the traditional learning paradigm. This would likely include the creation of standard educational tools that leverage machine learning to automate test grading and homework correction, and more advanced adaptive learning systems and intelligent tutors that provide real-time personalized feedback at a granular level. The current penetration rate of AI in China's K-12 education sector in the form of adaptive learning was approximately 4% in 2019 and is expected to increase to 19% by 2025. The market size of this sector is also expected to grow from RMB 30 billion in 2019 to over RMB 100 billion by 2025.

China and Global Higher Education

China's government has emphasized the need for indigenous innovation to reduce the country's dependence on other countries for high-end manufacturing. Having developed the largest workforce in the world, Chinese education and training have been pivotal to the country's unprecedented economic growth. Chinese workers and their labor productivity have grown tenfold over the past 30 years, even as the country's GDP has increased 13 times.

However, in recent years, China's enormous pool of cheap labor has begun to shrink as mass migration from agriculture to urban employment has slowed. Like much of the advanced world, China is now aging and the country's debt levels are rising. Given these challenges, the Chinese government has begun focusing on innovation in order to support rising productivity and improved skills development. In fact, as many as 220 million Chinese workers, or 30% of the workforce, may need to transition between occupations by 2030.

Over the last decade, China has increasingly concentrated on reforming its HE system with the aim of increasing the capacity, quality, and world ranking of its tertiary institutions. Current reforms are directed at encouraging greater self-reliance by building a system of Chinese HE that is independent of US, Canadian, British, Australian, and New Zealand universities while developing a system of quality HE that becomes a destination for international foreign students on its own right. With targeted scholarship programs for BRI countries and developing countries in Africa (Xu et al., 2021; Yodpet et al, 2023), domestic investments in Chinese education are driving changes outside China as well.

Beyond infrastructure and trade, Chinese investments in HE are catalyzing transformation across the broader education landscape. This includes greater emphasis on peer-reviewed research and the development of Chinese and English-language journals with targeted incentives to produce world-class scholarship, especially in science, technology, engineering, and math (STEM) but also in the social sciences.

Emerging as one of the largest hubs in the world for international education, China is establishing joint-venture programs with the aim of attracting international students through programs that involve student exchange and study abroad. Chinese universities have become "magnet institutions" for BRI developing countries with enrolments jumping 12 percent to 317,000 students.[7]

China has become both a source and a hub for international students over the past decade with over 31% coming from South Korea, and over 10% each from the United States and Thailand, and over 8% each from Pakistan, India, and Russia.[8] According to China's Ministry of Foreign Affairs, over half a million foreign students study in China making it the top destination in Asia, with over 50% of those students coming from neighboring countries.

In July 2016, the Ministry of Education issued the Education Action Plan for the Belt and Road, and signed a memorandum of international cooperation with 14 provinces including Gansu, Ningxia, Fujian, Guizhou, and other autonomous regions and municipalities, aiming to build a ministerial–provincial joint platform for BRI. The Chinese Academy of Sciences (CAS) alone, has provided over 1.8 billion yuan (about 268 million USD) for construction of science and technology projects in association with BRI since 2013.

The government's Silk Road Scholarship Program sponsors 10,000 new international students each year from BRI countries. Chinese Universities can apply for state funding to run a BRI talent development site for large cohorts. In fact, degree-seeking students became the majority (52.44%) of international students in China for the first time in 2018. This includes bachelor, masters, and doctoral students who study abroad for at least one year with the number of foreign degree-seeking students increasing by more than 350% from 36,387 in 2006 to 178,271 in 2018.

In 2015, China launched the University Alliance of the Silk Road which brought together more than 130 universities on five continents. Coordinated by China's Xian Jiaotong University, the alliance aims to develop cooperation among its members and promote BRI in HE. In addition to this, The School of Business and Management at The Hong Kong University of Science and Technology (HKUST Business School) and Russia's SKOLKOVO School of Management have joined forces to launch a new Executive MBA program for Eurasia.

The Chinese National Science Foundation (NSFC) and the National Social Science Foundation[9] have been established to award grants based on peer review, based on the North American model. Both foundations have been involved in high-level strategic dialogue with Science Europe and other international science bodies to strengthen collaboration in achieving carbon neutrality goals and the United Nation's sustainable development goals.[10]

Building on research in science and technology, innovation has become a critical factor in maintaining global competitiveness, especially in knowledge and technology-intensive industries. Funding nearly 18,000 young scholars through the Young Scientists Fund in 2019 (NSFC, Annual Report, 2019), the system of talent development is undergoing systematic reform in Chinese universities (Xue, Tian & Li, 2022).

Modern academic publishing in China lags behind the West but this may be changing. Aided by global science communication and the first electronic journals emerging in the early 1990s, the development of open access as well as the merger and acquisition of big publishers, China is now catching up. The number of Chinese English-language journals (CELAJs) has increased from 83 in 1980 to over 500 today, with a commensurate increase in the number of university presses and over 8000 journals. Large scholarly publishers such as China Science Publishing Group Co., Ltd (CSPG) and Social Sciences Academic Press (SSAP) of the Chinese Association of Social Science (CASS), account for much of this growth.

Indeed, according to the 2018 Science & Engineering Indicators, a report published by the United States National Science Foundation (NSF), China has left the United States behind to become the largest producer of scientific articles.[11] In 2016, China published more than 426,000 studies, which amounted to

18.6% of the publications indexed in Scopus (Elsevier's database). The United States, with 409,000 studies, is now positioned after China. Clarivate Analytics announced that China ranks third in the world in publishing academic papers that are a result of international collaboration. Nonetheless, China still lags behind the United States in terms of citations.

Interpreting Chinese Globalization

While China's focus on labor-intensive industries has followed other Asian economies, the country's ambivalence toward neoliberal (market-led) development prescribed by the Washington Consensus has enabled it to catch up to advanced economies, even as the vast majority of developing countries have made little progress. In fact, much of China's economic growth is rooted in the government's capacity to marshal the capabilities of its sprawling population.

China now graduates more than 8.7 million students each year (a ten-fold increase from the 0.87 million graduates in 1999). Public investment in Chinese education soared 50-fold between 1992 and 2018, from 2.7% of the GDP to 4.1%. In 1978, only 66% of children were covered by compulsory education; today that share is 100%. Gross enrolment in secondary education more than doubled from 41% to 95% over the same period, even as the number of college admissions increased from 3.7 million in 2000 to 9.1 million in 2019.

In its drive to reduce its technological dependence on the United States and other advanced economies, Chinese human capital development is becoming a prominent feature of national policy and planning. Innovation has become a critical factor in maintaining global competitiveness, especially in knowledge-intensive industries, and China's global technology prowess reflects this understanding. Supported by an expansive telecommunications infrastructure (5G) and an AI-mediated Chinese techno-state, China's development model may one day become the global standard.

Where the Western approach to development policy has often led to a scramble for access to top-ranked institutions—leaving nothing for the rest, China's approach is different. The Office of the United States Trade Representative notes the elements of China's development approach includes central planning, plan mobilization across all sectors, the leveraging of state resources and finance, civil-military integration and two-way transfer, backbone enterprises in technology development, technological breakthroughs in key areas, import substitution policies, and the promotion of Chinese industries in its domestic market.[12]

Over the past 25 years, development theory and development studies have undergone great reversals reflecting the rapidly changing global geopolitics that has favored the growth of emerging economies and especially the "BRICS countries" (Brazil, China, Russia, India, South Africa). Building on investments in global interconnectivity and overlapping research collaboration across HE institutions, the expansion of China's BRI across emerging economies represents a new Chinese-led development model.

Unlike US-led trade liberalization (neoliberalism), education is critical to what might be called "Chinese infrastructuralism". Chinese infrastructuralism represents a new stage in globalization and a new model of development. Against many different and competing conceptions of development, including (i) The Washington neoliberal model; (ii) "development as freedom" (Sen); (iii) "limits to growth" and sustainability (Bruntland); (iv) various Marxist and neo-Marxist critiques of underdevelopment, dependence, and world systems theory; (iv) "post-development" (Escobar), we can now add State-led infrastructure development in the form of Chinese development socialism.

Following the Chinese model, infrastructure investment and development is layered, including not only physical infrastructure such as the development of transport networks (ports and railways) but also people-to-people exchanges emphasizing the new digital Silk Road, university alliances and the development of educational and cultural exchanges. Building on the New Digital Silk Road, people-to-people exchange, and university alliances, Chinese infrastructuralism includes both "hard" and "soft" infrastructure in the development of skilled labor.

What began as an enormous infrastructure project has evolved to include a new series of goals overlapping culture and education—in the broadest sense, to form the "soft infrastructure" of a massive regional trading system. BRI represents a pillar of the "Chinese Dream", providing a new model of development with the potential to reshape both higher and vocational education across the Eurasian region (Peters, 2020). All of this reflects a broader shift undergirding the rise of Asia as a regional trading center. Even as many universities across Western countries expect declining student enrolment (Redden, 2019), the Chinese government has linked study in China to job opportunities across BRI countries.

Building on trade relationships across 130 countries, and with new strategic partnerships with universities in Russia and the European Union (EU), China's broader global impact could be substantial. Combined with generous scholarship programs and an enormous economy, China's impact on global HE could be enormous. Indeed, as the quality and capacity of Chinese HE continue to improve, Chinese universities will continue to absorb eager students from around the world.

As demand for education continues to increase, particularly across STEM subjects, China's attractiveness as a study destination for emerging economies will grow, impacting the global HE market more broadly. As China seeks to reduce its technological dependence on others, its capacities for supporting STEM education can be expected to grow in scale and quality. Building on Chinese "indigenous innovation" and "re-innovation" of foreign technologies through its 5-year plans, the National Medium and Long-Term Science and Technology Development Plan Outline (2006–2020) (MLP), and "Made in China 2025", China hopes to become a global technology leader.

In the continued evolution of BRI, we can imagine significant technology investments that build on Chinese AI in the emergence of "global China". Rooted in next-generation technologies such as AI, deep learning, smart cities, quantum computing, and the Internet-of-Things, Chinese trade and investments could enable the vast digital convergence and economic synergies that many have been theorizing over the past decade (Peters, 2012). Rather than an abstract idea, Chinese Infrastructure—both "hard" (engineering) and "soft" (education and culture)— could mean a dramatic acceleration in globalization in the rise of a complex multipolar system.

Conclusion

With over 149 countries involved in China's Belt and Road system and over a trillion dollars of Chinese investment planned for economic, digital and social development across multiple continents, BRI represents a uniquely Chinese approach to development. Belt and Road regions could contribute as much as 80% of global GDP growth by 2050, advancing three billion more people into the middle class. More than simply a global infrastructure project, BRI reflects a new stage in globalization in which multiple regions and geographies are now converging around a new era in Chinese-led globalization.

Together, the decline of American predominance and the rise of Asia as the new economic center of gravity underscores a fundamentally new global order. Much as China has become the manufacturing workshop of the world, the country's enormous soft infrastructure of education and training could be set to reconfigure the global HE sector as well. China has taken the lead in development across much of the world through its BRI project. What this suggests is that Chinese FDI is now underwriting a new multipolar order in which Chinese HE could be key to global integration across emerging and developing countries.

The rapid development of Asia as a sprawling regional system is also a reflection of BRI's social integration across a vast Eurasian trading system. The connection between HE, science and technology, and BRI is comprehensive. However, drawing far-reaching conclusions on the final impact of BRI may be premature. BRI is still in an early phase of development. Nonetheless, based on the research presented in this essay, it is possible to identify several trends and discuss preliminary conclusions with regard to the long-term trajectory of HE within a changing multipolar order.

Notes

1 In Africa, for example, Chinese conglomerates have already become positioned to capitalize on the continent's need for technology, trade, and manufacturing. China's investments encompass utilities, port construction and agriculture but also telecommunications. Chinese telecom providers now dominate Africa's billion-user mobile phone market.
2 According to the Chinese government, China's trade volume of goods with BRI countries is reported to have reached an eight-year high in 2021 totalling 11.6 trillion yuan, a new high over the past eight years and a year-on-year increase of 23.6 percent, accounting for 29.7 percent of China's total foreign trade. China's foreign direct investment in BRI countries, was nearly 139 billion yuan, up by nearly 8% over the previous year representing 15% of all outbound investment.
3 https://thediplomat.com/2019/02/made-in-china-2025-explained/
4 http://education.chinadaily.com.cn/2021-12/08/c_691677.htm
5 People's Republic of China, The State Council, XinhuaNet. "中共中央、国务院印发《中国教育现代化2035》(The CCPC and State Council Publishes 'China's Education Modernization 2035 Plan')", The State Council, 23 Feb. 2019. www.gov.cn/xinwen/2019-02/23/content_5367987.htm
6 People's Republic of China, The State Council, XinhuaNet. "中共中央办公厅、国务院办公厅印发《加快推进教育现代化实施方案(2018-2022年)》(TheCCPC and State Council publishes 'Implementation Plan for Speeding up Education Modernisation (2018-2022)')", 23 Feb. 2019. www.gov.cn/zhengce/2019-02/23/content_5367988.htm
7 https://www.scmp.com/news/china/society/article/2165892/why-foreign-students-along-belt-and-road-are-jostling-enrol
8 https://chinapower.csis.org/china-international-students/
9 The NSSF was established in 1991.
10 For example, in 2022 NSFC and the UK Research and Innovation (UKRI) held talks on the logic and landscape of the knowledge system and the role of interdisciplinary research. The emphasis in the reform for strengthening basic research has focused on improving evaluation mechanisms, encouraging originality and innovation, and strengthening the "academic ecology" featuring responsibility, credibility, and contribution.
11 https://nsf.gov/statistics/2018/nsb20181/report/sections/academic-research-and-development/highlights
12 On the basis of this strategy China aimed for 40% self-sufficiency by 2020 and 75% self-sufficiency by 2025 (Peters, 2019).These strategies have included the encouragement of development in STEM disciplines with a focus on key digital technologies in quantum computing (QC), supercomputing (SC), machine learning (ML), genomic science (GS), new materials science (NMS) and so on with the development the new range of strategic biodigital technologies that drives technological convergence focused on the emerging global digital economy and fintech.

References

Baty, Phil (2021) Asian universities are on the rise. This is what it means for the rest of the world, https://www.weforum.org/agenda/2021/07/asian-universities-on-the-rise-education-rankings-learning/

Bräutigam, D. (2010). *The dragon's gift: The real story of China in Africa*. New York: Oxford University Press.

Brautigam, D. & M. Rithmire (2021) The Chinese 'Debt Trap' Is a Myth. *The Atlantic*, 6 February 2021.
China AI Development Report. (2018). China Institute for Science and Technology Policy. Retrieved from: https://www.sppm.tsinghua.edu.cn/english/info/1032/1601.htm
d'Hooghe, I. (2021) China's BRI and International Cooperation in Higher Education and Research: A Symbiotic Relationship. In: Schneider, Florian (ed.), *Global Perspectives on China's Belt and Road Initiative: Asserting Agency through Regional Connectivity*. Amsterdam University Press, https://www.degruyter.com/document/doi/10.1515/9789048553952-003/html
Economist (2018). The Chinese century is well under way. October 26.
Economist (2019). How China could dominate science. January 12.
Jacques, M. (2009). *When China Rules the World: The End of the Western World and the Birth of a New Global Order*. New York: Penguin Books.
Khanna, P. (2019). *The Future is Asian: Commerce, Conflict, and Culture in the 21st Century*. New York: Simon & Schuster.
Li, J. & E. Xue (2022) Reimaging the panorama of international education development in China: A retrospective mapping perspective, *Educational Philosophy and Theory*, DOI: 10.1080/00131857.2022.2090927
Morrison, N.(2022) China's Universities are Hot on U.S. Heels as Investment Pays Off, Forbes, https://www.forbes.com/sites/nickmorrison/2022/04/25/chinas-universities-are-hot-on-us-heels-as-investment-pays-off/?sh=7c80779f34e0
NSFC. (2019) *Annual Report*. https://www.nsfc.gov.cn/english/site_1/pdf/NSFC%20Annual%20Report%202019.pdf
Peters, M. A. (2012). Bio-informational capitalism, *Thesis Eleven*, 110:1, 98–111.
Peters, M.A. (2019) Trade wars, technology transfer, and the future Chinese techno-state, *Educational Philosophy and Theory*, 51:9, 867–870, DOI: 10.1080/00131857.2018.1546109
Peters, M.A. (2020) *The Chinese Dream: Educating the Future. An Educational Philosophy and Theory Chinese Educational Philosophy Reader*, Volume VII. Routledge.
Peters, M.A., Benjamin Green & Steve Fuller (2022) China's rise, the Asian century and the clash of meta-civilizations, *Educational Philosophy and Theory*, DOI: 10.1080/00131857.2022.2032654
Redden, E. (2019, November 18). Number of enrolled international students drops. *Inside Higher Ed*.
Xu, R., Yodpet Worapot, Hongjun Tian, Xiyuan Zhang, Yi Zhang, Hazzan Moses Kayode, Michael Adrian Peters, Benjamin Green, Fazal Rizvi & Cathy Ping Xie (2021) International education in the Asian Century: Decline of Anglophone dominance?, *Educational Philosophy and Theory*, DOI: 10.1080/00131857.2021.2017885
Xue, E., Shixu Tian & Jian Li (2022) Doctoral cultivation system and mechanism of university think tank in China, *Educational Philosophy and Theory*, DOI: 10.1080/00131857.2022.2060815
Worapot, Yodpet, Amelio Salvador Quetzal, Nguon Siek, Fenny Vebrina Sihite, Paul John Edrada Alegado, Vishalache Balakrishnan, Benjamin Green, & Stephanie Hollings (2023) International education within ASEAN and the rise of Asian century, *Educational Philosophy and Theory*, 55:1, 21–34, DOI: 10.1080/00131857.2022.2080545

Zakaria, F. (2011). *The Post-American World: And The Rise Of The Rest*. New York: Penguin Books.

Zhang, D. et al. (2022). Artificial Intelligence Index report 2022. Stanford Institute for Human-Centered Artificial Intelligence (HAI), Stanford University, March 2022. Retrieved from: https://aiindex.stanford.edu/wp-content/uploads/2022/03/2022-AI-Index-Report_Master.pdf

Zhu, X. & Jian Li (2018) Conceptualizing the ontology of higher education with Chinese characteristics, *Educational Philosophy and Theory*, 50:12, 1144–1156, DOI: 10.1080/00131857.2018.1504707

PART III
Policy and Planning for the Augmented Future

13
A NEW GENERATION ARTIFICIAL INTELLIGENCE DEVELOPMENT PLAN

The State Council of the People's Republic of China

The rapid development of artificial intelligence (AI) will profoundly transform human society. In accordance with the requirements of the CCP Central Committee and the State Council, this plan has been formulated to seize the major strategic opportunity for the development of AI, to build China's first-mover advantage in the development of AI, and to accelerate the construction of an innovative nation and global power in science and technology.

13.1 The Strategic Situation

The development of AI has entered a new stage. After 60 years of technological evolution, especially in mobile Internet, big data, supercomputing, sensor networks, brain science, and other new theories and technologies, AI's development has accelerated under the joint impetus of powerful demands of economic and social development, displaying new characteristics such as deep learning, cross-domain integration, man-machine collaboration, the opening of swarm intelligence, autonomous control, etc. Together, big data-driven cognitive learning, cross-media collaborative processing, and man-machine collaboration–strengthened intelligence, swarm-integrated intelligence, and autonomous intelligent systems have become the focus of the development of AI. The results of brain science research inspired human-like intelligence that awaits action; the trends involving the chips, hardware, and platform have become apparent; the development of AI has entered into a new stage. At present, the development of a new generation of AI and related disciplines, theoretical modeling, technological innovation, hardware, software upgrades, etc., all advance, provoking chain-style breakthroughs, promoting the acceleration of the elevation of economic and social domains from digitization and networkization to intelligentization.

AI has become a new focus of international competition. AI is a strategic technology that will shape leadership in the future. For this reason, the world's major developed countries are advancing the development of AI as a major strategy to enhance national competitiveness and protect national security by intensifying the introduction of plans and strategies for this core technology. This includes developing top talent, standards, regulations, etc. in order to seize the initiative in a new round of international science and technology competition. At present, China's situation in national security and international competition is more complex, and [China] must, looking at the world, apply the development of AI at the national strategic level by taking the initiative in planning, firmly seizing the strategic initiative in the new stage of international competition in AI development, in order to create a new competitive advantage that opens up the development of a new space which effectively protects national security.

AI has become a new engine of economic development. AI has become the core driving force for a new round of industrial transformation, [that] will release the enormous energy embedded in previous scientific and technological systems. In this way, AI will create a new and powerful engine, reconstructing production, distribution, exchange, consumption, etc., with links to a spectrum of economic activities. This includes new demands taking shape from the macro to the micro within each domain of intelligentization; with the birth of new technologies, new products, new industries, new formats, new models; triggering significant changes in economic structure, profound changes in human modes of production, lifestyle, and thinking; and a whole leap of achieving social productivity. China's economic development enters a new normal, deepening the supply side of structural reform— a very arduous task, [but China] must accelerate the rapid application of AI, cultivating and expanding AI industries to inject a new kinetic energy into China's economic development.

AI brings new opportunities for social construction. China is currently in the decisive stage of constructing a moderately prosperous society. The challenges of population aging, environmental constraints, etc., remain serious. The widespread use of AI in education, medical care, pensions, environmental protection, urban operations, judicial services, and other fields will greatly improve the level of precision in public services, comprehensively enhancing people's quality of life. AI technologies can accurately sense, forecast, and provide early warning of major situations for infrastructure facilities and social security operations. It can also grasp group cognition and psychological changes in a timely manner, and take the initiative in decision-making and reactions—which will significantly elevate the capability and level of social governance, playing an irreplaceable role in effectively maintaining social stability.

The uncertainties in the development of AI create new challenges. AI is a disruptive technology with widespread influence that may cause: Transformation of employment structures, redesign of legal and social theories, violations of personal privacy, challenges to international relations and norms, and many other problems.

AI will have far-reaching effects on the management of government, economic security, and social stability, as well as global governance. While vigorously developing AI, we must attach great importance to the potential safety risks and challenges, strengthen the forward-looking prevention and guidance on restraint, minimize risk, and ensure the safe, reliable, and controllable development of AI.

China possesses a favorable foundation for the development of AI. The nation has deployed the National Key Research and Development Plan's key special projects, such as intelligent manufacturing; issued and implemented the "Internet +" and AI Three-Year Activities and Implementation Program, releasing a series of measures from science and technology research and development; and promoted applications and industrial development, and other aspects. As a result of many years of continuous accumulation, China has achieved important progress in the field of AI, with the number of international scientific and technical papers published and the number of inventions patented ranked second in the world while achieving important breakthroughs in certain domains of core crucial technologies. Leading the world in voice recognition and visual recognition technologies; initially possessing the capability for leapfrog development in adaptive autonomous learning, intuitive sensing, comprehensive reasoning, hybrid intelligence, and swarm intelligence, etc.; with Chinese information processing, intelligent monitoring, biometric identification, industrial robots, service robots, and unmanned driving gradually entering the practical application. AI innovation and entrepreneurship have become increasingly active, and a number of leading enterprises have accelerated their growth, receiving widespread concern and recognition internationally. Accelerating the accumulation of technological capabilities and massive data resources, the organization and integration of both the huge demand for applications and an open market, constitutes China's unique advantage in AI development.

At the same time, we must also clearly see that there is still a gap between China's overall level of development of AI relative to that of developed countries— lacking major original results in the basic theory, core algorithms, key equipment, high-end chips, major products and systems, foundational materials, components, software, interfaces, etc. Scientific research institutions and enterprises do not yet possess international influence across ecological cycles or supply chains. Lacking a comprehensive research and development system, cutting-edge talent for AI is far from meeting demand. Adapting to the development of AI requires the urgent improvement of basic infrastructure, policies and regulations, and standards systems.

Facing a new situation and new demands, we must take the initiative to pursue and adapt to change, firmly seize the major historic opportunity for the development of AI, stick closely to development, study and evaluate the general trends, take the initiative to plan, grasp the direction, seize the opportunity, lead the world in new trends in the development of AI, serve economic and social development, and support national security, promoting the overall elevation of the nation's competitiveness and leapfrog current development.

13.2 The Overall Requirements

13.2.1 Guiding Ideology

Comprehensively implement the spirit of the 18th Party Congress and 18th Central Committee's Third, Fourth, Fifth, and Sixth Plenary Sessions. Thoroughly study and implement the spirit of General Secretary Xi Jinping's series of important sayings and new concepts, new ideas, and new strategies for governing the country. According to the "five in one" overall layout and "four comprehensives" strategic layout, conscientiously implement the CPC Central Committee and State Council decision-making arrangements, deeply implement the innovation-driven development strategy to accelerate the deep integration of AI with the economy, keeping society and national defense as a primary line, which is to enhance the following: scientific and technological innovation capacity for a new generation of AI as the main direction of attack; intelligent economy development; smart society construction; protecting national security; building of knowledge clusters, technology clusters, and industry clusters mutually integrated with talent, system, and culture, for a mutually supporting ecosystem, advancing intelligentization as the center of humanity's sustainable development. Comprehensively enhance society's productive forces, comprehensive national power, and national competitiveness, in order to provide strong support to accelerate the construction of an innovative new-type nation and global science and technology power, to achieve the two centennial goals and the great rejuvenation of the Chinese nation.

13.2.2 The Basic Principles

Technology-Led. Grasp the global development trend of AI, highlight the deployment of forward-looking research and development, explore the layout in key frontier domains, long-term support, and strive to achieve transformational and disruptive breakthroughs in theories, methods, tools, and systems; comprehensively enhance original innovation capability in AI, accelerate the construction of a first-mover advantage, to achieve high-end leading development.

Systems Layout. According to the different characteristics of foundational research, technological research and development, industrial development, and commercial applications, formulate a targeted systems development strategy. Fully give play to the advantages of the socialist system to concentrate forces to do major undertakings, promote the planning and layout of projects, bases, and a talent pool, organically link already-deployed major projects and new missions, continue current urgent needs and long-term development echelons, construct innovation capacity, create a collaborative force for institutional reforms and the policy environment.

Market-Dominant. Follow the rules of the market, remain oriented toward application, highlight companies' choices on the technological line and primary role in the development of commercial product standards, accelerate the commercialization of AI technology and results, and create a competitive advantage. Grasp well the division of labor between government and the market, better take advantage of the government in planning and guidance, policy support, security and guarding, market regulation, environmental construction, the formulation of ethical regulations, etc.

Open-Source and Open. Advocate the concept of open-source sharing, and promote the concept of industry, academia, research, and production units each innovating and in principle pursuing joint innovation and sharing. Follow the coordinated development law for economic and national defense construction; promote two-way conversion and application for military and civilian scientific and technological achievements and co-construction and sharing of military and civilian innovation resources; form an all-element, multi-domain, highly efficient new pattern of civil–military integration. Actively participate in global research and development and management of AI, and optimize the allocation of innovative resources on a global scale.

13.2.3 Strategic Objectives

These are divided into the following three steps:

First, by 2020, the overall technology and application of AI will be in step with globally advanced levels, the AI industry will have become a new important economic growth point, and AI technology applications will have become a new way to improve people's livelihoods, strongly supporting [China's] entrance into the ranks of innovative nations and comprehensively achieving the struggle toward the goal of a moderately prosperous society.

- By 2020, China will have achieved important progress in a new generation of AI theories and technologies. It will have actualized important progress in big data intelligence, cross-medium intelligence, swarm intelligence, hybrid enhanced intelligence, and autonomous intelligence systems, and will have achieved important progress in other foundational theories and core technologies; the country will have achieved iconic advances in AI models and methods, core devices, high-end equipment, and foundational software.
- The AI industry's competitiveness will have entered the first echelon internationally. China will have established initial AI technology standards, service systems, and industrial ecological system chains. It will have cultivated a number of the world's leading AI backbone enterprises, with the scale of AI's core industry exceeding 150 billion RMB, and exceeding 1 trillion RMB as driven by the scale of related industries.

- The AI development environment will be further optimized, opening up new applications in important domains, gathering a number of high-level personnel and innovation teams, and initially establishing AI ethical norms, policies, and regulations in some areas.

Second, by 2025, China will achieve major breakthroughs in basic theories for AI, such that some technologies and applications achieve a world-leading level and AI becomes the main driving force for China's industrial upgrading and economic transformation, while intelligent social construction has made positive progress.

- By 2025, a new generation of AI theory and technology systems will be initially established, as AI with autonomous learning ability achieves breakthroughs in many areas to obtain leading research results.
- The AI industry will enter into the global high-end value chain. This new-generation AI will be widely used in intelligent manufacturing, intelligent medicine, intelligent city, intelligent agriculture, national defense construction, and other fields, while the scale of AI's core industry will be more than 400 billion RMB, and the scale of related industries will exceed 5 trillion RMB.
- By 2025, China will have seen the initial establishment of AI laws and regulations, ethical norms and policy systems, and the formation of AI security assessment and control capabilities.

Third, by 2030, China's AI theories, technologies, and applications should achieve world-leading levels, making China the world's primary AI innovation center, achieving visible results in intelligent economy and intelligent society applications, and laying an important foundation for becoming a leading innovation-style nation and an economic power.

- China will have formed a more mature new-generation AI theory and technology system. The country will achieve major breakthroughs in brain-inspired intelligence, autonomous intelligence, hybrid intelligence, swarm intelligence, and other areas, having an important impact in the domain of international AI research and occupying the commanding heights of AI technology.
- AI industry competitiveness will reach the world-leading level. AI should be expansively deepened and greatly expanded into production and livelihood, social governance, national defense construction, and in all aspects of applications, will become an expansive core technology for key systems, support platforms, and the intelligent application of a complete industrial chain and high-end industrial clusters, with AI core industry scale exceeding 1 trillion RMB, and with the scale of related industries exceeding 10 trillion RMB.

- China will have established a number of world-leading AI technology innovation and personnel training centers (or bases) and will have constructed more comprehensive AI laws and regulations, and an ethical norms and policy system.

13.2.4 Overall Deployment

The development of AI is a complex systemic project related to the overall situation, that must be arranged in accordance with "build one system, grasp the two attributes, adhere to the trinity, and strengthen the four supports" to form a strategic path for the healthy and sustainable development of AI.

Construct an open and cooperative AI technology innovation system. Target the weak foundation in original theories and the key difficulties and deficiencies in major products and systems. Establish foundational theories and a common technology system for a new generation of AI, laying out the construction of a major scientific and technological innovation base. Strengthen the high-end talent team in AI to promote innovation and cooperative interactions. Form a continuous innovation capability for AI.

Grasp AI's characteristic high degree of integration of technological attributes and social attributes. It is necessary not only to increase efforts in the research and development and applications of AI, maximizing the potential of AI, but also to predict AI's challenges, coordinate industrial policies, innovate in policies and social policies, achieve the coordination of encouraging development and reasonable regulation, and maximize risk prevention.

Adhere to the promotion of the trinity of breakthroughs in AI research and development, product applications, and fostering industry development. Adapt to the characteristics and trends of AI development. In addition, strengthen the deep integration of the innovation chain and industrial chain, the interactive evolution of technology supply, and market demand. Take technological breakthroughs to promote domain applications and industrial upgrading. Through application demonstrations, promote the optimization of technologies and systems. At the same time as greatly promotes technology applications and industrial development, strengthen long-term R&D layout and research and achieve rolling development and continuous improvement. Ensure that theory is in the front, the technological commanding heights are occupied, and applications are secure and controllable.

Fully support science and technology, the economy, social development, and national security. Drive comprehensive elevation on national innovative capability with AI technological breakthroughs. Lead in the process of constructing a global science and technology power. Through strengthening the intelligent industry and cultivating the intelligent economy, create a new growth cycle for China's next decade or even decades of economic prosperity. Through building an intelligent society, promote the improvement of people's livelihoods and welfare and implement people-centric development thinking. Through AI, elevate national defense strength and assure and protect national security.

13.3 Focus Tasks

Based on the overall picture of national development, accurately grasp the global development trends of AI, find the correct openings for breakthroughs and directions for the main thrust, comprehensively strengthen basic science and technology innovation capabilities, comprehensively expand the depth and breadth of application in focus areas, and comprehensively enhance the built-in intelligence levels of applications in economic and social development, as well as in national defense.

13.3.1 Build Open and Coordinated AI Science and Technology Innovation Systems

Focus on increasing the supply of AI innovation sources; strengthen deployments in areas such as advanced basic theory, key general technologies, basic platforms, talent teams, etc.; stimulate open-source sharing; systematically enhance sustained innovation capabilities; ensure that our country's AI science and technology levels ascend to the leading global ranks; and make ever more contributions to the development of global AI.

13.4 Establish Basic Theory Systems for a New Generation of AI

Focus on major advanced scientific AI questions; concurrently deal with present needs and long-term developments; make breakthroughs in basic AI application theory bottlenecks; give priority to deploying basic research that may trigger paradigmatic change in AI; stimulate the intersection and convergence of disciplines; and provide powerful scientific reserves for the sustained development and profound application of AI.

Make breakthroughs in basic application theory bottlenecks. Aim at basic theoretical orientations with clear applied objectives, which promise to trigger an upgrade of AI technology, strengthen basic theoretical research on big data intelligence, cross-media sensing and computing, human-machine blended intelligence, mass intelligence, autonomous cooperation, decision-making, etc. Focus on breakthroughs in big data intelligence, unsupervised learning, comprehensive deep reasoning, and other such difficult issues. Establish data-driven cognitive computing models with natural language understanding at the core, and shape capabilities to go from big data to knowledge, and from knowledge to decision-making. Focus on breakthroughs in cross-media sensing and computing theory, including theories and methods for low-cost and low-energy smart sensing, active sensing in complex landscapes, listening comprehension in the natural environment as well as language sensing, autonomous multimedia learning, etc.

Realize superhuman sensing and highly dynamic, high-dimensional, and multi-model distributed large-landscape sensing. The focuses on breakthroughs in blended and enhanced intelligence theory are theories on human-machine cooperative and blended environmental understanding, decision-making, and learning; intuitive reasoning and causal models, recall and knowledge evolution, etc.; realizing blended and enhanced intelligence where learning and reflection approach or exceed human intelligence levels. The focuses for breakthroughs in collective intelligence theory are theories and methods for the organization, emergence and learning of collective intelligence; establishment of expressible and computable mass intelligence incentive algorithms and models; and shaping Internet-based collective intelligence theory systems. The focuses for breakthroughs in autonomous coordination, control, and optimized decision-making theory are theories concerning coordination sensing and interaction aimed at autonomous unmanned systems; autonomous coordination control and optimized decision-making; knowledge-driven human-machine-object triangular coordination and interoperation, etc.; and shaping novel theoretical systems and frameworks for innovation in autonomous intelligence and unmanned systems.

Arrange advanced basic theoretical research. Aim for a direction that may trigger a paradigmatic change in AI, far-sighted arrange research on high-level machine learning, brain-inspired intelligence computing, quantum smart computing, and other such cross-domain basic theories. The focuses for breakthroughs in high-level machine learning theory are theories and methods concerning self-adaptive learning, autonomous learning, etc., and realizing AI with high interpretative and strong generalization capabilities. The focuses for breakthroughs in brain-inspired intelligence computing theory are theories concerning brain-inspired information encoding, processing, recall, learning, and reasoning; the creation of brain-inspired complex systems and brain-inspired control theories and methods; and the establishment of new large-scale brain-inspired intelligence computing models and brain-inspired understanding computing models. The focuses for breakthroughs in quantum computing theory are methods for quantum-accelerated machine learning; establishment of high-performance computing and quantum computing convergence models; and shaping high-efficiency, accurate, and autonomous quantum AI system setups.

Launch cross-disciplinary exploratory research. Promote the intersection and convergence of AI with neurology, cognitive science, quantum science, psychology, mathematics, economics, sociology, and other such related basic disciplines; strengthen basic theoretical mathematical research to guide the development of AI algorithms and models; focus on researching the basic theoretical questions of AI legal principles; support exploratory research that is strongly original, and where there is no consensus; encourage scientists to explore freely; dare to overcome front-line scientific difficulties in AI; create ever more original theory; and make ever more original discoveries.

13.5 Build a Next-Generation AI Key General Technology System

Focusing on the urgent need to raise China's international competitiveness in AI, next-generation AI key general technology R&D and deployment should make algorithms the core; data and hardware the foundation; and upping capabilities in sensing and recognition, knowledge computing, cognitive reasoning, executing motion, and human-machine interface the emphasis; in order to form openly compatible, stable and mature technological systems.

Knowledge computing engine and knowledge service technology. Key breakthroughs in knowledge processing, deep search, and visual interactive core technology; realization of automatic acquisition of incrementally growing knowledge; possession of concept discernment, object discovery, attribute prediction, evolutionary knowledge modeling, and relationship discovery capabilities; the formation of multi-billion-scale, multi-source, multi-disciplinary, multi-data type, and cross-medium knowledge maps.

Cross-medium analytical reasoning technology. Key breakthroughs in cross-medium unified indicators; relational understanding and knowledge mining; knowledge map structure and learning; knowledge evolution and reasoning; intelligent description and generation, etc., technology. Realization of cross-medium knowledge indicators, analysis, mining, reasoning, evolution, and utilization. Construct analytic reasoning engines.

Key swarm intelligence technology. Key breakthroughs on the basis of the popularization of the internet, mass collaboration, knowledge resource management, open sharing, etc.,. Building frameworks to display swarm intelligence knowledge. Realize the integration and strengthening of swarm intelligence-based knowledge acquisition and swarm intelligence under open development conditions. Support swarm perception, cooperation, and evolution at a national, tens-of-millions scale.

New architecture and new technology for hybrid and enhanced intelligence. Key breakthroughs in human-machine interaction for perception and execution integration models, new types of intelligent computing-fronted sensors, common use hybrid architecture, etc., core technologies. Build autonomous, environmentally adaptable hybrid enhanced intelligent systems, human-machine hybrid enhanced intelligent systems, and support environments.

Intelligent technologies of autonomous unmanned systems. Key breakthroughs in general technologies like autonomous unmanned system computing architecture, complex situational environment perception and understanding, real-time accurate positioning, adaptability, intelligent navigation in complex environments, etc. Unmanned and autonomously controlled systems including automobiles, ships, automatic driving in traffic, etc., intelligent technologies. Develop core technologies services like robots, special-purpose robots, etc., and support unmanned system application and manufacturing development.

Intelligent virtual reality modeling technology. Key breakthroughs in intelligent modeling technology for virtual counterparts. Increasing the sociality, diversity, and lifelike quality of virtual reality intelligent counterpart behavior. Realize the organic integration, high efficiency, and interactivity of virtual reality and augmented reality, etc., technologies.

Intelligent computing chips and systems. Key breakthroughs in high energy efficiency, reconfigurable brain-inspired computing chips, and brain-inspired visual sensor systems with computational imaging capabilities. Research and develop high-efficiency brain-inspired neural network architectures and hardware systems with autonomous learning capabilities. Realize brain-inspired intelligent systems with multimedia sensory information understanding, intelligence growth, and common sense reasoning capabilities.

Natural language processing technology. Key breakthroughs in natural language grammar logic, word-concept symbols, and deep semantic analysis core technologies. Advance effective human-machine communication and free interaction. Realize multi-style, multi-language, multi-domain natural language intelligent understanding and automated [results] generation.

13.6 Coordinate the Layout of AI Innovation Platforms

Construct AI innovation platforms. Strengthen the foundational support for AI research and development and applications. AI open-source hardware and software infrastructure platforms should focus on building and supporting unified computing frameworks for knowledge reasoning, probability statistics, depth learning, and other AI paradigms. Form and promote an ecological chain of platforms for interaction and synergies among AI software, hardware, and intelligent clouds. The group intelligent service platform should focus on the construction of knowledge resource management and the open sharing tools based on the large-scale cooperation on the Internet. Create a platform and service environment for the innovation of the industry and university. The hybrid enhanced intelligent support platforms should focus on the construction of a heterogeneous real-time computing engine supporting large-scale training and new computing clusters, providing a service-oriented, systematic platform and solution for complex intelligent computing. Autonomous unmanned system support platform focuses on the construction of autonomous system environmental awareness, autonomous collaborative control, intelligent decision-making, and other AI common core technology support systems. Create development and test environments for open, modular, reconfigurable autonomous unmanned systems. AI basic data and security detection platforms should focus on the construction of AI for the public data resource library, the standard test data set, cloud service platform, the formation of AI algorithms and platform security test evaluation methods, techniques, norms and tools, promoting the open sourcing and openness of all kinds of common software and technology platform. Promote military–civilian sharing and joint use for all kinds of platforms in accordance with the requirements of deep military–civil integration-related provisions.

13.7 Accelerate the Training and Gathering of High-End AI Talent

Make the construction of a high-end talent team of the utmost importance in the development of AI. Adhere to the combination of training and development. Improve the AI education system, strengthen the construction of a talent pool and echelons, and especially accelerate the introduction of the world's top talent and young talent, forming China's AI top talent base.

Cultivate high-level AI innovative talents and teams. Support and cultivate the development potential of leading AI talent. Strengthen professional and technical personnel training for basic research, applied research, operations, and maintenance aspects of AI. Pay attention to the training of compound talents, focusing on cultivating vertical composite talents for AI theory, methods, technology, products, and application, and compound talents who master the "AI +" economy, society, management, standards, law, and other horizontal areas. Through major research and development tasks and base and platform construction, converge high-end talents in AI. Create high-level innovation teams in a number of AI key domains. Encourage and guide domestic innovative talents and the teams to strengthen cooperation with the world's top AI research institutions.

Increase the introduction of high-end AI talent. Open up specialized channels and implement special policies to achieve the precise introduction of peak AI talent. Focus on the introduction of top international scientists and high-level innovation teams in neural awareness, machine learning, automatic driving, intelligent robots, and other areas. Encourage the use of flexible AI talent through project cooperation, technical advice, etc. Coordinate the use of the "Thousands Talents" plan and other existing talent plans to strengthen the field of AI talents, especially through the introduction of outstanding young talent. Improve enterprise human capital cost accounting and related policies. Encourage enterprises and scientific research institutions to develop AI talent.

Construct an AI academic discipline. Improve the disciplinary layout of the AI domain. Establish AI majors. Promote the construction of a discipline in the domain of AI. Establish AI institutes as soon as possible in pilot institutions. Increase the enrollment places for graduate and postgraduate degrees while working in AI and related disciplines. Encourage colleges and universities to broaden the content of AI professional education on an original basis. Create a new model of "AI + X" compound professional training, attaching importance to cross-integration of professional education for AI and mathematics, computer science, physics, biology, psychology, sociology, law, and other disciplines.

Strengthen cooperation in production and research. Most importantly, encourage universities, research institutes, enterprises, and other institutions to carry out the construction of an AI discipline.

Acknowledgment

The complete document has been translated by Graham Webster, Rogier Creemers, Elsa Kania, and Paul Triolo and can be found here: https://digichina.stanford.edu/work/full-translation-chinas-new-generation-artificial-intelligence-development-plan-2017/

14

US NATIONAL SECURITY COMMISSION ON ARTIFICIAL INTELLIGENCE

Eric Schmidt

Introduction

Artificial Intelligence (AI) technologies promise to be the most powerful tools in generations for expanding knowledge, increasing prosperity, and enriching the human experience. The technologies will be the foundation of the innovation economy and a source of enormous power for countries that harness them. AI will fuel competition between governments and companies racing to field it. And it will be employed by nation-states to pursue their strategic ambitions.

Americans have not yet seriously grappled with how profoundly the AI revolution will impact society, the economy, and national security. Recent AI breakthroughs, such as a computer defeating a human in the popular strategy game of Go1, shocked other nations into action, but it did not inspire the same response in the United States. Despite our private-sector and university leadership in AI, the United States remains unprepared for the coming era. Americans must recognize the assertive role that the government will have to play in ensuring the United States wins this innovation competition. Congress and the President will have to support the scale of public resources required to achieve it.

The magnitude of the technological opportunity coincides with a moment of strategic vulnerability. China is a competitor possessing the might, talent, and ambition to challenge America's technological leadership, military superiority, and broader position in the world. AI is deepening the threat posed by cyberattacks and disinformation campaigns that Russia, China, and other state and non-state actors are using to infiltrate our society, steal our data, and interfere in our democracy. The limited uses of AI-enabled attacks to date are the tip of the iceberg. Meanwhile, global crises exemplified by the global pandemic and

DOI: 10.4324/9781003230762-18

climate change are expanding the definition of national security and crying out for innovative technological solutions. AI can help us navigate many of these new challenges.

We are fortunate. The AI revolution is not a strategic surprise. We are experiencing its impact in our daily lives and can anticipate how research progress will translate into real-world applications before we have to confront the full national security ramifications. This commission can warn of national security challenges and articulate the benefits, rather than explain why previous warnings were ignored and opportunities were missed. We still have a window to make the changes to build a safer and better future. The pace of AI innovation is not flat; it is accelerating. If the United States does not act, it will likely lose its leadership position in AI to China in the next decade and become more vulnerable to a spectrum of AI-enabled threats from a host of state and non-state actors.

The Commission concludes that the United States needs to implement a strategy to defend and compete in the AI era. The White House must lead the effort to reorganize the government and reorient the nation.

Why Does AI Matter?

In 1901, Thomas Edison was asked to predict electricity's impact on humanity. Two decades after the development of the light bulb, he foresaw a general-purpose technology of unlimited possibilities. "[Electricity] is the field of fields", he said. "It holds the secrets which will reorganize the life of the world". AI is a very different kind of general-purpose technology, but we are standing at a similar juncture and see a similarly wide-ranging impact. The rapidly improving ability of computer systems to solve problems and perform tasks that would otherwise require human intelligence is transforming many aspects of human life and every field of science. It will be incorporated into virtually all future technology. The entire innovation base supporting our economy and security will leverage AI. How this "field of fields" is used—for good and for ill—will reorganize the world.

The Commission's assessment is rooted in a realistic understanding of AI's current state of development and a projection of how the technology will evolve.

AI is already ubiquitous in everyday life and the pace of innovation is accelerating. We take for granted that AI already shapes our lives in ways small and big. A "smartphone" has multiple AI-enabled features including voice assistants, photo tagging, facial recognition security, search apps, recommendation and advertising engines, and less obvious AI enhancements in its operating system. AI is helping predict the spread and escalation of a pandemic outbreak, planning and optimizing the distribution of goods and services, monitoring traffic flow and safety, speeding up drug and therapeutic discovery, and automating routine office functions.

Recognizing the pace of change is critical to understanding the power of AI. The application of AI techniques to solve problems is compressing innovation timescales and turning once-fantastical ideas into realities across a range of disciplines.

Deploying and adopting AI remains a hard problem. AI cannot magically solve problems. As AI moves from an elite niche science to a mainstream tool, engineering will be as important as scientific breakthroughs. Early adopters across sectors have learned similar lessons: Trying to employ AI is a slog even after the science is settled. Many of the most important real-world impacts will come from figuring out how to employ existing AI algorithms and systems, some more than a decade old. The integration challenge is immense. Harnessing data, hardening and packaging laboratory algorithms so they are ready for use in the field, and adapting AI software to legacy equipment and rigid organizations all require time, effort, and patience. Integrating AI often necessitates overcoming substantial organizational and cultural barriers, and it demands top-down leadership.

AI tools are diffusing broadly and rapidly. Cutting-edge deep learning techniques are often prohibitively expensive, requiring vast amounts of data, computing power, and specialized knowledge. However, AI will not be the provenance of only big states and big tech. Many machine learning tools that fuel AI applications are publicly available and usable even for non-experts. Open-source applications and development tools combined with inexpensive cloud computing and less data-intensive approaches are expanding AI opportunities across the world to state and non-state actors.

AI is changing relationships between humans and machines. In modern society, we already rely much more on machines and automation than we may be aware. The US military, for instance, has used autonomous systems for decades. However, as AI capabilities improve, the dynamics within human-machine "teams" will change. In the past, computers could only perform tasks that fell within a clearly defined set of parameters or rules programmed by a human. As AI becomes more capable, computers will be able to learn and perform tasks based on parameters that humans do not explicitly program, creating choices and taking actions at a volume and speed never before possible. Across many fields of human activity, AI innovations are raising important questions about what choices to delegate to intelligent machines, in what circumstances, and for what reasons. In the national security sphere, these questions will take on greater significance as AI is integrated into defense and intelligence systems. Across our entire society, we will need to address these new complexities with nuanced approaches, intellectual curiosity, and care that recognizes the increasing ubiquity of AI.

The Talent Competition

The United States is in a global competition for scarce AI talent.[1] The Commission is very concerned with current talent trends. The number of domestic-born students participating in AI doctorate programs has not increased since 1990, and competition for international students has accelerated, endangering the United States' ability to retain international students (Zwetsloot et al., 2019). For the first time in our lifetime, the United States risks losing the competition for talent on the scientific frontiers. Cultivating more potential talent at home and recruiting and retaining more existing talent from foreign countries are the only two options to sustain the US lead.

Competitors and allies recognize the importance of implementing AI talent strategies. Between 2000 and 2014, China's university system increased its number of science, technology, engineering, and mathematics (STEM) graduates by 360%, producing 1.7 million in 2014 alone (The Rise of China, 2018).[2] The number of STEM graduates in the United States' university system rose by 54% during the same time period, and many were international students (Science & Engineering Indicators, 2018). China's researchers now represent roughly 29% of top-tier deep learning talent in the world (The Global AI Talent Tracker, 2020).[3] China and other states have also taken steps to attract international talent with flexible immigration policies and incentives for tech talent (Staff Report, 2019).[4] The United States needs to invest in all AI talent pipelines in order to remain at the forefront of AI now and into the future. A passive strategy will not work in the face of the AI talent competition.

To achieve dominance in AI, the United States needs to train four archetypes to propel AI in America: Researchers, implementers, end users, and informed consumers.

Researchers: AI research engineers will focus on R&D of technologies that enable and advance semi- and fully autonomous systems. They serve as algorithm experts with up-to-date knowledge of modern AI research and may be involved in the inception of ideas and drive the development cycles from research to testing prototypes for a major project or component of a major project.

Implementers: They will be responsible for data cleaning, feature extraction and selection, and analysis; model training and tuning; partnerships with domain knowledge experts and end-users; and the discovery of local opportunities for exploitation. Developers require less training and education than AI experts, and will have training, education, and/or experience that is roughly equivalent to an associate or bachelor's degree; and that includes relevant ethics and bias mitigation in data processing and model training.

End users: They will have their daily business augmented/enabled by AI. The use of AI will strongly resemble the use of currently available software in that it will require some system-specific training, but, with the exception of some positions that manage data, little to no AI-specific expertise.

Informed consumers: This group of people needs the ability to make better consumer choices when purchasing technology and understand the importance of their actions in the market.

The Promise and Limits of Expanding STEM

Investments in STEM education are a necessary part of increasing American national power and improving national security. The United States ranks well overall on international measures of talent because of our ability to attract international talent, in spite of our uneven kindergarten to 12th grade (K-12) education system.[5] The United States must invest significantly in STEM education as an engine to drive the growth of AI talent in America. Investments in STEM education alone, however, will not be enough for the United States to win the international competition for AI and STEM talent. China is producing large numbers of computer scientists, engineers, and other STEM graduates (The Rise of China, 2018). For the foreseeable future, the United States' STEM education system does not have the capacity nor the quality to produce sufficient STEM or AI talent to supply the United States' markets or national security enterprise.[6] To compete, the United States must reform its education system to produce both a higher quality and quantity of graduates.

Pass a National Defense Education Act II. Motivated by fear that America had fallen behind in education and innovation after the Soviets launched Sputnik in 1957, Congress passed the National Defense Education Act (NDEA) the following year. The NDEA promoted the importance of science, mathematics, and foreign languages for students, authorizing more than $1 billion toward decreasing student loans, funding education at all levels, and funding graduate fellowships. Many students were able to attend college because of this legislation. In 1960, 3.6 million students attended college; by 1970 it was 7.5 million (Sputnik, 2020). This act helped America win the Space Race, helped power the microelectronics industry, and accelerated the United States' capacity to innovate, and, ultimately, played an important role in America's victory in the Cold War.

The Commission believes the time is right for a second NDEA, one that mirrors the first legislation, but with important distinctions. NDEA II would focus on funding students acquiring digital skills, like mathematics, computer science, information science, data science, and statistics. NDEA II should include K-12 education and reskilling programs that address deficiencies across the spectrum of the American educational system, purposefully targeting under-resourced school districts. The Commission also recommends investments in university-level STEM programs with 25,000 undergraduate, 5,000 graduate, and 500 PhD-level scholarships. Undergraduate scholarships should include credit hours at community colleges to ensure more Americans have access to affordable STEM education. Ultimately, the goal of NDEA II is to widen the digital talent pool by incentivizing programs for underrepresented Americans

Strengthen AI talent through immigration. Immigration reform is a national security imperative. Nations that can successfully attract and retain highly skilled individuals gain strategic and economic advantages over competitors. Human capital advantages are particularly significant in the field of AI, where demand for talent far exceeds supply (Zwetsloot et al., 2019).[7] Highly skilled immigrants accelerate American innovation, improve entrepreneurship, and create jobs (Kerr, 2013; Hanson and Slaughter, 2016; Zwetsloot et al., 2019). The United States benefits far more from the immigration of highly skilled foreign workers than other countries. In 2013, the United States had 15 times as many immigrant inventors as there were American inventors living abroad (Fink, 2013). By contrast, Canada, Germany, and the United Kingdom. all maintain a net negative inventor immigration rate (Miguelez and Fink, 2013). Compared with other United States advantages in the AI competition—such as financial resources or hardware capacity—this immigration advantage is harder for other countries to replicate.

Unfortunately, international students in the United States are increasingly choosing to study in other countries or return home (Zwetsloot et al., 2019).[8] One reason is the growing backlog of green card petitions (Kahn and MacGarvie, 2020). Indian immigrants face a particularly long wait. Many will spend decades on constrictive work visas waiting to receive their green cards, hindering both the technology sector's ability to recruit talent and Indian immigrants' quality of life. At the same time, other countries are increasing their efforts to attract and retain AI talent, including immigrants in Silicon Valley (Huang and Arnold, 2020).

While immigration benefits the United States, policymakers must also bear in mind the threat of unwanted technology transfer. However, restricting immigration is far too blunt a tool to solve this problem (Arnold et al., 2019). Restrictions harm United States' innovation and economic growth and only help our competitors by enabling their human capital to grow. They also incentivize US technology companies to move to where talent resides, whether right across our borders or overseas (Zwetsloot et al., 2019). Technology transfer will only get worse if significant components of the US technology sector move their research and development to China or other countries that are more vulnerable than the United States to technology transfer efforts.[9] A more effective strategic approach would pair actions to improve the United States' ability to attract top global talent with targeted efforts to combat technology transfer vectors. Changes to immigration policies should be paired with those recommendations.

Immigration policy can also slow China's progress. China's government takes the threat of brain drain seriously, noting that the United States' ability to attract and retain China's talent is an obstacle to the Chinese Communist Party's (CCP) ambitions (Zwetsloot, 2020).[10] Increasing China's brain drain will create a dilemma for the CCP—which will be forced to choose between losing even more human capital, further slowing their economic growth and threatening their advancement in AI, or denying Chinese nationals opportunities to study and work in the United States. At the same time, the United States should be cautious about potential adverse effects on talent pools in partner nations.

Broaden the scope of "extraordinary" talent to make the O-1 visa more accessible and emphasize AI talent. The O-1 temporary worker visa is for people with extraordinary abilities or achievements. Currently, adjudicators determine an applicant's eligibility through a subjective assessment. For the sciences and technology, this aligns largely with academic criteria such as publications in major outlets and is not well suited for people who excel in the industry.

Implement and advertise the international entrepreneur rule. The International Entrepreneur Rule (IER) allows US Citizenship and Immigration Services (USCIS) to grant a period of authorized stay to international entrepreneurs who demonstrate that "their stay in the United States would provide a significant public benefit through their business venture" (International Entrepreneur Parole, 2018).[11] An executive action could announce the administration's intention to use the IER to boost immigrant entrepreneurship, job creation for Americans, and economic growth. USCIS could also be directed to announce that it will give priority to entrepreneurs active in high-priority STEM fields such as AI, or in fields that use AI for other applications, such as agriculture. Entrepreneurs' ability to attract investors should be used as a screening criterion for entrepreneurs.

Expand and clarify job portability for highly skilled workers. The criteria for workers with H-1B, O-1, and other temporary work visas to obtain open market work permits for a one-year renewable period are too limited and ambiguous. Changes should clarify when highly skilled, nonimmigrant workers are permitted to change jobs or employers, increase job flexibility when an employer either withdraws their petition or goes out of business, and increase flexibility for H-1B workers seeking other H-1B employment.

Recapture green cards lost to bureaucratic error. Federal agencies generally issue fewer green cards than they are allowed. As of 2009, the federal government had failed to issue more than 326,000 green cards based on cumulative bureaucratic error (Citizenship and Immigration, 2010).[12] The Departments of State and Homeland Security (DHS) should publish an up-to-date report on the number of green cards lost due to bureaucratic errors. Using available authorities, both should grant lost green cards to applicants waiting in line. Congress should support the Departments of State and Homeland Security by passing legislation to recapture lost green cards.[13]

Grant green cards to students graduating with STEM PhDs from accredited American universities. Congress should amend the Immigration and Nationality Act[14] to grant lawful permanent residence to any vetted (not posing a national security risk) foreign national who graduates from an accredited US institution of higher education with a doctoral degree in a STEM-related field in a residential or mixed residential and distance program and has a job offer in a field related to science, technology, engineering, or mathematics. They should not be counted toward permanent residency caps.

Double the number of employment-based green cards. Under the current system, employment-based green cards are unduly scarce: 140,000 per year, fewer than half of which go to the principal worker (Kandel, 2020). This leaves many highly skilled workers unable to gain permanent residency and unable to transfer jobs or negotiate with employers as effectively as domestic workers. This decreases the appeal of joining the American workforce. To reduce the backlog of highly skilled workers, the United States should double the number of employment-based green cards, with an emphasis on permanent residency for STEM and AI-related fields.

Create an entrepreneur visa. International doctoral students are more likely than their native peers to want to found a company or become an employee at a startup, but they are less likely to pursue those paths (Roach, et al., 2019). One reason is the constraints of the H-1B visa system.[15] Similarly, immigrant entrepreneurs without the capital to use the EB-5 route to permanent residency are forced to use other visas that are designed for academics and workers in existing companies, not entrepreneurs (Kerr, 2020).[16] All of these issues make the United States less attractive for international talent, and, perhaps as important, reduce the ability of startups and other small companies—the main source of new jobs for Americans—to hire highly skilled immigrants, who have been shown to improve the odds that the business will succeed. Congress should create an entrepreneur visa for those who would provide a "significant public benefit" to the United States if allowed to stay in the country for a limited trial period to grow their companies (83 Fed. Reg. 24415, 2018). This visa should serve as an alternative to employee-sponsored, investor, or student visas and should instead target promising potential founders.

Create an emerging and disruptive technology visa. The National Science Foundation (NSF) should identify critical emerging technologies every three years. DHS would then allow students, researchers, entrepreneurs, and technologists in applicable fields to apply for emerging and disruptive technology visas. This would provide much-needed talent R&D and strengthen our economy (Etzioni, 2019).

Notes

1 Estimates on the gap of talent necessary to fill AI slots vary greatly, but it is agreed upon that the gap in talent currently is and will continue to be significant as nations compete for scarce resources. See Remco Zwetsloot, et al., Strengthening the U.S. AI Workforce: A Policy and Research Agenda, Center for Security and Emerging Technology at 2 (Sept. 2019), https://cset.georgetown.edu/wpcontent/uploads/CSET-Strengthening-the-U.S.-AI-Workforce.pdf ("The Research Institute at Tencent, a major Chinese technology company, asserts there are roughly 300,000 AI researchers and practitioners worldwide, with market demand for millions of roles. Element AI, a leading Canadian AI company, estimated in 2018 that there are roughly 22,000 PhD-educated researchers globally who are able to work on AI research, with only about 25% of those "well-versed enough in the technology to work with teams to take it from research to application". AI firm Diffbot estimates that there are over 700,000 people skilled in machine learning worldwide").

2 China also passed the United States in the global share of peer-reviewed S&E articles.
3 For these purposes "top tier" talent was defined by accepted papers at the prestigious AI deep learning conference Neural Information Processing Systems in 2019. This reflected approximately the top 20% of researchers in the field. China has placed a strong emphasis on deep learning, just one of the important components of AI.
4 For example, China's Thousand Talents Plan is part of a state-organized blueprint to be a global leader in science and technology by 2050.
5 See also Gordon Hanson & Matthew Slaughter, HighSkilled Immigration and the Rise of STEM Occupations in U.S. Employment, National Bureau of Economic Research at 1 (Sept. 2016), https://www.nber.org/system/files/working_papers/w22623/w22623.pdf.
6 As noted in Chapter 6 of this report, there were 433,116 open computer science jobs in the United States in 2019, while only 71,226 new computer scientists graduated from American universities in 2019. Code.org (last accessed Jan. 11, 2021), https://code.org/promote. See also Oren Etzioni, What Trump's Executive Order on AI Is Missing: America Needs a Special Visa Program Aimed at Attracting More AI Experts and Specialists, Wired (Feb. 13, 2019), https://www.wired.com/story/what-trumpsexecutive-order-on-ai-is-missing/.
7 According to one report, job listings for AI on one popular job website "increased more than fivefold between 2015 and 2017 and demand for "deep learning" skills increased by a factor of more than 30", while the number of people looking for jobs in the field grew much more slowly. This mismatch is slowing the adoption of AI. Most firms report that skills gaps are one of the top obstacles preventing them from adopting AI.
8 According to the Center for Security and Emerging Technology, in 2016, 14% of international students declined offers to study at US universities to study at home, and 19% decided to study in another country. In 2018, these numbers rose, with 39% staying at home and 59% studying in another country.
9 China is the world's largest single source of AI talent. Leading US technology companies such as Google and Microsoft have established cutting-edge research centers in China, in part to access that talent. This increases China's AI R&D capacity and potential for technology transfer, and, if the companies remain American, it reduces the American Intelligence Community's (IC) legal authorization to collect information about Chinese technology development. See The Global AI Talent Tracker, MacroPolo (last accessed Jan 17, 2020), https://macropolo.org/digital-projects/the-globalai-talent-tracker/; Roxanne Heston & Remco Zwetsloot, Mapping U.S. Multinationals' Global AI R&D Activity, Center for Security and Emerging Technology at 20 (Dec. 2020), https://cset.georgetown.edu/wp-content/uploads/CSET-Mapping-U.S.-Multinationals-Global-AI-RD-Activity-1.pdf.
10 ("[T]he head of the [Chinese Communist Party's (CCP)] Central Talent Work Coordination Small Group … complained that 'the number of top talents lost in China ranks first in the world'".); see also Joy Dantong Ma, China's AI Talent Base Is Growing, and Then Leaving, MacroPolo (July 30, 2019), https://macropolo.org/chinas-ai-talent-base-is-growing-and-then-leaving/?rp=m (noting that of the 2,800 Chinese NeurIPS participants between 2009 and 2018, about three-quarters of them were currently working outside of China).
11 There is currently no visa category well-suited to entrepreneurship in immigration statute. The IER, which relies on parole authority, was initiated after legislative avenues were exhausted. Legislative fixes would be preferable, but have so far they have proven politically infeasible.
12 A 2010 report to Congress indicated that some 242,000 unused family-based green cards were ultimately applied to the employment-based backlog, while Congress recaptured some 180,000 green cards via special legislation, leaving more than 326,000 green card numbers wasted.

13 Prior examples of Congressional action include provisions in the American Competitiveness in the 21st Century Act of 2000 and the REAL ID Act of 2005. See Pub. L. 106-313, 114 Stat. 1251, 1254 (2000) and Pub. L. No. 109-013, 119 Stat. 231, 322 (2005).
14 Specifically, 8 U.S.C. § 1151(b)(1).
15 Id. at 12.
16 EB-5 visas require a minimum $900,000 investment in a business in the United States.

References

83 Fed. Reg. 24415. (2018, May 29). Removal of International Entrepreneur Parole Program. *U.S. Department of Homeland Security.* https://www.federalregister.gov/documents/2018/05/29/2018-11348/removal-of-international-entrepreneur-parole-program

Arnold, Z. et al. (2019, September). Immigration Policy and the U.S. AI Sector: A Preliminary Assessment. *Center for Security and Emerging Technology*, 22. https://cset.georgetown.edu/research/immigration-policy-and-the-u-s-ai-sector/

Citizenship and Immigration Services Ombudsman: Annual Report 2010. (2010, June 30). *U.S. Department of Homeland Security.* https://www.dhs.gov/xlibrary/assets/cisomb_2010_annual_report_to_congress.pdf. The number today is likely higher, but DHS has not published updated statistics

Etzioni, O. (2019, February 13). What Trump's Executive Order on AI Is Missing: America Needs a Special Visa Program Aimed at Attracting More AI Experts and Specialists. *Wired.* https://www.wired.com/story/what-trumps-executive-order-on-ai-is-missing/

Fink, C. (2013, July 17). What Leads Inventors to Migrate? *World Economic Forum.* https://www.weforum.org/agenda/2013/07/what-leads-inventors-to-migrate/

The Global AI Talent Tracker. (2020, December 28). *MacroPolo.* https://macropolo.org/digital-projects/the-global-ai-talent-tracker/

Hanson, G. & Slaughter, M. (2016, September). Strengthening the U.S. AI Workforce, HighSkilled Immigration and the Rise of STEM Occupations in U.S. Employment. *National Bureau of Economic Research*, 23. https://www.nber.org/system/files/working_papers/w22623/w22623.pdf

Huang, T. & Arnold, Z. (2020, June). Immigration Policy and the Global Competition for AI Talent. *Center for Security and Emerging Technology*, 8. https://cset.georgetown.edu/research/immigration-policy-and-the-global-competition-for-ai-talent/

International Entrepreneur Parole. (2018, May 25). *USCIS.* https://www.uscis.gov/humanitarian/humanitarian-parole/international-entrepreneur-parole

Kahn, S. & MacGarvie, M. (2020, November). The Impact of Permanent Residency Delays for STEM PhDs: Who Leaves and Why. *Research Policy.* https://www.sciencedirect.com/science/article/abs/pii/S0048733319301982

Kandel, W. (2020, March 26). The Employment-Based Immigrant Backlog. *Congressional Research Service*, 4–5. https://fas.org/sgp/crs/homesec/R46291.pdf

Kerr, W.R. (2020). Global Talent and U.S. Immigration Policy: Working Paper 20-107. *Harvard Business School*, 14. https://www.hbs.edu/faculty/Publication%20Files/20-107_0967f1ab-1d23-4d54-b5a1-c884234d9b31.pdf

Kerr, W.S. (2013, August). High-Skilled Immigration, Innovation, and Entrepreneurship: Empirical Approaches and Evidence. *National Bureau of Economic Research*, 7–8. https://www.nber.org/papers/w19377

Miguelez, E.&Fink, C. (2013, May). Measuring the International Mobility of Inventors: A New Database. *World Intellectual Property Organization*, 16. https://www.wipo.int/edocs/pubdocs/en/wipo_pub_econstat_wp_8.pdf

The Rise of China in Science and Engineering. (2018). *NSF National Science Board*. https://www.nsf.gov/nsb/sei/one-pagers/China-2018.pdf

Roach, M. et al. (2019, September). Are Foreign STEM PhDs More Entrepreneurial? Entrepreneurial Characteristics, Preferences and Employment Outcomes of Native and Foreign Science & Engineering PhD Students. *National Bureau of Economic Research*, 1. https://www.nber.org/system/files/working_papers/w26225/w26225.pdf

Science & Engineering Indicators. (2018). *NSF National Science Board*. https://www.nsf.gov/statistics/2018/nsb20181/assets/561/higher-education-in-science-and-engineering.pdf

Sputnik Spurs Passage of the National Defense Education Act. (2020, December 28). *U.S. Senate*. https://www.senate.gov/artandhistory/history/minute/Sputnik_Spurs_Passage_of_National_Defense_Education_Act.htm#:~:text=The%20National%20Defense%20Education%20Act%20of%201958%20became%20one%20of,and%20private%20colleges%20and%20universities

Staff Report. (2019, November). Threats to the U.S. Research Enterprise: China's Talent Recruitment Plans. *U.S. Senate Permanent Subcommittee on Investigations*, 14. https://www.hsgac.senate.gov/imo/media/doc/2019-11-18%20PSI%20Staff%20Report%20-%20China's%20Talent%20Recruitment%20Plans.pdf

Zwetsloot, R. (2020). US-China STEM Talent "Decoupling": Background, Policy, and Impact. *Johns Hopkins Applied Physics Laboratory*, 19. https://www.jhuapl.edu/assessing-us-chinatechnology-connections/dist/407b0211ec4929960855132604148d4.pdf

Zwetsloot, R., et al. (2019a, September). Strengthening the U.S. AI Workforce: A Policy and Research Agenda. *Center for Security and Emerging Technology*, 1. https://cset.georgetown.edu/wp-content/uploads/CSET-Strengthening-the-U.S.-AI-Workforce.pdf

Zwetsloot, R., et al. (2019b, December). Keeping Top AI Talent in the United States. *Center for Security and Emerging Technology*, iii–vi. https://cset.georgetown.edu/wp-content/uploads/KeepingTop-AI-Talent-in-the-United-States.pdf

Zwetsloot, R. et al. (2019c, December). Keeping Top AI Talent in the United States: Findings and Policy Options for International Graduate Student Retention. *Center for Security and Emerging Technology*, 26. https://cset.georgetown.edu/wp-content/uploads/Keeping-Top-AI-Talent-in-theUnited-States.pdf

15
TRAINING THE "WORKFORCE OF THE FUTURE"

The Integration of New Technologies in Work-Based Higher Education Programs in Germany and the United States

Inez von Weitershausen

In recent years, digital technologies and Artificial Intelligence (AI) in particular have significantly modified job content and skill requirements (Eszell 2021). This development has triggered a debate about how to effectively train the "workforce of the future", and, in response, a proliferation of programs and initiatives by companies, governments, and educational institutions to promote both technical and social skills. The underlying rationale is that in order to be successful in the future, individuals need advanced skills in areas such as coding and electrical engineering, knowledge of cybersecurity and competencies to manage data centers and telecommunications networks (Eszell 2021), as well as the ability to act as creative problem-solvers, empathetic team-players, and innovative leaders.

In this context, Work-Based Higher Education (WBHE) constitutes a particularly promising option as it seeks to proactively align employers' needs and students' skills through the integration of theory and practice. As such, it also constitutes a valuable alternative to both traditional university degrees as well as digital skill development programs offered by alternative providers of education. Specifically, WBHE programs address the shortcomings of traditional degree programs which are often perceived as too theoretical in nature and, depending on the country, can be extremely costly. In comparison to digital skill development programs offered by alternative providers of education, such as technology companies or up-skilling agencies, WBHE is furthermore characterized by a commitment to ensuring a more general and transferable skill set that goes beyond the ability to use a specific product range. Despite their growing relevance today, however, WBHE programs are not a new phenomenon. With a long history in countries in different industrialized economies, they have long been considered a preferred route to obtaining relevant knowledge along with work experience.

DOI: 10.4324/9781003230762-19

In this chapter, we briefly elaborate on the development of WBHE in Germany and the United States before demonstrating its relevance in the face of rapid technological change and the proliferation of AI. In doing so, we draw on publicly available data on education and workforce development. In light of the fact that access to such data is considerably better in Germany, where organizations like the *Bundesinstitut fuer Berufliche Bildung* (BIBB) or the *Hochschulrektorenkonferenz* (HRK) systematically collect and administer relevant information,[1] we complemented our findings with insights from two higher education institutions (HEI): Cooperative State University Baden-Wuerttemberg (*Duale Hochschule Baden-Wuerttemberg, DHBW*) in Stuttgart, Germany, and Wentworth Institute of Technology (WIT) in Boston in the United States. Through internal and external reports,[2] syllabi, module descriptions and semi-structured interviews with students, alumni, faculty, and members of the administration of both HEI, we collected information about their cooperation with industry. Here, we focused on four areas – "Admission and Recruitment" (A&R), "Curriculum Design and Renewal" (CD&R), "Instruction and Training" (I&T), and "Assessment and Examination" (A&E), and considered in particular programs focused on the integration of AI. While practices of DHBW and WIT are not representative of the entirety of WBHE or work-based learning (WBL) in either country,[3] they both can serve as powerful illustrations of how dual study programs and co-op programs are typically organized and implemented in the different contexts.[4] Moreover, they share a sufficiently large number of characteristics[5] to lend themselves to a structured and systematic comparison of WBHE. Before elaborating on the practices at programs at both HEI, however, we first provide an overview of the German and US WBHE systems overall.

15.1 Work-based Higher Education in Germany and the United States

15.1.1 Germany

In Germany, WBHE has existed in the form of dual study programs since the early 1970s. Initiated by powerful corporations in the South-West of the country, they were a way to respond to demographic changes that also affected the industry's ability to access workers: In the 1960s and 1970s, Germany faced a growing number of high school graduates who wished to pursue a higher education degree.

To account for this change in preferences, the *Berufsakademien*, for example, in Stuttgart and Mannheim experimented with a new form of education that combined technical and academic skills. Drawing heavily on some of the key characteristics of Germany's Vocational Education and Training (VET) system, their efforts promoted the close integration of two places of learning,[6] quality control through competent institutions, the recognition of certificates among employers,[7] and legally binding work and salary conditions. In other parts of the country, universities of applied sciences (UAS) were created in an attempt to address companies' fears of a future shortage of employees with in-depth practical training and theoretical skills. (Niederdrenk 2013). Due to their focus on instruction rather than research, these novel institutions of higher education initially suffered from a reputation as second-order academic institutions. Today, however, UAS have now long outgrown traditional universities in numbers, and of the 396 HEIs that existed in Germany in 2018, 121 were universities, and 218 universities of applied sciences (HRK 2018).[8]

While UAS have significantly expanded their activities, frequently leading research efforts and taking on an increasingly powerful role in shaping the debate about the future of education and digitization (Niederdrenk 2013; UAS7 2018), their core feature continues to be their practically oriented study formats. Known as *Duales Studium* or dual study programs, they have long surpassed their initial existence and received widespread interest from policy-makers and potential participants in Germany as well as stakeholders internationally.

The turning point here was the early 2000s when the German government became aware of the potential of WBHE to address expected shortages of qualified workers, growing demand for knowledge and skills across many sectors, and challenges arising from an increasingly heterogeneous student body (Draeger and Ziegele 2014). Also, the assessment by education experts who underlined that WBHE could contribute to the academization of certain industries or occupations, the training of specialists in the fields of mathematics, computer science, science and technology (MINT), and the promotion of lifelong learning proved to be helpful for the proliferation of dual study programs in Germany (Berthold et al. 2009). Following the implementation of various official policies that formally raised the status of UAS, including (ongoing) initiatives to extend their competencies in the context of the Bologna reform, WBHE has thus seen a considerable increase in student enrollment from 2005, both overall as well as in relation to traditional university degrees and vocational education and training). Indeed, in 2016, the number of students enrolled in dual study programs for the first time exceeded 100,000, and in 2018 made up approx. 7% of enrollments overall. While this number is still low in comparison to enrollment in traditional degrees or VET programs, it was seen as a clear indication of the growing popularity of this comparatively new education format. Moreover, the number of educational programs grew, particularly in subjects like engineering, business administration, and computer science (BIBB 2017)—and with it the extent to which partnerships with companies were formed.

Perhaps the most striking change in the sphere of dual study programs has been the growing interest of highly qualified students. In the past, the intellectually most gifted high school graduates quasi "automatically" opted for a higher education degree at a traditional university, following the assumption that this would provide them with good career prospects. In recent years, however, this practice has been changing as students—especially in the STEM fields—begun to express a preference for programs with a greater weight on the applicability of course content. During the interviews conducted for this study, current students and recent alumni furthermore explained this shift in mindset with the hope for more interesting work, and the opportunity to become part of a team. Numerous students furthermore mentioned that they felt concerned about an increasingly insecure labor market and working conditions in the "gig economy", and therefore appreciated the prospect of establishing a relationship with an employer early on. The fact that these perceptions were also shared by particularly well-performing high school graduates and that studies have shown that the cognitive abilities of students in Germany cannot be determined by the type of HEI they opt for (Trautwein et al. 2006), thus suggests that dual study programs constitute an attractive educational pathway for a wider range of individuals than just those with a limited interest in or low likelihood of successfully completing a traditional degree program. Rather, it appears that both average students as well as "high performers", that is, students who are among the top 10% of high school graduates, are increasingly attracted to programs that offer a practice-oriented approach to learning along with the prospect of increased stability.[9]

Aware of this trend toward traditional universities have begun to include WBHE in their offerings. While absolute numbers are still comparatively low—in 2015, only 6% of all dual study programs were offered by universities (Thies 2015)—there appears to be a growing interest in bringing the dual study model to other HEI. At the same time, many UAS are becoming increasingly research-oriented. In light of this narrowing gap between the academic profiles of the different institutions, reputation no longer appears to be the key impediment to the proliferation of dual study programs among traditional universities. Rather, organizational challenges related to offering dual study programs have been identified as the main obstacle (Berthold 2009, p. 23–25).

15.1.2 The United States

Compared to the situation in Germany, work-based higher education in the United States is still an emerging field. This may—at least in parts be due to the fact that WBHE, also known as "cooperative education"—is still a rather poorly defined category, and is sometimes even seen as distinct from higher education. The Career and Technical Education Statistics by the National Center for Education Statistics (NCES), for instance, categorize "co-ops" as merely a form of work experience, along with programs such as internships, practicums, clerkships, externships, residencies, clinical experiences, and apprenticeships. Moreover, NCES refers to co-ops as a form of "training for working-class youth" in its Adults Training and Education Survey (ATES) (National Center for Education Statistics 2017). These definitions are problematic, however, in that they fail to appreciate the diversity of co-op programs that exist in the United States. They also neglect the fact that co-ops are frequently administered and were indeed founded by four-year institutions.

Initially established at the University of Cincinnati in the early 1900s, co-ops were based loosely on the United Kingdom's "sandwich courses" (Sovilla and Varty 2004) and reflected the idea that people learn best from experience and doing rather than mere abstraction, especially in the field of engineering. After an initial wave of "great resistance from both traditional educators and non-committed industrialists" (Haddara and Skanes 2007, p. 67), co-op programs soon expanded across the United States and increasingly triggered participation by a wide range of industries. Eventually, they also became part of the offerings of community colleges (CCs),[10] a particularly relevant part of the US education system. While today CC offers the majority of co-op programs and serves about 40% of all undergraduates (Ginder et al. 2017),[11] these programs are often associated with vocational education and training, or activities that "take time away from the classroom" (Crow 1997). This point of view is also reflected in the idea that co-ops are mostly a way to address the shortage of workers with "middle skills", that is, qualifications that go beyond what is learned at a high school, but do not match to those of a four-year degree (National Skills Coalition 2017).[12] This perception is problematic as it ignores the fact that a significant number of co-ops are run by four-year institutions which tend to have a much stronger focus on academic content than on practical skills.

Associating co-ops first and foremost with community colleges furthermore ignores the fact that—similar to their German counterparts—high-quality programs aim to promote a constructive and mutually beneficial partnership between the academic institution, the employers, and the trainee for a much longer time frame than the time it takes to get an associate's degree. These co-op programs are characterized by companies' promise to advance students' education while paying a reasonable salary in exchange for access to new talent, fresh perspectives, and the prospect of maintaining a well-trained workforce.[13] The fact that this crucial aspect does not feature in most official definitions suggests that there is a mismatch between the current status quo and the desired amount of collaboration between HEI and companies. It also points to the absence of national standards for the organization and classification of this type of education, despite the efforts by organizations such as the Association of Cooperative Colleges (ACC)[14] and the NCCE.[15]

While one may criticize the lack of a systematic and universally accepted way of classifying and categorizing the large number of programs and practices that shape the US WBHE space, it is noteworthy that the current system provides HEI with a lot of leeway and independence, especially when it comes to collaborating with companies. The subsequent section will further elaborate on this point.

15.2 Cooperation between HEIs and Companies in Work-Based Higher Education

While WBHE programs in the United States as well as in Germany are designed to integrate theoretical and applied knowledge through the close cooperation of HEI and companies, they do so in rather distinct ways. One way to understand these differences is by looking at four areas that are integral to the functioning of any HEI: Student Recruitment and Admission, Curriculum Design and Renewal, Training and Instruction as well as Assessment and Examination. This section investigates these areas with a view of the specific practices at Cooperative State University Baden-Wuerttemberg (*Duale Hochschule Baden-Wuerttemberg, DHBW*) in Stuttgart, Germany, and Wentworth Institute of Technology (WIT) in Boston in the United States. Specifically, it compares both institutions' approaches to promoting educational innovation, including in the field of AI, in and through cooperation with industry.

15.2.1 Student Recruitment and Admission

Student Recruitment and Admission describes the process of how individuals find and are selected for specific programs. In Germany, high school graduates who are interested in pursuing a dual study program at DHBW submit their materials directly to the company of their choice. They then undergo an often rather selective screening and selection procedure which, depending on the firm, may entail several rounds of assessment centers and in-person interviews. Often, this recruitment process resembles that used for candidates at other career stages, especially in larger companies.[16] Upon successful application to a company, students receive a training contract that serves as a prerequisite for their enrollment at the HEI. The latter, in turn, has a separate cooperation agreement with its practice partners. Students thus do not have to pass any additional (academic) requirements or tests to be admitted and enter into contractual relations with the HEI. Evidence that they hold the required high school graduation diploma (*Abitur* or *Fachabitur*) which enables them to enroll in a degree program suffices at this stage.[17] As a consequence, DHBW has little say in the composition of its student body and relies on the selection process defined by its industry partners. Moreover, DHBW does not charge tuition fees for its bachelor's and consecutive master's degree programs, and students merely pay a small enrollment or confirmation fee.[18] The university thus has no reason, or ability, to admit students from a particular socioeconomic background over others. As long as applicants fulfill the general admission criteria and there is capacity, they will "automatically" be accepted.

At WIT, by contrast, decision power in the field of admissions lies exclusively with the university and the latter's eligibility requirements. These can vary by discipline, but generally require a minimum grade point average (GPA), and a letter that demonstrates that the candidate's motivation is aligned with the university's mission and values and the specific degree program they are interested in. While companies can influence the selection process indirectly, for example, by offering (partial) scholarships for tuition to students of a specific demographic group, for example, minority students, they do not have a say in recruitment or admission service overall. The provision of financial aid can, however, be a powerful tool at an HEI like WIT which charges considerable amounts for its different programs.[19] As tuition fees constitute a key source of income, making applicants' "resourcefulness" a potential factor for selection. That being said, WIT faculty and administrators stressed throughout the interviews that students are "selected solely based on their motivation, likelihood of successful graduation, and fit with the program", and underlined that "generous scholarships are available to high-need students", who were described as "an under-tapped talent pool".

15.2.2 Curriculum Design and Renewal

Curriculum Design and Renewal refers to the "ongoing, cyclical, and analytical process, that continually strives to find new and effective ways to offer students learning experiences that are transformational, inspiring, and intellectually challenging" (Queens University 2019) and focuses on the identification and further development of learning outcomes and the choice of appropriate instruction methods. Generally speaking, WBHE in both countries seeks to engage with industry partners about strategic perspectives and skill demands. Differences exist, however, in how feedback on the quality and relevance of curricula is collected and integrated.

DHBW, for instance, entertains close relationships with companies and practitioners both through personal contacts of faculty and administrators as well as through a carefully designed and monitored organizational set-up. Indeed, DHBW's mission statement clearly states that "the participating companies and social institutions are involved as equal partners of the university" (DHBW 2015). This principle is reflected in the university's organizational structure, which promotes a close and continuous engagement among the different actors. A comprehensive set of codes and rules, agreed upon both by the university as well as the State of Baden-Wuerttemberg, thus foresee that industry representatives be integrated throughout the university's administration and governance structure. As a consequence, 50% of the members of the managing board and the senate at DHBW have an industry background, and eight of the 17 members of the supervisory board come from the private sector (DHBW 2019). Company representatives are furthermore foreseen to be a part of the *Fachkommissionen* (commissions of subject specialists), which oversee *inter alia* adaptations of the current curriculum.[20] In this context, it is important to note that all practitioners are asked not to speak exclusively to the interests of a specific company, but to provide recommendations based on the general direction and needs of "their" industry overall. This idea is supported by the fact that many of the industry representatives who are involved in curriculum- or governance-related decisions at DHBW tend to be rather senior figures in their respective organizations with broad expertise and knowledge.[21] A newly developed module on Risk Management and AI Data Analytics at DHBW has thus benefitted strongly from the leading academic's close cooperation with a senior industry expert.

WIT, too, has multiple channels to bring in practical expertise. Its governing body, the Board of Trustees,[22] for instance, is comprised exclusively of industry representatives, many of whom are also WIT alumni. Moreover, Industry Advisory Committees discuss a wide range of issues, including the performance and potential need for reform of specific programs[23] and there are 30–50 University Advisers who provide additional insights to the administration and trustees on issues of strategic importance.[24] In addition, faculty members regularly draw on their personal connections when seeking to integrate practitioners' perspectives in their courses. Yet, unlike DHBW, WIT does not have in place mechanisms to ensure that industry representatives promote learning content that represents the needs of an entire industry rather than a specific company.[25] This can be attributed to at least two factors: first, practitioners involved at WIT tend to be technical experts rather than senior managers, and therefore are most familiar with and focused on meeting their firm's immediate needs. Second, in the United States, business is generally characterized by a high degree of individualism—a fact also reflected in the lack of a tradition of sectorial bargaining. Given the potential for conflict between academic faculty, who wish to keep the curriculum broad and general enough to meet the demands of a wider range of firms, and practitioners, focused on the needs of specific firms, incentives for the joint development of courses are thus more limited at WIT than at DHBW. At the same time, industry input is still valued at specific points in time. The recent development and introduction of a new module focused on AI in the field of architecture illustrates this approach: the innovative program was co-developed by faculty members of two different academic disciplines, while industry representatives were invited to contribute in the form of guest lectures.

15.2.3 Instruction and Training

The Instruction and Training dimension of WBHE programs focuses on how didactical knowledge and subject-level expertise are combined through the careful selection and integration of instructors with practical expertise and the organization of theory-focused and practice-oriented learning phases. When it comes to the design of instruction and training in Germany, companies offering apprenticeship programs must present a strategic training plan, designed on the basis of an extensive set of rules which, assured by third actors,[26] outlines information on the factual and temporal structure (training plan) of each program.[27] While recent changes in its accreditation status have enabled DHBW to exercise greater power in ensuring alignment between the practical and academic dimensions of learning content,[28] its curriculum continues to have to meet standards overseen by different "outside parties".[29] In the United States, by contrast, the absence of a comparably extensively regulated structure means that co-op programs are anchored solely within the general accreditation guidelines of the university. This allows the university to determine independently whether and to which extent it wants to rely on external partners to provide feedback on or determine the contents of the curriculum. This leads to closer and more systematic integration of theory and practice in the German context than in the United States. The effect is further enhanced by the fact that at DHBW, only about 40% of courses are taught by the full-time academics of DHBW or partner universities. While these professors also tend to have a lot of industry experience,[30] most teaching staff are experts, employed mainly by partner companies or social institutions. This has implications for the teaching and instruction methods as it favors instruction with a strong reliance on real-world examples and case studies rather than abstract knowledge or theory. Indeed, the aforementioned new program in AI analytics draws heavily on "real-world" data and case studies.

More broadly, DHBW's instruction model is characterized by a highly formalized alternation of practical and theoretical phases which take place at different sites of learning. For instance, operating on a non-stop, 12-month schedule, the program grants vacation days as stipulated in the three-year employment contract signed between the student and the partner company at the beginning of the dual study program. Furthermore, following a clearly defined three-month rhythm, DHBW's *Blockmodell* (block model), which governs approximately 80% of all dual study programs in Germany, is perceived to be particularly effective at promoting a direct link between theoretical knowledge and practical skills.[31] At the same time, it provides ample opportunities to form relationships and experience the atmosphere at both a university as well as in the company.

At WIT, by contrast, students are mostly instructed by full-time academic faculty. While the latter can also have a background in industry, the latter is not a formal requirement. Rather, the focus lies on their teaching ability, the quality of their research, publications, and overall academic record.[32] Another major difference from the German system is the amount of time students at WIT spend at the university and in companies. Generally participating in only two (mandatory) co-op phases during the spring of the 3rd year and the fall of the 4th year respectively, students face instruction with a strong academic bias. While they can voluntarily complete the third co-op during the summer following their sophomore year to gain additional work experience, earn income, and acquire insights into the functioning of and corporate dynamics in companies,[33] doing so is an optional activity, and not applied toward the graduation requirement. To ensure high levels of work-integrated education, WIT faculty rely on hands-on projects, lab sessions, and workshops throughout the semester. This applies in particular to the newly developed educational offerings in the case of AI, where tools and real-world applications are considered highly beneficial.

15.2.4 Assessment and Examination

As in the instruction and training space, companies play a key role in the assessment and examination of students' performance in the DHBW system, in particular once students have acquired basic knowledge in key disciplines. Industry representatives thus oversee in-class projects, grade written reports, and conduct oral examinations. Company representatives frequently also act as mentors and student advisors and provide extensive feedback on students' performance. In German WBHE and at DHBW in particular students thus rely largely on their professional supervisors, and consult with professors predominantly on academic matters.[34] Even here, however, industry representatives can play a major role, namely when they teach courses and are responsible for assessing students' academic performance. This practice contrasts with that at WIT, where professors are clearly and solely in charge of evaluating students' academic performance.

Also with regard to the assessment of the practical phases of the programs, DHBW and WIT differ considerably. At DHBW, companies have to provide extensive feedback on the quality of the work done by the trainee as they move across departments and units, whereas, at WIT, performance during a co-op is assessed through a grade category ("satisfactory/unsatisfactory"), a self-evaluation and a short evaluation by the direct supervisor at the company site. While in both cases, companies may use the opportunity to distinguish themselves from others by providing better feedback and comment on both technical abilities as well as social skills, the very set-up of the assessment and examination component at DHBW and WIT reveals diverging fundamental priorities: Individuals attending DHBW have equal opportunities to learn about their work and themselves as students as well as employees and colleagues. Meanwhile, at WIT students receive extensive attention and feedback from their advisors and faculty members, but have comparatively fewer opportunities to experience how they will fare as workers. In the absence of an extensive report or numerical grade that could provide further insight into the quality of work done by WIT students, it is mostly their ability to obtain a position after graduation that serves as an indicator of their performance during the practical phases of their education. This form of indirect assessment is not without challenges, however, as fluctuations in the labor market and economy may prevent even well-performing candidates from acquiring a position upon completion of their studies.[35]

15.3 On the Potential of WBHE to Train the "Work of the Future"

Our analysis has demonstrated that WBHE in Germany and the United States differ considerably, despite their shared ambition to integrate theory and practice and their respective efforts to focus on new technologies. One major distinction lies in the engagement and influence of industry partners in areas such as admission, curriculum design, instruction, and assessment. WBHE programs in Germany can respond relatively easily to shifts in the labor market and firm demands due to the fact that representatives of different companies are invited to contribute both significantly as well as systematically across all of these aspects. Meanwhile, industry involvement in the United States is less structured and tends to depend largely on the preferences and connections of academic faculty. The integration of new content and technologies thus tends to be a consequence of individual efforts rather than as a general training and education strategy.

Related to this aspect is the question of who carries the associated costs. In the case of Germany, education—including training the "workforce of the future"—is generally perceived as a public good. Accordingly, the acquisition of academic knowledge at the university is covered by taxpayers, while corporations cover the costs for the practical training component, including students' salaries. In addition, public loan programs and privately funded scholarships are widely available and assist students with living expenses. Meanwhile, the majority of American co-op programs are financed through tuition fees and thus depend first and foremost on the resources of students or their families.[36] Despite the availability of generous grants and scholarships, especially for individuals from minority groups or particularly disadvantaged backgrounds, individuals interested in WBHE programs in the United States thus face similar challenges as students enrolled in traditional university degrees. At the same time, WBHE tends to not (yet) have the same reputational value as the latter, and awareness of their existence tends to be limited.

This may, inter alia, be a consequence of the fact that, in the United States, few regulations and official standards exist to ensure consistent quality among co-op programs and institutions, while WBHE programs in Germany have been subject to strict regulatory guidelines and public oversight. Moreover, extensive educational campaigns, including by political actors and by Universities of Applied Sciences themselves have ensured that qualified high school graduates and other potential candidates for WBHE programs tend to have a good understanding of the characteristics and advantages of these programs, notable the outlooks of combining paid work experience and a high -quality university experience.

Going forward, we thus recommend that efforts be made to promote transparency, visibility, and accessibility of WBHE programs in the United States. Widely communicated quality standards and new funding models could help this cause. The German system, by contrast, could benefit from a greater ability for HEI to distinguish themselves from others and demonstrate their innovative potential.

In both countries, WBHE should put a greater emphasis on enabling upskilling and retraining the existing workforce through continuing education. After all, the "workforce of the future" consists not only of tomorrow's students, but also of the large number of talented individuals who have yet to learn how to productively engage with new technologies and AI in particular.

Notes

1 In addition to databases such as *AusbildungPlus* (BIBB) and *Hochschulkompass* (HRK), other relevant sources of information in Germany include the *Bildungsbericht* by the *Leibniz-Institut für Bildungsforschung und Bildungsinformation*, and the *Akkreditierungsrat*. Meanwhile in the United States, it is mostly participating universities themselves which collect information on their activities.
2 These included documents on the organization and management of each institution as well as evaluation reports and legal guidelines governing higher education.
3 With a view of work-based learning, Carnevale et al. underline that "programs are often the same in name only" and "have different values at different institutions depending on the alignment between particular curricula and regional labor market demand, as well as on differences in program quality" (2015, p. 18).
4 Like most HEI in Germany, DHBW is a public institution that does not charge tuition fees, but draws on public funds and resources from its foundation to pursue its educational mission. WIT, by contrast, is a private school which relies largely on students' tuition and fees.
5 Both institutions are former trade schools which, over time, were granted "university" status and became recognized as innovative actors in the design and implementation of compulsory WBHE programs. Moreover, they both have excellent relations with local industry and are committed to improving their respective communities by providing a solid education to individuals from a wide range of backgrounds. Finally, both institutions offer undergraduate and graduate programs which combine on-the-job training and traditional academic studies in the STEM field, that is, subjects which are expected to offer particularly attractive opportunities for future employment in either country.
6 In the case of VET, these are (mostly) small and medium-sized companies and publicly funded vocational schools.
7 Apprenticeship certificates are issued by a chamber of industry and commerce, or of crafts and trades.
8 The remaining 57 institutions are Colleges of Art and Music.
9 A side effect of this change in student preferences has also been the greater openness of renowned institutions like the *Studienstiftung des deutschen Volkes*, which has long focused on supporting elite students at traditional universities, to accepting dual students into their mentorship and financial assistance programs.
10 Similarly, a notable university ranking, refers to co-ops as a form of training that "require(s) or encourage(s) students to apply what they're learning in the classroom out in the real world" (US News 2019) rather than as a way to acquire knowledge in a more integrated way.
11 Rather than for the important services they provide to many Americans, CCs are often known for their comparatively high dropout rates. As many of their graduates furthermore obtain an associate's rather than a bachelor's degree, community colleges have the reputation as being institutions of inferior quality.
12 Analyses of data by the Bureau of Labor Statistics has found that only 43% of US workers are trained for the 53% of US jobs that are middle skill (National Skills Coalition 2017).
13 The fact that this crucial aspect does not feature in most official definitions suggests a mismatch between the aspirations for and the actual extent of collaboration between HEI and companies.
14 Founded in 1926, the ACC is the first professional association for cooperative education.
15 In 1961, a study of cooperative education authorized and commissioned by the Ford and Edison Foundations resulted in the formation of the National Commission for Cooperative Education (NCCE), an organization dedicated to promoting and lobbying for cooperative education in the United States.

Training the "Workforce of the Future" 257

16 While especially internationally renowned German companies are frequently able to select among a large number of highly qualified candidates (Krone et al. 2019), it has been a specific feature of the German economy that also so-called "hidden champions", that is, small and medium-sized enterprises (SMEs) with a significant market share in a particular area, are seen as attractive training providers and employers.
17 Occasionally companies also require candidates to pass a six-months employment probation period before they are fully admitted into the firm's dual study program.
18 The fee is normally covered by the partner company.
19 In 2019, student fees for undergraduate and graduate programs were between $33,950 and $36,750.
20 Most commonly, a *Studiengangsleiter* (degree program coordinator) will identify a need for a and design a new module, before asking the relevant *Fachkommission* to review it.
21 Typical examples of this group are managers or executives of highly successful SMEs, so-called "hidden champions".
22 The Board of Trustees oversees policy making, planning, and the financial welfare of the school.
23 Industry Advisory Committees advise on the continuous development and evolution of study programs and advise departments of the professional requirements of the private and public sectors and the implications of those requirements upon the curriculum. Specifically, they provide a forum to discuss teaching, research, professional development, and academic excellence relative to the needs of the profession and related industries and assist with the development strategies for recruiting students to the programs and to internships, co-op, and permanent positions.
Composed of 10-20 individuals who meet between one to three times a year, IACs furthermore assist academic departments in locating funds and gifts for their educational and outreach programs.
24 For instance, byy participating in the Board of Trustee Committees, University Advisors can provide insights into "industry trends related to preparing the workforce of the future to ensure that the university remains at the forefront of student success and employer satisfaction, and students are properly prepared for full-time work" (WIT 2019).
25 At one industry advisory committee, companies even pay a fee to gain a seat on the table.
26 These actors are the German Chambers of Industry and Commerce, IHK and HWK.
27 All partner companies of DHBW thus have to show how the practical training components fit within and complement the academic contents of each learning module.
28 Since 2011, DHBW is able to conduct an internal review process, the "*Systemakkreditierung*" (DHWB 2011).
29 In addition to individual states' laws governing higher education, requirements of the Standing Conference of State Ministers (KMK), and the procedures for programs and system accreditations staff representation structures are a mechanism through which high standards are assured at the university level. Meanwhile, on the operational side, the Vocational Training Act ('*Berufsbildungsgesetz*', BBiG) and the Trades and Crafts Code (*Handwerksordnung*, HwO) are of particular relevance – at least with regard to apprenticeship-integrating programs.
30 The state law requires professors at universities of applied science to have at least five years of practical experience, three of which have to be outside the academic environment (Haug 2009).
31 Other HEI opt for different formats, including the *Rotationsmodell* (rotation model) and distance learning models with or without occasional presence phases at the place of learning (BIBB 2017).
32 Occasionally, academic positions at WIT are also filled by retired practitioners, interested in pursuing teaching as a second career and way to stay engaged, while passing on knowledge and experience.

33 This exception does not apply to students of Architecture, Applied Mathematics, and Electromechanical Engineering for which separate rules exist.
34 In line with this observation, our interviews suggest that the quality of the mentorship that trainees receive at the company and the degree to which they are integrated into a team early-on are indeed crucial contributors for their success across the program.
35 While the most appropriate way of comparing retention and integration into the labor market in both countries would be to look at how WBHE degrees perform in relation to graduates in the same subject who are enrolled in traditional programs, the absence of such data draws the author's attention to the different practices with which DHBW and WIT are involved in facilitating the job-finding process.
36 While universities or other actors may provide support through grants and tuition assistance, and companies pay a salary for services rendered during the co-op phases, students face the vast amount of expenditures.

References

Berthold, C. et al. (2009). *Demographischer Wandel und Hochschulen. Der Ausbau des Dualen Studiums als Antwort auf den Fachkräftemangel*. Gütersloh: CHE.

BIBB (2017). Empfehlung des Hauptausschusses des Bundesinstituts für Berufsbildung "Positionspapier der BIBB-Hauptausschuss AG zum dualen Studium", available at: https://www.bibb.de/dokumente/pdf/HA169.pdf

Carnevale, A. P. et al. (2015). Learning While Earning: The New Normal, Georgetown University. Center on Education and the Workforce, Washington, DC, available at: https://cew.georgetown.edu/wp-content/uploads/Working-Learners-Report.pdf

Crow, C. (1997). *Cooperative Education in the New Millennium, Cooperative Education Experience* (pp. 1–5). Columbia, MD: Cooperative Education Association (ED 414 433).

DHBW (2015). Leitbild der DHBW, available at: https://www.dhbw.de/fileadmin/user_upload/Dokumente/Broschueren_Handbuch_Betriebe/DHBW_Leitbild_2015.pdf

DHBW (2019). Zentrale Organisation, available at: https://www.dhbw-stuttgart.de/fileadmin/dateien/DHBW/Zentrale_Organisation.pdf

DHWB (2011). Die DHBW ist die erste systemakkreditierte Hochschule in Baden-Württemberg – erstklassiges Qualitätsmanagement bestätigt, available at: https://www.dhbw-stuttgart.de/themen/hochschule/meldung/2011/12/die-dhbw-ist-die-erste-systemakkreditierte-hochschule-in-baden-wuerttemberg-erstklassiges-qualitaets/

Draeger, J. and Ziegele, F. (2014). Hochschulbildung wird zum Normalfall Ein gesellschaftlicher Wandel und seine Folgen, available at: https://www.che.de/downloads/Hochschulbildung_wird_zum_Normalfall_2014.pdf

Eszell (2021). Assessing the State of Digital Skills in the U.S. *Economy*, available at: https://itif.org/sites/default/files/2021-us-digital-skills.pdf

Ginder, S.A., Kelly-Reid, J.E., and Mann, F.B. (2017). Enrollment and Employees in Postsecondary Institutions, Fall 2015; and Financial Statistics and Academic Libraries, Fiscal Year 2015: First Look (Provisional Data) (NCES 2017-024). U.S. Department of Education. Washington, DC: National Center for Education Statistics, available at: http://nces.ed.gov/pubsearch

Haddara, M., and Skanes, H. (2007). A Reflection on Cooperative Education: From Experience to Experiential Learning. *Asia-Pacific Journal of Cooperative Education*, 8(1), 67–76.

Haehn, K. (2019). Das duale Studium als Handlungsfeld betrieblicher Interessenvertretungen. In S. Krone et al., *Das Duale Studium – Und dann?* (pp. 243–353), available at: https://www.boeckler.de/5248.htm?produkt=HBS-007093&chunk=1&jahr=

Haug, V. (Ed). (2009). *Das Hochschulrecht in BadenWürttemberg*, 2nd edition. Heidelberg: Müller Jur.Vlg.C.F.

Hochschulrektorenkonferenz (HRK) (2018). Higher Education Institutions in Figures 2017, *Berlin*, available at: https://www.hrk.de/fileadmin/redaktion/hrk/02-Dokumente/02-06-Hochschulsystem/Statistik/2018-05-22_Final_Engl._Faltblatt_2018_fuer_Homepage.pdf

Krone, S. et al. (2019). Das Duale Studium – Und dann? p. 243–353, available at: https://www.boeckler.de/5248.htm?produkt=HBS-007093&chunk=1&jahr=

National Center for Education Statistics (2017). The Adult Training and Education Survey (ATES), available at: https://nces.ed.gov/nhes/ates.asp

National Skills Coalition (2017). United States' Forgotten Middle, available at: https://nationalskillscoalition.org/resources/publications/2017-middle-skills-fact-sheets/file/United-States-MiddleSkills.pdf

Niederdrenk, K. (2013). Zur Rolle der Fachhochschulen im deutschen Hochschulsystem.

Queens University (2019). Center for Teaching and Learning, Curriculum design and renewal, available at: https://www.queensu.ca/ctl/teaching-support/course-and-program-design/curriculum-design-and-renewal

Sovilla, E.S., and Varty, J.W. (2004). Cooperative Education in the USA, Past and Present: Some Lessons Learned. In R.K. Coll & Eames (Eds.), *International Handbook for Cooperative Education: An International Perspective of the Theory, Research and Practice of Work Integrated Learning* (pp. 3–16). Boston: World Association for Cooperative Education.

Thies, L. (2015). Das Beste aus zwei Welten. Duale Studiengänge als Brücke zwischen beruflicher und akademischer Bildung, available at: https://www.bertelsmann-stiftung.de/fileadmin/files/BSt/Publikationen/GrauePublikationen/LL_GB_Duales_Studium_150528.pdf

Trautwein, U., et al. (2006). Studieren an der Berufsakademie oder an der Universität, Fachhochschule oder Pädagogischen Hochschule?: Ein Vergleich des Leistungsstands, familiären Hintergrunds, beruflicher Interessen und der Studienwahlmotive von (künftigen) Studierenden aus Baden-Württemberg. *Zeitschrift für Erziehungswissenschaft*, 9(3), 393–412.

UAS7 (2018). Digitalisierung. Strategische Entwicklung einer kompetenzorientierten Lehre für die digitale Gesellschaft und Arbeitswelt. Die Position der UAS7-Hochschulen für angewandte Wissenschaften.

US News (2019). 2019 Internships/Co-ops – US News & World Report, available at: https://www.usnews.com/best-colleges/rankings/internship-programs

WIT (2019). Charter for University Advisers, available at: https://wit.edu/Charter/University/Advisers

16
HOW INDIA IS BUILDING LEARNING TECHNOLOGIES AT SCALE

Tarun Wadhwa

On November 8, 2016, India's Prime Minister Narendra Modi shocked the nation by announcing that the government would no longer recognize existing, commonly used high-denomination banknotes (Reserve Bank of India, 2016). This "demonetization" was done to reduce corruption and tax evasion by making financial transactions digital, standardized, and visible to the government. While initially producing chaos, upheaval, and hardship amongst the population, these dramatic actions set in motion a series of events that led to a revolution in India's financial technology sector. As a result, the country quickly evolved from being "data poor" to becoming one of the world's leading cashless societies—with an estimated $10 trillion in digital payments expected by 2026 (BCG, 2022).

In a similar fashion, the COVID-19 pandemic ushered in India's digital learning moment. On March 24th, 2020, the government stunned the nation by asking 1.3 billion Indians to stay home for 21 days to slow the spread of the virus (Chandrashekhar, 2020), kicking off a series of interventions that would lead to nearly 250 million students unable to access regular in-person instruction (UNICEF, 2021). In the midst of this crisis, India's technology companies, policymakers, and venture capitalists stepped up to fill the gap, resulting in an explosive Edtech market.

The landscape of online learning in India dramatically expanded, becoming a hotbed for digital learning innovation, experimentation, and user adoption. In 2020 and 2021 Indian Edtech companies raised a groundbreaking $5 billion in funding (Mitter, 2021), grew their user bases by multiples, and moved certain education fields, like online test preparation and online certifications, toward maturity (Toczauer, 2021).

DOI: 10.4324/9781003230762-20

In fact, since the start of the pandemic, India has generated at least six new Edtech "unicorns"—companies with a valuation of over 1 billion dollars. These include Unacademy, Eruditus, upGrad, Vedantu, and LEAD School. In addition, one existing Edtech giant has become a "decacorn"—a company valued at over 10 billion dollars, the pioneering Byju's. Together, these enterprises helped India emerge as a digital learning powerhouse.

By analyzing the rise, growth, and path to adoption faced by each of India's Edtech pandemic unicorns, we can draw lessons from the risks and rewards companies face in attempting to leverage connectivity, exponential technologies, and personalization to improve the capacity and potential of student learning globally.

Arriving at This Moment

The pandemic brought nearly a decade of change in user behavior and preference for technology in just a matter of months. While it may have served as the ultimate catalyst, these exponential advances have in fact been brewing for decades. The lockdowns began at a moment when many key technologies had already reached a point of widespread proliferation.

Indeed, in the last decade, India has come online in a major way. Mobile phones used to be objects of luxury, and landlines were once hard to secure—but now the country is flooded with over 750 million smartphones both powerful and affordable (Press Trust of India, 2022a). Since the launch of Reliance Jio and 4G mobile connectivity in 2015, billionaire Mukesh Ambani has reshaped the country by hooking the population on extremely cheap data plans. Through sheer ambition, he is turning the country into the world's top mobile data user (Sharma, 2021).

Since the launch of the Aadhaar identification program in 2009, there have been waves large-scale development of open-source governance and commerce platforms. These ground-breaking public-private efforts have come to be known as "India Stack". It has comprised a series of interconnected systems for identity, payments, documents, and digitally signed transactions which have supercharged digital adoption throughout the country (India Stack, n.d.).

At the same time, innovation has now globalized and so India's entrepreneurs have been able to tap into many of the same resources that are available to start-ups in San Francisco or Beijing.

Sophisticated storage, processing, and analysis technology that would once have cost millions to access are now available, cheap, and incredibly powerful. Artificial intelligence, machine learning, and cloud computing are now abundantly accessible through services offered by companies like Amazon, Google, and Microsoft. This enables the processing possible for scale, distribution, and complex individualized instruction tailored to specific needs.

Social media has made marketing far cheaper and more targeted for education companies. This allows them to reach customers they could not previously access and deliver content in form factors, languages, and formats that were never before possible, to diverse audiences across the country. Additionally, hardware-based systems that were once scarce such as virtual reality and sensor-based devices have now become obtainable. This has led to an explosion of creativity, although both technologies are still early in adoption in the learning context.

An Existing Crisis Made Worse

The enormity of the challenges that Indian education faced during the pandemic should not be understated (Delgado Martín & Larrú Ramos, 2022). India has the second largest school system in the world, after China. That includes nearly 10 million teachers and 265 million students across 1.5 million schools—the vast majority of which are in rural areas (Ministry of Education, 2022).

For all the progress the country has made in connectivity, gains have been unevenly distributed across the country's regions, populations, and income groups. According to an analysis by two major firms (Nielsen, 2014), only 11% of Indian households have computers such as desktops, laptops, and tablets. For the vast majority of the population, content consumption takes place on mobile devices. While 54% of urban residents reported having internet access, that was only true for 32% of rural residents.

There remain massive challenges related to infrastructure, power supply, and connectivity. One study by the non-profit group Oxfam India found that even amongst urban populations in private schools there were noteworthy issues. Although improving, internet signals, speeds, and mobile data cost still remain obstacles for many Indians (OxFam India, 2020). Data suggests that barriers to participating effectively in digital learning remains a challenge for large portions of India's students, especially those who are poor or have disabilities. One survey by Azim Premji University found that across five states, almost 60% of students surveyed could not properly access online learning opportunities. That was due to the absence of a smartphone, multiple users sharing one device, problems with the software, or other issues (Azim Premji University, 2020). Additionally, with these constraints, teachers reported finding themselves struggling to provide the emotional connection, assessment, and attention needed for adequate instruction.

In response, there was a surge of public and informal mechanisms to support students' remote learning efforts. These include using traditional tools such as textbooks, home visits and mass-communication tools, in addition to learning-enabling solutions such as midday meals, sanitation kits, and monetary support. The government's Ministry of Education made a large repository of learning curriculum and tools available while creating platforms for information sharing (UNICEF, 2021). Additionally, the Indian government highlighted its support for online education in the 2020 National Education Policy (Government of India, 2020).

The New Digital Learning Giants

The pandemic served to exacerbate many of the existing issues in India's education system and social-economic structures—creating both difficult conditions and an unprecedented need for digital learning solutions at the same time. If there was a market ripe for a digital learning transformation, it was India.

In the Indian cultural context, there is a large focus on education—and therefore parents are comparatively more willing to spend their disposable income on services for their children. As a developing nation, education is still seen as the most promising route to mobility. There is also widespread dissatisfaction with the status quo of most of the country's educational systems, so the existing options are insufficient. At the same time, Indian consumers have more practical access to cheap technology than ever before (Deloitte India, 2022).

The research firm CB Insights has identified 14 separate categories of product development occurring in the Edtech space: Broad online learning, learning management systems, career development, early childhood education, language learning, tech learning, study tools, course materials, school administration, next-generation schools, learning analytics, test prep, and classroom engagement, and offline tutoring (CB Insights, 2017). Nearly all of these areas are present in the Indian market. But the largest gains have been made in the fields of test prep, offline tutoring, and career development (Inc 42, 2021).

The existing potential in Indian education made the conditions suitable during the pandemic for an explosion in Edtech activity. In 2020, of the more than $10B raised by Indian startups, over 15% went to Edtech companies (Press Trust of India, 2021). The following year, in 2021, this more than doubled to $4.7 billion (Vanamali, 2022). The seven companies that rose to great heights in this era would come to define India's place in the digital learning landscape, forever altering the country's future growth trajectory.

Byju's

As of December 2021, Byju's was valued at $22B, making it the world's most valuable Edtech company and one of India's most valuable startups (Rai, 2022a). In many ways, Byju's has been groundbreaking for the entire Indian technology industry and digital learning as a whole. Many of the concepts, features, and business practices that Byju's pioneered, competitors would later adopt, advance, and bring to other markets and customer segments (Bhalla, 2021).

In some ways, the story of Byju's mirrors the story of India's rapid digitalization. Founded in 2011 by Byju Raveendran and Divya Gokulnath, the company's origins are in seeking to scale up video-based instruction so that it could reach larger groups of students, competing against traditional school instruction (Byju's, 2015). The country reached a turning point in late 2015 as Reliance Jio made the mobile internet affordable, creating the conditions for Byju's to raise over $100 million in funding. They used this funding to develop a groundbreaking learning app and scale to an extraordinary degree. The company claims to now have over 100 million registered users globally, spending an average of 71 minutes a day on the platform.

With a particular focus on math and science, Byju's has made great use of the freemium business model popularized by technology startups in the consumer space. That's when some content is available for no cost, but other knowledge is gated behind paid tiers. Byju's also has targeted the upper percentile of wealthy parents, given that they are the most likely to spend money on their children's supplemental education, positioning themselves as a premium offering.

More than any other Edtech player, Byju's has maintained dominance by aggressively expanding into new markets and building a global brand.

It has raised funding from top-caliber investors, including the Chan-Zuckerberg Initiative (Byju's, n.d.), and partnering with established corporations like Disney (Takahashi, 2021). It has focused on integrating and adopting new technologies, particularly live streaming for instruction, machine learning for personalized assessment and recommendation, and other forms of audiovisual display and storytelling (such as mobile interaction, computer vision, and augmented reality). The company has also been on a massive acquisition spree, spending over $3 billion on over a dozen companies, most notably White Hat Jr, which teaches coding, and Aakaash Educational Services, an established chain of physical coaching centers (Singh, 2021a).

Unacademy

Starting as a YouTube channel in 2010, Unacademy has grown into a platform and mobile app that currently hosts over 1 million videos from 10,000 educators across the country (Unacademy, n.d.). The company's primary focus is preparation for India's notoriously difficult entrance examinations (The Economist, 2022). Claiming to reach over 50 million learners, Unacademy states that 70% of their users come from Tier III cities. These areas, as defined by the Reserve Bank of India, have between 20,000 and 50,000 residents (Reserve Bank of India, n.d.)

Like Byju's, Unacademy's growth has been fueled by the usage of the freemium business model. In the case of Unacademy, most courses are free of cost, but to access live classes, personalized instruction, certain tests, and saving content offline requires a Plus level subscription. As the country has grown in its digital capabilities, Unacademy has been able to reach larger and more diverse segments of users.

Another pillar of Unacademy's advancement has been, like Byju, using aggressive consolidation and acquisitions for inorganic growth. Unacademy used its fundraising advantage and large userbase to expand into nearby verticals. This includes: Rheo TV, for online game streaming and monetization; Tapchief, for professional networking for students; and Mastree, for children's digital public speaking instruction (Sil, 2020).

Eruditus

Eruditus was founded in 2010 as an in-person executive education program, but the company floundered for several years before forming an online learning division, Emeritus.

In the process of the transition, the team learned how to build a full suite of services for their academic and corporate partners, eventually landing a partnership with business school INSEAD. This relationship created the momentum to partner with the University of Pennsylvania Wharton, MIT, Columbia Business School, and Dartmouth to offer in-person and online programs for senior executives in emerging markets (Eruditus, 2020). Eventually, the company adopted the Small Private Online Course model, a specialized form of Massive Open Online Courses which are used in a business-to-business context and feature executive peer-to-peer learning (Goral, 2013).

Eruditus has one key advantage that has helped fuel its growth: They have taken its cost savings and experience working in the Indian market abroad, and to great effect. Computing hardware is cheap everywhere now, powerful cameras and equipment cost just a fraction of what they did a decade ago. Since innovation has now globalized, savvy entrepreneurs have been able to use this arbitrage to fuel global expansion.

Much of their revenue is now driven by learners outside of India. Of the company's revenue in 2021, 36% came from the United States, 16% from Latin America, and 16% from Europe—a truly unique and global mix for an Indian Edtech company. With nearly double the staff of Coursera spread out around the world and working with local universities and partners, Eruditus seeks to grow by leveraging existing academic brands for its technology platform, while localizing student preferences in different regions (Talgeri, 2022).

upGrad

While the vast majority of offerings in the Edtech space are catered toward children and younger students, like Eruditus, upGrad caters to an older demographic—including higher education, working professionals, and corporate training.

Founded in 2015 by serial entrepreneur Ronnie Screwvala and two others, upGrad boasts an impressive list of partnerships including major domestic and international universities (upGrad, n.d.). With a particular focus on data science, IT management, and technology, upGrad has over 2 million registered learners. The company seeks to augment career growth with "upskilling", lifelong learning, and creating paths to obtain industry-relevant skills (Rai, 2022b). With the largest college-going population in the world, India has a huge need to improve the quality of graduates. upGrad seeks to achieve this by improving what these students are able to learn before they enter the workforce, and well as providing re-training to workers already mid-career.

upGrad has many common features seen in adult learning platforms around the world. That includes a steady stream of content from experts, different types of quizzes and assessment systems to measure performance, personalized learning tools and feedback on assignments, and machine-learning-informed guidance on filling in critical gaps. upGrad also uses common gamification techniques to encourage peer-to-peer learning and knowledge sharing. Additionally, the company seeks to also help students enter the workforce through interview preparation, career support, counseling sessions, and mock interviews, as well as hosting job fairs and setting up portals with hiring partners (upGrad, 2022).

upGrad's technology leverages the common building blocks around connectivity, personalized interaction, and asynchronous learning. They seek to differentiate by offering a stronger "student mentorship" experience. That includes providing support, context, and instruction to learners with online tools.

Vedantu

Founded by graduates of the Indian Institutes of Technology in 2014, Vedantu offers digital after-school tutoring. With a particular emphasis on exam prep and entrance exams for students in grades 4 to 12, Vedantu boasts over 35 million active users. The company focuses on live instruction, which has been shown to have a higher engagement rate than recorded lectures in the Indian market (Shrivastava & Peermohamed, 2019).

As a competitor to both Unacademy and Byju's with similar offerings, Vedantu differentiates by focusing on their personalized education platform, known as WAVE (Whiteboard Audio Video Environment).

WAVE uses machine learning, interaction technologies, and data-driven feedback loops to create a gamified experience between student and teacher with the goal to improve engagement and outcomes. Claiming to recognize over 70 parameters from the students' behavior and characteristics, Wave is said to combine inputs from whiteboard, content interaction, verbal, and facial recognition (Vedantu, n.d.). Vedantu serves to onboard new teachers onto the platform while maintaining a two-way rating system and sharing information between all parties involved. WAVE is designed to consume low amounts of data-driven bandwidth.

Additionally, the startup took advantage of India's improved connectivity by striking partnerships with telecom giants Airtel and Tata Sky to distribute their courses as part of a satellite television package at no cost to students (Singh, 2021b).

LEAD School

LEAD School, the most unique of the existing Edtech unicorns, is focused on bringing a "school in a box" to "small town India".

Founded in 2013, LEAD School has developed an integrated digital platform and learning management system for affordable private schools, particularly in rural areas (Pradeep, 2022). As opposed to circumventing the classroom, LEAD School is instead the largest provider of Edtech technology to schools and seeks to improve the education infrastructure by taking a systems-level approach to digitizing key aspects of classroom interaction (Singh, 2022a).

In a LEAD-powered school, teachers prepare for each class with pre-set lesson plans and curriculum obtained via smartphone or tablet. These lesson plans are then shared with the class via a Smart TV, where the teacher and students are both guided through group and individual practice. The learning kits the students are using as well are provided by LEAD. All outcomes are inputted into a database and shared with all involved parties.

Serving as the backbone for existing schools allows LEAD-powered schools to adapt to remote learning in a more seamless way (LEAD, 2021). Since this is where instructors post documents, host questions, and coordinate activities with their students, it allows for a more flexible form of learning in areas where that would not normally be possible. These platforms are also in a unique position to serve as catalysts for innovation—and when the time is right, they can leverage their existing customer base to roll out new features and functionalities.

Post-Lockdown Realities

EdTech has provided a unique bridge in managing Indian educational needs throughout the pandemic. However, with the end of the lockdowns has come a dramatic shift in the fertile conditions that fueled the ascent of Indian Edtech (The Ken, 2022). As physical institutions have opened their doors, the demand for online learning decreased. Meanwhile, macro conditions have changed. Markets have crashed, funding has dried up, there are widespread supply chain issues, and looming geopolitical instability. All of this has led to far more conservative investor attitudes toward taking risks.

The industry is in the midst of a rough correction (Subramaniam, 2022). There have been widespread layoffs, salary reductions, and resignations. With uncertainty ahead, companies have been doing whatever they can to extend their runways, which often means curbing previous ambitions. In a global recession, consumers are also cash-strapped. That means whichever parts of Edtech are not absolutely necessary will quickly fall by the wayside. Unsustainable business models will cease to work.

The problem is that going forward these companies now find themselves in a changing economic landscape. Digital learning has largely enjoyed conditions of high profits, low barriers to entry, good margins, and is easy scaling. Unfortunately, the economics of hybrid learning is not as advantageous. Unacademy is investing $200 million in opening physical tuition centers, while many other companies are doing the same or considering setting up physical touchpoints for sales and business development. These models are far from a sure thing (Abrar, 2022).

Perhaps this market adversity will give rise to alternatives to hypergrowth in the education space. It is not necessary that Edtech companies need to grow so quickly or be fueled by huge amounts of venture capital. As the rise of PhysicsWallah demonstrates, growth can be organic (Singh, 2022b). Unlike its predecessors, PhysicsWallah's rise has been fully driven by customer demand. As a YouTube channel, an online platform, and a close-knit science learning community, the company has been able to bootstrap its development while also becoming an Edtech unicorn. In fact, PhysicsWallah only sought outside funds well after it had achieved product-market fit and had established a loyal following.

There has also been a reckoning with some of the tactics used by high-growth companies to secure customers and upsell products.

Byju's in particular has been criticized for high-pressure work environments where employees have used aggressive tactics to sell parents (Inamdar, 2021). Courts have demanded Byju's return payments to dissatisfied students (Peter, 2022), legislators have warned the company about unfair trade practices (Press Trust of India, 2022b), and the media has taken note of the complaints. Perhaps in response, the industry is moving to self-regulate. In an effort to set a code of conduct and stave off more negative attention, Byju and several other key Edtech companies have become founding members of the India Edtech Consortium (India EdTech Consortium, n.d.).

While the pandemic succeeded in speeding up the adoption of all sorts of digital learning technologies, it's less clear whether Edtech actually succeeded in its ultimate goal of providing quality education to India's students.

Edtech does have a particular appeal to Indian parents and students (Basu et al., 2021), rooted in the flexibility, low cost, and capacity for personalization that it brings. The technology has also enabled entirely new formats of instruction and styles of teaching. But for all their advantage, education technologies still have a long way to go. Edtech tools fail often, can be tiresome to use, and bring their own unique drawbacks. Indeed, notwithstanding the value of Edtech, the best tool can only help those who can leverage it. Edtech is not a silver bullet. It can only go so far in driving learning and education. In fact, a survey by the Brookings Institution found that in the city of Chennai, only 1 in 5 children in the sample was enrolled in schools that did not offer any sort of remote instruction options at all (Vegas et al., 2021).

Lessons for the Future of Education

Notwithstanding the challenges that Indian education faces, the country remains at the forefront of the digital learning revolution. India's complex and combustible mix of language, religion, income level, and geography often allows it to serve as a policy laboratory of sorts for the rest of the world. Building the infrastructure for the future of education is full of pitfalls and false starts, hype and hyperbole, all of which make decision-making fraught with consequences. But by looking at India's experience in Edtech, we can potentially begin to sort the fads from genuinely useful developments.

During the pandemic, three major lessons came to light regarding how India harnessed digital learning:

1) **Balancing quality and scale.**
   The requirements of designing for the Indian consumer are high and rigorous. While that means that many ideas would never work in this sort of market, it also means that the ideas that do work are battle-tested and have potentially wide applicability. This sort of backdrop has made it difficult for companies to gain a footing at first but makes them more likely to last and deliver value when they do succeed. For the development of Edtech in these sorts of environments, it may be preferable to start in a narrow and restricted way, taking a piecemeal approach, rather than the all-encompassing routes that are often popular with Silicon Valley companies.

2) **Leveraging network effects.**
   The key to India's rapid advancement in technology is leveraging compound innovation through platform economics. That means that India has been able to leverage key inventions to create each next innovation by developing open ecosystems that are interconnected and can build off of one another. The proliferation of mobile phones, for example, made it possible to do identity authentication, watch long-form content, and send digital payments, each in successive waves as the technology advanced and got into more hands. Digital learning companies are built in the same way. The end result is a vibrant, digitally active nation that becomes the user base for each new learning idea.

3) **Protecting student interests.**
   With any sort of for-profit, high-growth venture, there are questions about how interests are being prioritized. When it comes to Edtech ventures that involve children, the concerns are even more heightened. Learning is too important to follow a trajectory like social media, where we had to make large mistakes in order to embrace network effects before taking corrective action. For example, we've seen China's government targeting Chinese technology and education industries for growing too powerful (Huang, 2022). Advancing Edtech will require proactive intervention by industry, government, and the public. We all need to watch how India builds feedback loops, legal frameworks, and enforcement authorities in Edtech to know what is working and what needs to be fixed.

Getting the creation, delivery, and regulation of Edtech right will be difficult, but there are huge upsides if the formula can be found. While we still need to sort through the hype, it's also clear that we are on the brink of creating powerful systems that could fundamentally shift how we organize our society, economy, and workforce. Across the world, the OECD estimates that improving educational performance will unlock over a trillion dollars in lifetime value (OECD, 2010). And a rapidly changing world now requires that we make education key to keeping our population competitive and productive. In order to meet the challenges ahead, Edtech will be critical to augmenting the systems and tools that we use to learn and educate ourselves in the 21st century. Fortunately, India offers a unique illustration of the promise and peril that we will face along the way.

References

Abrar, P. (2022, April 4). Edtech unicorns go hybrid to tap India's $180 billion education sector. *Business Standard*. Retrieved from https://www.business-standard.com/article/companies/edtech-unicorns-go-hybrid-to-tap-india-s-180-billion-education-sector-122040300968_1.html

Azim Premji University. (2020, December 15). *The Myths of Online Education*. https://azimpremjiuniversity.edu.in/field-studies-in-education/myths-of-online-education

Basu, R., Ramachandra, L., & Rathore, A. (2021). Reimagining learning with technology. *PwC India*. https://www.pwc.in/assets/pdfs/industries/education/reimagining-the-role-of-technology-in-education.pdf

BCG. (2022). *Digital Payments in India: A US$10 Trillion opportunity*. Retrieved May 10, 2022, from https://web-assets.bcg.com/be/3c/5bd90af6416a80b4496969ec0d1b/future-of-digital-payments-in-india.pdf

Bhalla, K. (2021, August 14). From Byju's to Eruditus — India now has four edtech unicorns, thanks to a $4 billion fund flowing in since 2020. *Business Insider India*. Retrieved from https://www.businessinsider.in/business/startups/news/india-now-has-four-edtech-unicorns-byju-unacademy-eruditis-upGrad/articleshow/85300757.cms

Byju's. (2015). *Meet Byju*. https://www.byjuslearning.com/pages/meet-byjus

Byju's. (n.d.) *Our Investors - Know Who are the Investors for BYJU'S*. https://byjus.com/our-investors/

CB Insights. (2017, June 21). *The Edtech Market Map: 100+ Startups Building the Future of Education*. https://www.cbinsights.com/research/ed-tech-startup-market-map/

Chandrashekhar, V. (2020, March 31). 1.3 Billion people. A 21-day lockdown. Can India curb the coronavirus? *Science*. Retrieved from https://www.science.org/content/article/13-billion-people-21-day-lockdown-can-india-curb-coronavirus

Delgado Martín, A. V., & Larrú Ramos, J. M. (2022). DEIFDC framework: Evaluation of digital education deployment in India in the midst of the Covid-19 pandemic. *Social Sciences & Humanities Open*, 6(1), 100281. https://doi.org/10.1016/j.ssaho.2022.100281

Deloitte India. (2022, February 22). *Deloitte's 2022 TMT Predictions for India | Press Release*. https://www2.deloitte.com/in/en/pages/technology-media-and-telecommunications/articles/big-bets-on-smartphones-semiconductors-and-streaming-service.html

Eruditus. (2020, October 26). 10 pivotal moments in Eruditus' 10-year journey. *Eruditus Executive Summary | Blog*. https://eruditus.com/executive-summary/10-pivotal-moments-in-eruditus-10-year-journey/

Goral, T. (2013, July). SPOCs may provide what MOOCs can't. *University Business*. Retrieved from https://web.archive.org/web/20160304190607/https://www.universitybusiness.com/article/spocs-may-provide-what-moocs-can%E2%80%99t

Government of India. (2020). *National Education Policy 2020 Ministry of Human Resource Development Government of India*. https://www.education.gov.in/sites/upload_files/mhrd/files/NEP_Final_English_0.pdf

Huang, Z. (2022, February 11). China's Edutech crackdown expands to high-school tutoring. *Bloomberg*. Retrieved from https://www.bloomberg.com/news/articles/2022-02-11/china-s-edutech-crackdown-expands-to-high-school-tutoring#xj4y7vzkg

Inamdar, N. (2021, December 7). Byju's and the other side of an edtech giant's dizzying rise. *BBC News*. Retrieved from https://www.bbc.com/news/world-asia-india-58951449.

Inc 42. (2021, June 1). *The Future of India's $2 Bn Edtech Opportunity Report 2020*. https://inc42.com/reports/the-future-of-indias-2-bn-edtech-opportunity-report-2020/

India EdTech Consortium. (n.d.). http://www.indiaedtech.in. Retrieved May 10, 2022, from https://www.indiaedtech.in/about-us.html

India Stack. (n.d.) *IndiaStack – Technology for 1.2 Billion Indians*. https://indiastack.org/

LEAD. (2021, October 1). School transformation, the LEAD way [Video]. *YouTube*. https://www.youtube.com/watch?v=8vH7bY-cxf4&ab_channel=LEAD

Ministry of Education. (2022). *UDISE+ Dashboard*. https://dashboard.udiseplus.gov.in/#/home

Mitter, S. (2021, August 3). Byju's, Unacademy grab ~76 pc of edtech funding in 2021; sector raises $1.9B since Jan. *Your Story*. Retrieved from https://yourstory.com/2021/08/byjus-unacademy-edtech-sector-funding-2021/amp

Nielsen. (2014, April 1). *The Rise of India's Rural Super Consumer*. https://www.nielsen.com/wp-content/uploads/sites/3/2019/04/nielsen-report-the-rise-of-indias-rural-super-consumer.pdf

OECD. (2010). *The High Cost of Low Educational Performance the Long-Run Economic Impact of Improving PISA Outcomes*. https://www.oecd.org/pisa/44417824.pdf

OxFam India. (2020, September 4). *Status Report: Government and Private Schools during COVID-19*. https://www.oxfamindia.org/knowledgehub/oxfaminaction/status-report-government-and-private-schools-during-covid-19

Peter, P. (2022, July 9). Bengaluru: Man sues learning app for poor service, gets Rs 99 thousand refund & Rs 30 thousand compensation. *Times of India*. Retrieved from https://timesofindia.indiatimes.com/city/bengaluru/man-sues-learning-app-for-poor-service-gets-99k-refund-30k-compensation/articleshow/92758055.cms

Pradeep, S. (2022, January 13). Lead becomes 2022's first Edtech unicorn with $100 Mn funding. *Inc42*. Retrieved from https://inc42.com/buzz/lead-becomes-2021s-first-edtech-unicorn-with-100-mn-funding/.

Press Trust of India. (2021, January 27). Indian startups attract $10.14 billion in funding in 2020: Report. *Business Standard*. Retrieved from https://economictimes.indiatimes.com/tech/funding/indian-startups-attract-10-14-billion-in-funding-in-2020-report/articleshow/80473418.cms?from=mdr

Press Trust of India. (2022a, February 22). India to have 1 billion smartphone users by 2026: Deloitte report. *Business Standard*. Retrieved from India to have 1 billion smartphone users by 2026: Deloitte report.

Press Trust of India. (2022b, July 1). Government warns edtech companies against unfair trade practices. *Economic Times*. Retrieved from https://economictimes.indiatimes.com/news/economy/policy/government-warns-edtech-companies-against-unfair-trade-practices/articleshow/92601700.cms

Rai, S. (2022a, June 28). Byju's said to offer over $1 billion for 2U to expand in US. *Bloomberg*. Retrieved from https://www.bloomberg.com/news/articles/2022-06-29/byju-s-said-to-offer-more-than-1-billion-for-2u-to-expand-in-us#xj4y7vzkg

Rai, S. (2022b, June 14). Education unicorn UpGrad doubles valuation with murdoch funding. *Bloomberg*. Retrieved from https://www.bloomberg.com/news/articles/2022-06-15/education-unicorn-upGrad-doubles-valuation-with-murdoch-funding

Reserve Bank of India. (2016, November 8). *Withdrawal of Legal Tender Status for ₹ 500 and ₹ 1000 Notes: RBI Notice*. https://rbi.org.in/Scripts/BS_PressReleaseDisplay.aspx?prid=38520

Reserve Bank of India. (n.d.). Details of tier-wise classification of centres based on population. *Reserve Bank of India*. https://rbidocs.rbi.org.in/rdocs/content/pdfs/100MCA0711_5.pdf

Sharma, N. (2021, September 7). Reliance Jio's cheap data turned India's internet dreams into reality. *Quartz*. Retrieved from https://qz.com/india/2055771/reliance-jios-cheap-data-turned-indias-internet-dreams-into-reality

Shrivastava, A., & Peermohamed, A. (2019, April 15). Edtech firms see money in live streaming classes. *Economic Times*. Retrieved from https://economictimes.indiatimes.com/startups/live-streaming-of-classes-online-is-likely-to-be-a-monetisation-tool-for-edtech-cos/articleshow/68894009.cms

Sil, D. (2020, September 2). India gets its second Edtech unicorn as unacademy joins the prestigious club. *Entrepreneur*. Retrieved from https://www.entrepreneur.com/article/355657

Singh, M. (2021a, April 5). Byju's acquires Indian tutor Aakhash for nearly $1 billion. *TechCrunch*. Retrieved from https://techcrunch.com/2021/04/05/byjus-acquires-indian-tutor-aakash-for-nearly-1-billion/

Singh, M. (2021b, September 29). Indian online learning platform Vedantu becomes unicorn with $100 million funding. *TechCrunch*. Retrieved from https://techcrunch.com/2021/09/29/indian-online-learning-platform-vedantu-becomes-unicorn-with-100-million-funding/

Singh, M. (2022a, January 12). India's Lead School becomes unicorn with fresh $100M in funding. *TechCrunch*. Retrieved from https://techcrunch.com/2022/01/12/lead-school-india-unicorn/

Singh, M. (2022b, April 7). India's PhysicsWallah becomes unicorn with $100 million funding. *TechCrunch*. Retrieved from https://techcrunch.com/2022/06/07/indian-edtech-physicswallah-becomes-unicorn-with-100-million-series-a-funding/

Subramaniam, N. (2022, June 19). The Indian Edtech Bubble Bursts as Byju'S, Unacademy & Co Feel the Heat. *Inc42*. Retrieved from https://inc42.com/features/indian-edtech-startup-bubble-bursts-as-byjus-unacademy-co-downturn/

Takahashi, D. (2021, July 13). Byju's launches Disney-based learning app for the U.S. *Venture Beat*. Retrieved from https://venturebeat.com/2021/07/13/byjus-launches-disney-based-learning-app/

Talgeri, K. (2022, March 13). How Eruditus built a global business around executive education — Organically. *Your Story*. Retrieved from https://economictimes.indiatimes.com/tech/funding/indian-startups-attract-10-14-billion-in-funding-in-2020-report/articleshow/80473418.cms?from=mdr

The Economist. (2022, May 26). *India's Exams are Plagued by Cheating*. https://www.economist.com/asia/2022/05/26/indias-exams-are-plagued-by-cheating

The Ken. (2022, June 16). *Was Edtech Just a Fool's Errand?* https://the-ken.com/edsetgo/was-edtech-just-a-fools-errand/

Toczauer, C. (2021). *Dragon Fire, Tiger Rising – Why India May Be the Next Edtech Investment Hub after China's Clampdown.* Www.onlineeducation.com. Retrieved May 10, 2022, from https://www.onlineeducation.com/features/india-and-edtech-investments

Unacademy. (n.d.) *Unacademy - India's Largest Learning Platform.* https://unacademy.com/about

UNICEF. (2021, October 1). *India Case Study Situation Analysis on the Effects of and Responses to COVID-19 on the Education Sector in Asia.* https://www.unicef.org/rosa/media/16511/file/India%20Case%20Study.pdf

upGrad. (2022, October 2). upGrad | Platform demo and walkthrough [Video]. *YouTube.* https://www.youtube.com/watch?v=B_UbDtoR16I&ab_channel=upGrad

upGrad. (n.d.). *About upGrad.* https://programs.upGrad.com/about

Vanamali, K. (2022, June 6). As pandemic boom fades, can ed-tech startups survive? *Business Standard.* Retrieved from https://www.business-standard.com/podcast/current-affairs/as-pandemic-boom-fades-can-ed-tech-startups-survive-122060600051_1.html

Vedantu. (n.d.). *Launching the New Vedantu Wave Platform.* Retrieved May 10, 2022, from https://www.vedantu.com/wave

Vegas, E., Shah, S., & Fowler, B. (2021). Ed tech and educational opportunity during the COVID-19 school closures. *Brookings Institute.* https://www.brookings.edu/wp-content/uploads/2021/08/Ed-tech-and-educational-opportunity-during-COVID-19-school-closures-FINAL-1.pdf

17
AI ≠ UBI

Income Portfolio Adjustment to Technological Transformation

Aleksandra K. Przegalinska and Robert E. Wright

17.1 Introduction

Business, economic, and technological change (BETC) occurs continuously but at variable speeds (Bakker et al., 2019; Lauterbach, 1977). While the cumulative effects of relatively rapid BETC, often termed "Revolutions" [e.g., Agricultural (Olmstead & Rhode, 2008), Communication (Albion, 1932), Financial (Sylla, 2002), Industrial/Industrious (De Vries, 1994), Institutional (Allen, 2011), Market (Majewski, 1997), Transportation (Seely, 2007)], have been substantial (Makridakis, 2017), they occur over years or decades. Automation waves in the 20th century also caused unsubstantiated fears of job loss (Terborgh, 1966).

Rapid change can create angst and stir predictions of dire results that induce specific interest groups to take direct actions to slow BETC for their own benefit, as Luddites (who destroyed installed machines in Britain between 1811 and 1817) and unions (who destroy machines before they are produced by means of union contracts protecting jobs) did (Donnelly, 1986). Nevertheless, changes in individual/familial life strategies consistently proved more effective than interest group action because they occur more quickly than even the fastest revolutions, adapting to BETC rather than trying to stop or slow it [see, e.g., (Hopkins, 1982); (Goolsbee, 2018)].

Individuals/families aspire to achieve goals that can be understood as a tradeoff between real (inflation-adjusted) consumption and leisure, that is, about how long and hard to work. Those goals adapt to BETC and life cycles (Childers, 2011; Dunn, 1979). Rational individuals (as defined by (Arrow, 2012)) form and update expectations about strategies most likely to achieve their life goals

(MacDonald & Peel, 1983). In essence, that means adjusting a portfolio of sources of real income (IPA), which stems from the five distinct[1] sources described in Table 17.1 below.

Proponents of AI = UBI concentrate on income sources four and five without sufficiently considering income sources one, two, and three. If AI causes employment to decrease, they reason, UBI ["periodic cash payment unconditionally delivered to all on an individual basis, without means-test or work requirement" (Haagh, 2019)] will be needed to meet the real income goals of unemployed/unemployable individuals. That reasoning, however, does not fully reflect reality for five reasons:

- AI is not yet as powerful as many believe. As a general purpose assistive technology (GPT), it generates new jobs and reskills existing ones.
- The net number of jobs continues to increase. Jobs that "disappear" do so because of the complex processes associated with BETC, not because of AI, the Internet of Things (IoT), or edge computing.
- *If* employment decreases in the future, individuals may prefer to respond via IPA, by increasing the importance of subsistence, proprietorship, and investment in their income portfolios over the acceptance of unilateral transfers.
- *If* individuals prefer unilateral transfers, options other than UBI abound and may prove preferable from policy and individual standpoints.
- *If* employment decreases dramatically and individuals prefer UBI, it can be implemented quickly at that time.

The numerically matching sections below explain those points in fuller detail.

TABLE 17.1 Sources of an Individual's Real Income

1. Subsistence	Joint production and consumption by the same individual or social unit, as in fishing, gathering, gardening, hunting, or trapping.
2. Proprietorship	Ownership and management of a business, from a nano-enterprise to huge enterprise with many employees and/or contractors.
3. Financial Investment	Ownership of financial securities like bank accounts, bonds, derivatives, equities, exchange-traded funds [ETFs], mutual fund shares, insurance policies, and so forth.
4. Employment	Working on behalf of a proprietor for fixed compensation based on time, perhaps augmented by performance measures like bonuses or commissions.
5. Unilateral transfers	True gifts, or one-way flow of resources, from a public or private donor to a recipient.

17.2 Artificial Intelligence Today

Artificial Intelligence is a general purpose technology (GPT), technologies, like the steam engine, electrification, and the Internet, that cause significant and widespread impacts on society and the workplace or that generate more specialized complementary innovations.

Current BETC, including the widespread application of AI, will impact how people live and work. The cumulative scope of AI-induced change must remain unknown, allowing alarmist dystopian visions of a future without human work even without evidence of trend changes. Automation changes the nature of work but AI's impact on the future of work remains unclear. Some researchers [e.g., (Acemoglu & Restrepo, 2017)] connect the adoption of AI and robots to reduced employment and wages, suggesting the need for UBI adoption. Others also claim that millions of jobs worldwide will automate quickly and significantly more jobs will disappear than be created (Furman & Seamans, 2019) (Crawford et al., 2016) (Goolsbee, 2018). Some business consultants concur but others predict the contrary. According to studies conducted by McKinsey, PricewaterhouseCoopers, and Skynet Today, AI will displace about one-third of the existing jobs worldwide within a decade, with the United States (up to 40%) and Japan (50%) among the hardest hit. According to the OECD AI Policy Observatory and Beyond Limits Study, however, AI will create more jobs than it destroys. Companies pioneering the development and scaling of AI have thus far not destroyed jobs on net and that trend will likely continue.

17.2.1 Working together with AI

Threats to jobs posed by AI and similar technologies can be assessed by examining core skill sets, that is, by distinguishing between durable jobs, those that will require reskilling, and those that will become obsolete (Latham & Humberd, 2018). Some jobs that were durable during previous periods of BETC will remain durable in the foreseeable future. Some workers will need significant reskilling but for others reskilling will be minor (Table 17.2).

TABLE 17.2 Durable, Reskillable, and Fragile Jobs

Durable Jobs:	Jobs requiring reskilling	Displaced jobs
Statistician, medical and health service managers, nurse practitioners, data scientists	Jobs in the scientific services, e-commerce, and manufacturing	Travel agents, cutters, trimmers, hand, data entry keyers, prepress technicians

Sources: https://www.bls.gov/ooh/fastest-growing.htm; https://www.bls.gov/news.release/ecopro.nr0.htm; https://www.bls.gov/emp/tables/fastest-declining-occupations.htm

Two parallel discourses regarding the future of work exist: (1) Automation of work leading to the replacement of humans; (2) so-called "cobotization", or collaboration between workers and assistive technologies, including AI.[2]

As David Autor (Autor, 2015) notices, machines both substitute and complement human labor. Substituting workers in routine tasks also amplifies the comparative advantage of workers in various problem-solving skills. Focusing on lost jobs, in other words, misses the fact that technology simultaneously increases "the value of the tasks that workers uniquely supply". Automation has already affected routine and low-skilled tasks, like industrial robots in manufacturing processes. AI's problem-solving, reasoning, and perception capabilities mean that it can perform some non-routine cognitive tasks, like summarizing computer science research papers. Recently, some companies have achieved productivity gains by using software robots to perform routine, rules-based service processes. If implemented well, such automation can result in high-performing human-robot teams, in which software robots and human employees complement one another. In some cases, automation substitutes labor (D. Autor & Salomons, 2018) but it also complements labor, raising output sufficiently to create higher demand for labor. It also interacts with adjustments in labor supply, say by increasing familial income enough to induce a spouse to leave the labor force.

Moreover, AI and automated tools usually replace tasks rather than jobs. Workplace productivity increases due to human-AI collaboration by assuming mundane tasks (Sowa, Przegalinska & Ciechanowski, 2021). Further applications of state-of-the-art AI focus on how people will work, and not driving people out of work. In other words, collaborative AI concerns the future of work, not the future of unemployment, the key consideration of many UBI proponents. A key insight from emerging collaborative AI research is jobs are bundles of tasks, some of which offer better applications for technology than others (Autor et al., 2000). Policymakers and researchers should think in terms of task replacement—potentially leaving more room for tasks that require strictly human labor, but also tasks that people enjoy engaging in—rather than unemployment. Some high-skilled professionals such as engineers, radiologists, or lawyers are at risk because most of the tasks they perform can be done by AI. Such highly educated professionals, however, may also prove capable of applying AI in a way that complements their work.

17.2.2 Future Artificial Intelligence

Major developments in AI, deep learning, natural language understanding, and machine vision led to new collaboration-oriented systems (Haenlein & Kaplan, 2019). Initially, AI systems such as AlphaStar, AlphaGo, or muZero (Vinyals et al., 2019; Wang et al., 2016; Shaikh, 2020; Schrittwieser et al., 2020) were created to prove that AI can compete with humans and actually beat them in complex games. Professional players, however, adapted rather than conceding defeat; their competition with AI led to significant performance improvement (Waters, 2018).

In the short- and medium-term, AI development will take two discrete paths. The first extrapolates what AI is today, highly specialized, deep learning algorithms applicable to clearly delineated problems in more complex, context-aware, and nuanced ways. Because of their capacity to learn highly nonlinear functions with near-automatic input space transformations, deep neural nets (DNNs) are currently the algorithms with very high economic potential at the frontier of task automation. DNN software can be extended to new domains formerly closed to digitization through transfer learning (Weiss et al., 2016; Torrey & Shavlik, 2010).

The second path entails the creation of AI systems capable of processing information in a manner similar to the human brain. Today, deep nets rule AI in part because of an algorithm called backpropagation (Hecht-Nielsen, 1992; Lillicrap et al., 2020) that allows deep neural nets to learn from data and thus gain capabilities like language translation, speech recognition, and image classification. Real brains, however, likely do not rely on similar algorithms. Human brains are capable of abstract reasoning and learning more efficiently than current AI systems can (LeCun et al., 2015). Geoffrey E. Hinton, Yoshua, and others have been thinking about more biologically plausible learning mechanisms that might match the success of backpropagation and expand AI's capacity to learn and adapt. Currently, feedback alignment, equilibrium propagation, and predictive coding seem particularly promising.[3]

The second path of biologically inspired AI development has a high potential of transforming AI's capabilities and overcoming its current limitations, creating more robust and complex systems capable of more abstract levels of reasoning. Like Singularity, however, it remains nascent and hence distant (Tegmark, 2017; McAfee & Brynjolfsson, 2017; McAfee & Brynjolfsson, 2016).

The first path may develop without the second, or alongside it. It will not affect the number of jobs per se, but rather, like earlier BETC "revolutions", it will produce a profoundly different economy. Network technologies, like the Internet, power grid, and highway system, will increasingly rely on AI as both solution complexity and demand increase.

Section 17.3 shows no indications at present that AI, or any other BETC, poses a threat to employment so long as human capital, from training programs to formal education, adapts, as it always has (Goldin and Katz 2010).

17.3 Long-Term Employment Trends

Real (inflation-adjusted) per capita income has trended steadily upward in much of Europe, Anglo-America, and the Far East for the last several centuries, subject only to booms and busts associated with wars, business cycles, and technological breakthroughs. Nations like Spain that lagged due to institutional deficiencies experienced rapid growth once growth-inducing institutions supplanted traditional ones. The overall trend is one of steady, though not monotonic, growth (Acemoglu & Robinson, 2012).

Note the use of a log scale in the following charts of US, UK, and Spanish real per capita income, which is standard when presenting long-term time series data so that year-over-year changes and long-term trends become visually evident. The Great Depression, Spanish Civil War, and World War II caused the big dip and subsequent fast growth. Note also how real per capita growth returned to the long-term trend line in the postwar period in both the United States and the United Kingdom and that institutional improvement, not technological change, drove Spanish income convergence (Figure 17.1).

Sustained increases in real per capita incomes stem only from productivity improvements, that is, creating more output from the same input, which is the point of BETC. Supply and demand conditions in labor and capital markets, along with public policies regarding taxation, unionization, and so forth, determine how the additional income is distributed among employees, proprietors, investors, and governments.

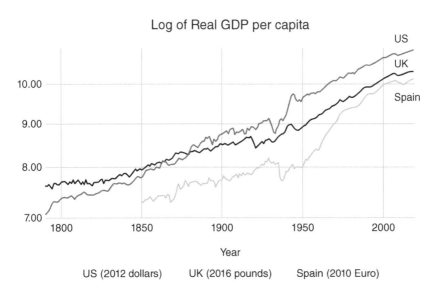

FIGURE 17.1 U.S., U.K., and Spanish Real GDP Per Capita.

Sources: Louis Johnston and Samuel H. Williamson, "What Was the U.S. GDP Then?" MeasuringWorth, 2021. URL: http://www.measuringworth.org/usgdp/; Ryland Thomas and Samuel H. Williamson, "What Was the Consistent U.K. GDP Then?" MeasuringWorth 2021. URL: http://www.measuringworth.com/ukgdp/; Leandro Prados-de-la-Escosura, "What Was Spain's GDP Then?" MeasuringWorth, 2021. URL: http://www.measuringworth.org/spaingdp/.

Private nonfarm business sector labor productivity in the United States has been climbing without interruption, though at variable rates of increase, for at least the last three decades and with minor reversals since at least World War II (Federal Reserve Economic Data, "Private Non-Farm Business Sector: Labor Productivity, Index 2012=100, Annual, Not Seasonally Adjusted" *FRED*, 2021. URL: https://fred.stlouisfed.org/graph/?id=MPU4910062). Similar metrics show similar trends for OECD (*Productivity - GDP per Hour Worked - OECD Data*, n.d.) and EU countries (Baily et al., 2020).

Nominal and real wage data suggest that labor productivity has been trending upward for over two centuries. The average nominal wage of manufacturing workers in the United States increased from 2 cents per hour in 1790 to $32.36 in 2019 (*Measuring Worth - Annual Wages in the United States*, n.d.). Real total compensation per hour for those same worker cycles sometimes stagnates for several years to a decade but also trends upward over the long term (Federal Reserve Economic Data, "Manufacturing Sector: Real Compensation Per Hour, Index 2012=100, Quarterly, Seasonally Adjusted" *FRED*, 2021. URL: https://fred.stlouisfed.org/series/COMPRMS.)

Long-term, workers responded to higher real compensation by working fewer hours. In the early 19th century, for example, female textile workers in Lowell, Massachusetts worked on average 12 hours per day, 300 days a year (Little, 2001). Although some professionals (attorneys, investment bankers, physicians, professors) continue to work 60 to 100 hours per week up to 50 weeks per year, most factory and office workers now work 40 or fewer hours per week and must receive a higher rate of compensation to induce additional hours of work.

Some claim that real compensation has stagnated or declined in the United States over the last few decades [see, e.g., (*Wage Stagnation in Nine Charts*, n.d.)] but only by conflating wages with total compensation. The latter includes benefits, including healthcare costs covered by employers and employer contributions to private retirement accounts (Federal Reserve Economic Data, "Nonfarm Business Sector: Real Compensation Per Hour, Index 2012=100, Quarterly, Seasonally Adjusted" *FRED*, 2021. URL: https://fred.stlouisfed.org/series/COMPRNFB). Rising healthcare costs due to America's inefficient, employment-based healthcare system have caused the divergence between wages and total compensation (Flynn, 2019). The magnitude of the problem is revealed by the fact that *half* of the unilateral transfers made by the US federal government to the poor cover healthcare costs (Feldstein, 2016).

As others have noted [e.g., (Autor, 2015)], total jobs (employees) has trended steadily upward in the United States since at least 1939, subject only to cyclical downturns or, at the extreme right of the graph, exogenous shocks like pandemics and the "lockdown" policies implemented in response (*The Effect of Lockdown Measures on Unemployment*, n.d.) (Figure 17.2).

For the last 20 years, between 2 and 8 million jobs have gone unfilled in the United States each year due to mismatches between worker skills and job

FIGURE 17.2 U.S. Nonfarm Workforce, 1939–2022.

Source: Federal Reserve Economic Data, "All Employees, Total Nonfarm, Thousands of Persons, Monthly, Seasonally Adjusted" FRED, 2021. URL: https://fred.stlouisfed.org/series/PAYEMS.

functions but also discrepancies between worker wage demands and what employers are willing to pay to fill open positions (Federal Reserve Economic Data, "Total Unfilled Job Vacancies for the United States, Persons, Monthly, Seasonally Adjusted" *FRED*, 2021. URL: https://fred.stlouisfed.org/series/LMJVTTUVUSM647S).

The Labor Force Participation Rate (LFP), the total percentage of the working-age population employed, has trended downward since its recent highs in the late 1990s but even at its nadir due to Covid lockdowns remained above its lows in the 1950s. The economic interpretation of the LFP is difficult because increases or decreases are not unequivocally good or bad. In poorer countries today, and in the early histories of the United States, the United Kingdom, and other core rich nations, the LFP was over 100% by today's definition of the labor force. Children as young as four worked, as did people now considered differently abled (blind, deaf, immobile, insane) or superannuated (too old to work). Similarly, the relatively low LFP in the 1950s and 1960s stemmed from America's relative economic strength and cultural mores. Many women remained out of the labor force because families could meet their life goals without them taking jobs (Toossi 2002). A low LFP due to a high percentage of people who want a job but cannot find one, by contrast, could signal economic trouble, like the big drop in the LFP during the 2020 pandemic and subsequent lockdowns (Bullard 2014). But secular declines in LFP like that which started circa 2000 might simply signal preferences for the other four income sources (Juhn and Potter 2006) (Figure 17.3).

Finally, Total Factor Productivity (TFP) measures increases in economic growth not explained by increases in labor and capital. It, therefore, proxies overall efficiency. In the United States and elsewhere, TFP has been increasing

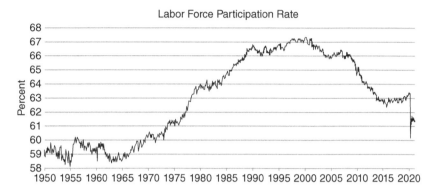

FIGURE 17.3 U.S. Labor Force Participation Rate, 1948–2022.

Source: Federal Reserve Economic Data, "Labor Force Participation Rate, Percent, Monthly, Seasonally Adjusted" FRED, 2021. URL: https://fred.stlouisfed.org/series/CIVPART.

FIGURE 17.4 U.S. Total Factor Productivity Index, 1954–2022.

Source: Federal Reserve Economic Data. "Total Factor Productivity at Constant National Prices for United State" FRED 2023 https://fred.stlouisfed.org/series/RTFPNAUSA632NRUG.

relatively slowly since the postwar period. If automation was truly transforming productive processes, one would expect TFP to increase more rapidly than it has been (Figure 17.4).

Section 17.4 describes how individuals (and families) try to meet their life goals by splitting their work time into subsistence activities, proprietorship, investment in financial assets, employment, and the receipt of unilateral transfers based on the relative costs and benefits of each income source.

17.4 Cost–Benefit Analysis of IPA

Simply because someone remains outside of the official labor force does not mean that they do not work. In 1950s America, for example, many married women engaged in subsistence activities in lieu of paid employment. Many in

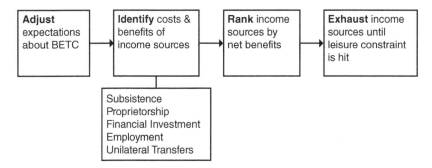

FIGURE 17.5   IPA Cost-Benefit Flowchart and Equation.

rural and suburban areas gardened and did their own washing, sewing, and so forth instead of buying vegetables and laundry services in the market. Like other rational actors, they compared the expected costs and benefits of each of the five main sources of income and chose the ones with the largest net benefits (Figure 17.5).

The flow chart above is more formally stated in Equation 17.1 below. [For more complex modelling of a portfolio of income streams with uncertain returns, see (Brennan, 1973).]

$$\sum_{n=1}^{5} w_n i_n \qquad (17.1)$$

Where:
n = income source counter
w = weight of each income source
i = income source.

Historical examples of such reasoning abound. In 1848, for example, Abraham Lincoln suggested that his stepbrother, John D. Johnston, should ease out of subsistence-only farming by growing some cash crops (proprietorship) and by going "to work for the best money wages … you can get" (employment), with the ultimate goal of buying bank and railroad shares (investment) (Guelzo, 2000). Similarly, trappers sometimes made their own clothes from the furs of the animals they trapped, a subsistence activity. Sometimes they sold the furs to furriers, making them proprietors. Other times they worked for a fur company for a salary, rendering them employees. Sometimes they purchased shares in fur companies, making them investors. Often, the same person engaged in all those activities serially, and sometimes even simultaneously, to adjust to BETC (Wright, 2019).

The major costs and benefits of each of the five main sources of income are described below. The costs and benefits vary in intensity over time and place, thereby inducing IPA (Mason, 2020; Rose, 2017). The existence of AI of course in no way limits the ability of human beings to engage in subsistence activities, proprietorship, financial investment, or to receive unilateral transfers. It may, however, enhance their ability to engage in such activities. AI is already used to reduce the costs of frightening deer away from gardens and of finding government grants, franchise opportunities, and investments (Biswal 2020). What it takes from employment, in other words, it may very well return to other sources of income.

17.4.1 Subsistence

Subsistence activities occur when individuals, families, or other social units make a good that they consume themselves (Elwert & Wong, 1980). For most of human history, subsistence activities like hunting and gathering, complemented by trade (proprietorship), constituted the main source of consumption. Subsistence may come to dominate again due to climatic or other shocks (Gowdy, 2020).

A major benefit of subsistence activity is control over the quantity and quality of consumption goods free from exogenous market shocks (Chibnik, 1978). During the Great Depression, for example, many people accustomed to buying poultry (chicken, ducks, rabbits, turkeys) at the market began to raise them for home consumption (Cook, 1998); hunting, fishing, and trapping activities increased (Wright, 2020).

Non-market shocks, like droughts or insect infestations, however, may decrease subsistence activities (Gowdy, 2020). Another major cost of subsistence activities is loss of gains from trade specialization, and scale economies (Kennedy, 1982). While raising chickens at home ensures access to eggs (barring non-market shocks), the opportunity cost per egg may be too high compared to the monetary cost of eggs produced at commercial scale. In 1900, for example, some 25% of US households produced their own eggs, compared with 1.6% today (Kidd & Anderson, 2019).

17.4.2 Proprietorship

Much early proprietorship emerged from individuals or families scaling up subsistence activities and selling their surpluses into markets. That added to the risk of exogenous market and non-market shocks but came with the benefit of some cash income (Johnson, 1998). Generally, proprietors enjoy more control over the terms of their work than employees do, including the number of hours worked and its intensity (Burke et al., 2008). Most non-farm proprietors do not consume the products of their labor themselves, but because they own their own businesses they earn or lose wealth as their businesses thrive or stagnate (Hamilton, 2000).

For those reasons, proprietorship was long a major goal, especially in the United States (Wright, 2017b; Wright, 2015). Tax (Nelson, 2008) and regulatory changes influenced its relative attractiveness over time and space (Goetz & Rupasingha, 2009). Self-employment, which constitutes a major type of proprietorship, has made several large swings since World War II but the overall trend, as a percentage of all workers, is down (Federal Reserve Economic Data, "Employment Level - All Industries Self-Employed, Unincorporated, Thousands of Persons, Monthly, Seasonally Adjusted" *FRED*, 2021. URL: https://fred.stlouisfed.org/series/LNS12027714).

17.4.3 Financial investment

Financial investors may engage in research to discern relatively inexpensive from relatively expensive financial assets and to forecast which asset classes are most likely to increase in value (bonds, derivatives, equities, insurance-linked securities, REITs, etc.) (Constable & Wright, 2011). It remains unclear, however, if such investors net of those research and forecasting costs actually earn higher risk-adjusted returns than investors who simply purchase diverse portfolios of financial assets (Malkiel, 2013). All investors are subject to the security market line, or the tradeoff between risk and return. In other words, financial investors can earn a low return with little risk of losing principal, or a high return with a commensurately high risk of losing principal, or anywhere in between (Modigliani & Pogue, 1974). One important benefit of investment is that it can consume very little time while generating market returns (Wermers, 2000), freeing people to engage in the other four main sources of income or leisure activities.

17.4.4 Employment

Employment means being paid for one's time, be it for each hour worked (hourly wage) or for a variable number of hours worked over a fixed amount of calendar time (salary). Performance bonuses or commissions may augment. Employment can be irregular but generally, only regular work is called a "job", which might be "fulltime" or "parttime" depending on hours worked each week (Asia, 1945). Employment may take place in facilities provided by the employer, in the employee's home, or elsewhere. The location of work has shown significant and interesting variation over time, suggesting that it often constitutes a major cost–benefit variable affecting the relative attractiveness of employment to both employers and employees (Juhász et al., 2020).

Employees give up part of their freedom in exchange for compensation. By definition, employees are subject to the direction of their employers during working hours, including, but not limited to, the pace of their work, the time they may use the toilet, acceptable political speech, and whether or not they may wear a mask (Anderson 2017). Employment was understandably considered akin to slavery in the United States in the 19th century (Wright, 2017). Accepting employment was something done when people could not meet their life goals via the other main sources of income (Steinfeld, 2001). Over time, however, an increasing percentage of the population moved from proprietorship (farming, shopkeeping) to employment as their major source of income as jobs became relatively less onerous and proprietorship relatively more so (Gallman & Rhode, 2020). In addition, many small proprietors found that they could no longer compete against larger enterprises by leveraging economies of scale in traditional proprietary sectors like farming and retailing (Bennett et al., 2020; Boyd, 1997).

17.4.5 Unilateral Transfers

One might think that everyone would always have a strong preference for receiving unilateral transfers because it appears to be all benefits and at no cost. In fact, acquiring and maintaining transfers can be difficult and time-consuming (Mould, 2020). In addition, most people have a strong aversion to receiving unilateral transfers (Parsell & Clarke, 2020). They know that they are taking resources from other people, sometimes voluntarily given but increasingly involuntarily through taxation (Misra et al., 2014). Even aid received after natural disasters may carry a stigma for some individuals (Fothergill, 2003; Stuber & Kronebusch, 2004).

Unilateral transfers follow the security market line in the sense that the larger they are, the more likely they are to be curtailed or even eliminated (Albert, 2000) for fear that they create dependence (Gottschalk & Moffitt, 1994). Many unilateral transfer recipients also fear that they may grow dependent on the transfers and hence beholden to the person, organization, or government providing the resources (Rank, 1994). A tailored approach to unilateral transfers may therefore better help people to achieve their life goals than a general policy, like UBI (Table 17.3).

TABLE 17.3 Tabular Summary of the Major Costs and Benefits of the Five Sources of Income

Income source	Costs	Benefits
Subsistence	Exogenous non-market shocks	Freedom from market shocks
Proprietorship	Exposure to market, non-market, and policy shocks	Autonomy; potential appreciation of the business
Financial investment	Risk-return tradeoff	Relatively low time commitment possible
Employment	Loss of autonomy	Known, steady income
Unilateral transfers	Funding risks increase with amount because taxpayers fear recipient moral hazard; risk of reduction or elimination of payments; potential stigma and other psychological effects like dependence	Something for nothing

17.4.6 Tabular Summary of the Major Costs and Benefits of the Five Sources of Income

Section 17.5 categorizes the major types of unilateral transfers and describes the strengths and weaknesses of each to demonstrate that if unilateral transfers become a more important part of IPA in the future, transfers other than UBI may be preferred by policymakers and recipients.

17.5 Cost–Benefit Analysis of UBI and Other Unilateral Transfer Policies

Calls for a UBI policy date back to at least Thomas Paine, who in *Agrarian Justice* (1797) argued that governments should compensate all citizens at adulthood because they had allowed private individuals to control all of Europe's land and hence constrained the ability of the landless to engage in subsistence or proprietary activities, effectively forcing them to rely on uncertain employment markets (Wright, 2021).

Friedrich Hayek (Rallo, 2019) and Milton Friedman (Milton Friedman on Freedom and the Negative Income Tax) also discussed, without embracing, the need for UBI-like policies as a more efficient means of taking care of society's poorest members by reducing the emotional costs and risks associated with certain types of unilateral transfers described in Section 17.4.5 (Bidadanure, 2019). The current US "welfare state" is extremely complex [see (Chaudry, Wimer, Macartney, Frohlich, Campbell, Swenson, Oellerich, and Hauan, 2016)], so switching to a single simple program promises significant administrative savings.

Numerous progressive pundits have discussed the pros and cons of UBI (Allegri & Foschi, 2021). Rivers (Rivers, 2019) rejects it because he believes it would "calcify poverty and class structure ... even more than the present arrangements". Nobel laureate Paul Krugman rejects UBI in favor of more targeted approaches (Malter & Sprague, 2019). After waffling on the subject in his book on income inequality (Stiglitz, 2013), Nobel laureate Joseph Stiglitz came out in favor of UBI, presumably because it reduces the stigma associated with receiving unilateral transfers and the costs of qualifying for assistance (Widerquist, n.d.).

Targeted UBI experiments in developing countries have been implemented on small and non-representative samples, rendering their results difficult to scientifically assess (A. Banerjee et al., 2019). Moreover, according to most recent studies (Stadelmann-Steffen & Dermont, 2020) the data collected through European Social Survey data in 21 countries indicated no association between risk of job automation and support for UBI. So-called Participation Income schemes that pay people for "participating" in civil society (voting, serving on juries, and such) do not solve the inherent problems with UBI while adding substantial administrative costs (Wispelaere & Stirton, 2007).

UBI's biggest strength is also its major weakness. While paying everyone the same sum may reduce the stigma sometimes associated with receipt of unilateral transfers (Williamson, 1974) and also seems to protect it from the political risk of reduction or elimination, its universality renders it fiscally impossible (Lee & Lee, 2021). Obviously, low-income people will gain from a UBI on net but UBI will only reduce the tax burden of high-income people, and necessarily by less than their taxes will have to increase to make the net unilateral transfer to the poor possible. In short, despite its superficial universality, UBI represents shallow accounting legerdemain. Ergo, like China's *dibao* (Chen & Yang, 2016), it might create as much stigma (Handler & Hollingsworth, 1969), shame (Parsell & Clarke, 2020), and other negative emotions (Goodban, 1985) in net recipients as other types of unilateral transfers induce. It might also create as much resentment in net donors (Marchevsky & Theoharis, 2000; Reese, 2005).

UBI implementation could also potentially threaten democratic traditions, especially if the number of net recipients (those whose UBI payments are greater than their taxes) ever exceeds 50% of the electorate because they could use their majority power at the ballot box to demand increases (P. Nelson, 2018). Even if UBI began at a modest level, unless net UBI recipients lost the power to vote, or UBI faced a hard cap impervious to popular pressure, it could easily balloon to levels that could foment a crisis, especially in countries, like the United States, already facing severe fiscal difficulties (US Government Accountability Office, n.d.).

In addition, UBI will not ensure the end of poverty because nothing will prevent net recipients from consuming more instead of saving for future exigencies (Goolsbee, 2018). Moreover, if net recipients can borrow against future UBI payments, some may consume their future UBI payments today, rendering them in need of aid in the future (Fleischer & Hemel, 2020). If not allowed to borrow, however, net UBI recipients will find it more difficult to invest using leverage or to begin their own businesses. If employment has decreased or disappeared, subsistence will be the only practical income option available if UBI payments are insufficient to meet their life goals. Society therefore may remain filled with people who are non-poor in absolute terms but still at the bottom of the income distribution and hence unsatisfied with their lives and structurally prevented from improving their lot, or their income ranking (Boyce et al., 2010).

None of this is to argue, of course, that unilateral transfers have no place in IPA, just that other types of unilateral transfers, especially more targeted ones that provide greater benefits to the poorest individuals/families (Goolsbee, 2018), may be preferable to policymakers, donors, and recipients. Generally, outcomes improve when individuals decide what best suits their needs rather than having decisions forced upon them by others (Banerjee, 2008; Reamer, 1983).

17.5.1 Private Charity

Private charity has a long history in the United States, dating back to its colonial period (Olasky, 1994). The number and diversity of nonprofit organizations supported by voluntary contributions of money, goods, and labor that helped others astounded early foreign visitors like Alexis de Tocqueville and Gustave de Beaumont (Noll, 2014). Cash loans or grants, clothes, education, food, fuel, healthcare, and lodgings flowed to the poor in sizable quantities that fluctuated with economic conditions. Some of the aid was "outdoor", given to individuals and families who lived in private residences. Some aid was "indoor", requiring residence in an "asylum" for the poor, blind, deaf, orphaned, or insane (Katz, 1984).

Often, charitable giving was done without direct aid from government, or with only modest and intermittent government inputs. During the Great Depression, however, government increased its role in unilateral transfers, some made via private charities but increasingly directly from government employees (Morris, 2009).

Governments presumably provided aid on an easier and fairer basis because government workers were not supposed to try to morally reform the poor the way that many private charities, even secular ones, often did. On the other hand, voluntary donations were more stable than political support for government unilateral transfers because donors felt they had more control over the disbursement of their funds, which were often directed toward groups thought most charity-worthy, like orphans or "lunatics" (Rothman, 2017), and away from shirkers (Charness & Rabin, 2002) and abusers of drink or drugs (Belletto, 2005; Carlson, 1998).

17.5.2 Government Vouchers

Major US government voucher programs include Supplemental Nutrition Assistance Program (SNAP), informally still referred to as "Food Stamps" for the form that the vouchers used to take.

Inflation-adjusted SNAP expenditures per recipient have more than doubled since 1970 (USA Facts, "Nutrition assistance (SNAP) average monthly benefit per person," *USAFacts.org*, 2021. URL: https://usafacts.org/data/topics/people-society/poverty/poverty-programs/nutrition-assistance-snap-avg-monthly-benefit-per-person/?adjustment=Inflation.)

SNAP grew because it allowed low-income individuals to purchase foods innocuously, through a government-provided debit card that creates less stigma than the older, more conspicuous stamp-like technology did.

In addition, the illegal secondary market for stamps reduced support for the program when the public learned that recipients could exchange their stamps for drugs. With SNAP, taxpayers feel more confident that their taxes are not being misused.

17.5.3 Government Cash

Governments also make outright grants of cash to low-income individuals. The major federal cash grant program, Temporary Assistance for Needy Families (TANF), supplanted the older Assistance for Families with Dependent Children (AFDC) program, which was criticized for incentivizing people to become dependent on "welfare" payments. Because TANF is distributed through states, payments vary across the nation, with some states paying a much higher percentage of the putative "poverty line" than others. Taxpayers still fear creating a permanent "welfare" class if payments are too generous and do not want their money spent on illicit drugs or luxury goods that they might not feel they can afford themselves (Center on Budget and Policy Priorities, "TANF Benefits Still Too Low to Help Families, Especially Black Families, Avoid Increased Hardship," *CBPP*, 2016. URL: https://www.cbpp.org/research/family-income-support/tanf-benefits-still-too-low-to-help-families-especially-black.) As a result, inflation-adjusted TANF payments have decreased in all but three states since 1996, and have declined by more than 30% in half of all US states.

17.5.4 Government Provision

Governments also sometimes directly provide goods for the poor, either gifting them to them, as in the case of expired surplus foodstuffs, or leasing them to them at a below-market rate, as in the case of government housing. Concern that the poor will use the resources for untoward purposes was thus minimized but federal housing projects were notoriously ugly, shoddy, and expensive (Allen Hays, 2012) and created significant neighborhood negative externalities.

Governments are inefficient producers, so taxpayers restrict direct provision (Levy et al., 2013). The US government, for example, did not make "government" cheese directly but rather contracted for its production as part of an expensive dairy price support program (Heien, 1977).

17.5.5 Summary of the Major Costs and Benefits of Different Types of Unilateral Transfers

The major costs and benefits of the major types of unilateral transfers are summarized in Table 17.4 below.

Even if AI or other BETC eventually destroy jobs faster than people can engage in IPA, and policymakers and recipients believe that government cash grants are the best type of unilateral transfer to implement in response, initiating UBI now is not indicated because, as the next section explains, it can be implemented quickly if ever needed.

TABLE 17.4 Tabular Summary of the Major Costs and Benefits of Different Types of Unilateral Transfers

Unilateral Transfer Type	Costs	Benefits
Private charity	Attempts at behavior or belief modification	Dollars donated, not overall popularity, drive available resources
Government vouchers	Vouchers do not always match recipient needs leading to deadweight losses	Funding is less at risk if secondary markets can be stifled because taxpayers are less fearful that their money is used to purchase alcohol, drugs, etc.
Government cash grants	Funding risks increase with the amount because taxpayers fear recipient moral hazard	Fungibility decreases deadweight losses from recipient need mismatches
Government provision	Often low quality, e.g., housing, education	Services and housing can be acquired at below-market prices

17.6 Limitations

This chapter extrapolates centuries-long trends into the near future because, as shown in Sections 17.1 and 17.2, AI thus far is simply another in a long line of new technology. It has not palpably affected job, productivity, or output trends. Moreover, as shown in Sections 17.3 and 17.4, individuals and families have long engaged in IPA and nothing inherent in AI changes their ability to do so.

That said, a transformative AI breakthrough capable of accelerating BETC faster than individuals and families can adapt remains possible. If that occurs, more economically developed nations can implement UBI as quickly as government stimulus checks and corporate bailouts were distributed during the global financial crisis and pandemics of 2008 and 2020, that is, within a few hours to weeks depending on the mechanisms employed and policy intent (Sahm et al., 2012; Wright, 2010; *The Fiscal Response to COVID-19 in Europe: Will It Be Enough?*, n.d.)

In short, implementing UBI *now* because of what AI *might* do to jobs in the future is not rational policy (Hoynes and Rothstein 2019; Commentary: Universal Basic Income Ma…; Would a universal basic income reduce…).

17.7 Conclusion

Claims that AI will, or should, lead to UBI display too little detailed knowledge of the limitations of AI (Section 17.2), the nature of BETC (Section 17.3), the adaptive solutions offered to individuals by IPA (Section 17.4), and alternative unilateral transfer policies (Section 17.5) to warrant high confidence, especially given that UBI could be adopted almost instantaneously if ever needed ((Section 17.6).

Specifically, AI is not nearly as powerful as widely believed and is unlikely to supplant humans in the foreseeable future. Jobs are not disappearing but even if they eventually do, individuals will have time to increase subsistence, proprietorship, and investment. Even if individuals desire to increase unilateral transfers as a percentage of their income portfolios, they may, in conjunction with policymakers, prefer other types of transfers over UBI, which suffers from several conceptual problems. Finally, in the unlikely scenario that AI ever proves rapidly destructive, countries can quickly adopt UBI.

Notes

1 Careful analysis may be needed to correctly differentiate between the five major sources of income, the legal definitions of which sometimes do not match underlying economic realities. A landlord is a proprietor whereas the owner of a real estate investment trust (REIT) is a financial investor. Similarly, a worker with a regular schedule paid a salary or a fixed wage based on time is an employee, but a worker paid solely by the task or contract fulfillment is an independent contractor, a form of proprietorship. Someone who grows her own tomatoes to eat engages in subsistence but when she sells her tomatoes she becomes a proprietor. An employee may simultaneously be an investor via an employee stock ownership plan (ESOP) (Pierce et al., 1991). A disabled person receiving a stream of income may be the recipient of a unilateral transfer (e.g., charity, or a publicly subsidized government disability program) and/or may be an investor in a disability insurance policy (Liebman, 2015). Correctly differentiating between income sources, however, is unimportant to the argument because most individuals engage in IPA, that is, flexible income portfolios that vary with their life goals (Green, 2021) and over their life cycles (Browning & Crossley, 2001).
2 Automation of work that includes (1) fixed automation, (2) programmable automation, and (3) flexible automation. It can be caused by robots or RPA software in addition to AI. https://www.britannica.com/technology/automation/Manufacturing-applications-of-automation-and-robotics
3 Take, for example, one of the strangest solutions to the weight transport problem, courtesy of Timothy Lillicrap of Google DeepMind in London and his colleagues in 2016. Their algorithm, instead of relying on a matrix of weights recorded from the forward pass, used a matrix initialized with random values for the backward pass. Once assigned, the values remain constant, so no weights need to be transported for backward passes, allowing the network to learn efficiently (Singh et al., 2019).

References

Acemoglu, D., & Restrepo, P. (2017). *Low-Skill and High-Skill Automation.* https://doi.org/10.3386/w24119
Acemoglu, D., & Robinson, J. A. (2012). *Why Nations Fail: The Origins of Power, Prosperity, and Poverty.* Crown Publishers.
Albert, V. (2000). Reducing Welfare Benefits: Consequences for Adequacy of and Eligibility for Benefits. *The Social Worker, 45*(4), 300–311.
Albion, R. G. (1932). The "Communication Revolution". *The American Historical Review, 37*(4), 718–720.

Allegri, G., & Foschi, R. (2021). Universal Basic Income as a Promoter of Real Freedom in a Digital Future. *World Futures*, 77(1), 1–22.

Allen, D. W. (2011). *The Institutional Revolution: Measurement and the Economic Emergence of the Modern World*. University of Chicago Press.

Allen Hays, R. (2012). *The Federal Government and Urban Housing*, 3rd Edition. SUNY Press.

Anderson, E. (2017). *Private Government: How Employers Rule Our Lives (and Why We Don't Talk About It)*. Princeton: Princeton UP. https://press.princeton.edu/books/hardcover/9780691176512/private-government

Arrow, K. J. (2012). *Social Choice and Individual Values*, 3rd Edition. Yale University Press.

Asia, B. S. (1945). Employment Relation: Common-Law Concept and Legislative Definition. *The Yale Law Journal*, 55(1), 76–116.

Autor, D. H. (2015). Why Are There Still So Many Jobs? The History and Future of Workplace Automation. *The Journal of Economic Perspectives: A Journal of the American Economic Association*, 29(3), 3–30.

Autor, D., Levy, F., & Murnane, R. (2000). *Upstairs, Downstairs: Computer-Skill Complementarity and Computer-Labor Substitution on Two Floors of a Large Bank*. https://doi.org/10.3386/w7890

Autor, D., & Salomons, A. (2018). *Is Automation Labor-Displacing? Productivity Growth, Employment, and the Labor Share* (No. w24871). National Bureau of Economic Research. https://doi.org/10.3386/w24871

Baily, M. N., Bosworth, B., & Doshi, S. (2020). *Productivity Comparisons: Lessons from Japan, the United States, and Germany*. Brookings Institution. January, 22. https://www.brookings.edu/wp-content/uploads/2020/01/ES-1.30.20-BailyBosworthDoshi.pdf

Bakker, G., Crafts, N., & Woltjer, P. (2019). The Sources of Growth in a Technologically Progressive Economy: The United States, 1899–1941. *Economic Journal*, 129(622), 2267–2294.

Banerjee, A., Niehaus, P., & Suri, T. (2019). Universal Basic Income in the Developing World. *Annual Review of Economics*. https://doi.org/10.1146/annurev-economics-080218-030229

Banerjee, A. V. (2008). Why Fighting POVERTY is Hard? *Unpublished, mIT (mimeo)*. https://www.bbvaopenmind.com/wp-content/uploads/2009/01/BBVA-OpenMind-Frontiers_Of_Knowledge.pdf#page=247

Belletto, S. (2005). Drink Versus Printer's Ink: Temperance and the Management of Financial Speculation in the Life of P.T. Barnum. *American Studies*, 46(1), 45–65.

Bennett, R. J., Smith, H., & Montebruno, P. (2020). The Population of Non-corporate Business Proprietors in England and Wales 1891–1911. *Business History*, 62(8), 1341–1372.

Bidadanure, J. U. (2019). The Political Theory of Universal Basic Income. *Annual Review of Political Science*, 22(1), 481–501.

Biswal, A. (2020). *7 types of Artificial Intelligence that you should know in 2020*. Simplilearn Solutions. https://www.simplilearn.com/tutorials/artificial-intelligence-tutorial/types-of-artificial-intelligence

Boyce, C. J., Brown, G. D. A., & Moore, S. C. (2010). Money and Happiness: Rank of Income, Not Income, Affects Life Satisfaction. *Psychological Science*, 21(4), 471–475.

Boyd, D. W. (1997). From "Mom and Pop" to Wal-Mart: The Impact of the Consumer Goods Pricing Act of 1975 on the Retail Sector in the United States. *Journal of Economic Issues*, 31(1), 223–232.

Brennan, M. J. (1973). An Approach to the Valuation of Uncertain Income Streams. *The Journal of Finance*, 28(3), 661–674.

Browning, M., & Crossley, T. F. (2001). The Life-Cycle Model of Consumption and Saving. *The Journal of Economic Perspectives: A Journal of the American Economic Association*, 15(3), 3–22.

Bullard, J. (2014). The Rise and Fall of Labor Force Participation in the United States. *Federal Reserve Bank of St. Louis Review* (First Quarter 2014), 1–12. https://files.stlouisfed.org/files/htdocs/publications/review/2014/q1/bullard.pdf

Burke, A. E., FitzRoy, F. R., & Nolan, M. A. (2008). What Makes a Die-Hard Entrepreneur? Beyond the "Employee or Entrepreneur" Dichotomy. *Small Business Economics*, 31(2), 93–115.

Carlson, D. W. (1998). " Drinks He to His Own Undoing": Temperance Ideology in the Deep South. *Journal of the Early Republic*, 18(4), 659–691.

Charness, G., & Rabin, M. (2002). Understanding Social Preferences with Simple Tests. *The Quarterly Journal of Economics*, 117(3), 817–869.

Chaudry, A., Wimer, C., Macartney, S., Frohlich, L., Campbell, C., Swenson, K., Oellerich, D., and Hauan, S. (2016). *Poverty in the United States: 50-Year Trends and Safety Net Impacts*. U.S. Department of Health and Human Services.

Chen, J., & Yang, L. (2016). Interactional Impacts on Claimants of Chinese Dibao. *The International Journal of Social Quality*, 6(2), 18–34.

Chibnik, M. (1978). The Value of Subsistence Production. *Journal of Anthropological Research*, 34(4), 561–576.

Childers, R. G. (2011). Being One'S Own Boss: HOW Does Risk Fit In? *The American Economist*, 56(1), 48–58.

Constable, S., & Wright, R. E. (2011). *The WSJ Guide to the 50 Economic Indicators That Really Matter: From Big Macs to "Zombie Banks," the Indicators Smart Investors Watch to Beat the Market*. Harper Collins.

Cook, S. R. (1998). The Great Depression, Subsistence, and Views of Poverty in Wyoming County, West Virginia. *Journal of Appalachian Studies*, 4(2), 271–283.

Crawford, K., Whittaker, M., Elish, M. C., Barocas, S., Plasek, A., & Ferryman, K. (2016). The AI Now Report. *The Social and Economic Implications of Artificial Intelligence Technologies in the Near-Term*. http://acikistihbarat.com/Dosyalar/AINowSummaryReport-artificial-intelligence-effects-in-near-future.pdf

De Vries, J. (1994). The Industrial Revolution and the Industrious Revolution. *The Journal of Economic History*, 54(2), 249–270.

Donnelly, F. K. (1986). Luddites Past and Present. *Labour / Le Travail*, 18, 217–221.

Dunn, L. F. (1979). Measurement of Internal Income-Leisure Tradeoffs. *The Quarterly Journal of Economics*, 93(3), 373–393.

Elwert, G., & Wong, D. (1980). Subsistence Production and Commodity Production in the Third World. *Review*, 3(3), 501–522.

Feldstein, M. (2016). Reducing Inequality and Poverty. *Project Syndicate*. https://www.project-syndicate.org/commentary/reducing-inequality-in-america-by-martin-feldstein-2016-08

Fleischer, M. P., & Hemel, D. (2020). The Architecture of a Basic Income. *The University of Chicago Law Review. University of Chicago. Law School*, 87(3), 625–710.

Flynn, S. M. (2019). *The Cure That Works: How to Have the World's Best Health Care – At a Quarter of the Price*. Simon and Schuster.

Fothergill, A. (2003). The Stigma of Charity: Gender, Class, and Disaster Assistance. *The Sociological Quarterly*, *44*(4), 659–680.

Furman, J., & Seamans, R. (2019). AI and the Economy. *Innovation Policy and the Economy*, *19*, 161–191.

Gallman, R. E., & Rhode, P. W. (2020). *Capital in the Nineteenth Century*. University of Chicago Press.

Goetz, S. J., & Rupasingha, A. (2009). Determinants of Growth in Non-Farm Proprietor Densities in the US, 1990-2000. *Small Business Economics*, *32*(4), 425–438.

Goldin, C., & Katz, L. F. (2010). *The race between education and technology*. Harvard University Press.

Goodban, N. (1985). The Psychological Impact of Being on Welfare. *The Social Service Review*, *59*(3), 403–422.

Goolsbee, A. (2018). *Public Policy in an AI Economy* (No. w24653). National Bureau of Economic Research. https://doi.org/10.3386/w24653

Gottschalk, P., & Moffitt, R. A. (1994). Welfare Dependence: Concepts, Measures, and Trends. *The American Economic Review*, *84*(2), 38–42.

Gowdy, J. (2020). Our Hunter-Gatherer Future: Climate Change, Agriculture and Uncivilization. *Futures*, *115*, 102488.

Green, J. M. (2021). *Diversify Your Income For Financial Independence*. Retrieved March 26, 2021, from https://www.thebalance.com/diversify-your-income-sources-357629

Guelzo, A. C. (2000). Come-outers and Community Men: Abraham Lincoln and the Idea of Community in Nineteenth-Century America. *Journal of the Abraham Lincoln Association*, *21*(1). https://cupola.gettysburg.edu/cwfac/32/

Haagh, L. (2019). *The Case for Universal Basic Income*. John Wiley & Sons.

Haenlein, M., & Kaplan, A. (2019). A Brief History of Artificial Intelligence: On the Past, Present, and Future of Artificial Intelligence. *California Management Review*, *61*(4), 5–14. https://doi.org/10.1177/0008125619864925

Hamilton, B. H. (2000). Does Entrepreneurship Pay? An Empirical Analysis of the Returns to Self-Employment. *The Journal of Political Economy*, *108*(3), 604–631.

Handler, J. F., & Hollingsworth, E. J. (1969). Stigma, Privacy, and Other Attitudes of Welfare Recipients. *Stanford Law Review*, *22*(1), 1–19.

Hecht-Nielsen, R. (1992). Theory of the Backpropagation Neural Network. In *Neural Networks for Perception* (pp. 65–93). Elsevier.

Heien, D. (1977). The Cost of the U.S. Dairy Price Support Program: 1949-74. *The Review of Economics and Statistics*, *59*(1), 1–8.

Hopkins, E. (1982). Working Hours and Conditions during the Industrial Revolution: A Re-Appraisal. *The Economic History Review*, *35*(1), 52–66.

Hoynes, H. and Rothstein, J. (2019). Universal Basic Income in the United States and Advanced Countries. *Annual Review of Economics*, *11*, 929–958. https://www.annualreviews.org/doi/abs/10.1146/annurev-economics-080218-030237

Juhn, C. and Potter, S. (2006). Changes in Labor Force Participation in the United States. *Journal of Economic Perspectives*, *20*(3), (Summer 2006): 27–46. https://www.aeaweb.org/articles?id=10.1257/jep.20.3.27

Johnson, T. (1998). *Farm Life Long Ago*. Steck-Vaughn Company.

Juhász, R., Squicciarini, M., & Voigtländer, N. (2020). *Away from Home and Back: Coordinating (Remote) Workers in 1800 and 2020*. https://papers.ssrn.com/abstract=3753983

Katz, M. B. (1984). Poorhouses and the Origins of the Public Old Age Home. *The Milbank Memorial Fund Quarterly. Health and Society*, *62*(1), 110–140.

Kennedy, L. (1982). The First Agricultural Revolution: Property Rights in Their Place. *Agricultural History*, *56*(2), 379–390.

Kidd, M. T., & Anderson, K. E. (2019). Laying Hens in the U.S. Market: An Appraisal of Trends from the Beginning of the 20th Century to Present. *The Journal of Applied Poultry Research*, *28*(4), 771–784.

Latham, S., & Humberd, B. (2018). *Four Ways Jobs Will Respond to Automation: The Level of Threat to a Given Profession Depends on Two Factors, the Type of Value Provided and how It's Delivered*. MIT Sloan Management Review.

Lauterbach, A. (1977). Employment, Unemployment and Underemployment: A Conceptual Re-Examination. *American Journal of Economics and Sociology*, *36*(3), 283–298.

LeCun, Y., Bengio, Y., & Hinton, G. (2015). Deep learning. *Nature*, *521*(7553), 436–444.

Lee, J.-H., & Lee, J. (2021, February 3). South Korea Premier Says Universal Basic Income "Impossible". *Bloomberg News*. https://www.bloomberg.com/news/articles/2021-02-03/south-korea-premier-says-universal-basic-income-is-impossible

Levy, D. K., McDade, Z., & Bertumen, K. (2013). Mixed-Income Living: Anticipated and Realized Benefits for Low-Income Households. *Cityscape*, *15*(2), 15–28.

Liebman, J. B. (2015). Understanding the Increase in Disability Insurance Benefit Receipt in the United States. *The Journal of Economic Perspectives: A Journal of the American Economic Association*, *29*(2), 123–150.

Lillicrap, T. P., Santoro, A., Marris, L., Akerman, C. J., & Hinton, G. (2020). Backpropagation and the Brain. *Nature Reviews. Neuroscience*, *21*(6), 335–346.

Little, J. I. (2001). A Canadian in Lowell: Labour, Manhood and Independence in the Early Industrial Era, 1840-1849. *Labour/Le Travail*, *48*, 197–263.

MacDonald, R., & Peel, D. A. (1983). The Life Cycle Hypothesis and Rational Expectations : Some Further Empirical Results. *Recherches Économiques de Louvain / Louvain Economic Review*, *49*(4), 381–390.

Majewski, J. (1997). A Revolution Too Many? *The Journal of Economic History*, *57*(2), 476–480.

Makridakis, S. (2017). The forthcoming Artificial Intelligence (AI) revolution: Its impact on society and firms. *Futures*, *90*, 46–60.

Malkiel, B. G. (2013). Asset Management Fees and the Growth of Finance. *The Journal of Economic Perspectives: A Journal of the American Economic Association*, *27*(2), 97–108.

Malter, J., & Sprague, K. (2019, April 23). *"I'm Not a UBI Guy': Paul Krugman Says Money Could Be Better Spent on More Targeted Programs*. CNBC. https://www.cnbc.com/2019/04/23/paul-krugman-on-universal-basic-income-im-not-a-ubi-guy.html

Marchevsky, A., & Theoharis, J. (2000). Welfare Reform, Globalization, and the Racialization of Entitlement. *American Studies*, *41*(2/3), 235–265.

Mason, A. (2020, March 25). *6 Ideas to Diversify your Income Streams*. https://thecollegeinvestor.com/16174/6-ideas-to-diversify-your-income/

McAfee, A., & Brynjolfsson, E. (2016). Human Work in the Robotic Future: Policy for the Age of Automation. *Foreign Affairs*, *95*(4), 139–150.

McAfee, A., & Brynjolfsson, E. (2017). *Machine, Platform, Crowd: Harnessing Our Digital Future*. W. W. Norton & Company.

Measuring Worth - Annual Wages in the United States. (n.d.). Retrieved March 25, 2021, from https://www.measuringworth.com/datasets/uswage/

Misra, J., Moller, S., & Karides, M. (2014). Envisioning Dependency: Changing Media Depictions of Welfare in the 20th Century. *Social Problems*, *50*(4), 482–504.

Modigliani, F., & Pogue, G. A. (1974). An Introduction to Risk and Return: Concepts and Evidence. *Financial Analysts Journal, 30*(3), 69–86.

Morris, A. J. F. (2009). *The Limits of Voluntarism: Charity and Welfare from the New Deal Through the Great Society.* Cambridge University Press.

Mould, T. (2020). *Overthrowing the Queen: Telling Stories of Welfare in America.* Indiana University Press.

Nelson, P. (2018). *Universal Basic Income and the Threat to Democracy as We Know It.* Business Expert Press.

Nelson, S. C. (2008). Tax Policy and Sole Proprietorships: A Closer Look. *National Tax Journal, 61*(3), 421–443.

Noll, M. A. (2014). Tocqueville's America, Beaumont's slavery, and the United States in 1831–32. *American Political Thought, 3*(2), 273–302.

Olasky, M. (1994). *The Tragedy of American Compassion.* Regnery Publishing.

Olmstead, A. L., & Rhode, P. W. (2008). *Creating Abundance.* Cambridge Books. https://ideas.repec.org/b/cup/cbooks/9780521673877.html

Parsell, C., & Clarke, A. (2020). Charity and Shame: Towards Reciprocity. *Social Problems.* https://doi.org/10.1093/socpro/spaa057

Pierce, J. L., Rubenfeld, S. A., & Morgan, S. (1991). Employee Ownership: A Conceptual Model of Process and Effects. *Academy of Management Review. Academy of Management, 16*(1), 121–144.

Productivity - GDP per Hour Worked - OECD Data. (n.d.). Retrieved March 31, 2021, from https://data.oecd.org/lprdty/gdp-per-hour-worked.htm

Rallo, J. R. (2019). Hayek Did Not Embrace a Universal Basic Income. *Independent Review, 24*(3), 347–359.

Rank, M. R. (1994). A View From the Inside Out: Recipients' Perceptions of Welfare. *Journal of Sociology and Social Welfare, 21*(2), 3.

Reamer, F. G. (1983). The Concept of Paternalism in Social Work. *The Social Service Review, 57*(2), 254–271.

Reese, E. (2005). *Backlash against Welfare Mothers.* https://doi.org/10.1525/9780520938717

Rivers, R. (2019, January 29). *A Progressive Rejection Of Universal Basic Income - Ron Rivers - Medium.* Medium. https://medium.com/@ronrivers/a-progressive-rejection-of-universal-basic-income-2604366c6d3a

Rose, J. (2017, November 2). 5 Ways To Generate Different Sources Of Income. *Forbes Magazine.* https://www.forbes.com/sites/jrose/2017/11/02/different-sources-income/

Rothman, D. J. (2017). *The Discovery of the Asylum: Social Order and Disorder in the New Republic.* Routledge.

Sahm, C. R., Shapiro, M. D., & Slemrod, J. (2012). Check in the Mail or More in the Paycheck: Does the Effectiveness of Fiscal Stimulus Depend on How It Is Delivered? *American Economic Journal. Economic Policy, 4*(3), 216–250.

Schrittwieser, J., Antonoglou, I., Hubert, T., Simonyan, K., Sifre, L., Schmitt, S., Guez, A., Lockhart, E., Hassabis, D., Graepel, T., Lillicrap, T., & Silver, D. (2020). Mastering Atari, Go, Chess and Shogi by Planning with a Learned Model. *Nature, 588*(7839), 604–609.

Seely, B. E. (2007). Economic History as Technological History: George Rogers Taylor's "The Transportation Revolution, 1815-1860". *Technology and Culture, 48*(4), 824–830.

Shaikh, M. D. S. (2020). *Insight of DeepMind Learning: Journey of Transformation from Natural Intelligence to Artificial Intelligence.* Amazon Digital Services LLC - KDP Print US.

Singh, A., Ramasubramanian, K., & Shivam, S. (2019). *Building an Enterprise Chatbot: Work with Protected Enterprise Data Using Open Source Frameworks*. Apress.

Sowa, K., Przegalinska, A., Ciechanowski, L., (2021) Cobots in Knowledge Work: Human – AI Collaboration in Managerial Professions, in: Journal of Business Research, Volume 125; 135–142, https://doi.org/10.1016/j.jbusres.2020.11.038.

Stadelmann-Steffen, I., & Dermont, C. (2020). Citizens' Opinions About Basic Income Proposals Compared – A Conjoint Analysis of Finland and Switzerland. *Journal of Social Policy*, 49(2), 383–403.

Steinfeld, R. J. (2001). *Coercion, Contract, and Free Labor in the Nineteenth Century*. https://doi.org/10.1017/cbo9780511549564

Stiglitz, J. (2013). The Price of Inequality. In *New Perspectives Quarterly*, 30(1), 52–53. https://doi.org/10.1111/npqu.11358

Stuber, J., & Kronebusch, K. (2004). Stigma and Other Determinants of Participation in TANF and Medicaid. *Journal of Policy Analysis and Management: [the Journal of the Association for Public Policy Analysis and Management]*, 23(3), 509–530.

Sylla, R. (2002). Financial Systems and Economic Modernization. *The Journal of Economic History*, 62(2), 277–292.

Tegmark, M. (2017). *Life 3.0: Being Human in the Age of Artificial Intelligence*. Knopf Doubleday Publishing Group.

Terborgh, G. (1966). *The Automation Hysteria*. W. W. Norton.

The Effect Of Lockdown Measures On Unemployment. (n.d.). Retrieved March 25, 2021, from https://www.richmondfed.org/publications/research/coronavirus/economic_impact_covid-19_09-04-20

The Fiscal Response to COVID-19 in Europe: Will It Be Enough? (n.d.). Retrieved March 31, 2021, from https://www.caixabankresearch.com/en/economics-markets/activity-growth/fiscal-response-covid-19-europewill-it-be-enough

Toossi, M. (2002). A Century of Change: The U.S. Labor Force, 1950-2020. *Monthly Labor Review* (May 2002), 15–28. https://www.bls.gov/opub/mlr/2002/05/art2full.pdf

Torrey, L., & Shavlik, J. (2010). Transfer Learning. In *Handbook of Research on Machine Learning Applications and Trends: Algorithms, Methods, and Techniques* (pp. 242–264). IGI Global.

US Government Accountability Office. (n.d.). *The Nation'S fiscal Health: After Pandemic Recovery, Focus Needed on Achieving Long-Term Fiscal Sustainability*. Retrieved March 25, 2021, from https://www.gao.gov/products/gao-21-275sp

Vinyals, O., Babuschkin, I., Chung, J., Mathieu, M., Jaderberg, M., Czarnecki, W. M., Dudzik, A., Huang, A., Georgiev, P., Powell, R., & Others. (2019). AlphaStar: Mastering the Real-Time Strategy Game StarCraft II. *DeepMind Blog*.

Wage Stagnation in Nine Charts. (n.d.). Retrieved March 25, 2021, from https://www.epi.org/publication/charting-wage-stagnation/

Wang, F., Zhang, J. J., Zheng, X., Wang, X., Yuan, Y., Dai, X., Zhang, J., & Yang, L. (2016). Where does AlphaGo go: From Church-Turing Thesis to AlphaGo Thesis and Beyond. *IEEE/CAA Journal of Automatica Sinica*, 3(2), 113–120.

Waters, R. (2018, January 12). Techmate: How AI Rewrote the Rules of Chess. *Financial Times*. https://www.ft.com/content/ea707a24-f6b7-11e7-8715-e94187b3017e

Weiss, K., Khoshgoftaar, T. M., & Wang, D. (2016). A Survey of Transfer Learning. *Journal of Big Data*, 3(1). https://doi.org/10.1186/s40537-016-0043-6

Wermers, R. (2000). Mutual Fund Performance: An Empirical Decomposition into Stock-Picking Talent, Style, Transactions Costs, and Expenses. *The Journal of Finance*, 55(4), 1655–1695.

Widerquist, K. (n.d.). *UNITED STATES: Nobel Laureate Joseph stiglitz Endorses Unconditional Basic Income*. Retrieved March 30, 2021, from http://basicincome.org/news/2015/09/united-states-nobel-laureate-joseph-stiglitz-endorses-unconditional-basic-income/

Williamson, J. B. (1974). The Stigma of Public Dependency: A Comparison of Alternative Forms of Public Aid to the Poor. *Social Problems*, 22(2), 213–228.

Wispelaere, J. D., & Stirton, L. (2007). The Public Administration Case against Participation Income. *The Social Service Review*, 81(3), 523–549.

Wright, R. E. (2010). *Bailouts: Public Money, Private Profit*. Columbia University Press.

Wright, R. E. (2015). *Little Business on the Prairie: Entrepreneurship, Prosperity, and Challenge in South Dakota*. Center for Western Studies.

Wright, R. E. (2017). *The Poverty of Slavery*. https://doi.org/10.1007/978-3-319-48968-1

Wright, R. E. (2019). America's Fur Business Parts I, II, and III. *Fur Traders & Rendezvous*. https://www.alfredjacobmiller.com/explore/americasfurbusiness1/

Wright, R. E. (2020). *History and Evolution of the North American Wildlife Conservation Model*. https://doi.org/10.2139/ssrn.3673178

Wright, R. E. (Ed.). (2021). *The Best of Thomas Paine*. American Institute for Economic Research.

INDEX

Pages in *italics* refer figures, **bold** refer tables and pages followed by n refer notes.

2020 National Education Policy 262

Aadhaar identification program 261
Academically Adrift: Limited Learning on College Campuses 190
academic research 3, 122, 126–127, 131
accountability 82, 129–130, 149
accuracy 6, 40, 87, 119, 139, 148
Adler, Mortimer 191
Adults Training and Education Survey (ATES) 248
aerospace engineers 82, 86
agriculture, aquaculture, and food 56–58
AI *see* artificial intelligence
AI Revolution 2, 5
AI Three-Year Activities and Implementation Program 223
AlphaGo 120, 277
AlphaStar 277
AlphaZero 120, 174
Amazon 110, 178, 261
Ambani, Mukesh 261
Araya, Daniel 1–9, 184
Aristotle 182–184
Arrhenius, Svante 91
artificial general intelligence (AGI) 105
artificial intelligence (AI) 1, 75, 90, 172, 188, 189, 191, 196, 198, 201, 203, 204, 206, 209–210, 215; advances 119–120; algorithms and systems 236; basic theory systems for a new generation 228–229; build a next-generation 230–231; capability maturity and data management 128; challenges and controversies 127; changing relationships between humans and machines 236; China's situation 222–223; cloud-powered academic research 126–127; and computing research 173; connected campus and student success 125–126; construct an AI academic discipline 232–233; cultivate high-level AI innovative talents and teams 232; current state of development 235; deployment 227, 236; development of 221; for education 137–138; in education 144–145; educator-supporting 141; enabled features 235; ethics of 139, 143; foundation of the innovation economy 234; frameworks 121–122; future 277–278; governance and ethics 128–130; guiding ideology 224; history 119; and human rights 143; implemented in education 139; increase the introduction of high-end AI talent 232; and information technology in education 120–121; innovation platform construction 231–232; intelligent navigation systems 86; learning about 142; machine learning tools 236;

Index

market-dominant 225; for mission design, planning, compliance, and space assistance 85–86; a new engine of economic development 222; open-source sharing 225; personal assistants in space 84; policy and planning 8; preparing for 142–143; and preventing potential space debris 86; to process satellite images 85; rapid technological change and the proliferation of 246; revolution 234–235; strategic objectives of China 225–227; strategic technology 222; student-supporting 140–141; for system monitoring 85; systems layout 224; system-supporting 139–140; talent competition 236–237; teaching and learning 122–125; and technological unemployment 173–175; technology 131; technology-led 224; today 276; for training systems 86; working together with 276–277
artificial narrow intelligence (ANI) 175
Arum, Richard 190
Assessment and Examination (A&E) 246, 250, 254
Assistance for Families with Dependent Children (AFDC) 290
Association for Institutional Research (AIR) 125
Association of Cooperative Colleges (ACC) 249
A-telic activities: freedom for 185–184; liberal arts and 184–185
augmented reality (AR) 35, 140, 231
augmenting human civilization 3
automation 5, 9, 30, 53, 65, 86, 88, 104, 106, 108–110, 108–113
autonomous unmanned systems 229–231
Autor, David 277
Azim Premji University 262

Bandura, Albert 197–198
Barr, Stringfellow 191, 192
Beall, Erica 201
Beane, Matt 113
Belt and Road Initiative (BRI) 7, 206
Bennett, Kate 199
Benzell, Seth 113
big data analytics 81
Big Tech: emergence of 177–178; freedom from 178; liberal arts and freedom from 180–181; VR/AR devices 179

bio innovation 49–51, 61–64; risks and issues 61–64
Bio Revolution 4, 49
Bloom, B. S. 123
brainbound 159–160
brain science 221
Brandeis, Louis 107
Brann, Eva 201
Bräutigam, Deborah 208
BRI see Belt and Road Initiative
Brynjolfsson, Erik 4, 103–115
Buchanan, Scott 191, 192
Bundesinstitut fuer Berufliche Bildung (BIBB) 246
Burmeister, Jon K. 6, 172–186
Business, economic, and technological change (BETC) 274; application of AI 276; cost–benefit analysis of IPA 282–287; long-term employment 278–282; UBI adoption 276
businesses 66–69
Byju's 263–264

California Privacy Rights Act (CPRA) 129
capital investment 111
Carbonell, Jaime 121
career opportunities: engineers in a range of disciplines 82–83; finding talent 83; scientists 81–82
Carnegie Mellon University 163
CAR T-cell therapy 59, 65–66, 71n18
Case, Anne 107
Ceylin Büyüksoy, Z. T. 121
challenge-based learning 32
Chalmers, David 158–159
Cheng, E. C. 121
China 206, 207–208; globalization 208–209, 213–215; global technology leader 210; higher education 210–213; human capital development 209–210
China Science Publishing Group Co., Ltd (CSPG) 212
Chinese Academy of Sciences (CAS) 211
Chinese Association of Social Science (CASS) 212
Chinese Communist Party's (CCP) 239
Chinese English-language journals (celajs) 212
"Chinese infrastructuralism" 214
Chinese National Science Foundation (NSFC) 212

Chui, Michael 48–72
civil engineers 82
Clark, Andy 158–160
climate change 4, 42, 49, 61, 70, 91–93, 95, 97–101
climate finance 98
climate problem: new technologies to address the 97; professional fields to address the 97–100; redesigning higher education for 100; as a societal problem 93–95; universities in addressing the 95–97
cobotization 277
collaboration 99
commercialization and diffusion 64–65
competency-based education (CBE) 38, 145
complex situations 13, 17–18, 230
Comprehensive and Progressive Agreement for Trans-Pacific Partnership (CPTPP) 208
computer-driven cathode-ray tube display 15
computer software and hardware engineers 82
conceptual framework: augmentation means 18; develop 17; *experimental methods* 23; *explicit-artifact* process capabilities 20; four basic classes 18; H-LAM/T system 20, 22; information-storage mechanism 21; memo-writing process 20–21; orient us toward the real possibilities 17–18; process-hierarchical structure 19; process hierarchies 19; radical innovations 24; system-engineering problem 22; writing machine 22
Cosmos Economy 4, 76–77
cost–benefit analysis: employment 285–286; financial investment 285; five sources of income **286**; flowchart and equation *283*; government cash 290; government provision 290; government vouchers 289; of IPA 282–284; limitations 291; private charity 289; proprietorship 284–285; subsistence 284; types of unilateral transfers **291**; of UBI and other unilateral transfer policies 287–288; unilateral transfers 286
COVID-19 lockdowns 9
COVID-19 pandemic 5, 36, 63, 69, 121, 127, 260

CRISPR-Cas9 48
cross-medium analytical reasoning technology 230
Crowder, Norman 120

Damon, Matt 203
data analytics and artificial intelligence 98
deaths of despair 107, 115n17
Deaton, Angus 107
deep neural nets (DNNs) 278
deep space exploration 80
de facto 196
Defries, Ruth 4, 90–101
Demleitner, Nora 203
demonetization 260
Departments of State and Homeland Security (DHS) 240
depth of knowledge 90, 99
Deresiewicz, William 190
differential privacy (DP) 129
DigComp Digital Competency Framework (2.2) 143
digital learning: Byju's 263–264; Eruditus 265; future of education 268–270; landscape 263; LEAD School 266–267; post-lockdown realities 267–268; transformation 263; Unacademy 264; upGrad 265–266; Vedantu 266
direct-to-consumer (DTC) 58, *68*
disaster preparation and response 98

Èapek, Karel 103
Earth observation 78
Earth System Science (ESS) 95
Economic Co-operation and Development (OECD) 39, 130
Edison, Thomas 235
EdTech 121, 130–131, 140, 261
education policies 4
Education Transformation Framework (ETF) 122
EDUCAUSE 125
electronic brain 108
electronics engineers 82
Encyclopedia of DNA Elements research consortium (ENCODE) 60
Engelbart, Douglas C. 3, 13–27
epistemology 196
Erskine, John 191
Eruditus 261, 265

ethics of AI&ED: creation AI programs 150–151; data ownership 146–147; effectiveness of AI in education 144–145; facilitate robust research 149–150; human rights 143–144; innovate around data privacy 148–149; personalized learning 145–146; preparing for AI 147–148; proprietary content and transparency 147
European Union (EU) 129, 214
Evers, Matthias 48–72

Facebook 173
FAIR 34–37
fairness 129, 139
Faraday, Michael 198
Federal Trade Commission (FTC) 146
Feng, S. 121
Finn, James 120
Fischman, Wendy 190
5G telecommunications 1
FLEXA 126
flexibility 24, 31–32, 87, 120, 141, 169, 174, 188, 268
Fogel, Robert 6
Foote, Eunice Newton 91
Forcier, L. B. 130–131
foreign direct investment (FDI) 208, 216n2
Francis, G. 144
free thinking 189, 196
free trade 112, 209
Friedman, Milton 287
functional analysis 16
Fung, Jin Michael 3, 30–44
future curriculum 169–170

Gallup/Bates College survey 189
Gardner, Howard 190
General Data Protection Regulation (GDPR) 129
general purpose assistive technology 275–276
general purpose technology 1
Generation Artificial Intelligence Development Plan 210
Generative Adversarial Networks (GANs) 142
gene therapies 53, 63
genetically modified organisms (GMOs) 58
Gilded Age 2
Global Age 2

globalization and localization 31
Gokulnath, Divya 263
Goldfarb, Avi 113
Google 261
Gouldner, Alvin 196
GPS technology 78, 180
grade point average (GPA) 250
Graide 141
graphical user interface (GUI) 3
Graphics Processing Units (GPUs) 126
"Great Books" 191, 192
greenhouse gas (GHG) emissions 49, 92
Gregg, Jack 4, 75–89
Griffiths, M. 130–131

Harris, Tristan 179–180
Hassabis, Demis 109
Hayek, Friedrich 287
HE *see* higher education (HE)
health 98
Heisenberg, Werner 198
higher education (HE) 206, 210–213; accessible 35; challenges 37–38; fit for purpose 35; inclusive 36–37; quality education 38–40; relevant/responsive 37
higher education institutions (HEI) 246, 250
Hinton, Geoffrey E. 278
H-LAM/T system (human using language, artifacts, methodology, in which he is trained): intelligence amplification 25–26; source of intelligence 24–25; two-domain system 26–27
Hochschulrektorenkonferenz (HRK) 246
Holmes, Wayne 6, 130–131, 137–153
Holzman, Jaq 199
Hong Kong University of Science and Technology (HKUST) 212
Hosseini, Samira 3, 30–44
Human Genome Project 51
human health and performance 56
human intellectual effectiveness 14
human intelligence 157–158; biological brain 160; distinctive features of 158–159; mental extensions 161–163
human-like artificial intelligence (HLAI) 103–105, 108
Huxley, Aldous 178
hybrid and enhanced intelligence 230

inclusiveness 36, 129
Indian Institutes of Technology 266
India Stack 261
individuals and consumers 69–70
Industrial Revolution 2, 5, 93, 191
innovators 66
inspiring professors 32
Instagram 173
Institute for Health Metrics and Evaluation's (IHME) 63
Institute for the Future of Education (IFE) 35
Instruction and Training (I&T) 246
intelligent agriculture 226
intelligent body 160–161
intelligent computing chips and systems 231
intelligent manufacturing 223, 226
intelligent tutoring systems 140
intelligent virtual reality modeling technology 231
International Baccalaureate Organization (IBO) 127
International Entrepreneur Rule (IER) 240
International Society for Technology in Education 151
International Space Station (ISS) 79–80
Internet of Things (IoT) 81, 179, 215, 275
investment in scientific research 64

"Johnnies" 196, 198, 199, 200
Johnston, John D. 283
Johns Hopkins 191
Joseph, Miriam 185
justice and equity sensitivity 99–100

K-12 classrooms 5
K-12 education 238
K-12 schooling 173
Kant, Immanuel 198
Keynes, John Maynard 2, 173
key swarm intelligence technology 230
Klinova, Katya 113
knowledge computing engine and knowledge service technology 230
Kongsgaard, Alex 199
Kronman, Anthony 196
Krugman, Paul 287
Kuznets, Simon 107
Kykalova, Alena 113

Labor Force Participation Rate (LFP) 281
La Greca, Jason 119–132

land use planning and architecture 98
Law, N. 121
LEAD School 261, 266–267
learning analytics 124, 146, 263
Leibniz, Gottfried Wilhelm 198
liberal arts education 6–7, 173, 176–177, 180–181, 186n3, 191, 202
longevity 31, 105
low Earth orbit (LEO) 75, 77–78
Luckin, Rose 130–131
lunar and planetary landing 78

machine learning 1–2, 6, 53–54, 85, 97–98, 110, 112, 119, 124, 128–129, 142, 152, 175, 179, 186, 210, 216n12, 229, 232, 236, 261, 264, 266
Magpies 158
Major, L. 144
Manyika, James 48–72, 113
Marber, Peter 1–9
Marcus, Gary 113
massive online open courses (MOOCs) 35
materials, chemicals, and energy 58–59
mathematics, computer science, science and technology (MINT) 247
McAfee, Andrew 113
McCarthy, John 119
mechanical engineers 82
mega-constellations 78
Mercier, Hugo 163
Merz, Ted 199
Meyer, Andrea 113
Meyer, Dana 113
Microsoft 261
Millennium Development Goals (MDGs) 38
Mitchell, Tom 110
Modi, Narendra 260
Montessori system 176
Moravec, Hans 108
Morrill Act of 1862 93
Musk, Elon 83

NASA 77
National Association of College and University Business Officers (NACUBO) 125
National Center for Education Statistics (NCES) 248
National Defense Authorization Act 8
National Defense Education Act (NDEA) 238
National Defense Education Act II 238

National Development and Reform Commission (NDRC) 208
National Key Research and Development Plan 223
National Science Foundation (NSF) 212, 241
natural intelligence 6, 157–158
Natural Language Processing (NLP) 120, 231
Nature Human Behaviour 169
neurocentric bias 161
new biological capabilities 51–54
Nicomachean Ethics 182
Nietzsche, Friedrich 175
Nilsson, Nils 105
Nisbet, Travers 48–72

Office of Responsible AI (ORA) 130
Organisation for Economic Co-operation and Development (OECD) 39, 130, 148, 270, 276, 280

Paine, Thomas 287
Papaspyridis, Alexandros 119–132
pareto optimal outcome 107
Pask, Gordon 120
Paul, Annie Murphy 157–170
payload launch 77
personal geographic mobility 13
personalized learning 122, 126, 132, 140, 144–146, 266
Personally Identifiable Information (PII) 129, 149
Peters, Michael A. 7
Polgreen, Lydia 199
policy and planning 7
predictive analytics 125
principles of brain extension: altering our mental state 165–166; create cognitively congenial situations 168; embedding extensions 168–169; generate cognitive loops 167; making it real 164–165; offloading 164; re-embody 166; re-socialize 167; re-spatialize 166
privacy & security 129
Przegalinska, Aleksandra K. 274–292
PSET CLOUD 140
public administration 98–99

Question Bot (QBot) 123–124

Rasmusson, Zach 199
Raveendran, Byju 263

Regional Comprehensive Economic Partnership (RCEP) 208–209
Reisberg, Daniel 162
reliability and safety 129
research and technological spinoffs 80
Responsible AI Strategy in Engineering (RAISE) 130
ribonucleic acid (RNA) *50*, 51, 56, 70n1
robotics 75; autonomous operation 86; humans *vs.* machines 86–87
Rock, Daniel 110
Rogers, Josh 199
Roksa, Josipa 190
Roosevelt, Mark 202
Rousseau, Jean-Jacques 176–177

safety and security 139
Santa Fe 191, 200, 202
SARS-CoV-2 pandemic 49
Sasse, Ben 199
Satellite Communications and Internet 77–78
Schaeffer, Jonathan 109
Schmidt, Eric 234–243
Schoener, Abe 199
School of Mines of Columbia University 93
science, technology, engineering, and mathematics (STEM) 237; create an entrepreneur visa 241; education system 238; employment-based green cards 240–241; international competition for AI and 238; job portability for highly skilled workers 240; strengthen AI talent through immigration 238
scientific research 64, 66, 77, 126, 223, 232
secure and connected campus 122
"self-efficacy" 197
shifting demographics 31
Shiohira, Kelly 6, 137–153
"Silk Road Economic Belt" 207, 208
SkillsFuture Singapore 31
Skills-OVATE 140
Smith, G. 127
social media 137, 143, 179, 197, 261, 269
Social Sciences Academic Press (SSAP) 212
Socratic inquiry 196
solar energy 75, 79, 84
space debris removal and mitigation 79–80

space mining and manufacturing 78–79
space tourism 80
SpaceX 77
special economic zones (SEZ) 207
Sperber, Dan 163
SQuAD reading comprehension test 120
St. John 191, 192, 196, 197, 198, 200, 202, 203
student success 122, 125–126, 257n24
Supplemental Nutrition Assistance Program (SNAP) 289
Sustainable Development Goals (SDGs) 39; environmental sphere 41–42; infrastructure sphere 42–44; social sphere 40–41
system of intellectaugmentation 14
systems and multidisciplinary approach 99
systems engineers 82–83, 85

tax policy 111
teaching and learning 33, 38, 122–126, 130–131, 139–140, 144–145, 148, 151, 210
Tec-21 model 32–33
Technical and Vocational Education and Training (TVET) 145
technological advancements and digital transformation 31
technological unemployment 173–175
Tecnologico de Monterrey 32, 35–36
Temporary Assistance for Needy Families (TANF) 290
"The Great Resignation" 189
"The New Program" 192, 200
"The Program" 191, 192, **193–195**
TikTok 173
TikTok's algorithms 179
total economic impact 59–61
Total Factor Productivity (TFP) 281, *282*
"transactional" perspective 190
transparency 6, 129, 131, 139, 144, 147–149, 255
transparency and interpretability/intelligibility 129
Tsapali, M. 144
Turing, Alan 103
Turing Trap 103–115
Turley, Helen 199, 199
Turley, Larry 199

UBI: payments 288; policy 287
UBI *see* universal basic income
Unacademy 261, 264
UNESCO 40–41, 130, 142
United Arab Emirates (UAE) 77
United Nations (UN) 38–39
universal basic income (UBI) 9, 172, 274–292
universities of applied sciences (UAS) 247
upGrad 261, 265–266
US Citizenship and Immigration Services (USCIS) 240
US Food and Drug Administration (FDA) 60
US Tax Code 111

Vedantu 261, 266
venture capital firms (VCs) 76
Vineyards, Duckhorn 199
virtual reality (VR) 35, 231, 262
Vocational Education and Training (VET) 246, 249
von Weitershausen, Inez 245–258

Wadhwa, Tarun 8
Wang, T 121
Watts, Shawn 203
Wegner, Daniel 163
Wentworth Institute of Technology (WIT) 246, 250, 252
Wetlaufer, John 199
Whiteboard Audio Video Environment (WAVE) 266
Williams, James 179–180
Winiarski, Warren 199
Woodcock, Amos 191
Work-Based Higher Education (WBHE) 245; assessment and examination 254; curriculum design and renewal 251–252; in Germany 246–248; instruction and training 252–253; student recruitment and admission 250–251; in United States 248–249; work of the future 254–255
work-based learning (WBL) 246, 256n3
World Economic Forum (WEF) 30
Wright, Robert E. 274–292

Xi, Jinping 206, 224
X5GON 141

Zheng, Alice 48–72